The Indian Heritage

The Indian

Victoria & Albert Museum
21 April – 22 August 1982

Court Life & Arts under Mughal Rule

Heritage

Cover illustration:
Shah Jahan as a prince
Mughal, c.1616-17
VAM : IM 14-1925
Cat. no.41

Designed by H M S O Graphic Design
Typeset by Hugh Wilson Typesetting
Printed by Balding + Mansell
ISBN 0 905209 20 6
Dd 8219629

Contents

Foreword

The major exhibitions at the V & A over the last few years have focused on the art of courts, up until now European, but this year, as our contribution to the Festival of India, we turn our attention to that of the Mughal Emperors. It is appropriate that we should stage such an exhibition as custodians of a large part of the collections of the old East India Company. It also reflects a major rôle of the Indian Department of the Museum, to present the visual heritage of the Indian sub-continent to the British public on behalf of the Asian communities now in this country. Our galleries already offer an introduction to Indian civilisation, but the exhibition will signal a new initiative, reflecting long-term planning for a more extensive display of the superb collections for too long in store.

The exhibition has been the work of Robert Skelton and his colleagues in the Indian Department, in conjunction with Brian Griggs, the Museum's designer, and the staff of the Exhibitions Section. They have been dependent throughout on the support of many institutions and individuals, but our particular thanks must go to Sir Michael Walker, Chairman of the Festival of India Trust and Mrs Pupul Jayakar, Chairman of the Indian Advisory Committee. In India a key rôle was played by Dr Kapila Vatsyayan, Joint Educational Adviser in the Ministry of Education and Culture, New Delhi, with the support of Mr H.S. Jassal of the Department of Culture and Mr I.D. Mathur, Acting Director of the National Museum, whose colleagues Mr L.A. Narain and Mrs Krishna Lal organised the collection and transport of the Indian loans. Also in India, we are deeply indebted to His Excellency Sir John Thomson, the British High Commissioner, and Lady Thomson; also Mr Robert Frost, Educational Adviser of the British Council in Delhi and his colleague Mrs S.K. Bahl, without whose support the exhibition would not have taken place.

We are grateful also to His Excellency the Indian Ambassador in Moscow, and to Dr H. Popov, Head of the Fine Arts Department, Ministry of Culture of the USSR.

In Britain, we have received much assistance from the former Indian High Commissioner His Excellency Mr A. Goray, and his successor His Excellency Dr V.A. Seyid Muhammad, as well as important help from Dr I.P. Singh, the former Deputy High Commissioner,

8 Mr J.M. Gugnani, First Secretary, Education and, more recently, from Mr N. Desai, Counsellor at the High Commission.

Valuable advice and assistance has been constantly available from the Cultural Relations Department of the Foreign and Commonwealth Office, especially from Mr John McRae and Mr W.T. Hull. Since his appointment as Director of the Festival Mr Stanley Hodgson has given us invaluable guidance. Throughout the preparations for the Festival, Miss Joanna Drew, supported by Geoffrey Watson, Catherine Lampert and Rosalie Cass have played a major rôle, without which our own task would have been infinitely more difficult.

Both Air India and British Airways have contributed generously towards the freight costs of loans from Delhi to London. We are also grateful to the World of Islam Festival Trust, Mr Robin Wigington and Mr Howard Ricketts for their donations towards the conservation of Tipu Sultan's tent, and to Mr Martand Singh and the Trustees of the Calico Museum of Textiles, Ahmedabad, who generously donated the body of no.519 for the exhibition. Finally, I must acknowledge with gratitude the support of Gaylords and Viceroy of India restaurants, and Chivite International, who have provided food and wine for events connected with the exhibition.

Sir Roy Strong
Director, Victoria & Albert Museum

Acknowledgements

We acknowledge with gratitude the lenders to the exhibition, without whose generous support it would not have been possible:

Her Majesty the Queen
The Duke of Buccleuch and Queensberry KT, VRD
The Marquess of Bute, JP
The Marquess of Tavistock and the Trustees of the Bedford Estate
The Rt. Hon. the Lord Reigate, PC
The Rt. Hon. the Earl Amherst
The Rt. Hon. the Earl of Powis
The Executors of the late Earl of Powis
Baron Thyssen-Bornemisza
Baron and Baroness Bachofen von Echt
Mr John R. Alderman
Mr and Mrs J.W. Alsdorf
Dr Mildred Archer
The Ashmolean Museum, Oxford
Mr Lalit Bashin
Catherine and Ralph Benkaim
Bharat Kala Bhavan, Benaras
Bibliothèque Nationale, Paris
Boston Museum of Fine Arts
The British Library, London
The British Museum, London
The Brooklyn Museum
The Burrell Collection, Glasgow
The Change Trust
Robert Chenciner Esq
The Chester Beatty Library, Dublin
The Cleveland Museum of Art
Mrs Edward Croft-Murray
The David Collection, Copenhagen
Simon Digby Esq
Miss V.M. Dominy
Dr and Mrs William K. Ehrenfeld
Robert Elgood Esq
The Hon. Robert Erskine
Richard Falkiner Esq
Sven Gahlin Esq
Dr H. Ginsburg
Roland Goodall Esq
Howard Hodgkin Esq
Mrs Lisbet Holmes
Mr Harold F. Horstmeyer
Mr Stephen P. Huyler

The India Office Library and Records
Mr James Ivory
Sri GK Kanoria
Mr Vishnu M. Lall
Mr Momim Latif
Mr and Mrs W.Z. Lloyd
Los Angeles County Museum of Art
Maharaja Sawai Man Singh II Museum, Jaipur
Patrick McMahon Esq
Metropolitan Museum of Art, New York
Jagdish and Kamla Mittal Museum of Indian Art, Hyderabad
Mr Bashir Mohamed
Musée des Arts Décoratifs, Paris
Musée Historiques des Tissus, Lyons
Museum of Art, Rhode Island School of Design
Museum Rietburg, Zürich
The Náprstek Museum, Prague
National Gallery of Art, Washington
The National Museum of Denmark, Copenhagen
The National Museum of India, New Delhi
The National Trust, Powis Castle
Mr S.L. Pasricha
Pilkington Glass Museum
M. M. Pincket
The Prince of Wales Museum of Western India, Bombay
Mme Krishna Riboud
Howard Ricketts Esq
The Rijksmuseum, Amsterdam
Robert and Lisa Sainsbury Collection, University of East Anglia, Norwich
Mrs V. Schreiber
Mr A.A. Soudavar
Staatliche Kunstsammlungen, Dresden
State Hermitage Museum, Leningrad
John Suidmak Esq
Edmund de Unger Esq
The Textile Museum, Washington
Mr Stuart Cary Welch
Robin Wigington Esq
Dr M. Zebrowski

Within the institutions included in the above list, we have received valuable support from many of our Museum colleagues in many countries including:

Amsterdam: The Rijksmuseum: Dr S.H. Levie, Director; Ms Pauline Scheurleer, Curator of Oriental Art
Banaras: Bharat Kala Bhavan: Mr O.P. Tandon, Dr Anand Krishna
Bombay: The Prince of Wales Museum of Western India: Mr S. Gorakshakar, Director, and Mr S. Andhare
Boston: Museum of Fine Arts: Mr Jan Fontein, Director; Mrs K.K. Hunter, Mrs V. Desai and Mr M. Kiernan
Brooklyn: The Brooklyn Museum: Mr M. Botwinick, Director; Mrs Amy Poster
Cleveland: The Cleveland Museum of Art: Mr Sherman E. Lee, Director; Stanislaw Czuma; D.G. Shepard
Copenhagen: The David Collection: André Leth, Director; The National Museum: Mr Torben Lundbaek, Chief Curator
Dresden: Staatliche Kunstsammlungen: Dr Schobel, Director
Dublin: The Chester Beatty Library and Gallery of Oriental Art: Dr P. Henchy, Mr D. James
Glasgow: The Burrell Collection, Camphill Museum: Dr R. Marks, Assistant Director, Ms R. Scott, Depute Keeper
Hyderabad: Mr and Mrs Jagdish Mittal; Mr Naozar Chenoy
Jaipur: His Highness The Maharaja of Jaipur; Dr Ashok Das, Director, Maharaja Sawai Man Singh II Museum; Mrs Chandramani Singh
Leningrad: Academician B.B. Piotrovsky, Director, State Hermitage Museum; Dr A Ivanov
London: British Library: G.E. Marrison, Director; Mr J.P. Losty British Museum: Dr D. Wilson, Director; Mr L. Smith, Keeper of Oriental Antiquities, Dr Michael Rogers; Mr K.R. Miller, Dept. of Coins and Medals; The India Office Library and Records: Mr Barry Bloomfield, Director; Mrs Pauline Rohatgi
Los Angeles: County Museum of Art: Dr Earl A. Powell III, Director; Pratapaditya Pal, Senior Curator of Indian and Islamic Art; Ms Sheila Canby
Lyon: Musée Historique des Tissus: M. J.M. Tuchscherer, Director
New York: Metropolitan Museum of Art: Mr Philippe de Montebello, Director; Mr S.C. Welch; Miss Nabuko Kajitani; Mrs Carolyn Kane; Colta Ives
Oxford: Ashmolean Museum: Mr D.T. Piper, Director; Dr J. Harle, Keeper of Eastern Art; Miss Mary Tregear
Paris: Bibliothèque Nationale: M Alain Gourdon, Mme Geneviève Lassalle Musée des Arts Décoratifs: M Francois Mathey, Director
Prague: Náprstek Museum: Dr Jana Součková, Director; Dr Hana Knižková
Rhode Island: Museum of Art: Dr S.E. Ostrow, Director; Glenn D. Lowry
Washington, D.C.: National Gallery of Art: Mr J. Carter Brown, Director; Mr J.V. Columbus, Textile Consultant; The Textile Museum: Mr Andrew Oliver, Jr., Director; Dr Mattiebelle Gittinger
Zurich: Museum Rietberg: Dr Eberhardt Fischer, Director

Within the Victoria and Albert Museum, I am particularly grateful to Brian Griggs, the exhibition's designer, and his colleagues; Michael Darby, Exhibitions Officer, Garth Hall and Mark Bowis; the Conservation Department, especially Sheila Landi, John Larson and their colleagues; Peter Macdonald and Brenda Norrish of the Photographic Studio; Nicky Bird; Simon Tait and the Press Office; Mr P. Daly, Mr C. Kennett, Mr H. Richardson and their staffs; and John Ayers, Harold Barkley, Claude Blair, Shirley Bury, Duncan Haldane, Michael Kauffmann, Santina Levey, John Mallet, Anthony North, Nathalie Rothstein, Charles Truman, all of whom were generous with help and advice over particular queries.

Outside the Museum, we received help from many quarters, and are particularly indebted to those who gave us the

10 benefit of their enthusiasm, knowledge and experience. They include Robert Alderman, Dr A. Bivar, Mitchell Crites, Simon Digby, Richard Falkiner, Bashir Mohamed, Howard Ricketts, Christopher Rowell, Robin Wigington and Mark Zebrowski. Mr E.A. Jobbins of the Geological Survey and Museum gave much helpful gemmological information on V & A jewellery and hardstones; Dr A.S. Melikian-Chirvani kindly made proofs of his forthcoming book available for entries 489 and 497, as well as reading inscriptions on other objects. Mr J. Burton-Page has given valuable advice and also generously provided material for the slide display in the exhibition. We have also received help from Major H.N. Williams of the National Trust at Powis Castle, and Mr Geoffrey de Bellaigue, Surveyor of the Queen's Works of Art, has provided valuable assistance.

Finally, I must thank my colleagues of the Indian Department: John Lowry, Andrew Topsfield, Veronica Murphy, Susan Stronge, Betty Tyers, Graham Parlett, Beth Stockley, Rosemary Crill, Shaun Kavanagh and Pamela Hudson, who know only too well how much I have relied on them

Robert Skelton
Keeper, Indian Department

Contributors

Initials after each entry indicate that it was written by one of the following:

RC	Rosemary Crill
SD	Simon Digby
ML	Momin Latif
AS M-C	Dr A S Melikian-Chirvani
VM	Veronica Murphy
RS	Robert Skelton
A SC	Anna Somers Cocks
SS	Susan Stronge
AT	Andrew Topsfield
RW	Robin Wigington

India in the
Mughal Age

One Monday in the summer of 1494, the ruler of Farghana – a pleasant valley east of Samarqand – was sitting near the wall of his palace overlooking a ravine watching his tame pigeons. Suddenly an attendant reported danger, but before he could even get his slippers on, Umar Shaikh, his pigeon house and the side of the building were hurtling to destruction. It is hardly surprising that his twelve year old son, Babur, who succeeded him was soon ousted from the small kingdom, but fortunately his lineage and education together with the support of loyal adherents preserved him through the many vicissitudes of fortune which ensued. These are faithfully recounted in Babur's *Memoirs* – a prose classic of the Chagatai Turkish language.

Babur was directly descended from the two great Central Asian scourges – Timur, whom we know as Tamburlaine, and Chingiz Khan. Before he lost his principality of Farghana, Babur's ambition was to rule at Samarqand, the capital of his illustrious forebear, Timur, but the growing power of the Uzbeg Turks baulked him in this aim and forced him to move down to Kabul. Nevertheless, Babur's brief visits to the metropolis and its sister city, Herat, served to deepen his appreciation of the brilliant cultural achievements that had blossomed throughout the century under Timur and his successors. With Uzbeg power undiminished by the death of Babur's prime enemy, the young prince settled for the more feasible prospect of retaining Kabul and once he was secure there he adopted the royal title of Padshah, thus claiming pre-eminence among Timur's descendants.

Frustrated by the loss of his ancestral lands, Babur turned his attention to India, where Timur had ferociously intervened in 1398 to destroy the power of the Tughluq sultans – a dynasty whose empire had once embraced much of the sub-continent. In the century and a quarter which had elapsed since Timur's raid, the inhabitants of India had witnessed contradictory changes. So far as central authority was concerned, it was an epoch of decline, as political disintegration robbed Delhi of its outlying provinces and independent dynasties arose in region after region. As Babur remarked after his arrival there, his immediate neighbours were five Muslim kings and two important Hindu rajas, besides many lesser Hindu chiefs in the hills and jungles. Yet despite these political divisions, in cultural matters there was a growing unity and fruitful interchange of ideas. Thus although today we have little more than the surviving buildings and literature as witnesses, there is growing evidence that the fifteenth century was one in which the intrusive culture of the Muslim aristocracy increasingly came to terms with the rich inheritance of classical Hindu civilization.

To Babur, sight-seeing in his new dominions after defeating the Lodi Afghan ruler near Delhi in 1526, the fruits of this cultural synthesis were not altogether agreeable. Having been brought up in the cooler climate and cultivated society of Turkistan he found Hindustan 'a country of few charms' and complains in his diary that 'of social intercourse, paying and receiving visits there is none; of genius and capacity none; of manners none; in handicraft and work there is no form or symmetry, method or quality; there are no good horses, no good dogs, no grapes, musk melons or first-rate fruits, no ice or cold water, no good bread or cooked food in the bazaars, no Hot-baths, no Colleges, no candles, torches or candlesticks.' Some of this is merely the home-sick grumbling of an expatriate, for Babur also recognised virtues in his new territory, particularly its abundance of wealth and the many trained artisans, whom he soon put to work laying out the gardens whose construction (no.24) was a corollary of his passion for nature. His descendants had no such complaints, for, in any case, they had the capacity and the inclination to ensure that every defect in his list was remedied, while the delights of Hindustan were understood and appreciated as a major element in their new heritage.

If Babur would have grown to love India, as the British did centuries later, he – like so many of them – was denied the chance by an early death. After only four years of Mughal rule the attractive but less capable personality of his son Humayun was to be tested by the sudden assumption of kingship. With alternate bursts of energy and lethargy he began the task of subduing neighbours and rivals, but among the Suri Afghans established eastwards along the Ganges he encountered Sher Shah, a rival of outstanding capacity, who first usurped the fledgling state of the Mughals and then in a reign of only six years proceeded to lay the administrative foundations of its future success. Humayan was forced to flee to Iran, where Shah Tahmasp's hospitality, laced with calculated slights, was the prelude to his guest's re-establishment in Kabul.

Meanwhile in India, Sher Shah's successors were not of the Suri ruler's quality and in 1555 Humayun seized the opportunity of regaining Delhi. Only six months later he slipped and fell down his library steps on hearing the call to prayer. Clearly his fall was less dramatic than Umar Shaikh's, but the result was the same. For the second time in the short history of the dynasty, a teen-aged prince was suddenly elevated to the throne. Akbar, however, was a very different youth from his grandfather. Whereas Babur was a highly literate twelve-year-old, Akbar's disturbed childhood, or perhaps the condition known as dyslexia, left him without formal literacy. In any case the solution of his immediate problems did not require the use of books. With Akbar and his guardian Bairam Khan away in the Punjab, a Hindu commander of the Suri Afghans retook Delhi, and it was largely by chance that the ensuing battle was settled in Akbar's favour. Now at last, with the aid of his protector, the young king could take up the work from which death had debarred his two predecessors. Adjoining areas began falling to the Mughal armies and as he became the master of more territory it also became necessary for

Akbar to throw off Bairam Khan's tutelage and then to master powerful factions within his own court. This was done without interruption to his empire-building, which together with the suppression of rebels exercised his military talents for the next four decades.

It is difficult to evaluate Akbar's personal qualities soberly, because although they are too admiringly enumerated by his minister, friend and biographer, Abu'l Fazl, in the official history of the reign (*Akbar Nama*, nos. 25-32 and 35), he was clearly a man of such exceptional energy, perception and practical wisdom, that he would appear to fit more readily into the role of a fictional hero than conform to the less idealised character that we properly expect of historical portraiture. Even some of his faults and foibles were such as to command respect and help to explain the effect his personality had on those surrounding him. If this was a man for whom a personality cult was unquestionably justified, his deliberate use of it, together with an ability to establish warm human contact, is further testimony to his political sagacity. This acumen is perfectly illustrated by his treatment of the Hindu rulers of Rajasthan, who, as powerful neighbours of alien faith and race, might well have provided the rock on which a newly arrived Muslim dynasty could founder. In the first place Akbar invested their impregnable fortresses with displays of superior military capacity (nos. 27, 31) but then he was quick to conclude family alliances and promote them to high positions of trust within his army and court. Turning his attention simultaneously to every function of state, he consolidated good relations with his Hindu subjects by a number of measures such as the removal of the poll-tax on them and the establishment of a translation bureau in the royal library in which the classics of Hindu scripture and legend were rendered into Persian – the court language – so that Mughal officers might better understand those subject to their administration. That modern India remembers his pioneering efforts in community relations with justifiable pride is not surprising, but racial and religious tolerance and understanding in India did not begin with Akbar and credit is also due to the Rajput chiefs themselves who defended their kingdoms gallantly but were also willing to compromise their proud lineage and caste purity by giving their daughters in marriage to the imperial family and placing their military and executive talents at its disposal.

It was through one of these Rajput princesses that Akbar gained a long-awaited heir, as was predicted by Shaikh Salim Chishti, who lived at the village of Sikri, near Agra. To benefit from the saint's auspicious presence, the birth took place at Sikri itself (no.28) and the child was named Salim in his honour. As a further expression of royal gratitude, Akbar commenced building a new capital at the site which he named Fatehpur, i.e. 'City of Victory' to commemorate his successes in war (nos. 29, 30). In its architecture (nos. 120, 136, 137) the city owes much to the employment of craftsmen from the maritime provinces of Gujarat and Bengal, which were added to the empire soon after the work commenced and contributed significantly to its growing prosperity.

Possession of the important sea-ports of Gujarat and Bengal placed Akbar in control of a network of trade routes that were virtually identical with those linking India with the outside world in ancient times. The focus of these was Agra, on the great waterway eastwards along the Jumna and Ganges rivers, and joined by the Grand Trunk Road through Malwa to Gujarat and the Deccan. From Lahore – Akbar's capital between 1584 and 1598 – trade flowed to the Near East and Central Asia through Afghanistan and Kashmir as well as to the Indian ocean via the Indus. In Roman times, the same pattern had existed with the Kushan capital of Mathura occupying the position taken by neighbouring Agra in Akbar's day.

There was, however, a new factor. In the year that the young Babur revealed his imperial ambitions by his temporary seizure of Samarqand (1497), Vasco da Gama was setting out for India around the Cape. By the time that Akbar had transformed Babur's intended revival of Timurid fortunes into solid reality, the Portuguese were firmly entrenched in Goa and other outposts around the coast of India, with dominance over the sea-lanes linking India with the Near and Far East. We recognise green or red peppers as India's most typical condiment but it is easy to forget that, like its name, the chilli is a South American import that was unknown in India prior to the age of maritime exploration.

Curiously enough, such evidence of foreign contact in India's material culture (see also nos. 4, 13, 41, 48, 63, 298, 299, 303, 323, 356, 375-377, etc.) is scarcely matched in Indian literature of the period and it is largely from the detailed writings of European travellers that we gain insight into a widening of Indian horizons at this time. That a new receptivity coincided with the establishment of a fresh imperial regime was clearly no accident and it is not unreasonable to suppose that Akbar's own personality was a factor in its development. His lack of formal education must surely have contributed to his ability to think independently. In any case he certainly saw the necessity for institutional learning and his limited ability to read and write was no bar to his passion for a knowledge of important literary works. As Abu'l Fazl tells us in the *Ain-i Akbari* (no.45), Akbar had books read to him daily and personally marked the place at the end of each reading. The Library was an important sub-department of state with a well organised staff and a considered system of classification. We know from the Dutch compiler, De Laet, that at Akbar's death, it contained 24,000 volumes and it is clear that a very large number of these were copied during Akbar's reign to the highest standard of contemporary book production (nos. 23-32, 35). A talented staff of scholars, headed by the polymath, Abu'l-Fazl, constituted a sort of imperial think-tank of which the translation bureau was a part.

Abu'l Fazl tells us in the *Akbar nama* (no.35) that in April 1590 a certain Padre Firmiliun came to the court from Goa and received high honour. As 'he possessed abundance of sense and knowledge', His Majesty 'made over some quick-witted and intellectual persons to be instructed by him in order that the translation of Greek books might be carried out' and 'varieties of knowledge were acquired'. The identity of this priest is uncertain but we do know that ten years earlier in 1580 Father Rudolph Acquaviva headed a Jesuit Mission to the court following Akbar's request to the Viceroy of Goa.

Whatever other motives he may have had in making this invitation the Emperor's ostensible purpose was to further his understanding of Christianity as part of his enquiries into various religious faiths. As one who had associated with mystics since his early years (no.25), Akbar had acquired a taste for religious speculation and from about 1575 he attempted to satisfy this by chairing theological disputations between Muslim scholars of different sectarian views. Their mutual intolerance disgusted him and he gradually extended his enquiries to include the opinions of Hindus, Jains, Parsees and Christians. The fruit of these discussions was an attempt to combine the best elements of these beliefs into a Divine Faith (*Din-i Ilahi*), which was clearly intended to promote religious harmony in the Empire but only gained a few adherents within the inner circle of the Emperor's associates.

There has been much controversy over the extent to which Akbar departed from the tenets and practice of Islam and adopted heretical practices such as worship of the sun, and insufficient attention has been given to the fact that Akbar's undoubted reverence for the solar body is consistent with a longstanding theme in Iranian literature concerning the opposition of good and evil as symbolised by the dualism of light and darkness. This cult of solar beneficence and splendour was not unconnected with Iranian concepts of kingship and the Mughals were well aware of regal pretensions in ancient Iran as transmitted in the form of anecdotes about the Sassanian kings in medieval Islamic manuals of statecraft. Akbar's father, Humayun, who dabbled in astrological and occult fancies, merely played with these ideas as when he veiled himself and received the plaudits of his courtiers on 'the rising of the sun' as the veil was removed from his face.

Akbar perceived a more serious function in fostering an imperial cult but the institution of such practices as his daily appearances to his subjects at a balcony window at daybreak stems from the same notion. This symbolism was taken up with a vengeance by Akbar's successor Salim, who adopted the title Nur al-Din Jahangir on his accession in 1605, thus associating in his own name both concepts, i.e. 'Light of the Faith' and 'World Grasper'. The culmination of Jahangir's use of the theme is found in a series of elaborate pictorial allegories (no.48) which clearly owe much to contemporary European theories of kingship as expressed in Mannerist paintings and prints, of which he was a collector (no.44).

A major theme of the European Imperial Cult was the emergence of an Augustan ruler, who, reinaugurating the first Golden Age, enables Justice – in the guise of Astraea/Virgo – to descend again to earth. Thus, as in Virgil's Fourth Eclogue, or in Semitic sources such as the Book of Isaiah, carnivore and herbivore may lie down together in peace. In the allegorical paintings of both Jahangir and his son Shah Jahan (nos. 48 and 56) these beasts are shown beneath the feet of the Just Ruler on the globe, which symbolises his universal dominion. One important feature of the Emperor's justice is his suppression of iniquity and in two of Jahangir's paintings this is symbolised by the ancient Iranian motif of light opposing darkness. A painting in the Chester Beatty Library (Arnold & Wilkinson, 1936, III, pl.62) shows Jahangir, nimbate as the personification of solar light, shooting arrows at the severed head of an Abyssinian enemy, whose dark visage represents the Night over whom Dawn triumphs daily. The other version of this theme (no.48) is even more curious, for the dark-skinned foe represents Penury, whose destruction clearly hints at an imperial preoccupation with economic policy.

There were times in the life of Babur when almost his only asset was the loyalty of a few followers with their horses and their weapons, and this in itself suggests the basis on which medieval Islamic states were founded. The possession of a kingdom, on the other hand, requires an administrative structure of some elaboration. The army remains a fundamental pillar of the state but loyalty must be fostered by the sort of remote control that had been developed in ancient Iran and continued throughout the Islamic period. Dynastic legitimacy has to be stressed (nos. 52-53) and regal pretensions manifested in ways that require the command of considerable economic resources. Similarly, if military success permits the control of territory, strategic routes and centres of population and trade, it also depends on the wealth that it reaps, since army loyalty is prompted as much by payment as by respect for the imperial myth.

Mughal India inherited the fiscal and administrative system of the sultanate period which was a combination of medieval Islamic and Hindu practice overhauled during Humayan's exile by Sher Shah. Under Akbar, the system was carefully reconsidered and took on the characteristics of meticulous record keeping that earned it the soubriquet *kaghazi raj* – 'government by paper' (nos. 75, 81). The administrative elite or *umara* (Arabic plural of *amir*) supervising this system was organised within a hierarchy of military ranks, founded by Akbar, whose members (*mansabdars*) were graded according to the number of troops and horses that they were supposed to maintain. Payment was either made in cash or by the assignment of revenue from lands (*jagir*) alloted to them on a temporary basis. Some of them – particularly the Hindu Rajas – were also hereditary landlords or *zamindars*, but all property was theoretically subject to escheat on the owner's death. Actual practice was governed by intricate regulations, frequently subject to revision or abuse, particularly as central authority waned.

These officers served in departments of state, in the army, or in the provincial administration and, with a few exceptions, were subject to transfer – often into quite different types of office from those previously held. The chief minister, known as the *Wazir*, was in charge of the Exchequer and other senior officials included the Military Paymaster (*Bakhshi*) and High Steward of the Imperial Household or *Khan-i Saman* (no.69). Officials concerned with Muslim law fell outside the *mansabdari* system but their income could also be provided directly from agricultural revenue (no.81). Most central functions were duplicated in the provinces where the principal powers were divided between the Governor (*Subahdar*) and the Treasurer (*Diwan*). An elaborate system of checks existed with newswriters constantly forwarding independent reports of local activities and conditions to the court. Steps were taken to foster agriculture and trade but, despite imperial disapproval, corruption and extortion by officers of all grades was the rule rather than the exception. This often resulted in the impoverishment of the peasantry and the concealment of wealth by members of the mercantile classes. Nevertheless, a flourishing banking community existed – particularly among the Jain and Marwari communities – and their bills of exchange (*hundi*) were honoured with surprising reliability over great distances.

The conspicuous consumption and display which attracted the attention of foreign travellers and prompted the legend of the 'Grand Mogul' in Europe, was mainly confined to the nobility and the court. Although the nobles were to some extent subject to sumptuary laws, particularly under Akbar's austere great-grandson Aurangzeb, the splendour of their apparel and accoutrements was encouraged by the regular custom of giving and receiving presents. Already under the Tughluq sultans of the 14th century it was a regular procedure for each of the imperial officers to be given a dress of honour twice a year and the resulting demand for large quantities of luxury fabrics was met by the establishment of workshops (*kar-khana*) which employed thousands of artisans. This custom was continued by the Mughals as was the practice of presenting robes of honour, jewelled daggers, saddles, pen cases and other costly items when officials presented themselves at court on the occasion of promotion or transfer (no.70). It was equally obligatory for the courtiers themselves to make costly gifts (*pishkash*) to the Emperor and other superiors, in addition to token cash presents known as *nazr*. The Emperor did not necessarily accept into his treasury all of the gifts made as *pishkash* but even

though some may have been returned to the presenter they constituted a considerable item in an officer's expenditure. Many *amirs* maintained their own workshops and also went to much trouble in seeking out rarities such as precious stones to offer at court. Supervision of the *karkhanas* and palace stores was carried out by the High Steward, whose clerks kept careful inventories of gifts at the time of their presentation (nos. 40, 69).

The quest for curiosities and objects of rare material or workmanship was especially encouraged by Akbar's son, Jahangir, whose inordinate appetite for the exotic and strange resembled that of his Habsburg contemporary Rudolph II. Although he inherited his father's intellectual curiosity it was diverted more towards natural phenomena than to practical and spiritual questions as is shown by comments in his Memoirs on the animals (no.46), birds, plants and artefacts which excited his attention. In a land where art responded to organic stimuli rather than to the cultivated artifice of taste, Jahangir was the first and ultimate connoisseur, who not only collected insatiably but also patronised the arts, especially painting (no.37), with active discrimination. His introduction of the flowering plant as a design motif following a spring visit to Kashmir revolutionised subsequent Mughal ornament but the artistic innovations of his reign (1605-27) ranged much further – from the cladding of buildings in marble (nos. 4, 125, 136) to the development of jade carving (nos. 349-354) or to changes in sartorial fashion (no.252).

As a ruler, Jahangir's chief success lay in his ability to maintain the *status quo* despite character defects such as an over-indulgence in opium and alcohol that would have ruined his health more speedily without the intervention of his strong-minded wife, Nur Jahan. His successor Shah Jahan (1628-58) possessed a more resolute political will than his father and his reign marked the apogee of Mughal achievement in nearly every sphere. His adoption of Timur's title 'Lord of the (auspicious planetary) Conjunction' signalled a leaning towards territorial aggrandisement which he exercised by turning his armies towards the North-West Frontier and the Deccan.

Qandahar was surrendered to him by its Persian governor in 1638 but regained a decade later by the Shah, who resisted Mughal attempts at its recapture (nos. 75, 77). Shah Jahan's attempts to reconquer the Timurid territories of Balkh and Badakhshan proved similarly futile and despite energetic campaigning by his capable third son, Aurangzeb, he was only partly successful in extending Mughal power in the Deccan.

The wealth at Shah Jahan's command was prodigious and despite enormous expenditure on an extravagant building programme that included the Taj Mahal, he could still maintain a court whose magnificence was the envy of all others. The summit of his ostentation was his commissioning of the celebrated Peacock Throne (no.57) which displayed the accumulated wealth of the imperial treasury. For a knowledgeable expert on jewels (no.41), who was himself a jewellery designer, his first entry into this gem-encrusted bower must have produced an untypical frisson of excitement in his somewhat cold and self-possessed demeanour.

Shah Jahan's haughty manners were inherited by his heir-apparent and favourite, Dara Shukoh (no.67), as were the mystical tendencies of his grandfather. Like Akbar, Dara showed an interest in religious eclecticism but with the advantage of a scholar's education which enabled him to translate Hindu scriptures and compile works on Sufism. His connoisseurship was directed to calligraphy rather than painting (nos. 58-62) and he was himself an accomplished penman (no.51). Despite many obvious gifts, however, he lacked practical wisdom, as is demonstrated by his credulity in matters of superstition. When the succession was contested during his father's illness in 1657 he was defeated in battle by his younger brother Aurangzeb (no.79) and subsequently executed for heresy. Adopting the title 'Alamgir ('World-Grasper'), Aurangzeb thus seized the throne.

Stigmatised by history as a cold and calculating religious bigot, Aurangzeb emerges from its pages as a somewhat tragic figure. Admittedly a fratricide, who imprisoned his aged father and other male relatives, he was rather a victim of his own overriding sense of duty than a tyrant. He maintained the imperial dignity of the court but tried to sweep away features which he found inconsistent with Muslim orthodoxy. His piety was beyond reproach but the simplicity of his personal life, demonstrated by his copying out the Qur'an for sale, was not without its inconsistencies. He was an enemy of those arts such as painting and music which broke the tenets of Islam but nevertheless permitted portraiture when it magnified his imperial status (no.78) or enabled him to check that an imprisoned relative was not rejecting doses of a debilitating drug.

His relentlessly pursued political aim was the subjugation of the Deccan sultanates, which he finally achieved with the conquest of Bijapur and Golconda in 1686-7. In the process he over-extended and impoverished the Empire so that despite his exertions as the dynasty's supreme bureaucrat he ended his reign with a confession of failure. In a letter to his son A'zam Shah, he wrote 'I came alone and am going alone. I have not done well to the country and the people, and of the future there is no hope.'

When Aurangzeb's grip was removed by his eventual death in 1707, the inevitable process of disintegration began and although their bombastic titles multiplied with their declining authority there was not one among his successors who deserved the adjective with which Europeans had prefixed the dynasty's name. *Wazirs* and *Subahdars* became king-makers or princes so that the title *Nawab* (honorific plural of *Na'ib* 'lieutenant') came to signify an independent ruler. In 1739, the pleasure-loving Muhammad Shah (no.85) was humiliated by the invader Nadir Shah and the capital sacked. The contents of the imperial treasury, including the Peacock Throne, were removed to Iran and in the wake of political anarchy, the British gradually took control. Still within the eighteenth century, some men of conspicuous ability such as Haidar 'Ali (no.411) in the southern Deccan or Ranjit Singh in the Punjab (no.571) could seize and maintain power, while others such as Siraj ud-Daula (no.567) and Haidar's son, Tipu (no.96, etc.), failed to stem the tide of foreign imperialism. With pathetic dignity, the last Mughal Emperor, Bahadur Shah (1837-58) attempted to maintain the traditions of his heritage both as a king (nos. 109, 307) and as a man of cultivated tastes. He gave patronage to the great Urdu poet Ghalib and was a poet and calligraphist himself. While Bahadur Shah strove to uphold the values of the past, many of his nominal vassals among the Maharajas and Nawabs gave themselves up increasingly to a taste for things European. Already before the Emperor's deposition in 1858, a new era had dawned.   RS

The European Vogue

The allure of novelty, which led European princes and nobles to stock their *Kunstkammers* and cabinets of curiosities with oriental exotica, also fascinated the Mughal rulers of India. The early Letter Books of the East India Company of London (founded 1600) list articles which would make suitable presents for the Grand Mughal or 'vent well' at his court. They include gloves, looking-glasses, pictures and 'toys' (in the contemporary sense of a trinket or curiosity). By 1616 the emperor Jahangir (1605-27) was referring with evident pride to the 'European screens' which adorned the sides of his Hall of Public Audience. This enthusiasm did not prevent him from noticing that the silver coach presented to him by Sir Thomas Roe, an ambassador from James I, was poorly finished, and having it dismantled and remade by his own workmen (Roe, p.322, note 3).

From the start it was clear that certain types of merchandise were always in demand: clocks, watches and automata. This still applied in the 1790s when what must be the world's best-known mechanical toy was made for Tipu Sahib, Sultan of Mysore (1782-99). 'Tippoo's Tiger', the 'Man-Tyger-Organ', or 'Musical Tiger', is a life-size carved and painted wooden tiger shown in the act of mauling a prostrate European, who waves a feeble arm and shrieks while the tiger growls. A door in the animal's flank opens to reveal a small organ keyboard, which can be played to provide a musical accompaniment. The bodywork, by local craftsmen, relates to painted wooden toys still produced at centres in South India; the mechanism was probably made by a French artisan in the Sultan's service. The French alliance is further stressed by the Sèvres porcelain (no.404) which Louis XVI presented to Tipu, whose European collections also included an English watch and telescope and ivory furniture (no.568).

The work of an unusually versatile craftsman, Ram Singh Malam, known as 'the Navigator', of Okhamandal, Kathiawar, led Mirza Maharao Lakho – 'Lakhaji' – of Kutch (1741-60) to take an interest in European objects long before his territory had any official contact with the East India Company. Ram Singh Malam had found his way to Europe as a boy and become expert in a wide range of crafts. Under Lakho's patronage he set up court workshops at the capital, Bhuj, training apprentices in skills which included glass-blowing, enamelling, tile-making, gun-casting, and watch-and clock-making. He made two return visits to Europe at the Maharao's suggestion, the second accompanied by apprentices. The *Aina Mahal*, an apartment of the new palace he designed at Bhuj, is filled with European-style objects, some made by Ram Singh and his apprentices, others, including 'elaborate pendant candelabra, with shades of Venetian glass' imported by him. Some of the prints and glass-paintings which line the walls were probably brought to Bhuj at this time.

By the 1790s the warlike Marathas had succumbed to the European craze. A British artist, James Wales, was commissioned to paint portraits of the Peshwa and his court at Poona. Wales made a long list of 'Europe articles' which seemed likely to have a sale at Poona. They included gold watches, painted glass windows, teapots, silk stockings and pianos. A few years later, the palace of Sindia, another great Maratha chief, at Ahmadnagar, was found by Colonel Welsh of the Madras Army to contain 'in two apartments only, several dozens of large handsome pier-glasses, two electrifying machines, an organ, a piano-forte, lustres, chandeliers, globes and many other similar luxuries . . .'. All these imported luxuries and many more besides could have been purchased in the major cities of India at the time. A single consignment advertised as a forthcoming auction in the *Calcutta Gazette* for June 8th 1786 ran to several hundred categories; the contents would have equipped a large and comprehensive emporium. They included many different kinds of looking-glasses and light-fittings. Even Sindia's electrifying machines were there. A generation earlier no Maratha leader need have been at the expense of shopping for consumer goods. Now the robber barons were beginning to stay at home; soon Sindia, Holkar and Bhonsle, like the Peshwa, would pay C.O.D. For personal shoppers Dring's Long Rooms – about 200 feet of them – in Calcutta's Lall Bazaar displayed a profusion of European luxury goods, patronised by British and Indians alike (no.105). Ghulam Hussain Khan, in his poem extolling Calcutta in 1780, seems to be expressing a commonly held view on the relative merits of Indian craftsmanship and imported goods:
You see, if you go to the bazaar,
The rare goods of the world there.
All the articles that exist in the four quarters of the globe,
You find in its bazaar without search.
If I were to depict the people of art therein,
The pen would fail to pourtray [sic] *such a picture,*
But it is well known to all
That pre-eminence in workmanship pertains to China and England.
(English translation of 1788)

Chinese artefacts, especially porcelain, had been prized at Indian courts for many centuries. The poet may, however, have had in mind more the vast array of charming and ingenious trifles which, when he wrote, were piling up in the *hongs* (warehouses) of Canton for export to the West via East India Company centres in India, and which were certainly to be found in the Calcutta bazaars along with the wares of Bilston and Brummagem. Sir Charles D'Oyly's verse satire *Tom Raw the Griffin* lists merchandise available at Dring's in 1821, which reads like an extract from the consignment of 1786, for example:
. . .stupendous lustres, And girandoles and chandeliers, that vie
With wall shades stuck around in sparkling clusters,
Which Doorga, often, for her annual nautches musters.
This refers to the entertainments put on by rich Hindu merchants such as Naba Krishna – D'Oyly's 'Nob Kishen' – for the annual Durga Puja or Dussehra festival. His guests included numbers of Britons,

who feasted on European delicacies and ogled their favourite nautch girls while inhaling the fumes of the *huqqa*, amid furnishings that were a blend of Eastern and Western taste (no.106).

It was at the court of Oudh, whose capital shifted from Lucknow to Faizabad and back at the whim of successive Nawabs, that Euromania entered its ultimate and definitive phase and where, paradoxically, it was to be seen in its most Indian manifestation. The association began quite soberly in the early 1770s when the able, rich and powerful Nawab Shuja-ud-daula (1753-75) decided to employ European officers such as the French Colonel Gentil (nos. 87, 89) to reorganise his army on European lines. In 1772, having heard favourable reports of the British painter Tilly Kettle, who had already worked for the Nawab of Arcot and was now seeking further commissions at the courts of India, he invited him to Faizabad to paint the family portraits. About the time of Kettle's arrival the East India Company finally succeeded in its attempt to wedge an official foot in the door of Oudh, a move which the astute Nawab had so far managed to circumvent. However, in 1773 he agreed, in return for certain concessions, to accept a permanent British Resident and maintain a troop of Company soldiers in addition to his own army. Under his successor, the ebullient and hedonistic Asaf-ud-daula (1775-97), the court of Oudh, now back at Lucknow, attracted crowds of European place-seekers and hangers-on to compete for the favours of the Nawab. If Asaf-ud-daula, who presided over the raffish and brilliant scene, was an eccentric whose flamboyant tastes ran to dressing up as an English admiral or clergyman, his colourful European associates included a number of five-star individualists, among them the French General Martin, who built himself a combined palace-mausoleum called Constantia or La Martinière, of great fantasy, where already in his lifetime the sepulchral lamps were lit to burn 'for ever'; and Colonel Mordaunt, the (technically) illegitimate eldest son of the Earl of Peterborough, who became commander of Asaf-ud-daula's bodyguard and his chosen companion in the non-stop carnival that pleased the Nawab. The intimacy of their relationship is immortalised in Zoffany's painting 'Colonel Mordaunt's Cock Match at Lucknow', commissioned by Warren Hastings in 1784.

The sad decline of Oudh from its days of greatness under the mighty Shuja-ud-daula, a ruler of stature in both senses of the word, the frittering of its vast resources in meaningless ostentation by his descendants, and their gradual dwindling, not merely into puppets of the East India Company, but into total incapacity, is not relevant to this account. Our theme is the culmination of Euromania at Lucknow under Ghazi-ud-din Haidar (1814-27) and Nasir-ud-din Haidar (1827-37). Ghazi-ud-din's cult of the European received a boost early in his reign when he secured the services of the Scottish artist Robert Home as Court Painter, an appointment which only terminated with the patron's death. Home was more than a mere painter. When

the Nawab Wazir, encouraged by the East India Company, assumed the title King of Oudh in 1819, Home was more than equal to the occasion. The enterprising Scot ransacked the Indo-European grammar of ornament to equip his patron with all the trappings of kingship. In these the fish symbol of state was often cunningly concealed, or alternatively flaunted. Crowns, regalia, coats of arms, flags (no.295), drapes, costumes, uniforms, thrones with griffins and sphinxes, pumpkin carriages, boats shaped like shells and swans and peacocks and mermaids and crocodiles: all sprang from the drawing board. The monarch approved; some of the things were certainly made, and seen by Captain Robert Smith on his visit to Lucknow a few years later, when he apparently met Home. Meanwhile the carnival continued, with fireworks every night.

The King liked to appear in public in his English-style coronation robes, including a mantle of purple velvet with ermine cape worn over his brocade *jama*. His favourite crown was a rather old-fashioned, spiky affair of the kind found in Christmas crackers and drawn by children. One of his countless wives – a European – was accommodated in a special European-style mansion in its own grounds, known as *Vilayati Bagh* – 'Blighty Park'. A Lucknow painting of about 1814 depicts him presiding rather gloomily over a profuse mixed-company banquet in a palace with its proper ration of lustre wall-shades, sporting prints, and mirror-frames topped with astonishing plumes of wire and stucco, while a European lady guest squints speculatively at the ceiling. His successor was painted in 1831 at a smaller party, dressed like a slimmed-down Ruritanan clone of George IV, festooned and bespangled with glittering orders, against a modest corona-domed backdrop which could double for a Muharram *taziyah* or a shell grotto in Dorset (no.107). This little pavilion is illuminated by a chandelier, a pair of triple-light girandoles, and two hanging lamps. The reality was bizarre, but more sinister: the Decline and Fall of the Roman Empire performed at the Brighton Pavilion. In 1837 Nasir-ud-din Haidar was poisoned, supposedly by his relatives. The fireworks were fizzling out, their light most lurid towards the end.

Home's work at Lucknow had a lasting influence. 'School of Home' designs, which cleverly adapted European styles and blended them with Indian elements, spread from Lucknow (nos. 186-87) to other cities including Benares (no.188) and Delhi, where in 1838 the last of the Mughal emperors was painted occupying a Home-style throne (no.109). The tradition survived longest in the palaces of Rajasthan. Regal furniture in the Home idiom, often encased in sheets of silver and occasionally gold, became standard issue for the Rajput princes of the middle and late 19th century, taking its place with the huge mirrors, sporting prints and drooping chandeliers so weighty that one Maharaja had an elephant experimentally hoisted to the ceiling first. Palace interiors of this kind can still be found in 1982.
VM

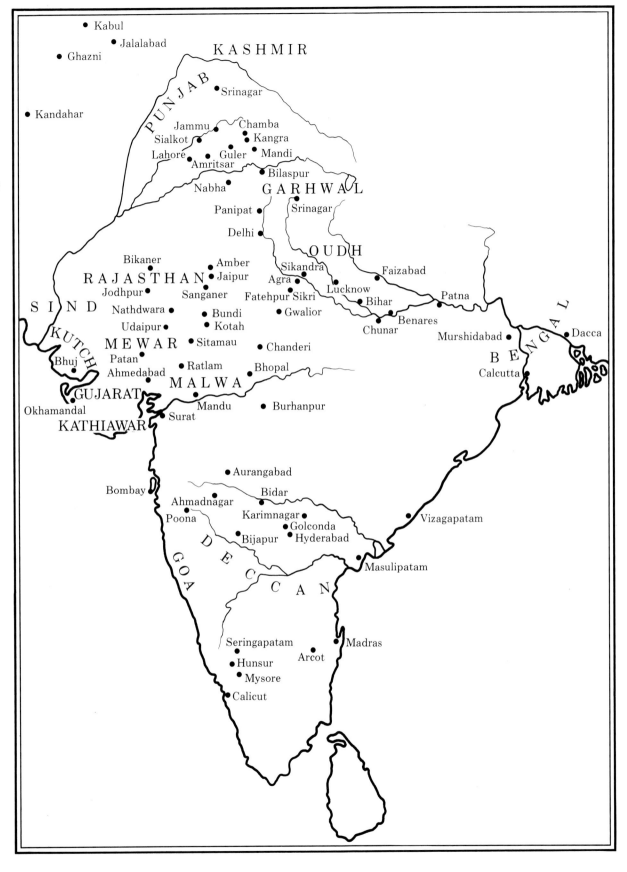

Chronology

1504
Babur occupies Kabul

1526
Babur defeats Ibrahim Lodi at Panipat

1527
Babur defeats Rajput chiefs at Kanwa near Agra

1530
Accession of Humayun

1540
Rebellion of Afghan chiefs causes Humayun to flee to Sind, Afghanistan and Persia

1555
Humayun returns and establishes himself at Delhi and Agra

1556
Accession of Akbar

1561
Malwa conquered

1564
Humayun's tomb built at Delhi

1565
Agra fort started

1568
Chitor falls to Akbar

1571-85
Building of Fatehpur Sikri

1573
Gujarat conquered

1580
First Jesuit mission to Akbar's court

1586
Kashmir falls to Akbar

1580-1627
Reign of Ibrahim 'Adil Shah II of Bijapur

1600
Founding of the East India Company

1605
Accession of Jahangir

1613
Akbar's tomb at Sikandra completed

1615-19

Thomas Roe's embassy to Jahangir's court

1620
Kangra taken

1628
Accession of Shah Jahan

1634-48
Building of the Taj Mahal

1638
'Ali Mardan Khan, Governor of Qandahar, surrenders it to Mughals

1640
Delhi fort started

1649
Qandahar occupied by Persians under Shah 'Abbas II

1649-53
Unsuccessful Mughal campaigns to regain Qandahar

1658
Accession of Aurangzeb

1668
Aurangzeb dismisses the Court musicians and prohibits all Hindu religious fairs

1686
Bijapur taken by Aurangzeb

1687
Golconda (Hyderabad) taken

1707
Accession of Bahadur Shah I (Shah 'Alam I)

1712
Accession of Jahandar Shah

1713
Accession of Farrukhsiyar

1719
Accession of Muhammad Shah

1739
Nadir Shah invades and occupies Delhi

1748
Accession of Ahmad Shah

1754
Accession of 'Alamgir II

1757

Battle of Plassey : Clive defeats Nawab Siraj ud-daula of Bengal

1759
Accession of Shah 'Alam II

1782
Accession of Tipu Sultan

1792
Accession of Ranjit Singh

1806
Accession of Akbar Shah II

1818
Rajasthani kingdoms accept British suzerainty

1839
Death of Ranjit Singh

1858
Bahadur Shah II, last Mughal Emperor, is deposed and goes into exile in Burma

Architecture & its decoration

The reputation of the Mughal Emperors, particularly Akbar, for fostering cultural unity in India has sometimes resulted in an over-emphasis on their role in creating a synthesis between Hindu and Muslim elements in Indian civilization. In actual fact this synthesis already existed during the pre-Mughal Sultanate period. If Akbar speeded the process, he was nevertheless heir to an advanced rapprochement in many spheres.

This is certainly true of architecture. Under the preceding Lodi dynasty (1451-1526) there were significant common features in secular buildings erected for both Hindu and Muslim patrons, while the transition from Lodi to Mughal architecture is scarcely perceptible. It is amazing how rapidly a new, aesthetically convincing, school of Islamic architecture arose in India during the first decades of the Delhi Sultanate (c.1200). Hindu masons, schooled in a tradition of trabeate (post and beam) construction were suddenly required to erect massive structures featuring the pointed arch and domed vault. Lacking experience of constructional technology that had originated in the riverine valleys of the Mediterranean and Near East, they were forced to imitate the appearance of arcuate structures by the indigenous device of corbelling across a void.

As Muslim rule was consolidated, the principles of the true arch and the vault were acquired and even found their way into some Hindu temple construction. Yet a creative tension between these two radically opposed building systems remained as a fruitful, if at times incongruous, element in the evolution of Indian architecture.

By the reign of Akbar (1556-1605), this unnatural alliance had produced many visually satisfying variations from the arch intersected by a bracketed lintel to assemblies of trabeated kiosks (chhatris) around a central dome. In Humayun's tomb (no.122) the Indian craftsmen's lithic mastery was brilliantly applied to forms derived partly from Iranian brick-built models, but Akbar's buildings at Agra and Fatehpur (no.137) exhibit a resourceful freshness in the adaptation of ancient principles of pillar, beam and bracket to structures of vigorously inventive design.

The bracket, in particular, was subjected to ingenious replication in courtyards modelled on those of Maharaja Man Singh Tomar's palace (c.1500) on the fortress rock of Gwalior, a building admired by Akbar's grandfather, Babur. Elaborate stone descendants of an early tradition of wooden brackets were a staple element of indigenous Indian architecture, imparting a particularly rich decorative effect to courtyards, whose overhanging eaves (chajja) served equally to protect adjoining rooms from the sun's rays and monsoon rain.

Under Akbar and Jahangir (no.2) these bracket lined courts continued to be built of the sandstones which Hindu masons had worked for countless generations. These were often combined with bold marble inlays, but in Jahangir's reign marble revetments began to be applied to the surfaces of whole buildings (no.124), permitting greater refinement of relief carving (nos. 1 & 131) and more minute control of colour through semi-precious stone inlays: pietra dura (eg. no.4).

Jahangir (1605-27), a less dynamic innovator than his father, is seldom credited with sensitivity to architecture, but this is almost certainly unjust. Instead, sovereignty of the age of marble is bestowed on that prodigious builder Shah Jahan, who tore down or altered the palaces of his immediate forebears in order to recreate the forts of Agra and Lahore before embarking on his great palace complex of Shahjahanabad, Delhi (nos. 95, 126, 132). If this reign established a norm for Mughal architecture thereafter, it also sowed the seeds of its decline as the over-refined lines of the High Mughal style (no.130) degenerated into flamboyant exaggeration (no.129). This was carried to its greatest excesses in the provincial courts of the late 18th and 19th centuries such as Lucknow (no.117), or in Rajasthan, where an originally restrained departure from Mughal sobriety (no.11) was finally abandoned in a riot of wild extravagance.

As with the buildings themselves, so with their decoration. Shah Jahan's reign (1628-58) marks the limits of Mughal innovation. From then on, their decorative evolution is only one of weakened proliferation, stereotyped repetition or rococo fantasy. Because of its eclectic origins, the development of this Mughal decorative style has a far more complex history than that of its slow decline and although buildings most often provide us with its chronological markers, it is relevant to our understanding of all the decorative arts.

One of the glories of Qutb ud-Din Aibak's great mosque screen (1199 AD) at Delhi, with which the story of Indo-Islamic architecture begins, is the sinuous scrolling plant stem, which unfolds itself around the sanctuary arcade. However superbly appropriate it may seem on this mosque façade, it is nevertheless entirely redolent of the lush vegetal embellishment with which Hindu temples proclaim their allegiance to the chthonic powers of fertility and growth. It was inevitable, of course, that the decoration of such monuments would soon take on a more overtly Islamic character particularly with the decline of temple building as a vehicle for artisan training. In some provinces, such as Gujarat, the Hindu decorative tradition remained powerful and had an important fertilizing influence on Mughal architecture when Akbar imported Gujarati masons to Agra and Sikri after his conquest of the province in 1572. Despite the persistence of an indigenous ornamental tradition in Indo-Islamic architecture, a more recognisably Islamic foliate decoration also came into use. It appears on an extension to Qutb ud-Din's mosque added by his successor Iltutmish (1211-1236) where, instead of flowing with organic rhythms, the scrolling stems interlace, and their leaves are stylised split palmettes of almost mechanically precise outline. This dynamic but austere classical arabesque, found throughout the world of Islam from Spain to Ghazni, had infinite variation but also possessed an almost canonical purity making which made it valid in buildings of all periods, even after new forms of arabesque gained currency. It is present in architecture throughout the Mughal period and in the minor arts it was especially favoured by the makers of armour and weapons (no.459) whether they were employed by Muslim, Sikh or Hindu patrons.

A more naturalistic type of floral arabesque developed under Far Eastern influence, following the Mongol invasions of the Near East in the thirteenth century, and this reached its most sophisticated development under the Timurids, whose works at Herat and Samarqand so strongly influenced the taste of Babur and his successors. This same artistic currency – in which the arabesque repertoire is enhanced by lotus palmettes, peonies and other flowers, together with a variety of leaf forms and Chinese cloud patterns – was also in vogue among the Mughals' Safavid and Ottoman contemporaries. Like the formal split-leaf arabesque this persisted throughout the Mughal period in architecture as well as in other arts such as book illumination (no.66), carpet manufacture (no.194), and objects in other media (no.419). It equally found favour in the kingdoms of the Deccan, where Ottoman and Iranian influences were particularly strong (no.491). As in Iran and Turkey, its Far Eastern constituents were also reinforced by the import of Chinese blue and white porcelain, of especial importance in India, where there was no indigenous tradition of fine ceramic manufacture.

If arabesques are a characteristic expression of Islamic ornament, geometric patterns are no less so and the two are closely linked, in their fundamental properties of infinite extension over a two-dimensional surface, in their mathematical organisation and in their shared tendency towards interlacement. At their most complex, both astonish and delight the eye with a visual counterpoint in which rhythmically organised pattern will emerge from or remingle with other kaleidoscopic shapes or intertwining lines. Baffling as it is to both eye and mind, Islamic geometric ornament is based on quite simple combinations of square and circle from which endless varieties of polygons may be constructed, either by connecting intersections or by omitting to do so. Such geometric schemes, in which the hexagon often played a major role, were especially suitable for openwork grilles (jali), which gave privacy and shade from sunlight, while encouraging the passage of cool air (nos. 15-17). In Mughal architecture, especially during the earlier reigns, geometric designs were also a major element in the decoration of wall surfaces, whether in the form of stone relief, cut plaster, tile mosaic or stone inlay. For obvious reasons they were particularly suitable for inlays (no.124) or for techniques such as architectural joinery, in which façades were built up from wooden panels (nos. 19-20). This bias towards geometric pattern is similarly found where inlay techniques are used for domestic objects in wood (no.554). Metal inlays never had this bias

due to their malleability and with the great advancement of lapidary skills under Mughal patronage even stone inlaying became freed from its dependence on geometric motifs.

However, the revolution, which resulted in the introduction of *pietra dura* towards the end of Jahangir's reign, was not simply due to the refinement of craft techniques but also to changes in the Mughal's decorative vision, which demanded more subtle manipulation of hard materials in the interest of a new eclecticism of design. As in the case of the means – *pietra dura* (no.4) and naturalistically modelled relief carving (nos.11 and 13) – the decorative result was influenced by an awareness of Italian Renaissance art, which by this date had spread through much of Europe and was being carried to India in the form of rarities in demand at the court (no.299), engravings (no.44) and itinerant craftsmen (nos. 375-377). A very clear indicator of this Renaissance influence is the sudden re-appearance of acanthus foliage (nos. 11, 13, 356 etc.), which had disappeared after India's early contact with the Graeco-Roman world. Less obvious is a new and more spacious arrangement of strapwork in cartouche panels, whose articulation derives from Italy's revival of the grotesque as modified by European interest in the 'Moorish' ornament of Venetian metalwork and seen in the designs of such engravers as Cornelis Floris or Balthasar Sylvius. Apart from its appearance on buildings in Shah Jahan's reign this new organization of arabesque panels influenced the development of trellis designs (nos. 195, 201) which became popular in this reign.

The most characteristic element of the High Mughal style is the repetition of the formal flowering plant, which owes its peculiar combination of stylisation and naturalism to European herbals (no.64) which were copied by Mughal artists following the Emperor Jahangir's trip to Kashmir in the Spring of 1620. Almost immediately, the border decoration of Jahangir's royal picture albums changed from decorative landscapes or arabesques (no.44) to flowering plants spaced out in rows (nos. 41, 50 & 67) as in some of the herbal engravings themselves. By Shah Jahan's reign this arrangement of flowering plants in rows or other combinations was becoming a dominant motif in architecture (nos.125-27) and soon invaded the decorative arts, particularly carpets and textiles (nos. 203, 218, 226, 282-83). It is difficult to see how it could be otherwise for the Mughals were schooled on the Memoirs of their ancestor Babur, whose passion for natural history was inherited by Jahangir. They were aware of the current vogue for floral decoration among their European contemporaries, and no other ornamental motif could have accorded more fully with their own refined sensibilities and inherited taste.

RS

25

1
Stele
White marble.
Height : 56cm, *Width* : 33.5cm
Inscribed with a Persian couplet of the Emperor Jahangir and the date AH 1027 corresponding to the 13th regnal year = 1618AD.
Lent by the British Museum, Department of Oriental Antiquities, 1956.5-19.4.
The slab has the outline of a cusped arch and is carved in relief with four lobed cartouches containing Persian inscriptions in *nasta'liq* script with flowers as space fillers. The top cartouche states the circumstance of the couplet's composition and the lowest contains the date. It was made on Jahangir's orders while the court was residing at Ahmedabad during the royal tour of Gujarat. In his Memoirs (*Tuzuk* II,30), the emperor records that 'In the middle of the garden of Khurram (Shah's Jahan's) residence there is a bench and a reservoir. On one side of that bench there is a Mulsari-tree (*Mimusops elengi*) against which to lean the back. As in one side of its trunk there was a hollow to the extent of three-fourths of a yard, it had an ugly look. I ordered them to cut a tablet of marble and fix it firmly in that place, so that one could lean one's back on it and sit there. At this time an impromptu couplet came to my tongue, and I ordered the stone-cutters to engrave it on that stone, that it might remain as a memento on the page of time. This is the couplet:
The seat of the Shah of the seven worlds, Jahangir, son of Akbar Shahinshah.'
The floral decoration on the slab is typical of the refinement achieved in Jahangir's reign and owes much to Timurid ornament.　　RS

2
Bracket
Sandstone
Height : 61cm, *Width* : 86.4cm
Mughal, Lahore, c.1617-18
VAM : I.S.1066-1883
The bracket is carved in the form of an elephant and rider (partly broken) between two horizontals with a lotus bud hanging from the upper one.
It comes from 'Jahangir's Quadrangle' (*Daulat khani-i jahangiri*) in Lahore Fort, which was started by Akbar but completed during Jahangir's reign. This bracket formed part of the frontage of carved columns and animal brackets, and reflects the same heritage of Hindu palace architecture as is found in the

early buildings of Agra and Fatehpur Sikri.
Bibliography : Khan (1958), pp.17-18, fig.6).　　RS

3
Colonnade
Serpentine
Height : 307cm
Mughal, 1st half of the 17th century.
VAM : I.S.3394-1883
The colonnade is of four twelve-sided columns and four half-columns each with bracket capitals and ornamental brackets in front.
It comes from a royal pavilion at Ajmer and may date from the reign of Jahangir, although the surviving pavilions on the Anar Sagar Lake were built by Shah Jahan.
The architectural style reflects the eclecticism of Mughal art in which the capitals of the column derive from Near Eastern prototypes, but the serpentine brackets with pendent lotus buds stem from Hindu tradition.　　RS

4a
Frieze panel (pietra dura)
Marble inlaid with carnelian, yellow and black marble and serpentine.
Height : 24.5cm, *Length* : 82.6cm
Mughal (Agra), c.1640
VAM : 1534-1855

4b
Panel (pietra dura)
Marble inlaid with yellow and black marble and carnelian.
Height : 14cm, *Length* : 91.5cm
Agra jail, c.1880 after original of c.1626
VAM : I.S. 1093-1883
This probably copies a detail from I'timad ud-Daula's tomb.　　RS

5
Thirteen tiles
Faïence.
Max. height : 19.7cm, *Width* : 22.2cm
Mughal, 2nd quarter of the 17th century.
VAM : I.M. 250, 263, 266, 268, 271, 278, 279, 283, 284, 287, 297 and 300-1923, and Circ. 1293-1923.
The tiles show various parts of several floral designs : four are of flowers within a trellis, three of sprays of flowers on a dark ground, one of flowers in a vase, one of flowers with a part of what may be a peacock, one a large flower with two leaves, and three border designs, of which two are of scrolling flowers and the other scroll with alternate lion masks and donkey heads.
The tiles are in *cuerda seca* technique,

in which the design is outline on the fired tile with a manganese-purple pigment mixed with a greasy substance which separates the areas to be coloured. These are then painted with a brush and the tile is fired a second time; the greasy lines disappear, leaving a dark outline separating the different colours.
These tiles come from the tomb of Madani, near But Kadal in Srinagar, Kashmir. The building itself dates from the mid-15th century, but was refurbished by a Mughal nobleman in Shah Jahan's time.
They show a strong similarity to the *haft rangi* (seven coloured) tiles of Safavid Persia, using the same range of colours that gave those of Persia their name.
Bibliography : Archaeological Survey of India, Annual Report for 1906-7, pp.162 ff., plates LVII-LIX.　　RC

6
Tile
Faïence
Height : 20.5cm, *Width* : 20.5cm
Mughal, 2nd quarter of the 17th century.
VAM : 1-1898 (I.S.)
The tile is made in the *cuerda seca* technique (see no.5) and shows two ibexes in front of a tree with a clump of flowers.
This tile, like the others exhibited, shows a strong affinity with contemporary Persian tiles, and may have been made by Persian craftsmen working in India. A pair of very similar ibexes is depicted on a tile panel in an Armenian church in Julfa, near Isfahan, the Safavid capital, one of the major centres of *cuerda seca* tile production.
Bibliography : Coomaraswamy (1913), fig.189; Carswell, J.: *New Julfa*, Oxford, 1968, pl.IV, pp.26-27.　　RC

7
Tile
Faïence
Height : 19.4cm, *Width* : 20.0cm
Mughal (Lahore), c.1645
VAM : 25-1887 (I.S.)
The tile, in *cuerda seca* technique (see no.5) shows a sprig of flowers against a yellow background, enclosed within a framework of scrolling leaves. It comes from the tomb of Asaf Khan, brother of the Emperor Jahangir's wife Nur Jahan, and father of Shah Jahan's wife Mumtaz Mahal. The tomb is at Shahdara near Lahore.
Bibliography : Brown (3rd ed.), pp.115-6; Vogel (1920), p.10.　　RC

8
Tile
Faïence
Height : 23.5cm, *Width* : 23.5cm
Mughal, probably Lahore, 2nd quarter of the 17th century.
VAM : 941-1873
The tile is painted in the *cuerda seca* technique (see no.5) with the figure of Layla visiting her lover Majnun in the desert. The emaciated figure of Majnun is only partly shown with his hand extended holding a fruit. The subject is taken from the Persian poet Nizami's poetical romance *Layla wa Majnun*.　　RS

9
Three tiles
Faïence
Max. length : 27.9cm, *Width* : 25.4cm
Mughal (Delhi), 2nd quarter of the 17th century.
VAM : 303 to 305-1890 (I.S.)
These *cuerda seca* tiles show two borders of scrolling floral design, one with chevronned borders, and part of a caparisoned ox with a flowering plant and Chinese clouds.
These tiles are from a building in Delhi, where a number of buildings have the remains of tile decoration of various types : tiles executed in the *cuerda seca* technique are found on the west wall of the tomb enclosure of Qutb ud-din Bakhtyar Kaki at Mahrauli, and may have been used elsewhere in the Delhi area, possibly imported from Lahore.　　RS

10
Four tiles
Faïence
Max. height : 23.5cm, *Width* : 23.5cm
Mughal (Lahore), 2nd quarter of the 17th century.
VAM : 46, 59, 71 and 76-1898
Three of these *cuerda seca* tiles show field patterns : lilies in a trellis (46-1898); part of a tree from which shoots are sprouting (59-1898); leaves and Chinese clouds (71-1898). The fourth (76-1898) is part of a border containing a plant scroll.　　RS

5

6

8

11

12

14

11
Architectural slab showing a banana plant
Marble
Length : 64cm, *Width* : 50.6cm
Amber, late 17th century
Lent anonymously.
The buildings of Amber Palace from the time of Mirza Raja Jai Singh I (1622-68) were influenced by the palace architecture of Shah Jahan, which provided models for Jaipur marble carvers until the present day.
The cusping of the arch with its counterpoint of acanthus leaves is characteristic of Mughal design, but the flamboyant banana plant and the *makaras* from which the arch springs are Rajput motifs. RS

12
Two stepping stones in the form of lotus flowers
Marble
Height : 16cm, *Diameter* : 34.7cm
Agra or Eastern Rajasthan, 17th-18th century
Lent by Mr Howard Hodgkin.
Stepping stones such as these were placed in marble water channels in Mughal or Rajput gardens from the reign of Shah Jahan onwards. RS

13
Throne for a deity (pitha)
Marble
Width : 74.2cm
Rajasthan, 18th-19th century.
VAM : IPN 14
The throne stands on four legs and resembles a Mughal throne with a lobed back and relief decoration of acanthus and smooth-edged leaves. On either side of the open front are two guardian figures seated holding staves. A similar throne is depicted in the painting of Maharana Jagat Singh at worship (no.144). RS

14
Hunting hound
Sandstone
Height : 47cm, *Length* : 33.2cm
Rajasthan, early 19th century.
Lent by Mr and Mrs J.W. Alsdorf, Chicago.
The dog is seated as though looking up at its owner and may be the stylised portrait of a favourite animal made for a Rajput nobleman. Similar hounds are commonly depicted in Rajasthani hunting pictures and occasionally are the subjects of individual portraits (see Tooth & Sons (1974), nos.14 and 64; *idem* (1975) no.49). RS

15
Seven openwork screens (jali)
Sandstone
Max. height : 69cm, *Max. width* : 132cm
Agra, 19th century
VAM : 1032 to 1035-1883, 1037-1883, 02172, 02173

16
Seven openwork screens (jali)
Sandstone
Max. height : 86.2cm, *Max. width* : 77.2cm
Agra, 19th century
VAM : 02186, 02187, 02189, 02190 & A,02192 (I.S.)
Bought from the Vienna Exhibition, 1873.

17
Three openwork screens (jali)
Sandstone
Height : 61cm, *Width* : 38.2cm
Mathura, Agra, 19th century.
VAM : 1 to 3-1889. Given by J.A.C. Vincent, Esq.

18
Doorway
Carved teak, studded with iron bosses.
Height : 278.4cm, *Width* : 157.2cm
Mughal, late 17th century.
VAM : I.S.20-1920
From a house at Agra, said to have been the residence of a Mughal court official. The door is in two leaves, the left being provided with an overlap bar. Each leaf is divided into five square panels, each carved with a spray of double poppy, iris or other flower within a circle formed by a double stem bearing flowers and leaves. The jambs, lintel and superstructure have mouldings and bands carved in floral, trellis and other designs in low relief. Above the lintel are three recessed rectangular panels with floral decoration. There are five short iron chains to secure the door from the outside. RS

18a
Painted panel: Ganesha and female deities
Gouache on wood
Height : 6.5cm, *Length* : 30cm
Southern Rajasthan, late 17th century.
Lent by the National Museum of India, New Delhi. 75-654.
The auspicious elephant god Ganesha appears in the centre of the panel, attended by his rat *vahana*, maids and Rajput noblemen. Different forms of the Goddess appear at either side,

including Sarasvati on a goose, and Devi on a lion. AT

19
Bay window
Deodar wood, with traces of red, green, blue and yellow paint.
Height : 119cm, *Width* : 92.1cm
Lahore, late 18th century.
VAM : I.S.431-1883
This window and no.20 are from the same house. The window openings on both are separated by baluster columns decorated with chevron patterns and have sliding shutters carved in openwork with geometric ornament. RS

20
Window
Deodar wood, with traces of paint of various colours.
Height : 210cm, *Width* : 204cm
Lahore, late 18th century.
VAM : I.S.432-1883.

21
A pair of doors
Wood with brass and iron fittings.
Height : 180cm, *Width* : 59cm
Punbjab Hills, mid 19th century.
Private collection.
Each door contains thirty carved panels containing foliage and birds, except for those forming the second row from the top which contain deities and their attendants. On the left door these are the Goddess Durga and two male figures. On the right are Ramachandra with Hanuman flanked by a man and a woman. The frames of the doors are decorated with brass studs. RS

22
Cupboard
Teak
Height : 143.6cm, *Width* : 77.6cm
Baroda, 19th century
VAM : 104-1883 I.S.
The cupboard has three shelves and eleven compartments, with foliated arches and a projecting carved cornice supported by two architectural brackets. It is painted in red, yellow and green. It probably came from the shop of an apothecary in Baroda. RC

Paintings
& the arts
of the book

Court painting in the Mughal period was both prolific in quantity and varied in character. During three centuries of imperial rule (c.1555-1857) artists found almost continuous employment at the Mughal court, whether at Agra, Fatehpur Sikri, Delhi or Lahore, or in the emperor's travelling camp on hunting expeditions and campaigns. The Mughal nobility and, from the 18th century, provincial rulers such as the Nawabs of Oudh and Murshidabad offered similar patronage. The independent Muslim Sultanates of the Deccan maintained their own graceful styles of painting until their subjection by Aurangzeb in the 1680s, and various diminished local styles continued thereafter. The numerous semi-independent Hindu rulers of the Rajput kingdoms of Rajasthan, Central India and the Punjab Hills also retained in some measure their bold pre-Mughal traditions of devotional and poetical manuscript illustration, while complementing these with local versions of court portraiture after the Mughal style. In the latter part of our period even the most minor local chiefs and *zamindars* frequently supported an artist or two, to make conventional likenesses of their patron or to produce series of *ragamala* scenes or other traditional subjects. The widespread influence of the imperial court style throughout North India and the Deccan was to some extent a unifying factor in this diversity of regional production. In its emphasis on official portraiture and court scenes it carried with it a more soberly naturalistic vision than had prevailed before in Indian art. But its conventions were often interpreted quite freely by provincial artists, who were by temperament rooted in their own longstanding local traditions of painting.

Like much else in Mughal India, the imperial style was above all the creation of the energetic personality of Akbar. Early in his reign he had brought together a large atelier of native artists under the direction of the two great Safavid masters, Mir Sayyid 'Ali and Abd us-Samad, whom his father, Humayun, had taken into employment when in exile in Persia. Under Akbar's close supervision, a vigorous style of epic and poetical manuscript illustration was rapidly formed, which combined Persian technical refinement with Indian intensity and feeling for nature, with an additional leavening of European naturalism, acquired from prints and pictures which had begun to reach the court through merchants and Jesuit missionaries. The Akbari style reached its maturity by about 1590 in the illustrations to a number of historical manuscripts, of which the *Akbarnama*, the official history of the reign by Abu'l Fazl, is an outstanding example (nos. 25-32).

Akbar's achievement as a patron was both consolidated and further refined by Jahangir, who sought quality more than quantity in the work of his painters. The direction of Mughal painting turned away from manuscript illustration to the production of choice individual pictures, usually portraits or animal and flower studies, which were mounted in splendidly decorated borders and bound in albums for the emperor's perusal. Much of this work shows a growing debt to European models. King James's ambassador, Sir Thomas Roe, records Jahangir's eager interest in the English portrait miniatures which he showed him, and his glee when Roe (who complains of the bad lighting provided) was unable at first to distinguish between an original miniature and the copies of it made by Mughal artists. These same artists attained unusual eminence in the life of the court, sometimes being given grandiloquent titles; Mansur (nos. 36, 46), who specialized in the animal and flower studies which served Jahangir's interests as an amateur naturalist, was known as 'Wonder of the Age'. Closely observed portraits and court scenes, both official and more informal in atmosphere, were painted by artists such as Govardhan (nos. 47, 52) and Bichitr (nos. 49, 50, 53). Towards the end of Jahangir's reign, as his health and powers dwindled, elaborate allegorical scenes combining Islamic, Hindu and European imagery were made to affirm his continuing glory (no. 48).

Little new direction was given to Mughal painting by the later emperors. Under Shah Jahan, who cared more for architectural projects and the lapidary arts, court portraiture hardened into a magnificent but stiffly official style (nos. 56, 57, 68, 71). Aurangzeb's deposition of his father and murder of his elder brother Dara Shikuh in 1658-9 was a further turning-point. Dara Shikuh (no. 67), who as the favourite son of Shah Jahan had devoted much of his time to learning, mystical thought and artistic patronage (nos. 58-62), was thus replaced in the Mughal line by a pious and puritanical soldier, who curtailed the extravagant luxuries of Shah Jahan's court and spent much of his long reign fighting futile and expensive campaigns in the Deccan. The Mughal artists were largely dispersed to provincial centres, and under Aurangzeb's effete and often short-lived 18th century successors their tradition slowly stagnated, although some masterly work was still done in the reign of Muhammad Shah (no. 85). An afterglow of the great period of Mughal painting continued at the courts of Oudh and Murshidabad (nos. 86, 92), but the increasing power of the British East India Company following Clive's victory in Bengal in 1757 led not only to the adoption of exotic occidental influences (nos. 93, 103, 104, 107, 108) but eventually to the transference of artistic activity to the so-called Company school of hybrid Europeanized painting. The earliest agents in its development were scholarly European enthusiasts of Indian culture such as Col. Gentil (nos. 87, 89) and Col. Polier (no. 90). They were followed as patrons by countless British residents and travellers who would commission or buy increasingly standardized series of illustrations of native crafts, castes, pastimes and festivals (nos. 100-102, 113-15) or of topographical views of the famous Mughal monuments (nos. 118-35).

Painting at the Deccani and Rajput courts owed much to Mughal example, while preserving distinctive differences of style and temper. The Deccani school, before it was cut short by Aurangzeb, had a delicacy and brilliance of colour and line and an atmosphere of aesthetic languor which was foreign to the more earnest, propagandist Mughal style; it reflected the proclivities of patrons such as Ibrahim Adil Shah of Bijapur (nos. 43-44) for whom music and the arts were a commanding passion. The numerous Rajput schools of painting, isolated in the deserts and hills of the north-west, enjoyed a greater longevity. After their submission to Akbar and Jahangir, the Rajput nobility had become increasingly exposed to the fashions and tastes of the imperial court. By the end of the 17th century most of them patronized more or less assimilated versions of Mughal portraiture and court scenes. Often these stock subjects were reinterpreted with freshness and originality. The school of Udaipur was perhaps the most versatile in this respect. From the beginning of the 18th century the Maharanas of Udaipur commissioned great numbers of unusually large pictures depicting life at their court, including formal durbars, religious festivals and also the private pleasures of the rulers (nos. 140-46, 149, 157). In a different, more intimate way, we are also offered a revealing view of the life of a minor Hill prince, Raja Balwant Singh of Jammu, whose gifted artist, Nainsukh, recorded his daily pursuits and devotions with unusual sympathy and candour (nos. 163-66). At the same time, earlier traditions of devotional and secular manuscript illustration also continued to develop at the Rajput courts: *ragamala* scenes, in which the musical modes (*ragas* and *raginis*) are visualized as male and female figures in conventional (often amorous) situations, were the most popular subject matter of all (nos. 138-39; 82 is a Deccani example).

The paintings in this exhibition are not intended as a representative display of the different regional schools. The main purpose in selection, which has been served by the inclusion of a majority of Mughal and Company pictures, is above all a social historical or documentary one: both to illustrate daily life in its public and private aspects at the Mughal and other courts, and to show the role of the court artists and craftsmen in maintaining that way of life and contributing to its splendour. The public sphere of court life is shown in the durbar and other formal scenes (nos. 40, 68, 78, 104, 109, 140, 155), as well as in the portraits imbued with imperial symbolism (nos. 48, 52, 53, 56, 57), and in scenes of war (nos. 27, 31, 77, 79, 84) and hunting (nos. 32, 34, 42, 80, 141, 151). The more private side of the rulers' life includes the pursuits of religion, whether Muslim (nos. 25, 55, 74, 83, 97, 110) or Hindu (nos. 142, 144, 149, 159, 163), of the patronage of learning and the arts of the book (nos. 35, 37-39, 43, 45, 51, 54, 58, 66), of music and dance (nos. 26, 36, 44, 82, 90, 103, 138-39, 165), and of the games and pastimes enjoyed in the closed world of the *zenana* (nos. 76, 86, 91, 101, 102, 147, 148, 154, 168). The Mughals' pursuit of connoisseurship and collecting is illustrated in those portraits where they are shown holding jewels or ornaments (nos. 41, 50, 67); many other Mughal pictures contain similar documentary evidence of the work of the court artisans. The crafts-men themselves appear in a number of pictures (nos. 23, 33, 65, 87, 100, 113-16, 169, 170), as do, more rarely, the bazaars and merchants

with whom their wares found an outlet (nos. 111, 152, 160-62). A section is devoted to craftsmen's designs and working patterns of the 18th and 19th centuries (nos. 89, 171-90), which in many cases in their emphasis on floral ornament continue to look back to the Mughal passion for flowers seen in the paintings, as in all the other arts, of the reigns of Jahangir and Shah Jahan.

AT

31

Mughal, Deccani & Company Schools

23
Zarir, the weaver of silk garments at his loom in Nishapur
From a manuscript of Zia' ud-din Nakshabi's *Tuti Nama* 'Tales of a Parrot'.
Gouache
Page height : 19.6cm, *Width* : 12.8cm
Mughal, c.1580-85
Lent by the Trustees of the Chester Beatty Library, Dublin: MS. 21 (f.79r).
The *Tuti Nama* is a collection of cautionary tales in which a parrot deters its mistress from infidelity. On the 17th night it relates the fate of a weaver who, failing to make a profit in Iraq, sets up his loom successfully in Nishapur but is robbed. Although the story sets this incident in Iran, the illustration depicts a contemporary Indian weaver at work.
Bibliography : Nakshabi (1978), p.179
D. James (1981).   RS

24
Babur supervises the construction of the Garden of Fidelity
by Bishndas, portraits by Nanha.
Gouache
Height : 21.9cm, *Width* : 14.4cm;
Height : 22.2cm, *Width* : 13.6cm
A double page from a *Babur Nama* manuscript.
Mughal, c.1590
VAM : I.M. 276 & A-1913
Babur was a habitual constructor of pleasant gardens in his long career of travels and conquests. He records in his memoirs that the Bagh-i Wafa (Garden of Fidelity) was laid out near Jalalabad (in Afghanistan) in 1508/9 'on a rising ground, facing south . . . There oranges, citrons and pomegranates grow in abundance . . . [In 1523/4] I had plantains brought and planted there; they did well. The year before, I had had sugar cane planted there; it also did well . . . The garden lies high, has running water close at hand and a mild winter climate.'
Bibliography : *Babur Nama* (1922), p.208; S. Crowe *et al.* (1972), pp.56ff. AT

32

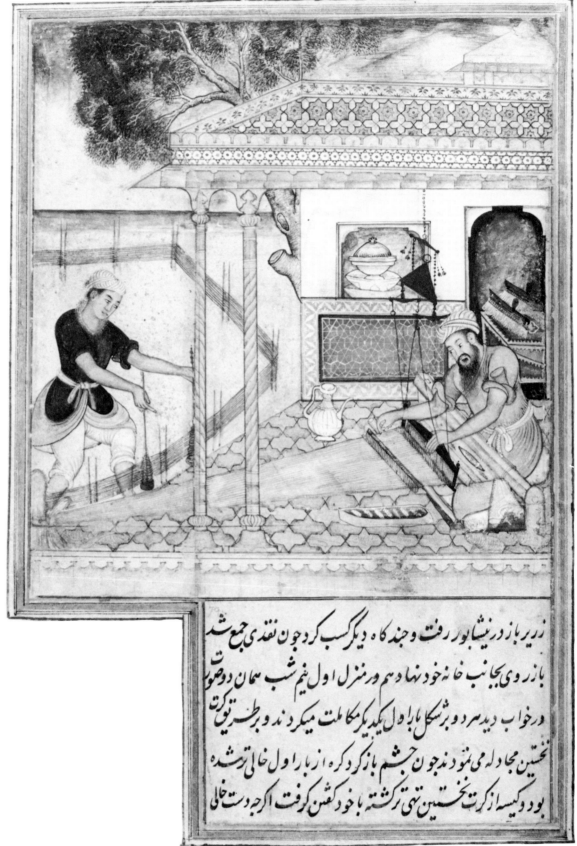

23

درختهای انا هم هست کردا کرد حوض تمام سبزه زار

بای عن باغ همین است در وقت زرد شدن با بجهار سیار

24

25
Akbar as a child visiting the saint Baba Bilas
Gouache
Height : 28.9cm, *Width* : 17.2cm
From an *Akbar Nama* manuscript.
Mughal, c.1590
Lent by the Trustees of the Chester Beatty Library, Dublin.
During their exile from India, the nine-year-old Akbar was sent to Ghazni by his father Humayun in 1551. He remained there six months and often visited the saint Baba Bilas, who is said to have discerned in him the marks of future greatness.
Bibliography : Arnold and Wilkinson (1936), vol.1, p.48; vol.3, pl.89.　　AT

26
Dancing girls taken from Baz Bahadur's place at Mandu perform a kathak dance before Akbar in 1561
Outline by Kesu Kalan, painting by Dharmdas.
Gouache
Height : 37.5cm, *Width* : 25cm
From an *Akbar Nama* manuscript.
Mughal, c.1590
VAM : I.S. 2-1896 (16/117)
Bibliography : *Akbar Nama* (1902), II, p.221.　　AT

27
Bullocks dragging siege-guns uphill during Akbar's siege of Ranthambor Fort in 1568.
Outline by Miskin, painting by Paras.
Gouache
Height : 37.5cm, *Width* : 24.5cm
From an *Akbar Nama* manuscript.
Mughal, c.1590
VAM : I.S. 2-1896 (72/117)
Bibliography : Stchoukine (1929), pl. XI; Welch (1963), no. 11b.　　AT

28
Rejoicings at the birth of Salim
Outline by Kesu Kalan, painting by Dharmdas.
Gouache
Height : 37.5cm, *Width* : 25cm
From an *Akbar Nama* manuscript.
Mughal, c.1590.
VAM : I.S. 2-1896 (78/117)
After Akbar had long remained without an heir, his first surviving son was born in 1569 at Sikri at the home of the Sufi Shaykh Salim Chishti. In his gratitude Akbar named the child (later the Emperor Jahangir) after the Shaykh, and subsequently erected the new capital city of Fatehpur Sikri on the spot (see nos. 29, 30, 136, 137).　　AT

29

Workmen building the royal city of Fatehpur Sikri
Outline by Tulsi Kalan, painting by Bhawani.
Gouache
Height: 37.5cm, *Width*: 24.2cm
From an *Akbar Nama* manuscript.
Mughal, c.1590
VAM: I.S. 2-1896 (86/117)   AT

30

Akbar inspecting the building of the new city of Fatehpur Sikri
Outline by Tulsi Kalan, painting by Bandi, portraits by Madhu Khurd.
Gouache
Height: 38cm, *Width*: 24cm
From an *Akbar Nama* manuscript.
Mughal, c.1590
VAM: I.S. 2-1896 (91/117)   AT

31

Akbar directing the siege against Rai Surjan Hada in Ranthambor Fort
by Khem Karan.
Gouache
Height: 37.5cm, *Width*: 25cm
From an *Akbar Nama* manuscript.
Mughal, c.1590
VAM: I.S. 2-1896 (73/117)   AT

32

Akbar hunting in an enclosure
Outline by Miskin, painting by Mansur.
Gouache
Height: 37.5cm, *Width*: 25cm
From an *Akbar Nama* manuscript.
Mughal, c.1590
VAM: I.S. 2-1896 (56/117)
The *battue* was a favourite Mughal form of hunting. An army of beaters (numbering fifty thousand on one occasion) formed a huge circle and drove the game towards its centre until it was concentrated in a small area. The *qamargah* or enclosure was then formed with screens, and the emperor began the carnage, which could last for days.
Bibliography: Welch (1978a), pl. 14. AT

33

Diwan-i Hafiz with border decoration showing a goldsmith at work
Manuscript
Height: 24.4cm, *Width*: 17cm
Text: Iran, first half of the 16th century.
Borders: Mughal, late 16th century.
Lent by the Marquess of Bute.
The border decoration added in India includes a variety of human, bird and animal figures in decorative cartouches. The craftsman uses an earthenware kiln resembling that in use today, blowing

33

the charcoal through a tube while introducing the work to the heat with tongs. A mortar, mallet and pincers lie to hand. An autograph note of the Emperor Shah Jahan states that this copy was written by the celebrated calligrapher Sultan 'Ali and although the colophon page is missing it seems unlikely that the emperor would have invented this. An earlier autograph shows that it also belonged to Jahangir, who quotes from the poems of Hafiz in his memoirs.
Bibliography : Skelton (1976), p.251. RS

 35

34
A falconer
Gouache
Height : 14.5cm, *Width* : 9cm
Mughal, c.1600
Lent by the Los Angeles County Museum of Art.
The nobleman wears a hawking glove and a full length hunting *jama*, embroidered with a *simurgh* and various fowl and different animals and their prey in a landscape setting.
Bibliography : Welch (1963), no.19.   AT

35
Abu 'l-Fazl presenting the first book (daftar) of the Akbar Nama to Akbar
Illustration from a royal copy of the *Akbar Nama*.
Gouache
Height : 24cm, *Width* : 13.5cm
Inscribed on the margin as being the work of Govardhan.
Mughal, c.1605
Lent by the Trustees of the Chester Beatty Library, Dublin : MS. 3. f. 177r.
This illustration to Abu'l-Fazl's postscript (*khatima*) appears at the end of his account of the first thirty years of Akbar's life, completing the first book of the 'Annals of Akbar' with events up to AD 1572. The actual presentation, however, could not have occurred until after April 1596 when Akbar's primeminister finished writing this *daftar*, which is in two parts, dealing with the history (I) up to and (II) after Akbar's accession.
In the painting, which forms half of a double-page, Abu'l-Fazl kneels before the emperor proferring one volume, with the other beside him. For illustrations from the royal copy of the first *daftar* which was evidently presented on this occasion see nos. 25–32.
Bibliography : *Akbar Nama* (tr.) II, pp.544-576; Arnold & Wilkinson (1936), I, p.10, II, frontispiece; E. Blochet (1929), pl.CLXXXII; L. Schulbert (1968), p.177; G. Hambly (1968), fig.9.
RS

34   *35*

36

Portrait of a vina player *(binkar)*
Gouache
Height : 9.2cm, *Width* : 7cm
Inscribed in Persian: *'amal-i mansur
naqqash* 'Work of Mansur the Painter'.
Mughal, c.1605
Private Collection.

This performer holding a *bin* or North
Indian *vina* is possibly Naubat Khan
Binkar the son-in-law of Akbar's celebrated musician Tansen. His name was
Misri Singh and his title suggests that
36   he may have been placed in charge of
the *Naubat Khana*, where kettle drums
(*naubat*) placed over the guardhouse
are played at certain hours of the day.
In 1607 this title passed to another
official (*Tuzuk* I., 111), perhaps after
Misri Singh's death.
Mansur was one of Jahangir's principal
artists who specialised in natural history
painting (cf. no.46).
Bibliography : S.C. Welch (1964),
p.164 no.18; A.K. Coomaraswamy
(1926), p.39, pl.XXVIII; Moti Chandra
and Khandalavala (1955-6), pp.19 &
23; A.K. Das (1974).   RS

37

Jahangir receives an artist in camp
Gouache
Height : 22.3cm, *Width* : 14.6cm
(*Page height* : 35cm, *Width* : 23.5cm)
Mughal, c.1605
Lent by the India Office Library and
Records : Johnson Album 27, 10.
The emperor sits with a few courtiers
on a terrace within the royal enclosure
of the imperial camp and reaches to
take a painting offered by a young artist,
as a court official reads from a document. Another member of the library
staff waits with a manuscript and a
musician plays a zither (*qanun*). It is
possible that this represents Jahangir's
patronage of painting shortly before his
accession.
Bibliography : T. Falk and M. Archer
(1981), p. 64, no. 53.   RS

38

The Emperor Babur seated reading
Gouache
Height : 18.2cm, *Width* : 11.3cm
Inscribed in margin : *shah babur*.
Mughal, c.1610
Lent by the Trustees of the British
Museum : 1921-10-11-03.
The emperor's pose, costume and
throne follow a Persian model but the
landscape details are characteristic of
the early Jahangiri school. It has been
perceptively suggested that this is by

or from the circle of the Khurasani immigrant Aqa Reza and the curious calligraphic device near the prunus sapling may conceal the name of the artist. The emperor's outer jacket is of interest in relation to number 252. However, it is not necessarily an embroidery and it is possible that an Iranian figured velvet or woven silk is represented.
Bibliography : E. Blochet (1929), pl. CIX; I. Stchoukine (1929), pl. XXXV; R. Pinder-Wilson (1976), no. 102.　　RS

39
Quatrain
Reverse of painted leaf from an album.
Ink and gold
Height : 15cm, *Width* : 7.9cm
Signed : *raqimahu sultan khurram sanah 1020* 'The writer, Sultan Khurram, year 1020/1611-12'
Mughal, c.1611-12 AD
Private collection.
This leaf is from a series from an album put together for Prince Khurram (later Shah Jahan) during his youth to preserve his writing exercises. Some of these were copies of inscriptions made by his father in manuscripts in the royal library and others, like the present example, were Persian love poetry with mystical connotations. He was 19 or 20 years old when he copied this poem. It may perhaps be translated :
Tonight, here am I with a like-minded companion :
An assembly adorned like a garden,
A cup of wine, pleasing sweetmeats and a musician are all here,
Oh, would that you were here and not all these!
Bibliography : R.W. Skelton (1976), pp.256-7, pl.126; A. Welch (1979), pp.182-3. no.78.　　RS

40
Jahangir weighing Prince Khurram on his sixteenth birthday
From an illustrated copy of the Emperor's Memoirs (*Tuzuk-i Jahangiri*).
Gouache
Height : 26.6cm, *Width* : 20.5cm
Inscribed in Persian with a line of the text (*Tuzuk* I, p. 115) and the names of the chief persons depicted.
Mughal, c.1615-25
Lent by the Trustees of the British Museum : 1948-10-9-069
The prince was weighed against gold, silver, etc. in July 1607 (6 Rabi' II 1016) on the occasion of his 16th lunar birthday and the money given to the poor. This took place during a day spent at Khurram's residence in the

Urta Garden at Kabul. Those present in the picture include the Khan-i Khanan, holding the pan of the scales, with (left to right) I'timad-ud-daula, Asaf Khan, Mahabat Khan and Khan Jahan Lodi behind him. The prince's presents to his father on this occasion are shown being listed by an official of the Steward's department. They include daggers, jewellery, gold vessels and silks, which are depicted with particular care.
Bibliography : Barrett and Gray (1963) pp.103-4; Pinder-Wilson, (1976), pp.68-9; S.C. Welch (1978a) pl.18.　RS

41
Shah Jahan as a prince, holding a jewel
From the Minto album.
Gouache
Height : 20.6cm, *Width* : 11.5cm
(*Page height* : 39cm, *Width* : 26.7cm)
Inscribed, top: *Shah Jahan*; right: *Auspicious Likeness of the Cynosure and Lord of Mankind*; lower border: *A good likeness of me aged twenty-five and it is the fine work of Nadir uz-Zaman.*
Mughal, c.1616-17
VAM : I.M. 14-1925
The prince stands in a flowery meadow richly jewelled and holding an aigrette of European design, (Evans pp. 98-9). In his girdle he wears a *jamdhar* dagger similar to an example in the Wallace Collection (Norman (1971) p. 1554 fig. 1) and several bow rings hang from a cord at his waist. It has been suggested that the inscription giving his title as Shah Jahan was added after the picture was painted (Beach, p. 90). This assumes that the phrase *bist a panj salagi man ast* means 'in my twenty-fifth year', i.e. 1024 AH (1615-16 AD) and that Shah Jahan is referring to his lunar birthday, in April 1615, when he became aged 24. In fact, the Mughals celebrated both lunar and solar birthdays and were not consistent in stating their age. Jahangir states that his son was 24 in January 1616 (*Tuzuk* I, p.306) and the prince became 25 by the solar reckoning in January 1617. It was in October of that year, while he was still 25, that he was given the title Shah Jahan. The artist Nadir uz-Zaman is known to have been travelling with the Imperial camp at this time and it is likely that he made this picture to commemorate Prince Khurram's elevation to the new title.
Bibliography : I. Stchoukine (1929), pl.XXXII; B. Gascoigne (1971), p.186; M. Beach (1978), p.90; Pinder-Wilson

(1976), pp.70-71; *Princely Magnificence* (1980), pp.5 and 131; J. Evans (1970), pls.98-9; A.V.B. Norman (1971), p.1554, fig.1.　　RS

42
'Abdullah Khan Uzbeg out hawking
From the Minto album.
Gouache
Height : 28cm, *Width* : 16cm
(*Page height* : 38.7cm, *Width* : 26.9cm)
Inscribed in Persian: *shabih-i 'abdullah khan uzbeg 'amal-i nadir al-zaman* 'Likeness of 'Abdullah Khan Uzbeg, work of Nadir uz-Zaman.'
Mughal, c.1618
VAM : I.M. 20-1925
'Abdullah Khan II of the Shaybanid dynasty ruled Transoxiana from his capital at Bukhara from 1583 to 1598. He is attended by a falconer with a hooded bird (see no.293) and at his saddle is a falconer's drum (see no.509). This composition exists in several versions and ultimately depends upon a Persian prototype. It is probable that Jahangir's interest in 'Abdullah Khan was stimulated by an old retainer of the Uzbeg ruler who visited the court in 1618 and pleased the emperor with his anecdotes. It was doubtless this visit which prompted the commissioning of the picture.
Bibliography : F.R. Martin (1912), pl.177; P. Brown (1924), pl.IX; Ivanov *et al.* (1962), pl.14; *Tuzuk*, II, p.30.　RS

43
Verses in nasta'liq script with surrounding decoration
From a manuscript of the *Kitab-i Nauras*, of Ibrahim 'Adil Shah.
Ink and gold on paper (re-marginated)
Height : 13.4cm, *Width* : 5.6cm
(*Page height* : 20.6cm, *Width* : 11cm)
Written by Khalilullah Butshikan.
Bijapur; AH 1027/1618 AD
Lent by Catherine and Ralph Benkaim.
The *Kitab-i Nauras* is a collection of songs in Dakhini Hindi by Ibrahim 'Adil Shah of Bijapur, who named his work after the nine sentiments, *nava rasa*, of classical Sanskrit prosody.
The present page from a copy made for Ibrahim by his leading court calligrapher, contains the last line of Song no. 40 in Nazir Ahmed's edition and the whole of Song 3b which personifies the musical mode Karnati as a beautiful woman suffering the pangs of separation from her lover.
The gold decoration surrounding the lines of text is a *tour de force* of minute refinement. On either side are trees

with delicate foliage filled with a variety of birds but the most inventive feature is the decoration between the lines. In descending order these are 1 running foxes, 2 cranes, 3 wisps of cloud, 4-7 swimming ducks. See detail below.
Bibliography : N. Ahmed (1956), pp.37, 114, 116, 140.　　RS

42

43

44a

44

A page from the Jahangir Album
Painting (recto) by Farrukh Beg, calligraphy (verso) by Mir 'Ali.
Gouache, ink and gold.
Height: 62.5cm, *Width*: 42.0cm
Mughal, c.1019 AH/1610-11 AD (with paintings, prints and calligraphy of the 16th and 17th centuries).
Lent by the Náprstek Museum, Prague.
Jahangir's painting album, started while he was a prince (c.1600) and continued until at least 1618, was a scrap book of which the unifying feature was the painted borders decorated with arabesques or inhabited landscapes.
Recto (numbered 97 at the bottom): Borders of gold arabesques, inspired by Chinese painted porcelain, and inhabited by animals and birds painted in colours, surround a painting mounted with two late sixteenth century Flemish engravings of the saints Francis and Teresa above it. The painting, which is the principle item on the folio, is a portrait of Sultan Ibrahim 'Adil Shah II of Bijapur (ruled 1590-1627) as a master musician. He sits against cushions resting on the trunk of a tree playing his lute (*tanbur*) while receiving the acclamation of three leading musicians seated before him. A youth attends the king with refreshments and in the distance are palaces and royal elephants. The inner border of the pictures is inscribed in Persian: (upper) 'God is great. The likeness of Ibrahim 'Adil Khan of the Deccan, ruler of Bijapur, who, in the knowledge of the music of the Deccan, considers himself superior to the masters of that art'; (lower) 'And (it is) the work of Farrukh Beg, in the fifth regnal year (i.e. of Jahangir) corresponding to the year 1019, written by the humble servant Muhammad Husain of the Golden Pen (in the service of) Jahangir Shah'.

The provenance and date of the painting is controversial, but there is no question that it is in the manner of an extremely accomplished artist who worked for Ibrahim 'Adil Shah at Bijapur, and is perhaps the ruler's leading painter, Farrukh Husain, who was praised in the prefaces to Ibrahim's *Kitab-i Nauras* (no.66). It has been suggested (Skelton, 1957), that Farrukh Beg worked for a while at Bijapur before returning to the Mughal court, and that he may have been known as Farrukh Husain during his stay in Bijapur. This view is supported by the style and inscription of the present painting and by the inscription on another unpublished page of the same album in Tehran which was painted by Farrukh *Husain* at Kabul in 992/1584-5 shortly before Farrukh *Beg* left there for the Mughal court on the death of his patron, Mirza Muhammad Hakim, in July 1585 (see Atabay, 1353 *shamsi*, p.357). If the present picture was made by Farrukh Beg in Bijapur and presented to Jahangir, it is likely to have been painted in about 1605 when Ibrahim was aged 25. In this case, the date 1019 (1610-11) is that of the inscription but a difficulty is presented by the fact that there is a gap between this and the signature of the scribe. If the date is that of the picture, we must presume that Farrukh Beg made a copy for Jahangir of the original that he made a few years earlier.
The musical instrument shown here is doubtless Ibrahim's celebrated *tanbur*, 'Moti Khan', which he praises in the *Kitab-i Nauras*.
Verso: A quatrain of Persian verse, written in *nasta'liq* by the 16th century Persian master Mir 'Ali, and remounted with a Mughal painting of two birds (early 17th century) within gold landscape borders. The partly coloured figures seated in the landscape are a Safavid prince and musician, a lapidary grinding or polishing a ruby on a bow lathe, an astrologer and a youth reading.
Bibliography: Hájek (1960), pp.70-74, pls.10-18; Ahmed (1977), p.24 ff.   RS

44b (detail)

46

47

45
Abu'l-Fazl : *Ain-i Akbari*
Manuscript with four pages of illustrations
Height : 34.2cm, *Length* : 21.5cm
Mughal, AH 1031/1621 AD
Lent by the Trustees of the British Library : Or. 2169.
The *Ain-i Akbari* 'Institutes of Akbar' is a survey, with statistics, of the Mughal Empire by Akbar's prime minister, completed in 1598 AD.
This copy has four full pages illustrating various weapons and personal ornaments of which the last is displayed here (f.351b.) and shows sixteen bracelets, rings, etc., as listed on the preceding folio. The facing page of Persian text begins the chapter on 'Workmen in Decorative Art' with a description of the Indian mode of gem setting followed by accounts of inlayers (*zarnishan*), gold encrusters (*koftgar*), enamellers (*minakar*), goldsmiths (*sadakar*), specialists in openwork (*shabakakar*), repoussé workers (*munabbatkar*) and granulation workers (*charmkar*). RS

46
A zebra
From the Minto album.
Gouache
Height : 18.3cm, *Width* : 24cm
(*Page height* : 26.9cm, *Width* : 38.7cm)
Inscribed in Persian in Jahangir's hand:
astari kih rumiyan az habashat bi-hamrahi-yi mir ja'far avardah budand sanah 1030 wa shabih-i inra nadir al-asri ustad mansur kashidah sanah 16 'A mule which the turks in the company of Mir Ja'far had brought from Abyssinia (in the) year 1030 (1620-21) and the Wonder of the Age, Ustad Mansur, has drawn it, (in the regnal year) 16.'
Mughal, c.1621
VAM : I.M. 23-1925
This zebra was among the gifts presented at the commencement of Jahangir's sixteenth regnal year in March 1616. Mir Ja'far served as governor of Surat and Cambay where he carried on trade as a merchant. The emperor records in his Memoirs 'At this time I saw a wild ass (*gur-khar*), exceedingly strange in appearance, exactly like a tiger. From the tip of the nose to the end of the tail, and from the point of the ear to the top of the hoof, black markings, large or small, suitable to their position were seen on it. Round the eyes there was an exceedingly fine black line. One might say that the painter of fate, with a strange brush, had left it on the page of the world. As it was strange, some people imagined that it had been coloured. After minute enquiry into the truth, it became known that the Lord of the world was the Creator thereof. As it was a rarity, it was included among the royal gifts sent to my brother Shah 'Abbas.'
Two other (unsigned) Mughal zebra studies are known, not necessarily of the same animal. It is clear from his remarks in the *Tuzuk* and inconsistency over its identity (mule or wild ass) that this was Jahangir's first encounter with a zebra.
Bibliography : *Tuzuk* II, p.201;
I. Stchoukine (1929), pl.XXVII; Alvi and Rahman (1968), p.34, pl.VI;
S.C. Welch (1978a), pl.27; A.K. Coomaraswamy (1926), p.51, pl.XLII;
Spink & Son (1980), p.37, no.70. RS

47
Music in camp
From the Minto album.
Gouache
Height : 23cm, *Width* : 16.7cm
(*Page height* : 38cm, *Width* : 27cm)
Inscribed : *'amal-i govardhan* 'Work of Govardhan'.
Mughal, c.1620-25
Lent by the Trustees of the Chester Beatty Library, Dublin : MS.7A no.11.
A singer accompanied by a *rababi* kneel near their tent on the outskirts of the imperial camp near a village on the edge of a tank. A Gorakhpanthi *yogi* and another man sit and listen while the activities of the camp followers continue in the background.
Unlike its Near Eastern precursor, the traditional *rabab* of Muslim India is a plucked instrument (cf. no.564).
Bibliography : Arnold and Wilkinson (1936) I. p.30, III. frontispiece;
S.C. Welch (1978a), pl.28; D. James (1981), p.39. RS

48

48
Allegorical portrait of Jahangir as the Just Ruler triumphing over Poverty
Gouache
Height : 24cm, *Width* : 15.25cm
(*Page height* : 36.75cm, *Width* : 24.25cm)
Inscribed in Persian: *surat-i mubarak-i hazrat-i a'la kih tir-i kazam nishan-i daliddr (ya'ni shakhs-i iflas) ra az 'alam bar andakhtand wa jahan ra bi 'adal wa dad bana'i az nau sakhtand* ''Auspicious likeness of His Exalted Majesty who discharged the voracious arrow at the target of Poverty and gave the world a new foundation with his rectitude and justice'.
Mughal, probably Abul Hasan, c.1625
Lent by the Los Angeles County Museum of Art : M.75.4.28.
Jahangir, nimbate, personifying the sun, shoots arrows into the figure of Poverty, an emaciated old man shrouded in darkness. Two *putti* hold a crown above his head and a third proffers arrows to the king. Jahangir's justice is symbolised by the chain of bells alternating with yak tails tied to a post set on a plinth and held up by a *putto* in the clouds. In emulation of the legendary Anushirwan, Jahangir ordered that these bells should be suspended from his apartments above the wall of Agra fort so that suppliants could gain his attention at any hour. Beneath his feet is the globe symbolising universal dominion on which the lion and sheep lie down together in tranquillity under his just rule. The world rests on the fish as according to Islamic legend but the old man resting on the fish holding his book of laws is Manu the Hindu lawgiver and first king of the solar line. The picture belongs to the end of Jahangir's reign and may reflect his mood in 1624 when he ordered that the blind, maimed or sick should be driven from his sight when he left the palace. The use of the Hindi word *dalidr* (=*daridr*) recalls the use of this word in the ceremony of driving away poverty in Hindu households during the Diwali Festival.
Bibliography : M.H. Kahlenberg (1972), pl.XCII; M.C. Beach (1978), p.92.   RS

49
Prince Salim with scholars and companions in a garden
From the Minto Album.
Gouache
Height : 28cm, *Width* : 20.2cm
(*Page height* : 38cm, *Width* : 27cm)
Inscribed in Persian: 'Work of Bichitr'
Mughal, c.1625

Lent by the Trustees of the Chester Beatty Library: MS.7 no.7.

The painting by one of the most accomplished 'official' painters who served Shah Jahan (see no.53), shows him already at the peak of his powers in the last years of Jahangir. With more developed pictorial resources available to serve his nostalgia, the deteriorating monarch was able to re-live the years at Lahore and Allahabad when he enjoyed convivial and stimulating company in better health and with fewer worries. Here, as in the inscription on one of his jade cups (no.351), his devotion to poetry and wine are combined. The stacked porcelain cups which he is draining without assistance are Chinese imported prototypes of another of his jade cups (no.350). Other evidence of the trade in imported luxuries is the use of European glass and an Ottoman velvet curtain. The *pandan* and spittoon are Indian and the green bowl curiously resembles another of Jahangir's hardstone vessels (no.372).

Bibliography: Arnold & Wilkinson (1936) I., p.29, III., pl.58; E. Blochet (1929) pl.CXCII; S.C. Welch (1978a), pl.36; D. James (1980), p.41, no. 51(e); P. Schulz (1914) II., pl.92.   RS

50

Prince Salim holding a mirror
From the Minto album.
Gouache
Height: 25cm, *Width*: 18.1cm
(*Page height*: 38.8cm, *Width*: 26.4cm)
Inscribed in Persian on the border by Shah Jahan: 'Drawing (*raqm*) by Bichitr.'
Mughal, c.1625
VAM: I.M. 28-1925
The picture shows Jahangir as a young man, as he was some 30-40 years before it was painted. He stands holding a mirror with a jewelled frame of European design. The knife (*kard*) suspended from his belt is unusual in having its hilt in the form of a human head and this may be a slightly distorted representation of the knife hilt which shortly afterwards was owned by Shah Jahan (no.406). For another late portrait of Jahangir as a young man see no.49.
Bibliography: G. Hambly (1968) p.72, fig.47; Pinder-Wilson (1976), p.77.   RS

51

Persian verses on a decorated page
From an album assembled for Prince Dara Shikuh.
Ink, gouache and gold.

Height: 18cm, *Width*: 9.1cm
(*Page height*: 40.1cm, *Width*: 26.2cm)
Signed in Persian Arabic and partly erased: *harrarahu dara shikuh* 'Written by Dara Shikuh'.
Mughal, c.1630
Lent anonymously.
This is the *verso* of a page of which the *recto* has a portrait of the Emperor Humayun seated on a terrace.
The verses, written in an accomplished *nasta'liq*, comprise two couplets ascribed to Mir Abu'l-Ma'ali, who is perhaps the Mir Shahi Abul Ma'ali who was a favourite of Humayun and wrote poetry under the pen name, Shahidi. They refer to the celebrated Sufi theorist 'Abd ul-Karim Jili, who died in the 15th century:
Shah Jili of felicitous stars:
His shadow stretches for ever!
For anyone in the shade of his bounty,
Sin is devotion and the enemy, a friend.
The calligraphy is executed on gold-dusted, marbled paper within cloud shaped panels surrounded by birds and flowers painted on a gold ground. It is mounted with blue outer borders decorated in gold with a large floral arabesque occupying cusped medallions. Dara Shikuh was a talented practitioner of the writing style of his great teacher 'Abd-ur-Rashid Dailami and the most noted calligrapher of his family. Like his father (cf. no.39) he had his exercises gathered together in at least one album of which this one was put together during or soon after the court stayed at Burhanpur (March 1630-March 1632) when the prince was 16-17 years old. It was possibly for this album rather than that named after him (nos. 58-62) that he composed a preface in which his appreciation of the art and its relation to painting is expressed in high-flown phrases.
Bibliography: Sotheby & Co. (11 April 1972), lots 84-86; R.H. Pinder-Wilson (1976), pp.79-80, no.140; A. Welch (1979), pp.188-89, no.81; B.J. Hasrat (1953), pp.160-67.   RS

52

Timur hands his imperial crown to Babur
From the Minto album.
Gouache
Height: 29.3cm, *Width*: 20.2cm
(*Page height*: 38cm, *Width*: 27cm)
Inscribed in Shah Jahan's hand: 'The work of Govardhan'.
Mughal, c.1630
VAM: I.M. 8-1925
The Amir Timur (Tamerlane) sits

between the first two Mughal Emperors, all three enthroned on a carpeted terrace beneath a triple canopy. Before each ruler stands his *wazir* leaning upon a staff: Mirza Rustam before Babur, Mirza Shah Rukh before his father Timur and Bairam Khan in front of Humayun.
The painting was made as the pair to no.53 and the two together emphasized the legitimacy of the Mughals as descendents of the great Central Asian conqueror, who had captured Delhi in 1498. This painting was at one time the first folio of one of Shah Jahan's royal albums. For a dagger similar to that worn by Jahangir see no.416.
Bibliography: S.C. Welch (1976), p.48. RS

41

52

53
Akbar transfers the Timurid crown to Shah Jahan
From the Minto album.
Gouache
Height : 29.7cm, *Width* : 20.5cm
(*Page height* : 38cm, *Width* : 27cm)
Inscribed on the footstool before Shah Jahan: *'amal-i ghulam ba-ikhlas bichitr sanah 3(?)* Work of the loyal servant, Bichitr, (regnal) year 3(?).
Mughal, dated in the 3rd (?) regnal year = 1039/40 (AD 1630-1)
Lent by the Trustees of the Chester Beatty Library : MS.7 no.19.
This companion painting to no.52 shows Akbar seated between his son and grandson on a carpeted terrace beneath a canopy decorated with birds of paradise. Motifs on the elaborate thrones include elephants on that of Akbar, and the allegorical motif of lion and sheep on the other two. Before each monarch stands his *wazir*: I'timad ud-daula, father-in-law of Jahangir, Khan A'zam ('Aziz Khan), foster-brother of Akbar and Asaf Khan, brother-in-law of Shah Jahan. At one time this was the last folio of an album of Shah Jahan but originally it may have been intended as a double-page opening with no.52.
Bibliography : Arnold and Wilkinson (1936) I, p.33, III, pl.65; E. Blochet (1929), frontispiece; D. James (1981), p.40. RS

54
Manuscript of the Kimya-i Sa'adat : the 'Chemistry of Felicity'
by al-Ghazzali.
Gold-speckled paper in a brown morocco binding painted in gold.
Height : 14.8cm, *Width* : 9.7cm
Inscribed on the first page *naskhat-i kimya-i sa'adat dar 'ilm-i akhlaq. muhammad ghazzali tusi* and signed by the scribe (f.128) *mohammad reza*.
The manuscript Persian or Indian, 16th-17th century; the binding Mughal, 1630-40, with later repairs to borders and spine.
Lent by Mr Bashir Mohamed.
This is a copy of a famous mystical work on the religious and moral duties of the true believer by the great Sufi master al-Ghazzali of Tus (1058-1111 AD). It is written in a fine *nasta'liq* on gold-sprinkled paper with gold margins. The Mughal binding is of gold morocco finely painted in gold with a lily and smaller flowering plants with Chinese clouds. RC

54

55
Ibrahim 'Adil Shah venerates a learned Sufi
Gouache
Height : 16.2cm, *Width* : 14.4cm
(*Page height* : 41.4cm, *Width* : 29cm)
Inscribed in Persian on a flask in the picture: *sihhat wa 'afiyat* 'Health and Prosperity'; and on the border: *mashshaqahu khanazad 'ali reza*. 'Drawn by the 'house-born' (servant) 'Ali Reza'.
Bijapur, Deccan, c.1630-40
Lent anonymously.
The Sufi Shaikh sits at ease in a room under a canopy from which ostrich eggs are suspended. He holds a scroll and a pair of pince-nez, a peach at his left side and a manuscript and scroll to his right. Lying on the manuscript is a small gold plaque decorated with a horseman and an elephant with riders. A youthful attendant stands behind him with a cloth with which to fan his master. Beside the Shaikh, but ignored by him, Sultan Ibrahim 'Adil Shah II adopts the role of cup-bearer, holding a flask (cf. no.501) and a large gold cup.
The painter 'Ali Reza is known by a few signed works of which this and a drawing in the Museum (no.D.398-1885) appear to be slightly later versions of subjects in the style of Ibrahim 'Adil Shah II's reign. Another painting, formerly in the Ardeshir collection, shows a blending of the mid-seventeenth century Mughal and Bijapur styles as does his portrait in the India Office Library (J.64 no.29).

55

A second portrait, formerly in the Khajanchi collection, shows that he entered the service of the Maharaja of Bikaner, who served in the Deccan wars. An inscription on this saying that he came from Delhi appears unreliable in view of the style of his earlier work together with the present inscription which suggests he was born in the service of the Bijapur court. His masterpiece at Bikaner was the record of his patron's dream of Vishnu, now in the Bharat Kala Bhavan, Banaras. Although Ibrahim 'Adil Shah II is known to have associated with various Sufi Shaikhs there is at present insufficient evidence to identify the main figure.
The picture is mounted on an eighteenth century album page with a floral diaper border. The inscription has evidently been recopied from the original border at the time of remounting.
Bibliography : Ardeshir (1940), fig.9; Sotheby & Co. (1973), lot 25; Soustiel and M.C. David (1974), no.30; Khandalavala, Moti Chandra, Pramod Chandra (1960), nos.83 and 113; Falk and Archer (1981), no.457; Eaton (1978), p.107 ff. RS

56
The Emperor Shah Jahan in Majesty
From the Minto album.
Gouache
Height : 24.6cm, *Width* : 16.3cm
(*Page height* : 38cm, *Width* : 27cm)
Inscribed in Persian by the emperor:

'Work of Bichitr'.
Mughal, c.1630
Lent by the Trustees of the Chester Beatty Library, Dublin : MS.7 no.16.
A typical example of Bichitr's work as an official painter producing an allegorical portrait of the emperor emphasizing his imperial power and glory. Richly jewelled and holding a turban ornament of European inspiration, the emperor stands on the terrestrial globe above the lion and sheep who lie down together under his just regime. His power and magnanimity are symbolised by the repentant figure of the Bundela raja, Jujhar Singh, who submitted to the emperor in 1629 after falling out of favour. Angels bear the dynastic crown above the imperial head and Muslim divines standing on clouds acknowledge his supremacy as the 'Shadow of God' on earth. It was Mughal custom for a defeated rebel to wear his sword round the neck as a sign of submission. The decapitated head of Jujhar Singh after his death in 1635 is illustrated in the Windsor *Padshah Nama* (f.175).
Bibliography : Arnold and Wilkinson (1936) I, p.32, III, pl.63. RS

42

57

Shah Jahan on the Peacock Throne
From a royal album of Shah Jahan
Gouache
Height : 16.7cm, *Width* : 12.6cm
(*Page height* : 37.9cm, *Width* : 26.7cm)
Mughal, c.1635
Lent anonymously.

The emperor sits against a cushion
holding a rose on the golden enamelled
and jewel encrusted throne which has
four legs and four columns supporting a
rectangular domed canopy with projecting cornice and two peacocks
perched above. The outer border of the
album page is particularly fine and
unusual, being a trellis of unequal
openings containing flowers and birds.
This celebrated throne was planned at
the beginning of the reign as a means of
displaying the immense wealth of jewels
in the royal treasury. It was completed
seven years later in time for the New
Year Festival of 1635 (A.H.1044). All
the literary accounts, whether of official
historians or European travellers, give
conflicting descriptions and valuations
of the throne but pictorial representations are more consistent. If we accept
the visual evidence, then Bernier was
wrong about the number of legs (six)
but right about the peacocks. Tavernier,
who appears to have examined it more
closely only mentions one peacock but
rightly mentions four legs. Tavernier
and Lahori in the *Padshahnama* des-
cribe twelve columns supporting the
canopy but it seems that these were
probably short supports for the eleven
panels which made up the sides. No
writer mentions four large columns
supporting the canopy and no painting
shows the 'trees' or bouquets of flowers
mentioned in association with the birds
by Lahori and Tavernier. According to
Bernier the peacocks were made by a
Frenchman, who may have been Austin
of Bordeaux. Brown's suggestion that
the throne may have been altered after
this picture was painted is borne out
neither by Lahori nor by its similar
depiction early in Aurangzeb's reign.
Bibliography : *Badshahnama*, II, p.62;
Ma'athir-ul-umara, I, pp.397-99;
F. Bernier (1891), pp.268-69; J.B.
Tavernier (1889) II, pp.303-5;
Manrique II, p.198-99; 'Abdul Aziz (n.d.),
pp.35-73; Brown (1924), p.90. pl.XXV;
I. Stchoukine (1935), no.VIII; S.J. Falk
(1973), pp.181, 208. For comparisons,
see S.C. Welch (1963), no.58;
A.A. Ivanov, *et al*. (1962) pl.34; Binney
(1973), nos.58 and 64.   RS

58a & b

**Binding and opening pages (ff.1-2)
of the Dara Shikuh Album**
The binding, morocco stamped with
gold; the pages painted in gold, with
inscriptions.
Height : (page) 32.5cm, *Width* : 23.5cm
Mughal, c.1635-40
Lent by the India Office Library and
Records. Add.Or.3129.
The Dara Shikuh Album was assembled
in c.1633-42 and the binding (A) is
contemporary, though recently restored.
The covers are of black morocco with a
panel of red morocco with a design of
strapwork and flowers stamped in gold.
The doublures are of red morocco with
a central medallion and gold openwork
cornerpieces on a blue ground.
The pages (B) are decorated in gold
with formal landscape settings with
animals and birds. F.2 bears the partially
obliterated dedication, dated 1640/1,
in Dara Shikuh's own hand to his wife,
Nadira Banu Begam. F.1 bears inscriptions from the reign of Aurangzeb,
when the obliteration of Dara Shikuh's
inscription was probably carried out
following his capture and execution by
Aurangzeb in 1659.
Bibliography : Falk and Archer (1981),
pp.72-74, 379.   AT

59

An iris plant and a butterfly
From the Dara Shikuh album.
Gouache
Height : 19.1cm, *Width* : 10.8cm
(*Page height* : 32cm, *Width* : 22cm)
Mughal, c.1635
Lent by the India Office Library and
Records : Add. Or. 3129, (f.41v).
The plant has evidently been copied
from an engraving from a European
herbal (cf. nos.63-64).
Bibliography : Falk and Archer
(1981), pp.79 and 391.   RS

60

A narcissus plant
From the Dara Shikuh album.
Gouache
Height : 19.2cm, *Width* : 10.8cm
(*Page height* : 32cm, *Width* : 22cm)
Mughal, c.1635
Lent by the India Office Library and
Records : Add. Or. 3129 (f.42r).
The plant is apparently based on a
European engraving from a herbal.
(Cf. nos.63-64).
Bibliography : I. Stchoukine (1929),
pl.XLVI b.; Falk and Archer
(1981), pp.78, fig.390.   RS

61

Flower study : exotic flowers with insects and gold clouds
Gouache
Height : 17.5cm, *Width* : 9.8cm
From the Dara Shikuh Album (f.49v).
Mughal, c.1635
Lent by the India Office Library and Records : Add. Or. 3129 (f.49v).
Bibliography : Falk and Archer (1981), pp.79, 394.   AT

62

Flower study: a pink rose, a blue iris, a pimpernel and other flowering plants
Gouache
Height : 16.9cm, *Width* : 10.1cm
From the Dara Shikuh Album (f.67v).
Mughal, c.1635
Lent by the India Office Library and Records : Add. Or. 3129 (f.67v).
This painting is attributed by Falk and Archer to the same artist as cat. no.40.
Bibliography : Falk and Archer (1981), pp.80, 399.   AT

63

A Martagon Lily
Small Clive Album f.1
Gouache
Height : 21cm, *Width* : 12.7cm
(*Page height* : 35.2cm, *Width* : 24cm)
Mughal, 17th century
VAM : I.S. 48-1956
The design has ultimately been derived from the 'Martagum Pomponeum' etched as plate 15 of Pierre Vallet's *Le Jardin du très Chrestien Henri IV* and provided the first conclusive evidence that Mughal flower studies were influenced by early seventeenth century etched and engraved herbals in their mode of presentation (see no.64).
This album was evidently given to Lord Clive by Nawab Shuja ud-daula of Oudh following the battle of Buxar in 1764. Clive sent it home to England soon afterwards. Unlike most Mughal albums, which alternate paintings with calligraphy, the variety in this case is provided by pairs of flower paintings at each alternate opening. These have plain borders but the other paintings have rows of stylised poppy plants in their borders. A page with this type of decoration in the Los Angeles County Museum of Art (72.889) has the seal of Ashraf Khan in the service of 'Alamgir I in 1078 (1667-68). Other versions of Vallet's Martagon were made by J.T. de Bry in his *Florilegium Novum* (1611) and by E. Sweert in a Florilegium published at Frankfurt in 1612.
Bibliography : R. Skelton (1972), p.151 and pl.XCI.   RS

64

A Martagon Lily
Height : 36.5cm, *Width* : 25cm
Le Jardin du très Chrestien Louys Treiziesme, f.15.
by Pierre Vallet
Paris 1624 (first edition 1608).
VAM
Pierre Vallet (b. Orleans, c.1575) was an etcher and engraver who was employed by Henry IV as *brodeur ordinaire* and dedicated his book, originally entitled *Le Jardin . . . du roy . . . Henri IV*, of botanical etchings and engraving to the Queen, Marie de Medicis, as an embroidery pattern book. His work influenced several engravers of herbals, and represents the naturalistic style of plant illustration which was emulated in India by Ustad Mansur and his followers (see no.63).
Bibliography : W. Blunt (1950), pp.88-91, pl.XVa.; R. Skelton (1972), p.151, pl.XC.   RS

65

A calligrapher at work
Gouache
Height : 10.5cm, *Width* : 7cm
(*Page height* : 31.9cm, *Width* : 23.1cm)
Mughal, c.1640
Lent anonymously.
One of the most intense portraits in all Mughal art, this study of a calligrapher has recently been ascribed to the end of Jahangir's reign but the presence of flowering plants on the end of his girdle makes a date after 1640 more plausible. He is evidently writing a *qit'a* or fragment of verse diagonally on a coloured page (cf. nos.39, 43) but it is curious that his reed pen has nearly reached the left edge of the sheet with no marks being visible. Even a Hindu painter working at the court would have known the direction in which Persian script was written. A number of distinguished penmen worked at the Mughal court in Shah Jahan's reign and the emperor was a connoisseur of calligraphy.
Bibliography : P. Brown (1924), pl.XLVIII 2; T. Falk (1976), p.194 no.118; S.C. Welch (1978a), pl.29; B.P. Saksena (1958), p.267.   RS

66

Book plate of Shah Jahan
Opening page from the Kevorkian album.
Gold and gouache
Height : 91.5cm, *Width* : 63cm
Inscribed in Persian *tughra* characters:
His Majesty, Shihab ud-din Muhammad Shah Jahan, the King, Warrior of the Faith, May God perpetuate his ki. dom and sovereignty!
Mughal, c.1645
Lent by the Trustees of the Metropolitan Museum of Art : 55, 121, 10, 39.
The bookplate takes the usual form of a circular polylobed medallion or rosette containing floral arabesque on a gold and blue ground. This is encircled by a halo of blue arabesque tracery containing small gold radiating medallions and the surrounding paper is decorated in gold with a *simurgh* in each corner and other birds flying against a background of plant tufts and cloud forms. Shah Jahan's ex libris inscription is written in white on the gold central medallion. This type of opening decoration, known as a *shamsah* 'little sun', is typical of Persian manuscripts from the end of the 13th century and the present example follows a Safavid prototype. The surrounding decoration of birds resembles that of a manuscript of Sa'di's *Kulliyat* (B.L. Add.24944), illuminated in Shiraz in 1568/9, which changed hands in Delhi in 1149/1736-7 and may have been known to the illuminator of Shah Jahan's album in the same city a century earlier. Similar *shamsahs* of Shah Jahan's reign, but without the decoration of birds, occur in the Windsor Padshahnama (unpublished) and the ex-Rothschild collection (M.C. Beach (1978), no.21 and cover).
Bibliography : S.C. Welch (1978a), pl.30; A. Welch (1979), no.85; F.R. Martin (1912), pl.260; C. Rieu (1881), II, pp.594-98.   RS

67

Dara Shikuh with tray of jewels
From the Minto album.
Gouache
Height : 24.7cm, *Width* : 16cm
(*Page height* : 38.8cm, *Width* : 27cm)
Inscribed on the picture: *sanah* 105 (probably for 1055 = 1645-6 AD) and below in Persian by Shah Jahan: *shabih-i khub-i baba dara shikuh 'amal-i chitarman* 'A good likeness of Baba Dara Shikuh, work of Chitarman'.
Mughal, c.1645-6 AD
VAM : I.M. 13-1925.
Shah Jahan's heir apparent and favourite son is shown richly attired holding up a jewel taken from a tray which also contains a portrait cameo (see nos.376-79).   RS

68

Shah Jahan holding court
Gouache
Height : 30.5cm, *Width* : 22cm
Mughal, c.1650
Lent by the India Office Library and Records : Add. Or. 3853.
Shah Jahan sits at the throne balcony of a Hall of Public Audience (*Diwan-i Am*) corresponding neither with that of Delhi nor Agra. The emperor holds a jewel from a tray held by a youth in front of him; an officer and two youths attend with fly whisks. Prince Aurangzeb is presented by two courtiers and performs *taslim* faced by a row of senior Rajput and Mughal officers with standard-bearers behind them. One of the standards has a lion as its emblem (see no.515). Judging from the age of the main figures this may represent Aurangzeb's appearance at court in Lahore on the occasion of his promotion in January 1649 or his visit in November of the same year.
Bibliography : T. Falk and M. Archer (1981), p.84, no.80, pl.5; J. Sarkar (1952), I, p.63.   RS

69

The Lord Steward (Khan-i Saman) of the Mughal Household
From a royal album of Shah Jahan.
Gouache
Height : 19.5cm, *Width* : 11.1cm
(*Page height* : 38.4cm, *Width* : 26.4cm)
Mughal, c.1650
Lent by Dr and Mrs William K. Ehrenfeld.
The distinguished polymath Mulla 'Ala al-Mulk Tuni came to India from Iran in 1633-4 and was eventually appointed *Khan-i Saman*, with jurisdiction over the royal household and its workshops. The border of the painting alludes to his supervisory role over subordinate stewards, shown with inventories, and the storekeepers of porcelain, jewels and brocades. He died in 1663 approaching the age of seventy. For other pages from this album, see nos.70, 73.
Bibliography : Spink & Son (1980), pl.73; Martin (1912), pl.187; *Ma'athir* I, p.550 ff; J. Sarkar (1952), pp.40-44.   RS

44

65

45

67

68

70

70
Portrait of Rustam Khan
From a royal album of Shah Jahan.
Gouache
Height : 20.5cm, *Width* : 13.2cm
(*Page height* : 38.4cm, *Width* : 26.4cm)
Inscribed in Persian: 'Portrait of
Rustam Khan Bahadur Firoz Jang,
work of Hunhar'.
Mughal, c.1650
Lent by the Trustees of the Chester
Beatty Library, Dublin : MS 7B no.35.
Rustam Khan (d.1658) was a Circassian
who became chief swordsman of the
ruler of Ahmednagar and was granted
the title of Muqarrab Khan. Following
his defection to the emperor in Shah
Jahan's fourth year, he enjoyed a
distinguished military career and was
given the title of Firoz-i Jang 'Victorious
in War' in 1649/50 after service in the
Qandahar campaign. The picture
evidently commemorates his return to
court after the attempt on Qandahar,
when he was honoured with various
gifts including a turban ornament, a
jewelled dagger and a jewelled sword.
Rustam Khan is shown holding a *firangi*
sword with *khanda* hilt and is girt with
shield and *talwar*. The border depicts
members of his entourage including a
Deccani youth holding a *firangi* sword,
alluding to Rustam Khan's early skill
with this typical Deccani weapon.
Above and below, store-keepers are
appraising jewellery and weapons,
including a jewelled sword. The jewels
are stored in an inlaid wooden chest
(cf. no.555).
Bibliography : Arnold & Wilkinson
(1936), I p.37, III pl.71; Maathir-ul-
umara (tr.), II 2, pp.625-29.   RS

71
The reception of an envoy in camp
Probably from a manuscript of the
Badshah Nama of 'Abd ul-Hamid
Lahori.
Gouache
Height : 34.3cm, *Width* : 24.1cm
Inscribed in Persian: *'amal-i fateh chand*
'Work of Fateh Chand'.
Mughal, c.1650
Lent by the Bharat Kala Bhavan,
Banaras.
The Emperor Shah Jahan embraces an
envoy from Iran or Transoxiana during
the progress of the imperial camp
through hilly country. A formal *darbar*
is being held in an enclosure formed by
floral *kanats* beneath a gold brocade
canopy. The incident has not yet been
satisfactorily identified but the visitor
is clearly a person of high status for
whom a silver cushion has been placed
on the floorspread facing the Emperor's
gold cushion. The formal reception
takes place outside the camp, which is
laid out in the distance, around the
royal tentage which is coloured red.
If the event took place late in the reign,
the central figure may not be the
Emperor, but one of the royal princes,
who resembled their father more as
they grew older.
The name of the artist, Fateh Chand,
also appears on the re-painted portion
of a page from the *Tuzuk-i Jahangiri* in
the Reza Library, Rampur. An
eighteenth century painter of this name
is known and attributions to an earlier
Fateh Chand must at present be treated
with caution.
Apart from its graphic representation
of the distant camp, the picture shows
the richness of effect created by textiles
in court assemblies.
Bibliography : Rai Krishnadasa (1955),
pl.6; *Chhavi* (1971), pl. H.   RS

72
Sultan 'Abdullah Qutb Shah of Golconda
Gouache and gold
Height : 21.5cm, *Width* : 12.4cm
Inscribed (incorrectly) on border in
Persian *tana shah* and in a European
hand *Tannah Shaw*.
Golconda, c.1650
VAM : I.S. 18-1980
'Abdullah Qutb Shah (1626-72) stands
richly dressed against a blue back-
ground holding a *firangi khanda* and a
muslin kerchief. Divine sanction of his
kingship is indicated by rays of light
from the sky which form a golden
nimbus around his head.
It was under 'Abdullah's patronage that
Golconda painting reached its height
before declining after the Mughal
conquest of Golconda during the reign
of his successor Tana Shah.
For comparable portraits see Sotheby
& Co. (7 April 1975), lot 156 and
Christie's (24 April 1980), lot 54.   RS

73
Portrait of Maharaja Udai Singh of Jodhpur
From a royal album of Shah Jahan.
Gouache
Height : 38.5cm, *Width* : 26.5cm
(*Page height* : 16.6cm, *Width* : 10.15cm)
Inscribed in minute characters on the
picture with the artist's name : Payag.
Mughal, c.1650
Lent by the Trustees of the Chester
Beatty Library, Dublin : MS.7B no.34.

Udai Singh, nicknamed 'Mota Raja', (the Fat Raja) of Jodhpur (ruled 1583-94) was Shah Jahan's maternal grandfather and a leading officer in the service of the Emperor Akbar. He stands in a landscape in which two *faqirs* sit against a hillside. The border shows Rajputs from his entourage, two of whom remove *jamdhar* daggers from a mother-of-pearl inlaid casket.
Bibliography: Arnold and Wilkinson (1936) I.p.36. RS

74
Qur'an
Arabic manuscript
Height: 30.5cm, *Width*: 21.6cm
Inscribed on ff.3r. and 469 v. with identical royal *waqf* inscriptions, both erased, but apparently recording its donation to a religious institution in 1061 AH (1651 AD).
Mughal or Deccani, early 17th century
VAM: 23.9.1890
The manuscript is written in a fine *suls* hand, eleven lines to the page and has 471 folios of which two are blank. It opens with an illuminated double-page frontispiece and the text pages have decorated chapter headings and rosettes on burnished paper which has gold foliate ornament painted on its edges.
The text is followed by two pages (ff.468 v. and 469 r.) decorated with a peony and a rose painted on a gold ground with illuminated quarter medallions at the corners. These appear to have been painted when the manuscript was donated as a *waqf*. The contemporary gold block-stamped morocco binding has been repaired at a later date. RS

75
Letter (nishan) from Prince Dara Shikuh. Dated 14 muharram 1063 (15th December 1652)
Height: 33cm, *Width*: 25cm
Lent by the India Office Library and Records 3-I.O.4678a.
This *nishan*, written in *nasta'liq* script, bears the seal of Dara Shikuh, engraved in the seventeenth regnal year of Shah Jahan (1054 AH/1644 AD). The top of the document, containing the name of the addressee, has been lost, but it was evidently written to an imperial officer, and concerns the supply of immense quantities of food to the troops engaged in the Qandahar expedition and siege of 1652-3 (see no.77 for the siege of 1649, which in fact had to be abandoned for lack of supplies).

80,000 ox-loads of wheat and other provisions are to be supplied at Multan by two *banjaras*, a tribe of merchants and carriers who, since ancient times, had been travelling traders in Central India, the Deccan and Rajasthan and who acted as commissariat to the Afghan and Mughal armies.
The addressee is urged to ensure that no-one obstructs the arrival of the supplies for reasons of tax (*zakat*) or the cattle-census (*gavshumari*). RC

76
Playing cards
Paper, painted and lacquered.
Diameter: 6cm
Deccan, mid-17th century
Lent by the National Museum, Copenhagen.
Cards and card games are thought to have been introduced into India by the Mughals. Both Babur and Humayun are known to have played cards (*ganjifa*), and according to Abu'l Fazl Akbar himself took a hand in revising the composition of the *ganjifa* pack. Very few early sets of cards survive; this set, for which a Royal Danish Kunstkammer inventory date of 1674 is recorded, is perhaps the earliest extant example. 74 cards survive of what would have been a standard Mughal *ganjifa* pack of 96, divided into 8 suits: *taj* (crown), *safed* (silver coin), *shamsher* (sword); *ghulam* (servant); *chang* (harp), *surkh* (gold coin), *barat* (document) and *qimash* (pillow). Each suit has two court cards (king and vizier) and ten numeral cards. In this pack the court cards of the *surkh* suit feature respectively Solomon, flanked by two *jinns*, and the embodiment of popular wisdom, the Mullah Nasr ud-Din, on his donkey.
Bibliography: Dam-Mikkelsen and Lundbaek, pp.128-30; von Leyden (1982). AT

77
An incident at the siege of Qandahar
by Payag (unsigned).
From a manuscript of the *Badshah nama* (3rd volume completed by 'Abd al-Waris).
Gouache
Height: 34.3cm, *Width*: 23.9cm
Inscribed in the border in Persian (side) *qal'ah-i qandahar yurish burdan sipah-i hind* 'The assault on Qandahar by the Indian Army' and (below) the names of six leading officers of the Mughal forces.
Mughal, c.1650-5
Lent anonymously.
The Mughal army is shown in a mountainous landscape laying siege to a fortified hill on the outskirts of the city of Qandahar in Afghanistan. Three forces of infantry converge on the fort towards stockades erected for their protection while the commanders hold a consultation at the head of cavalry and elephants lower down the hill. Within the fort, a magazine is exploding. The Mughal commanders are listed, from left to right, as Qulij Khan Bahadur, Sa'id Khan Bahadur, Raja Jaswant Singh Rathor Afghan, Dilir Khan (facing left), Bahadur Khan Afghan and Rustam Khan Dakhini (facing right).
The fortress city of Qandahar was alternately occupied by the Mughals and the Safavid Shahs of Iran ever since its seizure by Babur and was a bone of contention between the two dynasties. In 1638 it was surrendered to Shah Jahan by its Persian governor, but recaptured by Shah 'Abbas II in 1649. Shah Jahan immediately sent a large army to regain it under Prince Aurangzeb but with the approach of winter the siege was abandoned. A second attempt failed in 1652 as did a third under Dara Shikuh in the following year (see no.75).

If the inscriptions are correct, this picture represents the 1649 campaign in which Bahadur Khan died of asthma, and the incident is perhaps the attempted storming of the Chilzina Hill, when some of the Rajputs erected a stockade, as shown in the picture. A problem is presented by the portrait of Jaswant Singh which accords with his age at the time but not with his distinctive profile. A somewhat similar siege picture by the same artist in the Windsor *Badshahnama* manuscript (f.101 v.) represents the siege of a different fort of Qandahar, in the Deccan in 1631.
Bibliography: Blochet (1930), pl.XXXV; Welch (1973), pp.110-11, no.66; *idem*. (1978), pl.33; Beach (1978), pp.81-82, 84; Saksena (1958), p.227. RS

78
The Emperor 'Alamgir (Aurangzeb) holding an audience
Gouache
Height: 19.1cm, *Width*: 21.4cm
Mughal, c.1659
Lent anonymously.
The emperor is shown at the beginning of his reign enthroned under a canopy decorated with birds of paradise. He supports a hunting falcon on his gloved hand and is faced by Shayista Khan, also wearing a falconer's glove, 'Alamgir's son Muhammad A'zam and two other courtiers. The decoration of the throne, parapet, carpet, coats and sashes show the predominance of the formal flowering plant as a decorative motif at this date.
In the second half of 1659 Shayista Khan was granted the special favour of having his drums beaten in the royal presence, soon after which he was appointed to the governorship of the Deccan. The painting was perhaps made shortly before he took the appointment in the winter of that year. It is now attributed by S.C. Welch to the painter, Hashim.
Bibliography: Marteau and Vever (1913) vol.1, pl.20; S.C. Welch (1959), fig.19, idem (1963), no.59; R. Skelton (1972), pl.LXXXV; S.C. Welch (1978a), pl.37; M.C. Beach (1978), no.67; *Ma'athir-ul-umara*, vol. 2, part 2, p.832. RS

76

79

The Battle of Samugarh
Black line with gold and colour.
Height : 22.6cm, *Width* : 32.7cm
Inscribed in Persian with the names of
the participants: *dara shikuh, aurangzeb
'alamgir padshah, murad bakhsh,
najabat khan, bahadur khan, ram singh
rathor.*
Mughal, c.1660
Lent anonymously.
On the 29th May 1658 the heir-
apparent, Prince Dara Shikuh, was
defeated by his younger brother
'Aurangzeb on the plain of Samugarh,
eight miles from Agra. This drawing,
evidently made soon after the battle
shows the moment when Dara's fortunes
turned towards defeat. On the left, with
his left flank in disarray and his
elephant-mounted musicians fleeing
towards the camp, Dara dismounts
from his elephant surrounded by the
cavalry of his central force. His Rajput
contingent on the right flank under Ram
Singh and others is pursuing the forces
of Murad Bakhsh whose elephant
retreats. Aurangzeb on his elephant
occupies the right centre with Bahadur
Khan on a smaller elephant and behind
his line of guns, while his general
Najabat Khan who led the vanguard is
seen at the top.
The painting formerly belonged to
Warren Hastings and passed into the
possession of the celebrated bibliophile
Sir Thomas Phillipps (1792-1872).
Bibliography : S.C. Welch (1976),
pp.54-5, no.21; Sotheby & Co. (1968),
lot 391; J. Sarkar (1912) I,pp.239-253. RS

80

**The Mughal Emperor 'Alamgir
(Aurangzeb) and his principal
officers on a lion hunt**
Gouache
Height : 29cm, *Width* : 42.3cm
Mughal, c.1670
Lent by the Trustees of the Chester
Beatty Library, Dublin : MS 11B, no.28.
'Alamgir and his third son A'zam Shah
attended by *amirs* occupy the howdah
of one of three elephants preceded by
beaters riding Gaur buffaloes. The
emperor aims his matchlock at a pair of
lions at bay in front of him. In the
background two other elephants are
attacked by lions within the rope fence
guarded by hunting attendants. According to Bernier, the emperor shot lions
from outside the nets but this does not
appear to have been the general practice.
Bibliography : Arnold & Wilkinson
(1936), I. p.48, III, pl.91; Bernier
(1891), p.378. RS

81

**An edict (firman) issued by the
Emperor Aurangzeb, dated 4 zu'l-
qa'da 1088 (19th December 1677)**
Height : 88cm, *Width* : 48cm
Lent by the India Office Library and
Records 6-I.O.4370.
At the top of the *firman* is the *bismillah*,
and underneath it a Qur'anic verse
written in *tughra*, the style of hand-
writing characterised by bold upright
lines overlapped by horizontal strokes
which was often used for the imperial
signature. Then comes the imperial seal
of Aurangzeb, of the type containing
the genealogy of his Timurid ancestors
(see no.00), engraved during his twelfth
regnal year, 1080 AH/1669 AD.
The main part of the document, written
in *nasta'liq*, concerns the appointment
of the *mulla* Muhammad 'Asim as *qazi*
of the *pargana* (district) of Jajmau, in
the *subah* (province) of Allahabad. It
grants him land measuring 100 *bighas*,
and sets out fifteen duties required of
him as *qazi*, such as propagation of
Islamic law (*sharia*), division of legacies,
inducing people towards religious
devotions, enforcement of penal laws
and safeguarding the property of
orphans. It ends by saying that the
inhabitants of the *pargana* should from
now on treat as authentic all letters,
deeds and decrees written and sealed
by him. RC

82

**Miftah al-sarod (a treatise on music)
by Qazi Hasan**
Persian manuscript
Height : 16.9cm, *Width* : 10.2cm
(*Page height* : 24.6cm, *Width* : 16.1cm)
The colophon states that the copy was
written in *zu 'l-qa'da*, 1102 AH (July-
August 1691 AD) in the district of Indur
(modern Nizamabad).
North Deccan, 1691 AD
VAM : I.S. 61-1977.
The *miftah al-sarod* is a *ragamala* or
'garland of musical modes' based on the
system of *Ksemakarna* but modified so
that the *Shri Raga* has six wives and
nine sons instead of the usual five wives
and eight sons. Thus the total number
of *ragas* (male) and *raginis* (female) is
eighty-six, of which eighty-three illustrations remain in the manuscript. The
double-page illustration exhibited
(numbered ff.44-45) is of *Kumbha Raga*
(no.66), one of the sons of *Shri* and
depicts him as a king wearing a jewelled
crown seated on a throne with male and
female attendants.
The manuscript is a provincial copy
written in a careless *nasta'liq* hand,
fifteen lines to the page, and was
completed twenty years after its composition by Qazi Hasan son of Khwaja
Tahir son of Khwaja Muhammad Qazi
at Antur in the Daulatabad district of
the Deccan.
Bibliography : Ebeling (1972), p.206,
no.109. RS

83

**Prince Muhammad 'Azim ush-shan
leading the prayers in a mosque**
From the large Clive album. Gouache
Height : 28cm, *Width* : 37cm
(*Page height* : 32cm, *Width* : 47.5cm)
Inscribed in Persian; *muhammad 'azim
al-shan.*
Mughal, early 18th century
VAM : I.S. 133-1964 f.38r
Muhammad 'Azim ud-din, *alias*
Muhammad 'Azim ush-shan (1664-
1712) was the third son of Muhammad
Mu'azzam (Bahadur Shah I). He was
appointed Viceroy of Bengal, Bihar and
Orissa by 'Alamgir in 1697 and resided
at Patna which was re-named 'Azima-
bad after him. He leads the congre-
gation in bowing (*rak'at*) towards the

80

48

direction of Mecca indicated by the pulpit (*mimbar*), whose steps project from the left. The picture is a provincial work, perhaps from Azimabad itself, and foreshadowing the Murshidabad style. The artist has evidently altered the axis of the picture because the mouldings of the mosque plinth would normally be parallel to the *qibla* wall as would the sanctuary arcade.

The album was evidently assembled for Nawab Shuja ud-daula of Oudh and presented to Lord Clive in 1764 after the battle of Buxar.

Bibliography : B. Gray, *et al.* (1981), fig.162. RS

84
Manuscript of the Kitab hidayat al-rami ('The Archer's Guide') by Muhammad Budha'i (fol. 6b)
Gouache on paper
Height : 29.5cm, *Width* : 19.1cm
Mughal, dated 1722
Lent by the Marquess of Bute.
This treatise on archery was originally written in AD 1500 for Husayn Shah, ruler of Bengal, and this copy was made by Sayyid Nur al-Din Muhammad 'Ali in 1722. This page shows the methods of bracing the oriental bow (see no.450) on horseback and seated or standing. This type of bow is highly reflexed and its form must be totally reversed during stringing. This is quite a skilled operation and manuals such as this would have been valuable for instruction.
Bibliography : Paterson (1972), p.83. RC

85
Muhammad Shah in a throne palanquin
Gouache
Height : 38.3cm, *Width* : 42.5cm
Mughal, c.1735
Lent by the Museum of Fine Arts, Boston.
The emperor, who earned the soubriquet 'Rangila' (Pleasure-lover), is carried by eight attendants in a golden palanquin in a garden near a pavilion resembling the *Diwan-i-Khas* of the Red Fort at Delhi. He is equipped for the hunt, with a falcon perched on his hand and a sword and quiver strapped to the *palki*. The painting illustrates the mode of supporting canopies (*shami-yana*) and curtains (*purdah*) around the verandahs of Mughal buildings.
Bibliography : S.C. Welch (1963), no.78; *idem*. (1978), pl.39. RS

86
Playing cards
Painted ivory
Diameter : 8cm
Murshidabad, c.1759-60
Lent by the National Trust, Powis Castle.
These exceptionally large and finely painted ivory cards formerly belonged to Robert Clive. They may have been presented to him by Nawab Mir Jafar, whom he had installed as ruler of Bengal after the battle of Plassey in 1757. The pack is a standard Mughal *ganjifa* of 96 cards, with 12 additional duplicate cards, and is unusual in that many of the court cards are portraits of the Mughal emperors and their Timurid ancestors.
Bibliography : von Leyden (1982), cat. no.32. AT

87
Map of the Bidar district, with illustrations of Sufis and bidri manufacture
Water-colour
Page height : 38cm, *Width* : 55.5cm
From an Atlas prepared for Col. Gentil at Faizabad, 1770.
Lent by the India Office Library and Records : Add. Or. 4039.
Col. Jean Baptiste Joseph Gentil (1726-99) was a French officer who served as military adviser to the Nawabs of Oudh from 1763-75. During the ten years he spent at Faizabad he employed a number of local artists, including Niwasi Lal and Mohan Singh, to illustrate his Atlas of India, compiled from literary sources, and the encyclo-paedic album, *Receuil de toutes sortes de Dessins. . .* (cat no.89). The map of the *subah* of Bidar is illustrated with representatives of the different Sufi orders and, below, with a scene of a bidri craftsman chiselling a round *huqqa* bowl (inscribed: *fabrique de Beder ou on incruste en or et argent*) and a group of typical *bidri* products, including *pandans, pikdans, huqqa* bowls and mouth-pieces, a ewer and basin, a back-scratcher, a candle-stick and other vessels.
Bibliography : M. Archer (1978), *passim*; Falk and Archer (1981), pp.135ff. AT

83

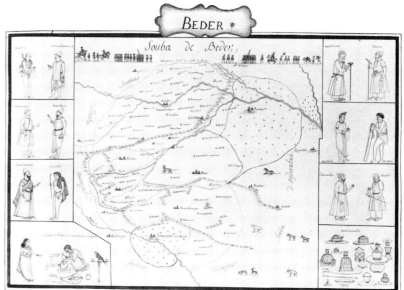

87

87 (detail)

88
View of the tomb of Akbar at Sikandra
Gouache
Height : 54.5cm, *Width* : 37.9cm
Mughal, c.1770
Lent anonymously.
Bibliography : Welch (1978b), no.60. AT

89
Illustrations of female jewellery
From an album of pictures by Nevasilal Mansingh and others, illustrating the customs and practices of the people of Hindustan compiled by Col. J.B.J. Gentil.
Watercolour on European paper
Height : 38.2cm, *Width* : 55.5cm
VAM : I.S. 25-1980, f.48
During a long stay in Faizabad and Lucknow, Gentil (see no.87) carried out various researches on the history and culture of Northern India and finally returned to France in 1778. The present album is entitled *'Recueil de toutes sortes de Dessins sur les Usages et coutumes des Peuples de Hindoustan ou Empire Mogol d'apres plusieurs peintres Indiens Nevasilal, Mounsingue etc. au service du Nabab Visir Soudjaat daula Gouverneur général des provinces d'Eleabad et d'Avad lequel recueil a été fait par les soins du Sr Gentil Colonel d'Infanterie; en 1774 a Faisabad.'*
In the absence of soundly documented jewellery from Northern India at this time the precision and range of Gentil's visual survey is particularly valuable. RS

88

90

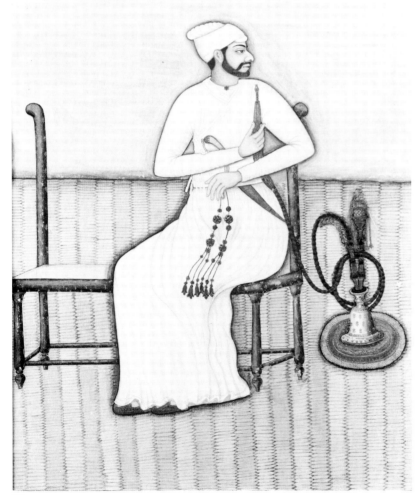

92

90
Col. Antoine Polier watching a nautch
Gouache
Height : 25cm, *Width* : 32cm
Lucknow, c.1780, after a presumed painting by Tilly Kettle, Faizabad, 1772.
Lent by Mr Michael Archer and Mrs Margaret Lecomber.
This painting, by an Indian artist, is a copy of an unknown work by a European. It is thought that the original artist was Tilly Kettle, who was in India from 1770 to 1777.
Polier was a native of Lausanne who was engineer and architect to the Nawab Wazir of Oudh from 1771 to 1776. He lived at Faizabad and Lucknow in an extravagantly Oriental style, and was an enthusiastic collector of Persian and Sanskrit manuscripts and Indian miniatures (see no.95). After his death, his collection passed to William Beckford, and most of it is now in Berlin (see Hickmann, 1979). Polier also retained a strong interest in European art and was a patron to several European artists, particularly John Zoffany, who visited India in 1783-90. In a painting by Zoffany now in the Victoria Memorial, Calcutta, he is portrayed in his house at Lucknow surrounded by European oil-paintings (see M. Archer, 1979, fig.96).
Bibliography : M. Archer (1972a); Welch (1978b), no.36; M. Archer (1979), pl.39, p.84.   RC

91
Design for a game of Snakes and Ladders
Drawing with colours
Height : 65.5cm, *Width* : 67.5cm
Lucknow, c.1780-82
Lent by the India Office Library and Records, Johnson Album 5, no.8.
The board comprises 72 numbered squares, proceeding from bottom left to top left. Each square is inscribed in Sanskrit and Urdu with the names of gradually ascending spiritual states or conditions. The game is a Pilgrim's Progress from states of worldly illusion to the abodes of Brahma, Vishnu and Shiva (squares 67-69, with cusped arches). As in the English children's game, ladders bring rapid promotion and snakes (and scorpions) demotion. Thus if one's counter reaches *Tapasya* (religious austerity: 10), one is promoted to *Svargah*, the heaven of Indra (marked with a flower: 23). *Daya* (compassion: 17) brings swift promotion to

the abode of Brahma (69), while *Ahankarah* (the vice of egoism: 55) leads all the way back to *Maya* (illusion: 2). If, towards the end, one overshoots to the *guna* of *Tamas* (darkness inertia: 72), one is demoted to *Prithvi* (the earth: 51). For a more elaborate version of the game, see Pargiter (1916).   AT

92
Nawab Muhammad Reza Khan seated with a huqqa
Gouache
Height : 28.6cm, *Width* : 23.2cm
Inscribed on the back in an 18th century English hand: *Portrait Nawab Mahomed Reza Kaun of Cossimbazaar.*
Murshidabad, c.1780-90
Lent by Mr Robert Alderman and Dr Mark Zebrowski.
The Nawab, a minister of the Nawab of Murshidabad, sits on a green lacquered wooden seat, with his *huqqa* on a woven grass matted floor. In 1787 it was said of him that 'his chest is so broad, his body so erect, his tone of voice so very loud, and his eyes so very full of fire at the age of seventy that he seems to have yet thirty years to live'. Green and gold lacquered furniture was characteristic of N.E. India (cf. no.567).
Bibliography : *The Seir Mutaqherin* (1975), vol. III, pp.148-50.   RS

51

93

52

93
Odalisque
Gouache
Height : 27.5cm, *Width* : 38.5cm
(*Page height* : 34cm, *Width* : 45cm)
Mughal, probably Lucknow, beginning
of the 19th century.
Lent by the Chester Beatty Library,
Dublin, MS.69 no.19.
A European woman dressed in an
eighteenth century 'Turkish' mode
reclines against cushions in a curtained
alcove between two columns and feeds
her tame cockatoo with fruit from a
small Turkish table. The room is furnished in the Empire style with figures
of the three Graces, or perhaps three of
the nine Muses, standing on an ornate
mantel. The European engraved source
of this picture has not been identified.
It is mounted on a gold-flecked page
border with gold-painted blue border of
late 18th century Lucknow type.   RS

94
Tipu Sultan on his throne
Water-colour
Height : 38.5cm, *Width* : 53.2cm
Mysore, c.1800
Lent by the National Trust, Powis
Castle.
Tipu sits holding his sword on his
golden throne with protruding tiger
head, jewelled tiger head finials (see cat
no.346) and a *chatri* with a jewelled
huma bird. The throne was broken up
at the Fall of Seringapatam; the *huma*
bird and large tiger head are now in the
Royal Collection at Windsor (no.347).
This depiction of the throne may err in
endowing the central tiger head with a
neck and feet.
Bibliography : Forrest (1970), pls.14a,
14b, 15a, 15b.   AT

94

95

The Red Fort at Delhi
Gouache
Height : 29.2cm, *Width* : 41.5cm
(page *Height* : 32.5cm, *Width* : 44.5cm)
Mughal, Lucknow, c.1785
Lent by the India Office Library and
Records : Add. Or. 948.
This bird's-eye view looks west from
outside the wall overlooking the Jumna
river. In the centre, projecting from the
emperor's private apartments is the
domed Musamman Burj containing the
balcony window (*jharokha*) at which the
emperor appeared to the public.
In the painting this is wrongly centred
on the garden court with the Hall of
Public Audience (*Diwan-i Am*) backing
on to it (roof and railing visible only).
In between this and the covered bazaar
leading from the Lahore Gate (centre
distance) is the Hathi Pol gateway surmounted by the musicians' balcony
(*Naqqar Khana*). To the right of the
private apartments the emperor (*Shah
'Alam*) and his attendants approach the
Hall of Private Audience (*Diwan-i Khas*)
and in the centre-right are two domes of
the Moti Masjid. To the left of the
Private Apartments is the Rang Mahal
looking over the courtyards of the
Zanana which extend towards the Delhi
Gate at the far left. Another version is
in an album of panoramic and court
scenes made for Colonel Anton Polier,
now in the Indische Museum, Berlin
(I.5005/11). A third is in the Royal
Ontario Museum (924.12.143).
Bibliography : T. Falk and M. Archer
(1981), pp.160 and 446, no.343; M.C.
Beach (1979), p.32, no.31.   RS

96

Tipu Sultan
Gouache
Height : 26.5cm, *Width* : 18cm
Mysore, c.1795-1800
VAM : I.S. 266-1952
Bibliography : Forrest (1970), pl.1.   AT

97

Calligraphic mihrab in Kufic script
Ink on paper
Height : 20.6cm, *Width* : 13.6cm
Hyderabad (?), c.1800
Lent anonymously.
This inscription in the archaic and
stylized Kufic script would have served
a protective or talismanic function. The
text is from the *Qur'an* (*Sura* 68, 51-2) :
'And lo! those who disbelieve would
fain disconcert thee with their eyes
when they hear the Reminder, and they
say : Lo! he is indeed mad; when it is

naught else than a Reminder to
creation.' (Pickthall tr.)
Bibliography : Welch (1976), no.38,
pp.17, 79. cf. A. Welch (1979), no.88. AT

98

**The Sadullah Chowk, a market
street in Old Delhi**
Gouache
Height : 27.6cm, *Width* : 43.3cm
Inscription on the back in Hindi and
Persian with a description of the
subject.
Delhi, c.1810
Lent by Mr James Ivory.
The inscriptions have been read as
follows: 'A picture of Shah Jahanabad
(Delhi); showing the Sadullah Khan
Chowk; with the Delhi Gate, the
Mosque of the Nawab Bahadur, and
opposite, in the distance, the Nimudhar
Kila'.
Bibliography : Welch (1978b), no.44. RS

99

A courtyard covered by a shamiana
Water-colour
Height : 43.6cm, *Width* : 65.4cm
Patna, c.1815
Lent by the India Office Library and
Records : Add. Or. 992.
Bibliography : M. Archer (1947), pl.8;
M. Archer (1972), p.109; Welch
(1978b), no.27.   AT

100

A lapidary's wife at work
From a volume of crafts and trades.
Water-colour
Height : 17.2cm, *Width* : 12.6cm
Inscribed in Persian: *zan-i hakkak nag
durust* (?) *numanad* (?) 'The lapidary's
wife causes a gem to look right.'
Company School, Lucknow, c.1815-
1820
VAM : 7970, f.13.
The wife of a hardstone carver (*hakkak*)
polishes a gemstone on a wheel oper-
ated by a bow string. The wheel on its
spindle is held between two wooden
posts and she uses a polishing powder
kept in the bowl at her side.
The paintings in the album are on
European paper which in the case of
f.46 is watermarked 'J. Whatman 1814'.
Bibliography : M. and W.G. Archer
(1955), p.62, fig.32.   RS

101

Ladies playing pachisi
Gouache
Height : 17.5cm, *Width* : 13.7cm
From an album of illustrations of crafts
and pastimes. Lucknow, c.1815.

VAM : 7970 (93.D.11)
Pachisi ('Twenty-five') is one of the
most popular Indian games. It is a race-
game, played either by four persons,
forming two sides, with four men each,
or by two persons each with eight men.
Moves are determined by the throw of
cowrie shells. See H.J.R. Murray
(1952), p.135.   AT

102

**A woman and child playing with
toys**
Gouache
Height : 17.5cm, *Width* : 13.8cm
From an album of illustrations of crafts
and pastimes. Lucknow, c.1815.
VAM : 7970 (93.D.11)
For similar lac-stained ivory toys, (see
cat. nos.539-542).   AT

103

**A nautch party in a European
mansion**
Gouache
Height : 28.5cm, *Width* : 36.2cm
Delhi, c.1820
VAM : I.S. 9-1955
Bibliography : M. Archer (1962) p.248,
Rawson (1972) pp.152-3.   AT

104

**Procession of Ghazi ud-Din Haidar
through the streets of Lucknow**
Gouache on paper, restored and
mounted on canvas in three sections.
Height : 123cm, *Width* : 483cm
Lucknow, c.1820-25

VAM : I.M. 2-1909
A self-indulgent and irascible ruler,
Ghazi ud-Din's friendly relations with
the British led to his being created King
of Oudh and to a prolific patronage of
British artists and artefacts. Robert
Home, his court painter, designed his
regalia as well as richly ornamented
furniture, carriages, howdahs and
pleasure boats : many of his designs for
these are preserved in the V & A. The
contemporary Engish vogue for panoramic paintings was also imitated by
Lucknow artists, in this case with a cast
of thousands.   AT

103

105

105

Taylor & Co's Emporium in Calcutta
by Sir Charles D'Oyly, c.1825-28.
Water-colour
Height : 18.1cm, *Width* : 23cm
An illustration, omitted in the published version, to D'Oyly's satirical poem, *Tom Raw, the Griffin*, (London, 1828). VAM : I.S. 1-1980.
'There is in Loll-Bazar a splendid shop. . .', known in D'Oyly's day as Taylor & Co, selling all manner of imported European furnishings and household goods. Fashionable ladies and gentlemen are shown parading in the shop's long colonnaded hall, watched by native attendants. Imported crockery stands on a table to the right, and elaborate chandeliers hang from the ceiling.
Bibliography : M. and W.G. Archer (1955), pp.33ff.; M. Archer (1970).   AT

106

Nob Kishen's nautch party
by Sir Charles D'Oyly, c.1825-28.
Water-colour
Height : 17.4cm, *Width* : 23cm
An illustration, omitted in the published version, to D'Oyly's satirical poem, *Tom Raw, the Griffin*, (London, 1828). VAM : I.S. 2-1980
Nob Kishen (Nawab Kishan), seen from behind sitting in a European chair, is entertaining a fashionable party of Europeans to a nautch performance. The furnishing of his music room bears out D'Oyly's satire on his indiscriminate

predilection for European artefacts:
'. . . the pampered Baboo has been lurking
Whole months at auctions, and at foreign shops,
At green glass lustres amorously smirking,
And licking at French mirrors his fat chops. . .'
(*Tom Raw*, lines 3665-68)
Nob Kishen would clearly have been a regular customer at the emporium of Taylor & Co (cat. no.105).   AT

107

Nasir ud-Din Haidar (King of Oudh 1827-37) entertaining British Guests
Gouache
Height : 35cm, *Width* : 24.8cm
Lucknow, c.1831
Lent by the India Office Library and Records: Add. Or. 2599.
Bibliography : M. Archer (1972) p.163, pl.56, where it is suggested that the British officer may be Lord Bentinck, who with his wife visited Nasir ud-Din Haidar in 1831.   AT

108

108

General Allard and his family
Gouache
Height : 20.6cm, *Width* : 26.9cm
Lahore, 1838
Lent anonymously.
General Jean Francois Allard was born at St Tropez in 1785. Enlisting at 18, he served in Napoleon's armies until Waterloo. Seeking a further military career in the East, he finally arrived at Lahore in 1822, where Maharaja Ranjit Singh employed him to train his army. In 1834-36 he revisited St Tropez with his Kashmiri wife and their children, and an oil painting of the family, now in the St Tropez Museum, was made by his nephew. A copy of the picture seems to have accompanied Allard when he returned alone to India, and to have served as a model for the Indian artist of this painting. Allard is shown taking tea with his family in front of their house at Anarkali, a suburb of Lahore. He is wearing Ranjit Singh's Bright Star of the Punjab (see cat. no.302) above the French Legion of Honour. Allard died soon after the painting was made, in January 1839.
Bibliography : Welch (1978b), no.55. AT

109

The last Mughal Emperor Bahadur Shah II enthroned
Gouache
Height : 32cm, *Width* : 38cm
Inscribed in Persian with the names and titles of the four subjects of the portrait

and its date; 'In the month of *Rabi* I, 1254 *Hijri* corresponding to the year 1 of the exalted accession.'
Mughal, Delhi, dated May-June 1838.
Private collection.
The Emperor sits on a golden chair of state with lion supports in front of the marble *jali* window incorporating the scales of justice in the *Khas Mahal* (Private Apartments) of the Red Fort at Delhi. He is attended by his two sons Fakhr ud-Din Mirza, the heir apparent, on his right and the young Mirza Farkhanda on his left. Behind the throne stands Mirza Beg Khan Bahadur waving a *morchhal*. The Emperor holds the stem of a large *huqqa* and wears a jewelled gold crown (cf. no. 307).
Bibliography : S.C. Welch (1978), pl.40; *idem*. (1978b), no. 52; Y.D. Sharma (1964), pl.XXIV.   RS

109

111

110

Qur'an manuscript
Written in *naskhi* script on 119 leaves;
covers missing.
Height : 5.1cm, *Width* : 3.8cm
North India, first half of the 19th
century.
VAM : I.M. 18-1912
This tiny *Qur'an* is said to have been
taken by Sir Theophilus Metcalfe from
under the pillow of Bahadur Shah II in
his private apartments in the Delhi Fort
after the siege of 1857. See also cat.
no. 534.   AT

111

**A dak-runner delivering letters to
shroffs (bankers)**
Gouache
Height : 19cm, *Width* : 23.7cm
Sind or Lahore, c.1850.
Lent anonymously.
The painting is inscribed in English:
'a Hurkurah (?dak runner) delivering
a letter to Shroffs/Bankers of Nourie
Hinduos (*sic*)'; 'Nourie' has been identi-
fied as a village in Sind. The *shroffs* are
shown at work on their bulging ledgers.
Bibliography : Welch (1978b), no.72. AT

112

**Nawab Muzaffar ud-Daula seated,
with a huqqa and a manuscript**
Gouache
Height : 36.5cm, *Width* : 25cm
Delhi, 1852
Lent anonymously.
Nawab Muzaffar ud-Daula Nasir al-

Mulk Mirza Saif ud-Din Haidar Khan
Bahadur Saif Jang was a prominent
nobleman in pre-Mutiny Delhi and a
friend of the poet Ghalib. He sits on a
black and gilt chair of the Bareilly type
in a room of his palace, with a *huqqa*
and spittoon at either side, and Bohe-
mian painted glass lamps suspended
above. The Mutiny of 1857 was to cause
his downfall. His deserted palace was
burnt down, and the Nawab himself was
summarily shot by the British.
Bibliography : Welch (1978b), no.53. AT

113

**A pile-carpet loom at Hunsur,
(Mysore)**
Pen and ink and water-colour.
Height : 44.9cm, *Width* : 62.8cm
Mysore, 1850
Lent by the India Office Library and
Records : Add. Or. 7555.
The picture is inscribed in English :
'Plan and Elevation of a Carpet loom
with five men at work. Grazing Farm.
Hoonsoor. 1st November, 1850.'
According to Mildred Archer, 'The
Amrit Mahal cattle-breeding establish-
ment was at Hunsur . . . Until 1864 it
had a large tannery, blanket manu-
factory and timber yard maintained by
the Madras Commissariat. This drawing
may well have been sent to the East
India Company together with a speci-
men carpet for the Museum.'
Bibliography : M. Archer (1972), p.58;
Welch (1978b), no.76.   AT

114

**A block-printer (chhipi), printing
floral motifs in a trellis pattern**
Gouache
Height : 22.8cm, *Width* : 18.5cm
Benares, mid-19th century.
VAM : 8042.13   AT

115

**A naichaband, or huqqa-snake
maker**
Gouache
Height : 22.8cm, *Width* : 18.5cm
Benares, mid-19th century.
VAM : 8042.19
The *naichaband* was a craftsman
making the stems or coiled tubes
(snakes) for *huqqas*. According to Hoey
(1880), pp.153-54, snakes 'are of two
kinds, (1) *satak*, a short coil used with
the *huqqa* called *bidar farshi* and (2)
pechwan, the long and heavy coil used
with a large *gargari*. Both are made in
the same way. The workman takes a
long, round, thin slip of wood, winds
round it spirally a thick cord or fine
rope and then over this he coils zinc
wire. Outside this he binds the bark of a
tree called *Bhoj pattar* and over this
again cloth, and he finally secures all
with silk, *kalabatun* [spangled embroid-
ery], and fine wire.'   AT

116

Four drawings of craftsmen at work
by Lockwood Kipling, 1870.
Pen-and ink, pencil and wash.
Height : 26.5cm, *Width* : 35.5cm

VAM : I.S. 0929 (24, 30, 40, 55/56)
(a) Gold fringe making (Delhi)
(b) Gold embroidery (Delhi)
(c) Loom for silk-weaving (Agra)
(d) A *bidri* worker (Lucknow)
From a series of 56 drawings of the
crafts of North-west India. Lockwood
Kipling (1837-1911) worked as a potter
in Staffordshire, before studying art at
South Kensington. From 1865-75 he
was Architectural Sculptor to the Bombay School of Art. From 1875-93 he
was Principal of the Mayo School of
Art, Lahore, and Curator of the Central
Museum, Lahore: the latter institution
appears in the early chapters of his son
Rudyard's classic Indian novel, *Kim*.
Bibliography : Tarapor (1980).   AT

117

**The Mosque of Asaf ud-Daula at
Lucknow**
Gouache
Height : 41.5cm, *Width* : 54cm
Murshidabad, c.1800
VAM : I.S. 11-1887 (14/49)
Bibliography : Sharar (1975), fig.8.   AT

121

118
Entrance gateway to the Taj Mahal, Agra
Water-colour
Height : 53.3cm, *Width* : 73.7cm
Delhi or Agra, c.1808
Lent by the India Office Library and
Records : Add. Or. 928.
Bibliography : M. Archer (1972),
pp.172-73.   AT

119
Amar Singh's Gate, Agra Fort
Water-colour
Height : 82cm, *Width* : 64cm
Delhi or Agra, c.1808
Lent by the India Office Library and
Records : Add. Or. 931.
Bibliography : M. Archer (1972),
pp.172-73.   AT

120
The Buland Darwaza, Fatehpur Sikri
Water-colour
Height : 66.7cm, *Width* : 77.5cm
Delhi or Agra, c.1808
Lent by the India Office Library and
Records : Add. Or. 935.
Bibliography : M. Archer (1972),
pp.172, 174.   AT

121
View of Agra Fort from the river Jumna
Water-colour
Height : 30.1cm, *Width* : 95.5cm
Delhi or Agra, c.1820
Lent by the India Office Library and
Records : Add. Or. 539.
Bibliography : M. Archer (1972),
pp.179-80; Welch (1978b), no.49.   AT

122
Mausoleum of Humayun, Delhi
Water-colour
Height : 53.3cm, *Width* : 71.1cm
Delhi or Agra, c.1820-22
Lent by the India Office LIbrary and
Records : Add. Or. 1809.
Bibliography : M. Archer (1972),
pp.181-84, pl.66.   AT

123
Entrance gatehouse to the mausoleum of Akbar at Sikandra
by Latif
Water-colour
Height : 53.4cm, *Width* : 71.1cm
Agra, c.1820-22.
Lent by the India Office Library and
Records : Add. Or. 1803.
Bibliography : M. Archer (1972),
pp.181-84.   AT

124
Mausoleum of Itimad ud-Daula, Agra
by Latif
Water-colour
Height : 53.3cm, *Width* : 71.1cm
Agra, c.1820-22
Lent by the India Office Library and
Records : Add. Or. 1799.
Bibliography : M. Archer (1972),
pp.181-83.   AT

125
Interior of the Khas Mahal (private apartments) at Agra Fort
by Latif
Water-colour
Height : 53.3cm, *Width* : 71.1cm
Agra, c.1820-22
Lent by the India Office Library and
Records : Add. Or. 1797.
Bibliography : M. Archer (1972),
pp.181-83.   AT

126
The Diwan-i Khas (hall of private audience) at the Red Fort, Delhi
Water-colour
Height : 26.3cm, *Width* : 36.5cm
Delhi or Agra, c.1820-25
Lent by the India Office Library and
Records : Add. Or. 1797.
Other versions of this scene belong to
the V & A and the Royal Institute of
British Architects.
Bibliography : M. Archer (1972),
pp.185-86; Welch (1978b), no.50.   AT

126

127
Side view of the tomb of Shah Jahan, Taj Mahal, Agra
by Latif
Water-colour
Height : 53.3cm, *Width* : 71.1cm
Agra, c.1820-22
Lent by the India Office Library and
Records : Add. Or. 1794.
Bibliography : M. Archer (1972),
pp.181-83.   AT

128
The tombs of Akbar, Sikandra, and Shah Jahan, Taj Mahal, Agra, seen from above
by Latif
Water-colour
Height : 53.3cm, *Width* : 71.1cm
Agra, c.1820-22
Lent by the India Office Library and
Records : Add. Or. 1795.
Bibliography : M. Archer (1972),
pp.181-83.   AT

129
Mausoleum of Safdar Jang
Water-colour
Height : 53.3cm, *Width* : 71.1cm
Delhi or Agra, c.1820-22
Lent by the India Office Library and
Records : Add. Or. 1810.
Bibliography : M. Archer (1972),
pp.184-85.   AT

130
Taj Mahal, Agra, from the river
Water-colour
Height : 48.5cm, *Width* : 70.8cm
Delhi or Agra, mid-19th century
VAM : A.L.4201   AT

131
Marble relief panel with pietra dura border decoration
Water-colour
Height : 38cm, *Width* : 59.5cm
Delhi or Agra, mid-19th century.
VAM : 9232K   AT

132

Pietra dura panels with birds, Diwan-i Am, Delhi Fort

Water-colour

Height : 25.3cm, *Width* : 19.8cm

Delhi, mid-19th century.

VAM : 292-1871　　　　　　　　　AT

133

Sixteen details of pietra dura floral decoration at the Taj Mahal, Agra

Water-colour; various sizes.

Agra, mid-19th century.

VAM : 291-1871　　　　　　　　　AT

133

134

The Khas Mahal (private apartments), Agra Fort

Water-colour

Height : 42.5cm, *Width* : 75.5cm

Delhi or Agra, late 19th century.

VAM : I.M. 185-1920　　　　　　　AT

135

The mausoleum of Akbar at Sikandra

Water-colour

Height : 34.8cm, *Width* : 66.2cm

Delhi or Agra, late 19th century.

VAM : I.M. 187-1920　　　　　　　AT

136

Panoramic view of Salim Chishti's tomb at Fatehpur Sikri

Gouache

Height : 516.5cm, *Width* : 609.4cm

(without border *Height* : 426.3cm, *Width* : 516.5cm)

North India, c.1870

VAM : (no number)

This painting of the tomb of the Sufi saint Shaikh Salim Chishti (1479-1572) may have been made as an exhibition backdrop. The borders (not shown) are based on geometric relief carving from Fatehpur Sikri.　　　　　　　　RC

137

View of the Diwan-i Khas (Hall of Private Audience) at Fatehpur Sikri

Gouache

Height : 505cm, *Width* : 939.5cm

(without border *Height* : 462.3cm, *Width* : 850.6cm)

North India, c.1870

VAM : (no number).

This painting forms a pair with no.136.

RC

Rajasthani & Central Indian Schools

138

Bhairava raga

Gouache

Height : 25.2cm, *Width* : 15.1cm

Early Bundi school, painted at Chunar, 1591.

VAM : I.S. 40-1981

The musical mode *Bhairava raga* is personified as the god Shiva taking his ease with ladies in a palace chamber. He sits holding a *vina* beneath a suspended elephant skin, attended by two maids. The *ragamala* series (now dispersed) to which this painting belongs was made by artists who had received training at Akbar's court. It served as a model for almost all later Bundi *ragamala* paintings.

Bibliography : Beach (1974), pp.6ff.; Skelton (forthcoming).　　　　　AT

139

Vilaval ragini

Gouache

Height : 19.6cm, *Width* : 14.6cm

Malwa, c.1640

Lent by the Trustees of the British Museum.

The musical mode *Vilaval ragini* is personified as a lady anxiously adorning herself in a mirror as she awaits her lover. This painting shows little Mughal influence and recalls pre-Mughal North Indian conventions of colour and line.

Bibliography : W.G. Archer (1958), pl.4; Dahmen-Dallapiccola (1975), p.202; Topsfield (1981), fig. 173.　　　AT

140

Maharana Sangram Singh II receiving a Dutch embassy in durbar

Gouache on cloth

Height : 159cm, *Width* : 120cm

Udaipur, c.1711

VAM : I.S. 09405

The Maharana (centre, with nimbus) sits in the Amar Vilas (or Bari Mahal) apartments in the palace at Udaipur, attended by *sardars* and servants. Before him sits a party of Dutch East India Company officers, led by J.J. Ketelaar (fourth from right of the group, facing left). Ketelaar's party passed through Udaipur in the spring of 1711 on its way to seek trading privileges from the Mughal Emperor at Lahore. According to a letter from Ketelaar, they were well received by the Maharana. A related cloth-painting also in the V & A shows the Dutchmen being entertained by the Maharana with animal fights and other spectacles.　　AT

141

Maharana Sangram Singh practising archery by the Udai Sagar

Gouache

Height : 48.5cm, *Width* : 75.5cm

Udaipur, 1720

Private collection.

The Maharana is seen twice, in his camp by the Udai Sagar (lake), firing arrows at water-fowl and at a water-buffalo in the fast-flowing stream to the left. He is attended in both scenes by nobles and servants. His private apartments, with red *qanats* and canopies, are seen, and nearby, servants husking rice by the river and preparing a meal, and tethered horses, camels and elephants. A long inscription on the border gives the date 1720 AD (V.S. 1777) and identifies the noblemen present. For later versions of this composition, cf. O.P. Sharma (1974), fig.35; Topsfield (1980), no.129.　　　　　　　AT

142

Maharana Jagat Singh watching the Rasalila

Gouache

Height : 60.5cm, *Width* : 44.7cm

Udaipur, 1736

Private collection.

The Maharana sits with a young son and *sardars*, smoking a gold *huqqa* in the form of a woman or child, and watching female dancers perform a *Rasalila* play enacting the youthful deeds of the cowherd god Krishna. A dancer in the role of Krishna, with

peacock crown and tiered skirt, is seen twice, fluting as he supports Mt. Govardhana on his finger near a canopy depicted with Indra on his elephant, and dancing before the Maharana with a *gopi* (milkmaid). Musicians provide accompaniment. The *sardars* (leading away from the Maharana) are : Raja Raghodev, Baba Takhat Singh, Nathji, Prince Pratap Singh, Baghji, Bakhat Singh, Sardar Singh and Baba Bharath Singh. In the courtyard below, servants sleep, chat and make music. The painting belongs to a series of at least ten very similar compositions showing different *Rasalila* scenes, by different artists and all dating from 1736. See Topsfield (1980), nos.113-14.　　AT

143

Maharana Jagat Singh boating near a lake palace

Gouache

Height : 52cm, *Width* : 30cm

Udaipur, c.1740-45

Private collection.

The Maharana passes one of the smaller lake palaces on an excursion in a royal barge on the Pichola Lake at Udaipur. His minister (Bihari Das Pancholi?) and son Pratap Singh and two *sardars* stand before him. Servants carry arms, the royal parasol, a chowry and the jewelled *huqqa* from which the Maharana smokes. The barge is painted with fish, turtles and water-fowl.　　AT

143

57

58

1 *(entry 29)*
Workmen building the royal city of Fatehpur Sikri
From an *Akbar Nama* manuscript.
Mughal, c.1590
VAM : IS 2-1896 (86/117)

2 *(entry 40)*
**Jahangir weighing Prince Khurram
on his sixteenth birthday**
Mughal, c.1615-25
Lent by the Trustees of the British
Museum : 1948. 10-9.069

59

144

145

146

144
Maharana Jagat Singh at worship
Gouache
Height : 37.5cm, *Width* : 22cm
Udaipur, c.1740-50
Lent by Mr and Mrs Ralph Benkaim.
The Maharana, in a saffron *dhoti*, sits
bare-headed in a palace chamber (cf.
Topsfield, 1980, no.126). He performs
his private *puja* (worship), waving an
arati lamp and ringing a small bell.
Before him are images of a *caturmuk-
halingam* with a Nandi, of Krishna and
Radha in a swing, and of Rama, Sita,
Lakshman and Hanuman. An empty
throne for an image stands nearby (cf.
cat. no. 13). Flowers, fruits, *pans*, lamps
and vessels are placed before the
images. Two servants stand in attend-
ance and a musician plays a *vina*.   AT

145
**Maharana Jagat Singh dismissing a
Rathor nobleman**
Gouache
Height : 23.5cm, *Width* : 30cm
Udaipur, c.1745
Lent anonymously.
The Maharana hands a *pan* as token of
dismissal from his presence to a Rathor
nobleman, Chatar Singh, who bows in
deference. The Maharana's voluminous
muslin skirts are held up by Rawat
Fateh Singh, revealing his fleshy calves.
AT

146
**Maharana Jagat Singh II receiving
two sardars**
Gouache, encrusted with pearls and
precious stones.
Height : 45.5cm, *Width* : 43cm
Udaipur, c.1745-50
Lent by Mr Gopi Krishna Kanoria.
The Maharana, who is shown wearing
real pearls and fragments of gemstones,
appears at a draped balcony with two
sardars; he holds the tube of a *huqqa*
and a bouquet of flowers. All the figures
wear flowers in their turbans, suggesting
that they are celebrating the New Year
Festival of Flowers (cf. Topsfield
(1980), no.128). This picture is to some
extent based on an earlier example,
showing Maharana Sangram Singh,
alone and similarly encrusted with
jewellery, which is also in the collection
of Mr Kanoria.   AT

147
**Maharaja Madho Singh playing
chess**
Gouache
Height : 35.4cm, *Width* : 24.1cm
Jaipur, c.1760
Private collection.
The Maharaja reclines against bolsters
on a bed, while a servant massages his
foot. Three kneeling courtiers oppose
him at chess and another servant
swings the *punkah*.   AT

148
Girl flying a kite
Gouache
Height : 17cm, *Width* : 10.5cm
Jodhpur, c.1760
VAM : I.S. 555-1952

149
**Maharana Ari Singh attending a
buffalo sacrifice**
by Bakhta
Gouache
Height : 61cm, *Width* : 44.5cm
Udaipur, 1761
Private collection
The autumnal martial festival of Naur-
atri was celebrated by the Rajputs with
worship of the sword and daily animal
sacrifices (Tod, vol.2, pp.679ff). The
Maharana and his *sardars* stand before
a Durga temple, while a buffalo is be-
headed with a sword blow. Courtiers
and a group of *sadhus* appear in the
foreground. The painting is ascribed to
the artist Bakhta and is dated *Paus sudi
12 V.S. 1818.*   AT

150

153

150

Maharaja Surat Singh (1787-1828) with courtiers
Gouache
Height : 13.9cm, *Width* : 13cm
Bikaner, late 18th century
Private collection.
Bibliography : Welch and Beach (1965), no.63, pp.98, 124.   AT

151

Raja Dalel Singh shooting boar at Gajner
Gouache
Height : 24cm, *Width* : 35.5cm
Bikaner, late 18th century
Lent by the Trustees of the British Museum.
Bibliography : Topsfield (1981), fig.178. AT

152

Seth Gordhandas, a cloth merchant
Gouache
Height : 19.3cm, *Width* : 12.4cm
Jaipur, c.1798
Lent by the Sawai Man Singh Museum, Jaipur.
Seth Gordhandas was a prominent cloth merchant supplying the Jaipur court; cat. no. 278 is an example of a textile purchased from him.
Bibliography : Cf. Chandramani Singh (1979), pl.10b.   AT

153

Maharaja Jagat Singh of Jaipur
Gouache
Height : 76cm, *Width* : 56cm
Jaipur, c.1810
Lent by Gopi Krishna Kanoria.

154

Maharaja Man Singh (r.1804-43) on a ferris wheel
Gouache
Height : 60cm, *Width* : 39cm
Jodhpur, c.1830
Lent by the Hon. Robert Erskine.
The Maharaja (with nimbus) and three nobles are shown drinking wine with ladies as they ride in a ferris wheel to the accompaniment of musicians on a day in the rainy season. Diminutive royal barges are moored on a lake in the foreground.
Bibliography : Cf. Lee (1960), no.48. AT

155

Maharaja Jai Singh III of Jaipur receiving Maharana Jawan Singh of Mewar in his camp
Gouache
Height : 46.3cm, *Width* : 54.8cm

Jaipur, c.1830
Lent by Mr Robert Alderman and Dr Mark Zebrowski.
The Maharaja (with nimbus, right) receives the Maharana in durbar within a chintz tent with large floral motifs, against a background of velvet *qanats*. The two rulers sit facing one another on a carpet beneath a *shamiana*; the two parties of Mewar and Jaipur noblemen sit on either side on a white floor-spread.   AT

156

Maharana Jawan Singh
Gouache on cloth
Height : 210cm, *Width* : 150cm
Udaipur, c.1835
Lent by the Change Trust.
The Maharana stands facing right against a green background. He holds a gold wand in one hand and the jewelled hilt of his sword in the other. In his *patka* he wears a dagger with gold elephant hilt, and a sword with silver ram's head hilt protrudes from behind (cf. no. 422a). He carries a painted hide shield. A comparable life-size study of his successor, Sirdar Singh, is in the collection of Mr G.K. Kanoria: see W.G. Archer (1962), no.84.   AT

157

Maharana Sarup Singh in durbar and feasting with his sardars in the Gordhan Vilas garden
Gouache
Height : 69cm, *Width* : 56cm
Attributed to Tara.
Udaipur, 1859
Private collection.
At lower left, the Maharana is shown eating with his *sardars*; he eats from gold vessels and they from leaf plates. His son, Shambhu Singh, waits on him, wearing a mask over his mouth, as do the servants and the cooks who are preparing kebabs, bread, jalebis and other sweetmeats. Courtiers, musicians and ladies riding on a ferris wheel appear in the foreground. Above right, the Maharana sits in durbar; his son Shambhu Singh stands before him with a *morchhal*. The painted palanquin to the rear, or one very like it, can still be seen in the City Palace Museum at Udaipur. The painting may be attributed to Sarup Singh's leading artist, Tara. AT

3 *(entry 49)*
Prince Salim with scholars and companions in a garden
Mughal, c.1625
Lent by the Trustees of the Chester
Beatty Library : Ms7 no.7

62

4 *(entry 160)*
**A marriage procession passing
through a bazaar**
Bilaspur or Mandi, c.1680
Lent by Mr Howard Hodgkin.

158

159

158

A nobleman in European uniform
Gouache on card
Height : 80.5cm, *Width* : 54.5cm
Gwalior or Indore (?) c.1840
Lent by Mr Robert Alderman and Dr
Mark Zebrowski.
This unidentified nobleman, possibly a
Maratha ruler from Central India, wears
a dramatically exaggerated European
style uniform with elaborate frogging,
braid and epaulettes. He sits in a
painted chair with fluted arm-rests of
European type and holds a European
pocket-watch. A Lucknow enamelled
sword with tooled leather scabbard
rests at his side.   AT

159

**Maharaja Ram Singh II of Jaipur at
worship**
Gouache
Height : 10.5cm, *Width* : 11.6cm
Jaipur, c.1870
Lent anonymously.
The Maharaja is shown seated in
padmasana, facing the viewer as he
would an image of a deity during worship. According to a contemporary
European report, he combined such
traditional observances with a high
regard for European ways 'and was
wont to acquit himself unexceptionably
as Lady Mayo's [dancing] partner at the
vice-regal balls at Simla.'
Bibliography : Welch (1978b), no.64. AT

Punjab Hill Schools

160

**A marriage procession passing
through a bazaar**
Gouache
Height : 32cm, *Width* : 49cm
Bilaspur or Mandi, c.1680
Lent by Mr Howard Hodgkin.
The youthful bridegroom, mounted on a
horse at the right side of the picture, is
escorted by foot-soldiers, an elephant,
noblemen, mounted and walking
musicians, and two *naqqara* drummers
who bring up the rear. The populace
watches this *tamasha* from the roof-
tops. Seven bazaar shops are also
shown in unusual detail: from left to
right, they are selling *lotas* and other
vessels; *pans*; sweetmeats; ceramic and
glass vessels; knives, daggers and
sword-hilts; textiles; grains and pulses.
Bibliography : Digby (1973).   AT

161

A bazaar scene
Gouache
Height : 20.5cm, *Width* : 26.5cm
Guler, c.1720
Lent by the Ashmolean Museum,
Oxford.
Bibliography : Oxford: Ashmolean
Museum (1981), no.409.   AT

162

A caravanserai at night
Gouache
Height : 19.9cm, *Width* : 11.3cm
Punjab Hills (obtained at Jammu), mid-
18th century.
Lent by the Jagdish and Kamla Mittal
Museum of Indian Art, Hyderabad
(76.277).
This unusual genre painting gives a
vivid detailed impression of nocturnal
life in a caravanserai in the Punjab
Hills. The main doors have been closed
for the night, and are watched over by
sentries around their fire. Inside, many
of the travellers are already sleeping,
either in their individual cells around
the walls, or stretched out on the
ground in the main enclosure, apparently undisturbed by the many activities
that are still going on. Men are buying
food from the permanent booths set up
within the caravanserai to cater to the
travellers' needs, and others are
cooking over open fires or drawing
water from the well.
As well as the many male merchants,
travellers and grooms, there are several
ladies present, two of whom are cooking,
while the rest are closeted in their
rooms. Some of them are travelling by
pardarath or curtained carriage, in
order to keep them from the eyes of
strangers on the road. The oxen who
draw the carts are tethered nearby, as
well as horses and the camels of trade
caravans. In the background, beyond
the caravanserai, are distant towns
under a starry sky.
Jammu and other places in the Punjab
Hills were on an important trade route,
especially in the eighteenth century
under Ranjit Dev (see no. 167), when
the usual routes of travel to Kashmir
and the North-West through the plains
had become unsafe due to disruptions
following the invasions by Nadir Shah
in 1739, and trade was diverted to the
hills (see Hutchison & Vogel (1933),
vol.II, p.542).   RC

167

169

163

Raja Balwant Singh at worship
by Nainsukh.
Gouache
Height : 18.5cm, *Width* : 26cm
Jammu, c.1750-55
VAM : I.S. 29-1980, purchased by subscription in memory of Dr W.G. Archer.
According to the inscription, the Raja is doing *puja* before a *salagrama* shrine. The *salagrama*, a type of river pebble (or fossilized mollusc shell) sacred to Vishnu, is covered by a cloth decorated with garlands and a peacock crown, conch, discus, mace and lotus, all emblems of Vishnu. Two servants hold *morchhals* while another prepares a brazier. AT

164

Raja Balwant Singh inspecting a horse
by Nainsukh.
Gouache
Height : 24.6cm, *Width* : 34.2cm
Jammu, c.1750
VAM : I.S. 8-1973
The Raja sits, smoking a *huqqa*, on a richly decorated throne with tiger head arm-rests. Attended by courtiers and servants, he considers the points of a stallion.
Bibliography : W.G. Archer (1952), fig.38; Khandalavala (1958), no.92; W.G. Archer (1973), 'Jammu', no.34. AT

165

Raja Balwant Singh listening to singing-girls and musicians
by Nainsukh.
Gouache
Height : 19cm, *Width* : 33.5cm
Jammu, c.1750-55
Lent by the Trustees of the British Museum.
The figure in the middle of the front row is thought to be Ladvai, the principal singer in Raja Balwant Singh's service.
Bibliography : W.G. Archer (1973), 'Jammu', no.36. AT

166

Raja Balwant Singh performing his toilet before retiring
by Nainsukh.
Gouache
Height : 28cm, *Width* : 37,7cm
Jammu, c.1754
Lent by Baron John Bachofen von Echt.
On a winter evening, Raja Balwant Singh sits on a low chair near a brazier in a verandah room of his country palace at Saruin. He holds a cup, and an attendant standing before him holds a bottle slung in a white *rumal*. A basin filled with herbs, lotas and ewers for ablutions, a basket of linen with a book, and a partially covered *huqqa* stand nearby, and his curtained bed stands on the right. In the foreground the singer Ladvai (see cat. no. 165) performs a song appropriate to the hour of night, strumming a *tanpura* for accompaniment.
Bibliography : W.G. Archer (1952), fig.39; idem (1973), 'Jammu', no.49. AT

167

**Raja Ranjit Dev of Jammu receiving   65
Raja Amrit Pal of Basohli**
Gouache
Height : 22.3cm, *Width* : 29.3cm
Jammu, c.1760
Lent by Baron John Bachofen von Echt.
Raja Ranjit Dev sits smoking a *huqqa* on a garden terrace; his *talwar* lies beside him. His elder son sits beside him, a hawk on his gloved wrist. The youthful Amrit Pal sits facing right, with a younger son of Ranjit Dev behind him, wearing a dark indigo Kashmir shawl with a poppy border.
Bibliography : W.G. Archer (1973), no.57. AT

168

A lady with a yoyo
Gouache
Height : 19cm, *Width* : 11.5cm
Chamba, c.1765
Lent by the Trustees of the British Museum.
Bibliography : W.G. Archer (1956), pl.14; idem (1973), 'Chamba', no.32. AT

169

A block-printer at work
Gouache
Height : 16.5cm, *Width* : 11cm
Kangra, c.1790-1800
Lent by the Rietberg Museum, Zurich.
The block-printer (*chhipi*) is shown printing the mantric formula *sri ram* on rectangles of cloth. Behind him cloths printed with a floral diaper hang from a rail. A mallet for beetling the cloth during the finishing process (calendering) lies near a dye vat. In the background, a woman brings a meal to a man in a *dhoti* who stirs a pot of dye over a fire. RS

5 *(entry 166)*

a) **Raja Balwant Singh performing his toilet before retiring**
Jammu, c.1754
Lent by Baron John Bachofen von Echt.

5 *(entry 155)*

b) **Maharaja Jai Singh III of Jaipur receiving Maharana Jawan Singh of Mewar in his camp**
Jaipur, c.1830
Lent by Mr Robert Alderman and Dr Mark Zebrowski.

6 *(entry 62)*

a) **Flower study from the Dara Shikuh album**
   Mughal, c.1635
   Lent by the India Office Library and
   Records : Add. Or. 3129f 67v.

6 *(entry 219)*

b) **Velvet**
   Mughal, mid-17th century
   Lent by the Chester Beatty Library :
   81 : 6/43.

170
A goldsmith (zargar) at work
From an album depicting trades in Kashmir.
Gouache
Height : 34.2cm, *Width* : 24.7cm
Inscribed in corrupt Persian with descriptions of tools and methods of work.
Company school, Srinagar, c.1850-60
Lent by the India Office Library and Records : Add. Or. 1679.
The page is divided into two halves with a general heading in Persian at the top. In the upper registar the *zargar* hammers an unbent gold bracelet (*karah*) on a beaked anvil held in a wooden block on which another anvil stands. In the lower register he melts gold over a bowl of coals with the aid of a blowpipe and tongs. The tools in front of him include a perforated plate and pliers for wire drawing, a wire brush for cleaning tools, cutters, a file, the blowpipe, tongs and vessels (used in refining gold?). Below him are an ingot of gold, gold on a dish and a touchstone. Above his head are a basin of water and a balance in its case. To the right are a container for molten gold, an anvil, a mould or die for embossed decoration and the finished bracelet on the beaked anvil.
Bibliography : M. Archer (1972), pp.232-35.   RS

Craftsmen's patterns

171
Book of floral designs
Gouache and gold on paper.
Height : 21.2cm, *Width* : 17.2cm
(*Page height* : 28.1cm, *Width* : 17.2cm)
Mughal or Deccan, early 18th century
VAM : 4779-1854
The volume contains 95 leaves of floral motifs covering a wide range of diaper and border patterns suitable for use by textile designers.
The pages have gold decorated margins and the morocco binding has gold-painted cartouches and borders.   RS

172
Nine floral designs
Drawings, some coloured. Varied sizes mounted on a sheet.
Mughal, 18th century
Lent by the India Office Library and

Records : Add. Or. 834-842.
These designs and those in no. 173 are some of a group of floral patterns assembled by a painter or decorative craftsman. A 19th century note states that they were used for cabinets, presumably painted or inlaid boxes. They could equally well have been used by the makers of textiles or metal objects.   RC

173
Seven floral designs
Ink and colour; varied sizes mounted on a sheet.
Mughal, 18th century
Lent by the India Office Library and Records : Add. Or. 879-885.
From the same series as no. 172. The first three are conventional Mughal flowering plants but the remainder appear to be derived from Chinese floral decoration. This is probably taken from blue and white porcelains, whose import (see nos. 401-3) accounts for an element of chinoiserie in Mughal art.   RS

174
A sheet of floral designs
Gouache with gold on paper.
Height : 25cm, *Width* : 20.6cm
Murshidabad, c.1760
Lent by the India Office Library and Records : Johnson Album 22, no.1.
Floral motifs such as these were part of the general repertoire of decorative elements used in textile and metalwork design as well as in the embellishment of albums (*muraqa'at*), for which these examples were probably intended.
Bibliography : Falk & Archer (1981) no.371.   RC

175
Designs for sword-fittings
by Mangat Ram
Wood-block prints
Height : 4cm, *Width* : 7.5cm
Height : 7cm, *Width* : 6.6cm
Srinagar, Garhwal, c.1760-70
VAM : I.S. 187 & A-1955
The two designs show a panther pulling down a stag, and peacocks with plant motifs. They were acquired by J.C. French from Balak Ram, the great-great-grandson of the artist, at Garhwal in 1930.
Bibliography : J.C. French (1931), p.57, pls.XIX, XX.   AT

176
Two flower designs
by Mola Ram
Gouache
Height : 10.5cm, *Width* : 11cm
Garhwal, c.1790
VAM : I.S. 188-1955
These two stylized poppy designs, one on a salmon pink and the other on a gold background, were painted by the well-known Garhwal artist Mola Ram, according to his great-grandson Balak Ram, from whom they were acquired by J.C. French in 1930.
Bibliography : J.C. French (1931), p.58. AT

177
Design for block-printed cottons
Water-colour
Length : 19cm, *Width* : 14.5cm
Masulipatam, 1796
VAM : D. 77-1907
The design is a diaper of flower sprays, all different, mainly in shades of blue and red on a white ground. Cf. no. 179. AT

178
Design for a circular panel
Brush drawing 21.2cm square
Jaipur, c.1800
VAM : I.S. 418-1952
The design consists of flowers surrounding a central medallion containing Durga mounted on her lion. RC

179
Design for block-printed cottons
Water-colour
Length : 23cm, *Width* : 14cm
Masulipatam, 1810
VAM : D.76-1907
The design is a trellis of leafy stems and flower-heads, mainly in shades of red and blue on a white ground. Like no. 177, it is probably a design for piece-goods (yardage), intended for costume items and in the contemporary English taste.   AT

180
Design for a dagger handle in the form of a horse's head
Brush drawing
Height : 14.2cm, *Width* : 9.8cm
Rajasthan, c.1820
VAM : I.S. 370-1952   AT

181
WITHDRAWN

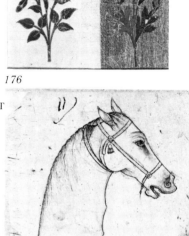

176

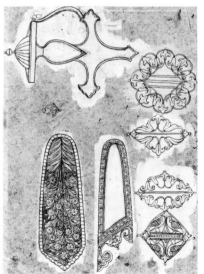

180

182

68

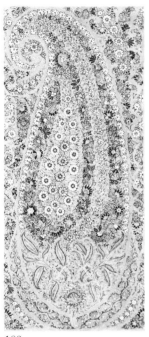

183

185

188

182
Drawing of designs for hilt and scabbard mounts of a talwar
Line and black wash on paper primed with body colour.
Height : 21.6cm, *Width* : 28.5cm
Probably Rajasthan, late 18th/early 19th century
Private collection.

183
Kashmir shawl design
Gouache
Height : 34.5cm, *Width* : 15.5cm
Collected in Kashmir by William Moorcroft, 1823.
Lent by the Metropolitan Museum of Art, the Elisha Whittelsey Collection, the Elisha Whittelsey Fund, 1962.
A multi-coloured design of mixed flowering plants within an elongated cone (*buta*); made for the North Indian market. William Moorcroft, who collected a number of these designs (see no. 184), was a veterinary surgeon employed by the East India Company. During his travels in Kashmir and the Himalayas in 1820-23 he made the first survey of the Kashmir shawl industry. His manuscript reports in the India Office Library give a picture of a highly organized industry catering for wide-ranging markets in India and abroad.
Bibliography : Karpinski (1963), col. pl.2; Irwin (1973), fig.10.   AT

184
Kashmir shawl design
Gouache
Height : 33.4cm, *Width* : 12.7cm
Collected in Kashmir by William Moorcroft, 1823.
Lent by the Metropolitan Museum of Art, the Elisha Whittelsey Collection, the Elisha Whittelsey Fund, 1962.
A multi-coloured design of mixed flowering plants within an elongated cone (*buta*) on a dark grey ground; made for the Persian market.
Bibliography : Karpinski (1963), col. pl.1; Irwin (1973), fig. 7.   AT

185
Design for an enamelled buckle
Gouache
Height : 10.5cm, *Width* : 12cm
Jaipur, mid-19th century.
VAM : I.S. 194-1952
The design is executed in preliminary colours without additional drawing, and includes flower motifs, elephants and horseman.   AT

186
Design for an armchair, carved with a lion's head, doves and fishes.
Pen and ink and water-colour
Height : 13cm, *Width* : 8.4cm
Lucknow, mid-19th century.
VAM : E. 276-1967
Exotic furniture of this kind (see also no. 187) was a product of the later Oudh rulers' passion for European style arte-facts, which came to a head in the reign of Ghazi ud-Din Haidar (r.1814-27) with the appointment of the British artist Robert Home as court painter. The Home Album, in the V & A's collection, includes many of his designs for regalia, furniture, carriages and state barges in the hybrid idiom favoured by his patron.   AT

187
Design for a settee, with an antelope arm-rest
Pen and ink and water-colour.
Height : 11.9cm, *Width* : 19.9cm
Lucknow, mid-19th century
VAM : E. 280-1967   AT

188
Design for an armchair with tiger arm-rests and floral ornament
Water-colour
Height : 25cm, *Width* : 18.5cm
Benares, c.1880
Lent anonymously.
The extravagant ornament of this chair shows some similarity to the earlier, Kedleston sofa (no. 572).
Bibliography : Welch (1978b), no.67. AT

189
Designs from a Kashmir shawl-weaver's pattern book
Ink on paper, with colour notes; various sizes.
Collected in Kashmir, 1881

VAM : I.M. 32-1924
The designs, mainly floral arabesques and long swirling cones typical of this late period of shawl design influenced by European entrepreneurs, are by a pattern-maker (*naqqash*) and the colour notes by an assistant (*tarahguru*). Acquired for his private collection by C. Purdon Clarke, (first Keeper of the Indian Section of the South Kensington Museum, subsequently Director of the museum and of the Metropolitan Museum of Art, New York) on his official purchasing tour of India, 1881-2. With other designs acquired on the same tour, they were presented to the museum by his son, C. Stanley Clarke, also Keeper of the department, in 1924. VM

190
A Kashmir shawl-weaver's coded pattern-guide (ta'lim) and colour scheme
Lithographs and pen and ink; various sizes.
Srinagar, Kashmir, 1881
VAM : I.M. 33-1924
The complex shawls of the mid-19th century were woven in separate sections by different craftsmen and finally joined by professional darners (*rafugars*).
Bibliography : Irwin (1973), fig.4.   AT

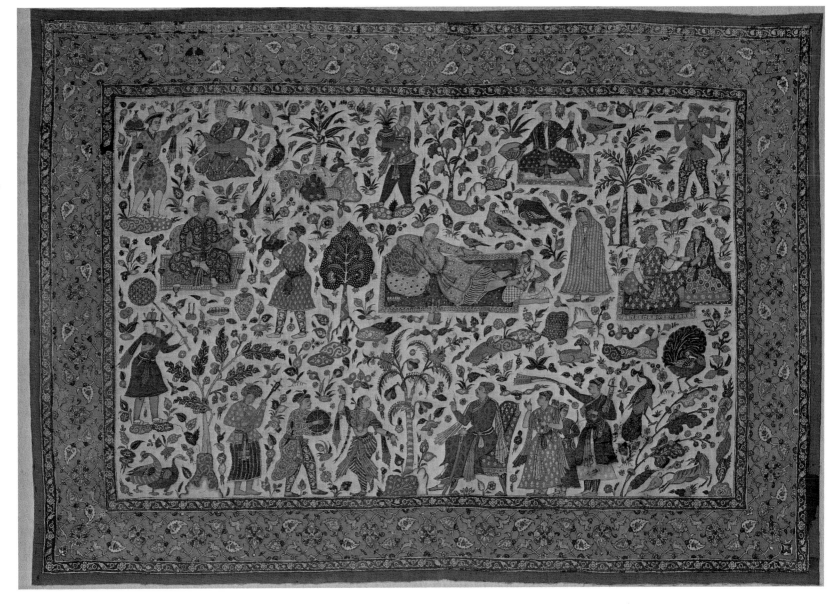

7 *(entry 241)*
Rumal; cotton painted and dyed
Golconda; c.1625-50
Lent by the Metropolitan Museum of
Art, New York : 28.159.1.

8a

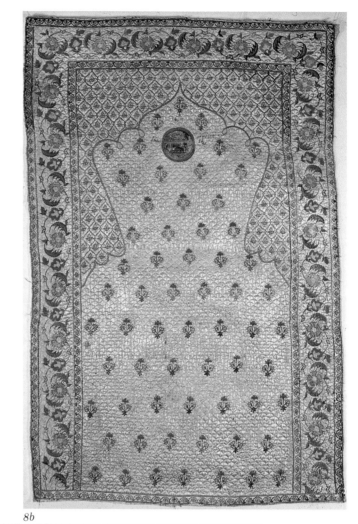

8b

8 *(entry 198)*
a) **Prayer rug**
 Mughal, second quarter of the 17th
 century
 Lent anonymously.

8 *(entry 233)*
b) **Prayer mat**
 Provincial Mughal, 18th century
 Lent by Mrs L. Holmes.

8 *(entry 196)*
c) **Carpet** (detail)
 Mughal, c.1625
 Lent by the National Gallery of Art,
 Washington

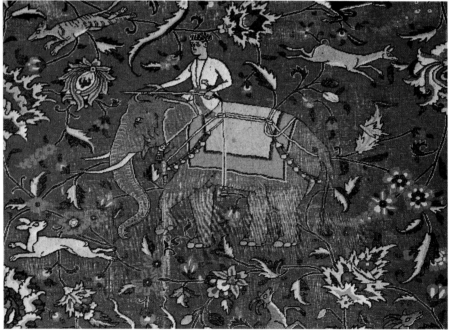

8c

Carpets

Carpet-weaving is not an art native to India : the hot damp climate makes the use of woollen pile rugs as floor-coverings both unnecessary and impractical. It is not known exactly when the first carpets were made in India, but the art was probably introduced by the Mughal emperors rather than by earlier Muslim rulers. Babur (1526-1530) was certainly familiar with their use, from his Central Asian upbringing and from visits to such towns as Herat, and his son Humayun (1530-1556) spent a year as a guest of Shah Tahmasp in Persia seeking assistance to regain his kingdom. This re-inforced his appreciation of Persian art and enabled him to bring back two of the leading court painters with him to India, where they helped to establish the Mughal school of painting. The work of Mir Sayid 'Ali in particular shows a complete mastery of the principles of Safavid decorative design, and these leading artists must have helped Indian designers to become more familiar with the current repertoire of Persian ornament.

However, there is no documentary evidence that carpets were being made in India until Akbar's time (1556-1605), when his chief minister Abu'l-Fazl relates in his chronicles of Akbar's reign, the *A'in-i Akbari,* how the Emperor '. . . has caused carpets to be made of wonderful varieties and charming textures; he has appointed experienced workmen, who have produced many masterpieces. The carpets of Iran and Turan [Turkestan] are no longer thought of . . . All kinds of carpet-weavers have settled here, and drive a flourishing trade. They are found in every town, but especially in Agra, Fatehpur and Lahore.' Akbar probably imported his weavers from Herat, in present-day Afghanistan, which was still an important centre of Persian culture as it had been under his Timurid ancestors. During the 16th and 17th centuries, Persian influence on Mughal textiles, including carpets, was naturally very strong, to such an extent that in some cases a Persian or Indian provenance is difficult to establish. This is especially true of the so-called Indo-Isfahan or Indo-Herat group (see cat. no.194) where sometimes only the colour-scheme gives a clue to the origins of a piece.

The Mughal style, in both painting and the decorative arts, became strongly established by Jahangir's reign (1605-1627) and most of the finest carpets date from this period. There was great emphasis on excellence in painting at Jahangir's court, and this is reflected in the design of carpets : animals, human figures and plants tend to be represented naturalistically. Carpets continued to be woven on the lines of traditional Persian schemes with repeating symmetrical patterns but often were designed as if they were indeed pictures. The pictorial carpet in the Boston Museum, the Widener carpet from Washington (cat.no.196) and the Peacock rug in Vienna are outstanding examples of this style, the latter showing such affinities with miniature painting that it may have been designed by Mansur, Jahangir's court painter who specialised in natural history subjects (see no.46).

Many examples of fine floral carpets also date from this period, and on into Shah Jahan's reign (1628-1659). One of the most well-known is the Girdlers' Carpet dated 1634, which was made for an Englishman, Robert Bell, who was Master of the Girdlers' Company. The design incorporates heraldic shields and the coat of arms of the Girdlers' Company. Another carpet of the period commissioned for an English client is the Fremlin Carpet (VAM : IS 1-1936) : this has a design of animals in a landscape, with the Fremlin family's arms woven into the field and border.

The Lahore floral rugs (see cat. no.203) date from the mid-17th century and can be compared with architectural decoration in such buildings as the Taj Mahal (see no.131) and an unusual tree rug in the Frick Collection, with fragments in the Victoria and Albert Museum and the Metropolitan Museum of Art, New York, is datable to about 1630. This rug shows rows of trees with flowers growing from their bases, an apparently unique design.

Also from Shah Jahan's reign are floral prayer rugs (cat. nos.198 & 199) which show a large flowering plant flanked by smaller plants in a niche and are perhaps the most typically Mughal of all carpet designs.
During the reign of Aurangzeb (1658-1707) carpets of good quality continued to be made, for example the millefleurs prayer rugs. But Aurangzeb was not such a avid patron of the arts as his predecessors, and as his court became more austere, so the standard of carpet design and execution began to decline. Many were still made for export to European countries, particularly England, through the East India Company which had started importing carpets in the 17th century. Lack of patronage became even more marked as the Mughal court itself went into decline after Nadir Shah's invasion of 1739. As carpet-weaving had never been an indigenous art form in India there were no traditional or village designs to re-vitalize the craft at a popular level. Lack of new ideas from the skilled designers at court meant that the old carpet designs were merely copied repeatedly, becoming increasingly debased and stereotyped as time passed. A revival of high-quality carpet-weaving in the 19th century was due to activities of European firms catering for the Western demand for imitations of classical Persian patterns.

RC

191

193

191
Fragment of an animal carpet
Wool
Length : 129cm, *Width* : 100cm
Mughal, late 16th/early 17th century.
Lent by the Textile Museum, Washington. R.63.00.20A.
Controversy still surrounds the dating and iconography of the carpet or carpets of which these two fragments were part. A pre-Mughal date of as early as 1500 has been suggested (see Bode & Kuhnel p.161), but the style of the plants and animals seems to indicate a date of the late 16th century at the earliest. The design is grotesque and enigmatic: the existing pieces do not fit together to form a distinguishable pattern, but there are recurring elements such as the six-headed bird and the leopard mask with menacing fangs. The subject of the design is usually described as deriving from the legend of the talking tree of Alexander the Great (the *waqwaq*), but in depictions of the tree in painting it always has a recognisably tree-like form, with animal and human heads appearing only at the ends of the branches, or as leaves. Here the actual structure of the pattern is all made up of animals and birds, which suggests an affinity with the motif, popular in paintings in manuscripts of the 16th century onwards, of a mythical animal whose composite parts are actually other creatures, often issuing from each others' mouths, as so many of them are in these fragments. The rows of animal heads with long-necked creatures sprouting from them such as in the Glasgow piece (cat.no.192) shows a similarity to the Vase carpet pattern, with heads in place of vases. This would also explain the lack of a central medallion.
Other fragments of the same design are in Detroit, Boston, the Louvre, the Metropolitan Museum, Copenhagen, Leningrad and San Francisco.
Bibliography : Welch (1963), pl.21; Erdmann (1970), fig.221; Beattie (1961), p.162; Eiland, (1979), p.143. RC

192 WITHDRAWN
Fragment of an animal carpet
Wool
Length : 256cm, *Width* : 256cm
Mughal, late 16th/early 17th century.
Lent by the Burrell Collection, Glasgow. 9-1.
This fragment is discussed under the entry for no.191, as they are part of the same carpet or group of carpets. RC

193
Fragment of an animal carpet
Wool
Length : 119.3cm, *Width* : 160cm
Mughal, c.1600
Lent by the Musée des Arts Décoratifs, Paris. Inv.5212.
The disembodied animal heads on this fragment give a bizarre effect similar to that of the red ground fragments (nos.191 and 192), but here the arabesque follows more conventional lines, being based on scrolling vine stems on which the animal heads replace leaves and bracts. The stems themselves are sensitively drawn in a manner which recalls the border of a famous Persian medallion rug in the Metropolitan Museum of Art, New York (Dimand (1963), cat.no.7).
This carpet, of which only a few other fragments remain, is more finely knotted than the red ground pieces. Fragments of its border, surviving in Paris and Hanover, are decorated with a more formal interlacing arabesque, recalling early Mughal architectural relief carving.
Like the red ground fragments, it has been given a pre-Mughal date (see Pope, no.1172), but there is now general agreement that it dates from the end of Akbar's or the beginning of Jahangir's reign. These pieces of the carpet have been re-arranged during the present century.
It has a foundation of silk warps of various colours, as in the case of the Aynard rug (no.199) and the Vienna millefleurs rug, it has a silk warp of various colours, which appears to be a feature of some Indian carpets. The design of arabesques incorporating animal heads was already in use in Persian manuscripts of the late 14th century.
Bibliography : Martin (1908), fig.89; Pope (1939), pl.1172 & 1173; Aga-Oglu (1931), p.3, fig.2; Pinder-Wilson (1957), no.95; Zebrowski (1981), fig.212. RC

194
Carpet
Wool, with gold and silver threads.
Length : 256.5cm, *Width* : 149.8cm
Mughal, late 16th or early 17th century.
Lent by His Grace the Duke of Buccleuch and Queensbury, KT, VRD.
The provenance of the 'Indo-Isfahan' or 'Indo-Herat' group of carpets, to which this one belongs, is still somewhat in dispute, but this example has some characteristics that seem to place it in India. In particular, its relatively empty

background is a typically Mughal feature.

The palmette design and Chinese cloud-band decoration are characteristic of the group; the serrated sickle-shaped leaves which are frequently a part of the design are absent in this rug. It is unusual also in that the focal point of the pattern is markedly central.

The use of gold and silver thread in this carpet may have been influenced by court taste of the Shah Abbas period (1588-1629) in Persia when it was used extensively in the so-called 'Polish' rugs.
Bibliography : London, V & A (1914), cat.no.41. RC

195
Carpet fragment
Silk
Length : 204cm, *Width* : 133cm
Mughal, c.1625
Lent by the Musé des Arts Décoratifs, Paris. Inv.4407.
The field design is a complex trellis ultimately derived from Mannerist strapwork. Sprigs of a naturalistic flowering plant occupy diagonally alternate compartments to form horizontal rows. The other compartments are further divided into four smaller units, each of which contains four fritillary blossoms radiating from a central tie.

The floral arabesque of the main border has a refinement which recalls 16th century North-West Persian carpets. The juxtaposition of these Iranian

195 (detail)

elements with the Mughal field design suggests that the carpet belongs to a transitional phase of Mughal design development in Jahangir's reign.
Bibliography : Martin (1908), fig.222; Paris, Grand Palais (1977), no.686. RS

196
Animal carpet
Woollen pile, cotton warps and wefts.
Length : 403.5cm, *Width* : 191.2cm
Mughal, c.1625
Lent by the National Gallery of Art, Washington.
The design of this carpet (part of the Widener collection), dating from the reign of Jahangir (1605-1627), shows the influence of the fondness for naturalism prevalent amongst the court painters at the time. It is asymmetrical and filled with action. The animals and figures dominate the carpet rather than being used as abstract elements of design. However, their apparently random dispersal throughout the field is in fact the basis of a skilfully organised series of focal points (the rhinoceros at the top, the fighting camels, the central elephant, fighting tigers and bottom elephant) enclosed by a sinuous double meander whose key elements are the crocodile in the upper half of the carpet, and the dragon in the lower. The design of the fighting camels is based on a well-known painting by the fifteenth century Persian artist Bihzad which found its way into the Gulistan Library portion of the Jahangir Album together with a copy by the Mughal painter Nanha (see Binyon et al. (1933), nos.132 and 133).

The border is made up of ogival cartouches alternately containing natural birds and animal masks and palmettes within arabesques. The motif of the mask flanked by animal heads is found in manuscript borders, carpets and tiles (see no.5).
Bibliography : Dilley (1959), pl.35; Erdmann (1970), p.75; Dimand (1973), pp.119-120; London, Hayward Gallery (1976), cat.no.99. RC

197
Carpet fragment
Wool
Length : 78.8cm, *Width* : 86.4cm
Mughal, 2nd quarter of the 17th century.
Lent by the Textile Museum, Washington. R.63.00.13.
This fragment was probably part of a large carpet with animals. It shows two elephants in combat, a typically Indian theme that occurs in painting and also

in architecture. There are panels showing fighting elephants on the walls of the fort in Lahore, where this piece may have been made. The elephants are being urged on by elephant goads (*ankus*).
Bibliography : Vogel (1920), no.7; Welch (1963), pl.40; Erdmann (1970), pl.II, p.75 RC

198
Prayer rug
Silk
Length : 155cm, *Width* : 100cm
Mughal, 2nd quarter of the 17th century. Private collection.
Mughal carpet-weaving reached its zenith with carpets such as this prayer rug. The design of a single flowering plant within a niche representing the *mihrab* was a typically Mughal one, also seen on velvets, silks (cf.no.206), and embroideries (no.232) as well as in architectural decoration, and the detailed and naturalistic execution of

196

the plant is also a characteristic of Mughal carpets. The extraordinary fineness of the weave (1935 knots per square inch) is surpassed only by that of a small fragment of a rug of a very similar design in the Metropolitan Museum, New York, which has 2552 knots per square inch. Apart from the Aynard rug (cat.no.199) the only other genuine survivor of this group of Mughal prayer rugs is one in the Metropolitan Museum, which also shows a chrysanthemum in a niche, but which is more brightly coloured and more coarsely woven (728 knots per square inch) and less masterly in design.
Bibliography : Ganz (1925), pl.33; Ellis (1969), fig.26; Brussels, Musées Royaux, (1969) n.175; Denny (1979), pp.106-7, pl.25; Allgrove (1980), pl.XVII. RC

199
Prayer rug
Woollen pile, silk warps and wefts.
Length : 124.5cm, *Width* : 90cm
Mughal, 2nd quarter of the 17th century.
Thyssen-Bornemisza Collection, Lugano.
This prayer rug, known as the Aynard rug after a previous owner, shows a flowering plant within a niche (*mihrab*), as in no.198, and has the deep colouring associated particularly with Mughal carpets. In this rug, the plant is flanked by cypress trees, a characteristic of many prayer rugs, notably those of the 'millefleurs' type of the early 18th century, of which the most famous example is in Vienna. A further similarity between them is the use of multi-coloured silk warps, a technique also found in the blue-ground animal fragments (cat.no.193).
Although it dates from the same period as no.198, this one incorporates some Chinese motifs which are totally absent in the other, for example the clouds inserted as space fillers between the flowers and the edge of the field, and the stylised rocks and ground at the bottom of the niche. It has been suggested (Beattie, 1972) that this rug may originally have been part of a multiple prayer rug (*saf*), and indeed it does seem to have been repaired in several places with patches from an identical or very similar piece. Also, the width and pattern of the borders are more in keeping with a *saf* than a single prayer rug.
The knotting of the rug is extremely fine (1058 knots per square inch/174 per square centimetre) and this combined with the use of fine lustrous *pashm*, the wool used in making Kashmir shawls, gives the effect of a sumptuous velvet rather than a wool rug.
Bibliography : Migeon (1903), pl.83; Beattie (1972), pp.67-72, pl.IX; Arts of Islam (1976), no.100.   RC

200
Carpet
Wool, with silk warps and wefts
Length : 142.2cm, *Width* : 88.9cm
Mughal, mid 17th century.
VAM : T.403-1910
The design of flowering plants within a lattice was very popular in Shah Jahan's time (1628-58), and several examples still exist. This piece is in fact a large fragment, and a piece showing the border of the same carpet is in Dusseldorf Museum.
Some of the elements, both of the border and the field, have points of similarity with the Altman carpet in the Metropolitan Museum of Art in New York (Dimand (1973), cat.no.60), where they form part of a more elaborate design. In both carpets, the lozenge shape and serrated outline of the trellis appear to be derived from sixteenth century Turkish brocades which were imported in large numbers to the Mughal court.
The carpet has 598 knots per square inch.
Bibliography : Eiland (1979), fig.109; Erdmann (1970), fig.140.   RC

201
Fragment of carpet
Wool, with cotton warps and silk wefts.
Length : 94cm, *Width* : 79cm
Mughal, mid 17th century.
Private collection, England.
This finely-knotted fragment is made up of several pieces. A smaller fragment of the same design is in the Victoria and Albert Museum (IM 153-1926). The flowers are very naturalistically depicted, and the trellis-work, made up of curling leaves and stems, shows strong European influence.
Bibliography : Spuhler (1978), cat.no.60.   RC

202
Carpet
Silk
Length : 360cm, *Width* : 135cm
Mughal, mid 17th century.
Lent by the Musée Historique des Tissus, Lyon.
This rug (in fact a piece of a formerly larger carpet) is rare, if not unique amongst Mughal carpets as it depicts birds and trees which have been reduced to stylised, almost abstract, motifs in a rigid, geometrical pattern. Though each element has been meticulously drawn, the overall effect is unusually stiff, with a symmetrical design along an axis that runs the length of the rug.
Bibliography : Erdmann (1970), fig.223; Bennett (ed.), (1977), pp.126 & 128.   RC

203
Floral carpet
Wool pile with cotton warps and wefts.
Length : 467cm, *Width* : 309cm
Mughal, Lahore, mid 17th century.
Private collection.
Carpets of this pattern form quite an extensive and distinct group. They date from the reign of Shah Jahan (1628-58) and were mostly made in Lahore. Like most of the group, this one comes from the Jaipur *Toshkhana*, where their origin is documented. The naturalism of the flowers is a characteristic of these Mughal carpets, as is the use of a bare red background. Apart from the guard stripes, the design owes nothing to Persian influence but is an expanded version of the decoration on revetment panels on buildings of Shah Jahan's reign. Ultimately this use of flowering plants arranged in rows appears to be inspired by European herbal engravings (see Skelton (1972) pls. LXXXVI and XCI).
Bibliography : Spuhler (1978), cat.no.59.   RC

204
Floral carpet
Wool
Length : 210.8cm, *Width* : 147.3cm
Mughal, Lahore, early 18th century.
Lent by the Ashmolean Museum, Oxford.
The repeating floral pattern of this rug with its symmetrical groups of flowers and serrated lancet leaves is a compressed derivative of the classical 'Herati' pattern. The border of lotus buds and flowers is unusual, though the same design is found on two similar rugs in the Metropolitan Museum, New York and one from a private collection which was sold recently at Christie's. This rug has multi-coloured silk warps, as does the one sold at Christie's, whereas the two New York pieces have cotton warps. It is also more finely knotted, having 780 knots per square inch.
Bibliography : American Art Association (1902), lot 1284; Dimand (1973), cat. nos.65 & 66; Christie's (1981) lot 41; Cleveland Museum of Art (1969), p.240.   RC

76

199

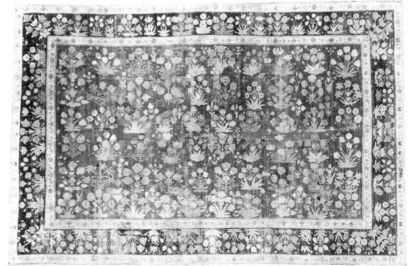

203

Textiles

Textiles

India was already the world's best-known source of luxury textiles many centuries before the coming of the Mughals. References by Greek and Roman authors imply that Indian cottons, above all the transparent 'Gangetic muslins' of Banaras and centres in Bengal, were recognised and admired throughout the ancient world. Permanently dyed cottons, probably South Indian chintzes, were sufficiently familiar to be mentioned proverbially by St. Jerome in his Latin Vulgate of the 4th century AD. In India itself, Sanskrit texts indicate the existence of silk-weavers' guilds in the early centuries of our era, while the equally early origin of techniques such as the *ikat* and *bandhana* processes is proved by their appearance in the cave paintings of Ajanta, c. 5th century AD.

The advent of the Mughal dynasty gave an undeniable boost to the production of up-market textiles, as to other crafts. Textiles are singled out for mention by Abu'l Fazl, the minister and biographer of Akbar (1556-1605), in his *A'in-i-Akbari,* compiled in the 1590's, as a subject in which the emperor took particular interest. Akbar favoured woollen garments – the chosen wear of *Sufis* (Muslim mystics) – 'from his indifference to everything that is worldly' in preference to richer stuffs. His penchant for wool is also indicated by the steps he took to improve shawl manufacture, especially in relation to dyes and width of fabric. The same *A'in*, p.97, goes into fascinating detail on the manner of classifying garments in the imperial wardrobe (*toshkhana*). Textiles were arranged according to the date of entry, which was recorded, sometimes with other information, on a label tacked on to the piece (a practice which survived in provincial *toshkhanas* into the 20th century). Price, colour and weight were also taken into account. Within these boundaries, textiles took precedence according to the nature of the day, astrologically auspicious or otherwise, on which they were received. A further refinement took into account the colours, of which thirty-five are listed in order of precedence. Abu'l Fazl further records that imperial workshops had been set up in the cities of Lahore, Agra, Fatepur Sikri and Ahmedabad, where the best of the local craftsmen were requisitioned to supply the needs of the court. Persian masters were brought in to teach improved techniques. It is questionable whether the Hindu weaver had much to learn from Persia in his traditional fields of cotton and silk weaving. What does seem likely is that pile carpet manufacture was introduced from Persia at this time (see Carpets introduction), while the shawl industry which Akbar improved may itself have been a foreign import to Kashmir by Muslim craftsmen from Turkestan as late as the 15th century. Whatever the impact of Persian intervention in the technical field – and *A'in* p.94 states that many categories of textile formerly imported from abroad could now (in the 1590s) be made in the royal workshops – there can be no doubt that by far the greatest transformation took place in the field of design. The finest early Indian textiles were often plain, as with the clear muslins which won acclaim in the cities of the Roman world. The garment pieces represented in Hindu/Buddhist sculptures and murals tend to be plain or geometrically patterned with chequers, stripes or chevrons, sometimes worked in diagonal bands alternating with processions of *hamsas* (sacred geese) and stylized rosettes. Furnishing fabrics such as hangings for temples and palaces would have been of the band or compartment design seen in nos.205, 209 and 210.

During the Mughal period all this changed. A naturalistic flowering plant motif, quite different from anything seen in earlier Indian art, distinct even from the semi-naturalistic flowers of earlier Persian manuscripts, emerged to become the dominant theme in Mughal arts and crafts from the mid-17th century on. The style was almost certainly heavily indebted to the European herbals known to have been circulating at the Mughal court in the early part of the century; it appears to have crystallized as a result of the ecstatic reaction of the Emperor Jahangir (1605-27) to the flora of Kashmir in the spring of 1620. The motif reached its zenith under Shah Jahan (1627-58), from whose reign may date the sumptuous gold and silver ground textiles with flowering plants woven or embroidered, which have come to epitomize the culture of the Mughal court (nos.207, 218). Paintings from the earlier years of Aurangzeb (1658-1707) show lavish use of 'cloth of gold' ground textiles in furnishings and costumes though towards the end of his reign increasing bigotry made him adopt a puritanical attitude towards luxuries. The flowering plant motif in many forms continued to dominate textile design throughout the 18th century, with increasing stylization. It appeared as a diaper of flower sprigs in court coat fabrics (nos.257, 279, 280), and as a row of single flowering plants at the ends of shawls and court girdles (nos.268, 282, 283). As a large flowering plant framed in a niche, it was the usual theme of furnishings such as prayer mats (no.232) and tent hangings (nos.206, 208, 211-214, 217), which like Mughal court dress represented a culture often originally alien to that of the craftsmen – weavers, embroiderers, chintz-painters – who made them, and whose adaptability had long proved itself a prime asset. The distinctive High Mughal style which had evolved by the mid-17th century, while owing its initial inspiration to the flower cult of the aesthete Jahangir, could not have come into being without the skills, the artistry and interpretative genius of Indian craftsmen, most of them anonymous.

Abu'l Fazl's informed account of the trappings and ceremonial of Akbar's court, seen from the inside, was followed by those of European travellers such as Bernier (1670) and Tavernier (1679), recording the impact on Western eyes of Mughal splendours under Aurangzeb. Bernier in particular painted a vivid picture of the court, in which lives of paralyzing routine as formal and humdrum as any thing known in contemporary Europe were rigidly organized and lived out in a setting of intoxicating beauty created by the hands of man. Much of the court's time was spent on the move, on campaign

282 Shawl fragment; Kashmir, late 17th/early 18th century

or progressing from one royal city of North India to another, along the Imperial Highway which would become known to the British in later centuries as the Grand Trunk Road. This nomadic life – the Mughals were descended from Central Asian nomads – was compatible with all the ceremonial of a court, because the imperial camp was not just a handful of tents and waggons, but a city and virtually its whole population on the move, down to the beggars and criminals. The capital was the court; when the court moved the people had no choice but to accompany it, if they wanted to eat; and life in the camp continued as at home.

Abu'l Fazl, in *A'in* pp.47-50, described the layout of the camp and in particular the tents of the royal enclosure, which were set up according to a plan which never varied, and which remained the same when Bernier accompanied a progress of Aurangzeb from Delhi to Lahore and Kashmir in 1665. The buildings of state which constituted the royal apartments in the palaces of the Mughals were represented by large and elaborate tents, some with an upper storey, set in a great square walled in by *qanats*, textile screens seven or eight feet high, supported by poles set into the ground at regular intervals, the outside usually of red cloth – the imperial colour – and the inside 'lined with printed Indian calico [chintz], representing large vases of flowers' (Bernier, ed. Constable (1891), p.360). The 'spacious and magnificent' royal entrance opened in the middle of one side said to be of chintz finer and richer than the rest. Within this square the ruler's private tents were enclosed by smaller *qanats* 'of the height of a man, some lined with Masulipatam chintz, painted over with flowers of a hundred different kinds, and others with figured satin, decorated with deep silken fringes' (*ibid.*, p.361). The tents of the women's

quarters were similarly enclosed by rich *qanats*. The principal tents in the royal enclosure, as with the *qanats* which defined its boundaries, were covered outside with red cloth – in the case of the tents 'ornamented with large and variegated stripes' (cf. no.213) – and 'lined with beautiful hand-painted chintz, manufactured for the purpose at Masulipatam, the ornamentation of which is set off by rich figured satin of various colours, or embroideries of silk, silver and gold, with deep and elegant fringes. Cotton mats, three or four inches in thickness, are spread over the whole floor, and these again are covered with a splendid carpet, on which are placed large square brocade cushions to lean upon.' (*ibid.*, p.362). All these tents, *qanats* and other necessary equipment were duplicated so that one complete set could travel a day ahead of the emperor, ensuring that on the arrival of the imperial party it would find the mobile city laid out and only awaiting occupation. Abu'l Fazl states that to service a short journey, the camp required 100 elephants, 500 camels, 400 carts, 100 bearers, 500 troopers, numerous officials, 1000 labourers, 500 pioneers (whose job it was to level the selected site), 100 water-carriers, 50 carpenters, tent-makers and torch-bearers, 30 leather-workers and 150 sweepers. Outside the royal enclosure were set up numerous tents regarded as belonging to the quarters of the monarch; tents for the royal guard, for the royal weapons, for the state trumpets, kettledrums and cymbals, for harnesses, for *khil'ats* (dresses of honour bestowed on favoured subjects), for storing various kinds of food (in addition to 15 or 16 kitchen tents), for stabling horses, elephants, hunting cheetahs, birds of prey, and assorted beasts for display or contests. As with the state apartments, all were arranged in a precise order. The 'vast assemblage of red tents' was placed in the centre of the accompanying army. The royal bazaars were laid out in the form of streets intersecting each other and cutting through the encampment of the troops. As night approached the tall beacon 'Lamp of the Sky' – 'upwards of 40 yards high' (*A'in* pp.51-52) was lit in the royal enclosure, to guide stragglers through the pall of smoke from countless fires of green wood, camel and cow dung, to the camp and supper.

The great vassals, many of them Rajput princes, who accompanied the progress, kept a state almost equal to that of the Mughal. Their encampments, on sites allotted by the emperor's quarter-master, and ensuring that a particular noble was placed in his proper situation relative to the royal enclosure, were scaled-down versions of the imperial camp. They also had two sets of everything, including their own bazaars, though they could also use the royal bazaars 'where indeed everything may be procured, almost the same as in the capital' (Bernier, p.366). Trouble occasionally arose when the amirs and rajas in their pride erected tents of a height rivalling those of the emperor. Bernier saw such a tent dismantled on the orders of Aurangzeb. Significantly, a number of important tent-hangings in this catalogue are described as 'formerly in the Amber/Jaipur *toshkhana*' (nos.207, 208, 210, 211, 212), besides other choice textiles including the knuckle-pad covers for shields (no.249) and the girdle of fine *pashmina* (shawl fabric) with gilded details (no.291). The Rajas of Amber, (subsequently of Jaipur), in Rajasthan, took service with the Mughals and emulated their mode of life, including the establishment of workshops and stores.

We know from Abu'l Fazl that in Akbar's reign imperial workshops were established in several leading cities of India. The list was extended in the 17th/early 18th centuries, when, for instance, many of the finest Bengal muslins were woven exclusively for the use of the Mughal court, and when the camp of Aurangzeb was furnished, as we have seen, with 'Masulipatam' chintzes (actually made at Golconda and centres further south, of which Masulipatam was the commercial capital and port). These workshops may be regarded as out-stations of those others attached to the court itself, where artisans of many kinds came to work daily at their hereditary crafts. Bernier streses that for Muslim as well as caste Hindu craftsmen the crafts tended to be automatically hereditary.

As we have seen, workshops organized on imperial lines were also attached to the courts of the great subject-princes. Like their imperial prototypes, they housed craftsmen whose work was not dependent on a regional peculiarity such as the need, real or fancied, for access to the water of a particular river. On the whole, it appears to have been indoor crafts, relatively economical of space, which occupied workers in these *kharkhanas*, though the presence of a carpet factory in the Amber palace prior to 1640 is indicated by a reference in an unpublished MS at Jaipur (Singh (1979), p.xlv, note 10). Another literary source mentions workshops of thirty-six

departments at Amber/Jaipur under the great Sawai Jai Singh II (d.1743) (*ibid.*, note 11).

The other provincial *toshkhana* which figures most prominently in this catalogue is that of Hyderabad, the city founded near the ancient capital of Golconda in the Deccan by Asaf Jah I, Nizam-ul-Mulk (1724-48), who was also for a short time prime minister to the emperor Muhammad Shah (1719-48). Most of the Hyderabad textiles described here reputedly date from his reign. Predictably, they include chintzes from Burhanpur (nos.225, 257 and 280), his headquarters. Other items from the Hyderabad collection include the splendid saddle-cloth of appliquéd velvet on a ground of couched silver-gilt thread (no.236), a brocaded court girdle, possibly Safavid in origin but bearing the Nizam's seal dated 1746 (no.267), a muslin girdle embroidered in orange and dark blue silk and silver-gilt thread, of great charm and distinction (no.274), and a dress fragment of printed and painted muslin minutely patterned with stripes of muted violet and gold (no.281). The visions of slender, tight-trousered zenana belles which this conjures up, though factual enough, are counter-balanced by the picture of a stout official of the East India Company, painted at Lucknow in the 1780's relaxing in an Indian-style coat of similar fabric (Welch (1978), pl.37).

Another *toshkhana* well represented is that of the great Tipu Sahib, Sultan of Mysore (1782-99), part of whose 'tent of fine chintz' is no.213 of the catalogue. The tent was made at Burhanpur, which with centres in the hinterland of Masulipatam (no.211) and others such as Agra and Sironj in the north, furnished the best chintz tent-hangings. Other textiles from Tipu's collection include a magnificent saddle-cloth of red velvet, massively embroidered in couched gold thread, wire and spangles (*zardozi* work, no.237), his red velvet shoes embroidered with silver thread and wire (no.256) and his *jama* of self-striped white muslin with applied sprigs of flattened silver-gilt wire (no.255).

From unidentified *toshkhanas*, one Muslim, the other probably Hindu, come the fresh and lively prayer-mat (dated 1801-2) of white satin, shell-quilted in undyed silk and rather coarsely embroidered with trellised spandrels and flower sprigs in reds and greens (no.233); and the tent-hanging, equally robust but of totally different character, of dark blue cotton embroidered in vibrant pink and yellow silk with a design in which the standard Mughal plant in a niche has been transformed into the flowering tree of textiles made for the European market (no.217). It was probably made for a small Rajput court in Western India.

A more conventional Mughal design is seen in the Burhanpur chintz yardage (no.279) with ink inscription written in the *toshkhana* of a Hindu raja in 1772. This closely parallels the motif on the *jama*, also of Burhanpur chintz, made up at Hyderabad (no.257) and that of the fragment (no.280) from the same source. These are only a few of the many items in the catalogue which were made for provincial *toshkhanas* under Mughal influence.

In spite of the monsoon climate of India, many of these textiles emerged from their traditional storage in relatively good condition, into the hands of the great collector-dealers of the earlier 20th century. Among these the names of Schwaiger and Heeramaneck are outstanding. Our debt to the *toshkhanas*, where the textiles continued to be housed long after they had ceased to be used, and to the men who at length re-discovered them and made them known, would be hard to overstate.

VM

82

205

205

Tent hanging (part of a larger piece)
Woven silk.
Height : 172.5cm, *Width* : 93.8cm
Western India, probably Ahmedabad;
c.1600.
Lent by the Cleveland Museum of Art;
53.474. A gift of George P. Bickford.
Red satin ground, with design mainly in
yellow and white. Field pattern of four
horizontal bands, each containing a
procession of three mounted Rajputs
under a vestigial niche, each group led
by a warrior on foot with shield and
raised sword. The bands are divided by
narrow borders patterned with simple
rosettes. A separate woven silk textile
with another horizontal design – a
broad band of repeating stylized lotus
medallions surrounded by a series of
narrow bands of repeating small rosettes
– has been joined to the warrior silk as a
top and bottom border.
Other portions of these or related
hangings in public collections include
pieces in the Boston Museum of Fine
Arts, Los Angeles County Museum of
Art, the Textile Museum, Washington
D.C., and the Calico Museum,
Ahmedabad. Some show additional
design elements including a highly
stylized symmetrical flowering tree with
birds and confronted animals, and
elephants with riders.
A typically Hindu design with human
and animal figures in horizontal compartments, possibly made for the
emperor Akbar who was interested in
and sympathetic towards Hinduism.
Cf.no.206, also probably the product
of an Ahmedabad royal workshop, in a
completely Muslim idiom.
Bibliography : Irwin in Ashton (ed.)
(1950), pl.69; Jayakar (1955-6),
pp.108-112; Ward (1956), p.65; Cleveland (1969), p.241.　　　　　　VM

206

Tent hanging
Woven silk.
Height : 212cm, *Width* : 97cm
Mughal, probably woven at Ahmedabad
under court patronage; mid-17th
century
Keir Collection.
Red ground, with design in white,
yellow and green. Stylized narcissus
plant in a cusped and tasselled niche.
An almost identical hanging from this or
a closely related set is in the Museum
für Indische Kunst, Berlin (acc.no.1.
364) and another in the Calico Museum
of Textiles, Ahmedabad.
An archetypal Mughal composition, this
design contrasts strikingly with the
Hindu style hanging no.205, which was
also probably made in the imperial
workshops at Ahmedabad.
Bibliography : Berlin (1971), no.150;
Spuhler (1978), p.202-3, no.124.　　VM

207

Tent hanging
Cotton, embroidered with silk and
silver-gilt thread.
Height : 165cm, *Width* : 192cm
Mughal, from the Amber/Jaipur
toshkhana; mid-17th century or later.
VAM : I.M.48-1928
Two niches from a set of *qanats*, cut
down and bordered to make a floorspread. Repeating design of elegantly
curved, naturalistic rose sprays in
shades of pink with yellow centres and
lime green foliage outlined in indigo, in
floss silk, mainly satin stitch, against a
background entirely covered with
silver-gilt thread, laid horizontally with
yellow silk worked in a chevron or
herringbone pattern. Borders with
scrolling rose stems, niches cusped with
acanthus edging in lime with indigo outlines.
A High Mughal style embroidery of
unsurpassed refinement and sensibility,
this hanging originally formed part of a
set comprising a tent (or tents) and
associated multi-niched qanats in the
Amber/Jaipur *toshkhanas*. It was probably made by Gujerati embroiderers
with experience in the Mughal court
workshops. With the decline of this
patronage as Aurangzeb (1658-1705)
gradually turned against the arts, many
such craftsmen were recruited by the
Rajput princes who frequented the
Mughal court and followed Aurangzeb
on his campaigns in the Deccan, and
who wished to emulate Mughal
sophistication at their own courts.
Because of its style and quality, this
much-published embroidery is usually
attributed to the reign of Shah Jahan
(1627-58). At Jaipur it is traditionally
associated with another set of tent-
hangings of rich red velvet, stencilled
and painted in gold leaf with a stylized
poppy plant and niche design, with
poppy and cypress borders (see
no.208). The related sets appear to
have comprised a tent – perhaps more
than one – with the velvet on the
outside, and the gold and silk inside.
In addition there were multi-niched
qanats matching both sets. Jaipur
tradition associates the tent with Man
Singh (1590-1615) or Jai Singh I (1622-
68) Maharajas of Amber (the capital

was moved to the new city of Jaipur nearby in 1728). While the reign of Man Singh is too early a date for either of the textiles, the silk and gold hanging by itself might well date from the reign of Jai Singh I, who served in all Aurangzeb's campaigns in the Deccan and was well placed to employ redundant Mughal craftsmen.

The difficulty arises in relating the embroidery to the velvet. It is possible to identify gold-painted red velvet textiles in 17th century paintings, usually with arabesque and medallion patterns. As niche-and-plant tent hangings, the technique has not been identified in any painting earlier than about 1720-30 (Falk and Archer, 1981, no.160). The velvet ground fabric, of very narrow weave, is probably European; a technical specialist has suggested a link with Dutch stamped velvets of a type made only in the second quarter of the 18th century. It is presumably possible that the two textiles, though used together, are not of the same date, and that a velvet tent of the 18th century could have been lined with a 17th century embroidery which in the interval had remained in the stores unused, having perhaps been commissioned by Jai Singh I shortly before his death.

If the two textiles are contemporary, the probability is that they date from the reign of Jai Singh II (1699-1743), arguably the greatest Rajput prince of any dynasty, a mathematician and astronomer of international reputation, and the founder of Jaipur. Gold-painted velvets like the Jaipur set were in fashion at the Mughal Court in the reign of Muhammad Shah (1719-48) (ibid), with whom Jai Singh II stood in high favour. It was a time when gold ground silk embroideries of a high standard still flourished. Jai Singh II maintained court workshops of 36 departments at Jaipur. Following his death and the decline of his dynasty during the Mahratta supremacy, it is unlikely that tent hangings of such extent and splendour would have been made; before long they were going out of fashion. Two more *qanat* niches of this embroidery are in the Calico Museum, Ahmedabad (acc.no.644, Irwin and Hall, 1973, no.1, colour plate II), one in the Boston Museum of Fine Arts (acc.no.66.861) and one in the Los Angeles County Museum. Other portions remain at Jaipur.
Bibliography : Irwin in Ashton (ed.), London (1950), no.1006; Irwin (1950), pl.3. VM

208
Tent Hanging
Velvet, stencilled and painted with gum and gold leaf.
Height : 184cm, *Width* : 138cm
Rajasthan, from the Amber/Jaipur *toshkhana*; probably 18th century.
VAM : I.M.30-1936
Red ground, with gold design of a stylized poppy plant in a niche. From a large tent, of which remaining sections include one in the Calico Museum, Ahmedabad (acc.no.252, Irwin and Hall, 1971, cat.185, pl.87), and a superb five-niche hanging in a private collection in New York. These retain borders with an alternately repeating flowering plant and cypress pattern, missing in our hanging, but seen in a red velvet textile with gilded trellised ground, with a London dealer in 1981, and thought to be from the roof of the same tent. A similar border edged the doorway.

Red velvet textiles with gold-painted patterns appear in many Mughal and Rajput miniatures. They include *qanats* of several niches in a Jaipur painting of about 1830 (no.155), a Kotah painting of about 1850 (Falk, 1978, no.71), and a door curtain, of which only the upper part is visible, in a Mughal painting of about 1720-30 (Falk and Archer, 1981, no.160).

The tent of which the present hanging is a section is traditionally associated at Jaipur with a much-published set of gold and silk-embroidered hangings dating from about the middle of the 17th century (no.207). It is, however, unlikely that the probably European velvet from which the outer tent is made dates from before about 1725.
Bibliography : Irwin in Ashton (ed.) London (1950), no.1003. VM

209
Hanging
Cotton, stencilled, painted and dyed.
Height : 155cm, *Width* : 202cm
Madras-Pulicat region, 17th century (after 1630).
Lent by Mme. Krishna Riboud.
Fine white ground, with pattern in reds, violets, brown, black, etc., typical of this school. The hanging is pieced together from fragments of a larger one. The arrangement now consists of three horizontal bands, a broad one across the top and bottom and a narrower one between. In the uppermost seven cusped niches, broad and narrow, surmounted by the high stepped roofs of South Indian temple pavilions, frame

scenes of Hindu palace life. In a central scene a princely figure stands with male attendants. On either side he appears in two slightly different interpretations of a durbar scene, enthroned with a consort beside him, and female attendants below the dais. More females crowd the narrow niches between these sections. Many of the attendants carry the insignia of royalty and an array of banners. The broad band at the bottom is divided down the middle. To the left are more niches, one containing another scene of the prince on his dais, another with a group of dancing girls, and three smaller ones with female attendants. Flower garlands hang from the roofs of all the niches in both bands. To the right of the bottom row the ruler, mounted on a massively built horse, rendered in a style evidently influenced by European engravings of the 1620s-30s, rides in procession attended by male followers on foot. One, near the front, carries a drawn sword; others bear the insignia of royalty, including a *chhatri* (state umbrella) and a large *panka* (fan), and numerous banners, some garlanded with flowers. Across the middle of the hanging is a narrow strip in which the prince – shown near the right side, empty-handed, his arms supporting the long elaborate sash then fashionable in the Deccan – sets out on foot with his followers who carry swords and long guns. Hunting and wild-fowling rather than war are suggested by the presence of two falconers, each carrying his bird.
Probably made for a Hindu court in the

Deccan, this hanging is related to the group published by Irwin, (1959), one of which is included in this catalogue (no.210). The practice of depicting figures and incidents in strip picture form, with or without captions in the local script, is an old Hindu tradition found in several regions of India (cf.no.205). In the south it appears in temple murals as at Lepakshi (Irwin (1959) figs.26 and 27), and survive in the painted cotton temple cloths of Kalahasti and other centres. VM

208

209

210

Tent hanging

Cotton, painted and dyed.
Height : 251.3cm, *Width* : 96.5cm
Golconda, formerly in the Amber
Palace *toshkhana*, Rajasthan, c.1630-40.
Lent by the Brooklyn Museum :
14.719.2.

White ground with design in red, blue,
brown and purple. Beneath an architectural frieze of 'onion' domes, a tall
niche encloses four horizontal strip
pictures of figures in Portuguese dress,
the central figure in each row seated on
a dais in a formal *darbar* pose. From a
set of seven hangings, originally joined,
apparently illustrating the 'Kings of the
Earth' theme which interested the
Mughal emperors and their vassals, and
originally from the Amber Palace collection.
Bibliography : Culin, 1918, pp.133-147;
Irwin, 1959, pp.38-40, pl.VI, fig.6.   VM

211

Tent hanging

Cotton, stencilled, painted and dyed.
Height : 295cm, *Width* : 207cm
Golconda, formerly in the Amber Palace
toshkhana, Rajasthan; probably early
18th century.
Lent by the Rhode Island School of
Design, 37.010. Gift of Miss Lucy
Aldrich.
Design in reds, violets, blue, green,
yellow, brown and white. Three niche
hanging from a *qanat* set. In the centre
on a white ground a tall palm tree with

clusters of hanging fruits is realistically
rendered, except that a little over half
way down its trunk is seen to merge into
an elongated waisted vase, growing in
its turn from a low mound of patterned
rocks. A fantastic flowering plant with
foliage and flowers of mixed species,
including enormous chrysanthemum
heads, emerges from the wide neck of
the vase on either side and branches to
fill much of the field. A smaller exotic
plant grows from miniature rocky
mounds to flank the tree. The upper
part of the field is patterned with small
detached plant motifs and 'Chinese
clouds'. To the left is a niche with red
ground, in which is a tall chequered
vase from which emerges a roughly
symmetrical arrangement of fantastic
flowering sprays, again flanked by a
pair of plants, this time springing from
either side of a range of rocks on which
the vase stands. A purple ground niche
enclosing a vase with broad base and
narrow neck supports a plant with huge
heads like tulips or turbans, with
smaller flowerheads, mixed foliage and
a few nuts. This is again flanked by a
pair of plants at the base. The background of the purple ground niche is
closely filled with minute flowers and
also leaf tendrils. The spandrels and
borders separating the niches are patterned with scrolling leaf and flower
motifs in several colours on a yellow
ground. The narrow guard borders are
red with scrolling stems, leaves and
flowerheads in yellow, brown and white.

Broad borders run along the top and
bottom of the hanging, with a repeating
pattern of cartouches and crosses filled
with floral arabesques, in the manner of
the Golconda rumals (nos.239-242).
Above the upper band of this border is
a heading patterned with a row of
identical flowering plants, the main
bloom with reflexed petals and projecting stamens, and below it a pair of
crocus-like buds and four gracefully
curved strap-like foliage; this design is
in the idiom of chintz girdles in the
Calico Museum (e.g. Irwin & Hall 1971,
pl.52A).
The tent hanging with its sumptuous
colourings, retains the rich colour
palette, much of the feeling and certain
motifs of earlier Golconda cotton paintings (cf.nos.239-242). Other sections
from this *qanat* set include one niche in
the Cooper-Hewitt Museum, New York
(1952-111-1), one in the Textile
Museum, Washington (TM6.129) and
one in the Los Angeles County Museum.
Bibliography : Mailey (1952), p.139f;
Cavallo in Boston (Heeramaneck,
1966), no.261; Beer, (1970), no.1.   VM

212

Tent hanging

Coarse cotton, stencilled, printed,
painted and dyed.
Height : 182.9cm, *Width* : 106.7cm
North India, formerly in the Jaipur
toshkhana; 18th century.
Lent by Mrs L. Holmes.
White ground, with design in red, two
greens and yellow; outlines black and
red. Much restored due to damage where
the black mordant has eaten away the
fabric.
A bold and striking variant of the flowering plant in a niche theme (cf.nos.198-
9). The proportions have been falsified
by a reduction in height during restor-
ation, apparent when this hanging is
compared with others in the same set.
At least eight more niches survive, most
of them separately, except for a run of
three still joined and retaining attach-
ments for support poles, in a private
collection in London. In addition, two
more niches from this or a matching set
are in the Calico Museum (acc.no.801,
Irwin & Hall 1971 pl.10) and there is
another in the Baroda Museum (acc.no.
I.A.764)   VM

213

**Tipu Sultan's tent (roof and one
wall)**

Cotton, printed, painted and dyed.
Approx 630cm square

Khandesh (Burhanpur), mid-18th
century.
Lent by the Trustees of the Powis
Estate.

White ground, patterned with a row of
niches each enclosing a vase of flowers
mainly in reds and greens (the latter
now appearing too blue due to the
partial disappearance of the fugitive
yellow overpainting). Series of leaf-and-
flowerhead borders. A band of black
and white merlons or battlements runs
along the top. The roof segments are
painted with vases and flowers similar
to those of the *qanats*, with here and
there pieces of another chintz fitted in
to fill gaps. The outside of the tent is a
separate layer of coarse whitish cotton.
The roof is edged with a band of red
and white patchwork, with another
around the central pole, on top. A
toshkhana stamp appears on one of the
red edging strips.
Possibly the 'tent of fine chintz' in
which Lord Cornwallis and his entourage were formally received by Tipu's
two small sons, the hostage princes, on
27th February 1792. The complete
tent, of which only part is shown here,
was among Tipu relics acquired by the
2nd Lord Clive, son of Clive of India,
and his connoisseur-collector wife, the
Powis heiress, during his Governorship
of Madras, 1798-1803.
The design is closely paralleled by a
tent hanging of 7 niches in the Calico
Museum (acc.no.222, Irwin and Hall,
1971, no.18) though the borders are
different. A hanging in the VAM
(I.S.131-1950) is also very like it, with
almost identical narrow triple borders
and broad borders similar except for
the addition of parrots perching on the
stems. The border and top merlon
design occur again in VAM I.S. 51 and
52-1950. A more decorated version of
the broad border appears on a chintz
picchavai in the Calico Museum, acc.no.
139, Irwin and Hall, 1971, no.68.   VM

211

212

213 (detail)

215

217

214
Tent hanging
Cotton, quilted and embroidered in silks.
Height : 178cm, *Width* : 70cm
Mughal, 18th century
Lent by Mr Vishnu M. Lall.
Dark red ground, closely quilted all over in red silk and embroidered with a niche design of a flowering plant in a vase, in white, blue and yellow. Broad borders of scrolling stems and flower-heads.
Two more niches from this set are in the Calico Museum, Ahmedabad, acc. no.142, Irwin & Hall (1973), no.9, colour plate III, and two more in the Metropolitan Museum of Art, New York, acc.no.33.65.9.
Lined and quilted hangings were some-times used to curtain off the open colonnades of palaces in the cold season (see also nos.216 and 217).   VM

215
Part of a tent hanging
Cotton, quilted and embroidered with silk.
Height : 88.5cm, *Width* : 84.5cm
Mughal, probably late 18th century.
Private collection, Eire.
White ground, with chain stitch em-broidery in coloured silk; architectural design obviously inspired by the *pietra dura* inlay of marble colonnades such as those of Agra. (See also nos.214 and 217).   VM

216
Miniature coverlet
Silk and cotton fabric, satin faced, quilted and embroidered in silk.
Length : 98cm, *Width* : 65cm
Mughal, 18th century
Private collection, Eire.
White ground, embroidered in coloured silk with a design based on a central cusped medallion filled with scrolling stems and flowerheads; a quarter medallion is repeated in each corner of the field. At either end of the quilt runs a band of arcading in the style of a Mughal colonnade, with a flowering plant in each of its seven niches. Widely spaced flower sprigs are dotted about the field at regular intervals, two at each end and two on either side. Diagonal lines of white quilting run from all four sides to enclose the central medallion in a multilinear lozenge, reminiscent of the impressed trellis compartments seen on many Mughal garment pieces. The embroidery is well preserved, with unfaded colours. The satin face of the fabric is very worn.

Possibly intended as an infant's cot quilt, or a blind for a small window. Textiles with an arcaded design like this are often seen in doors and win-dows in paintings of the period.   VM

217
Tent hanging
Cotton, embroidered with silks, lined and wadded.
Height : 205cm, *Width* : 113.5cm
Western India, probably late 18th/early 19th century.
VAM : I.S.1-1965
Dark blue (indigo) ground of coarse cotton, with flowering tree design flanked by two vases of flowers under a broad flattened niche, in pink, yellow, etc., mainly in a rather coarse chain stitch. The presence of a half-cypress on either side suggests that the panel is one section of a multi-niche hanging. Probably made for a minor Rajput court, this robust and lively provincial interpretation of Mughal idiom has transformed the conventional flowering plant motif into a full-blown flowering tree of a kind usually associated with work for the European market.
For other tent hangings wadded and lined for winter warmth see nos.214-5.   VM

218
The Northesk Bearing Mantle
Woven silk and silver-gilt thread.
Length : 117cm, *Width* : 110.5cm
Probably woven at Ahmedabad.
Mughal or Persian, second or third quarter of the 17th century.
Lent by the Rt. Hon. the Earl of Northesk.
Gold ground, with repeating pattern of poppy plants in pale orange with darker outlines, and lime green foliage outlined in dark blue. This 'cloth of gold', with its staggered rows of pale nodding poppies, is said to have been used to carry a Stuart prince to his christening. It is certainly of a quality which the Mughal emperors, intensely interested in the concept of kingship and the brotherhood of monarchs, might have thought worthy to present to a ruler. The flowering plant, rendered with a degree of naturalism hitherto unknown in Mughal decoration, became a dominant ornamental theme following Jahangir's ecstatic experience of the Kashmir flora in 1620. The movement drew further inspiration from the flower illustration in European herbals which found their way to the Mughal court. After 1620, Mughal palace scenes in

paintings began to include sumptuous gold or silver ground brocades with realistic flowers in staggered rows. An early depiction of such a textile is no.40. A parallel development in Safavid Persia seems to have begun slightly later in the century. Although this textile has hither-to been attributed to Iran, related examples have been found in India and the treatment of the plants accords more with Mughal than with Safavid design principles, in which 'the strong curves and the interlocking motifs make the rose less obvious' (Kahlenberg (1973), p.25).   VM RS

219
Velvet
Length : 85cm, *Width* : 56cm
Mughal, mid-17th century
Lent by the Chester Beatty Library, 81.6/43
Cream ground, with design mainly in red, yellow, green and violet, of large and small flowering plants alternately, in two rows, one placed end-on to the other. Inner border of scrolling stems with leaves and flowerheads, outer border of stylized rosettes making a semi-geometric design. Possibly in-tended as a book cover. Closely related designs appear in the marble dado panels of Mughal buildings of the Shah Jahan period, such as the *Diwan-i-Khas* at the Agra Fort.   VM

220
Velvet
Silver brocaded ground.
Height : 118cm, *Width* : 88cm
Mughal, probably second half of 17th century.
Keir Collection.
Silver ground with pattern of two semi-naturalistic flowering plants, one an iris, repeating alternately in staggered rows, mainly in red, green and white. Border patterned with double rows of flattened S-shaped detached leafy scrolls and flowerheads. Possibly a curtain or blind.
A *zari* ground velvet curtain with a somewhat similar plant design and almost identical border in the Jaipur collection was received from Lahore in 1696 (Singh (1979), plate 48). See also the border of no.219.
Bibliography : Spuhler, (1978), no.123.   VM

221
Piece of furnishing fabric
Velvet and gold brocade.
Length : 82cm, *Width* : 46cm
Persian for export to an Indian court, mid-17th century.
Private collection.

The design is of staggered alternate rows of cypresses flanked by pairs of female figures, alternately facing inwards and outwards, accompanied by small dogs. Although their costume is eclectic, they are possibly intended to be European women. The cypresses are entwined by prunus saplings – a traditional Persian motif – and grow at the edge of small pools. The field also contains flowering plants.

In technique and general conception, this is typical of Safavid velvets, associated with the pictorial style of Reza Abbasi, but in this case the weavers have copied the costume detail of imported Golconda painted cottons (see nos.239-242). Safavid velvets were much in demand in Indian courts, indeed many of the surviving examples originate from the Jaipur *toshkhana*. Indian figured velvets of the period are unknown and it appears that the Persian suppliers have here adopted figure designs which they supposed would appeal to their customers. Another fragment of this textile is in the Los Angeles County Museum of Art (see Kahlenberg (1973), pl.28).
Bibliography : Spuhler (1978), no.119, col. plate p.209. RS RC

221a
Velvet border
Length: 298cm, *Width* : 158cm
Mughal; probably mid-17th century.
VAM : 320-1898
Cream ground, patterned with a row of flowering plants in which an orange and red reflexed lily alternates with a yellow and blue narcissus. Green foliage.
The sumptuous cut velvet, its flowers depicted with a typically Mughal naturalism, consists of two border lengths probably intended as part of a floorspread, but now joined together.
Bibliography : London (1976), no.94 and illus. VM

222
Floorspread
Velvet
Mughal, probably 2nd half of 17th century.
Lent by Mr R. Chenciner.
Deep red ground, with symmetrical design mainly in white and blue-green, of scrolling stems, leaves and flower-heads, based on a central acanthus-edged medallion, with a quarter-medallion in each corner of the field. Broad border with pattern similar to that of the field, surrounded by two guard borders with a small floral scroll, and four with a continuous X pattern. There is a virtually identical floor-spread in the MMA, New York (acc.no.41.190.256), in much better condition. A Safavid velvet fragment in the VAM (733-1892) is of related pattern and colour scheme. VM

218 (detail)

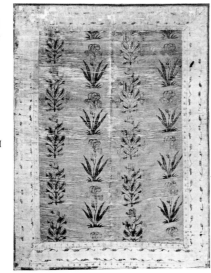

220

222

223

223
Floorspread
Velvet.
Length : 203cm, *Width* : 116cm
Mughal, probably late 17th century.
VAM : I.S. 16-1947
Cream ground, with 3-row pattern in green, red and blue, each row comprising a central formal cypress tree flanked by a pair of fanciful flowering plants. The cypress motif, with a symmetrical arrangement of stiff graduated leaf sprays sprouting from its outline, and a large stylized rosette superimposed on the slender trunk, is reminiscent of a turban ornament. The main border, a large floral scroll, is missing at one end, and the guard borders contain a small different scroll. Velvets with this kind of pattern often carpet the royal dais in miniature paintings of the period.
Bibliography : Irwin in Ashton (ed.), (1950), no.1005, pl.65.   VM

224
Fragment of a floorspread
Velvet
Length : 82cm, *Width* : 46cm
Mughal, probably 17th century
Lent by Mr B. Mohamed.
Green ground with flowered and foliated cusped octagonal medallion pattern mainly in red and white. Main border of large scrolling leafy stems and flowerheads, scaled down in the guard borders.
Another portion of this velvet was exhibited in the Royal Academy Exhibition of Persian Art in 1931 (no.202) and illustrated in the Survey of Persian Art (pl.1080) where it is discussed in conjunction with a more clearly Iranian example in the Metropolitan Museum of Art (*ibid*. p.2138, pl.1068.)   RS VM

225
Floorspread
Cotton, printed, painted and dyed.
Length : 245.8cm, *Width* : 102.5cm
Burhanpur, Khandesh, 18th century, probably 2nd quarter; made for the Hyderabad *toshkhana*.
VAM : I.M.69-1927
Two stylized rosettes, the larger a red chrysanthemum type, the smaller light green and of indeterminate species, repeating alternately in a trellis of delicate curving stems with buds and tendrils in shades of green on a dark blue ground. (The amount of dark blue in this chintz is unusual for Burhanpur work, and may indicate areas where yellow overpainting, now vanished, was used to produce dark green). Central and corner medallions patterned with scrolling leafy flowered stems in green and yellow on an undyed ground. Broad borders patterned as field but with trellis and ground colours reversed. Two guard borders of merlon (battlements) design, two repeating the medallion scroll. In each corner of the border is a square compartment containing a green rose spray, diagonally placed and surrounded by a delicate fern or seaweed filler pattern in light red with tiny white quatrefoil florets on a dark red ground.
Said to be a *dastar-khana*, the cloth on which dishes were placed at mealtimes, this floorspread from the Hyderabad *toshkhana* is believed to be associated with the reign of Asaf Jah, the first Nizam (1724-48), whose headquarters were at Burhanpur, which during this period of freedom from the incursions of the Mahrattas regained something of its old status as a crafts centre. The floorspread shows a version of the standard Mughal flower-and-trellis design perhaps more suggestive of woven and embroidered textiles than chintz, but it is closely paralleled by many of the 264 trellis patterns on a Burhanpur chintz designer's sample sheet of 1041 different designs in the Textile Museum, Washington D.C. (acc.no.6.140). The sheet also includes 272 variants of the diagonally placed flower in a square compartment with background filling of light and dark red or purple fern tracery with minute white florest. A Burhanpur chintz of style and colour scheme comparable to the floorspread was used as a wall-covering and bed curtains in a Dutch dolls' house of the 1670s in the Rijksmuseum (Irwin, 1970, fig.24). A more elaborate version is seen in no.76, pl.74b, of the same book. The Burhanpur conventions of (a) rendering flowerheads as highly stylized circular forms in a trellis of foliage, and (b) using light and dark red fern tracery with tiny white quatrefoil florets as filler patterns, are noticeable features of Tipu Sultan's tent (no.213), and of the prayer mat (no.231).   VM

225

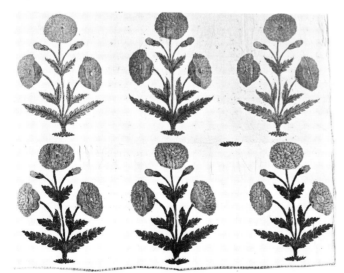

226 (detail)

226
Part of a floorspread
Cotton, painted and dyed.
Length : 106.7 cm, *Width* : 137 cm
Probably Burhanpur, late 17th/early
18th century.
VAM : I.M.69-1930
White ground, with pattern mainly in
red and green with black and red
outlines.
Archetypal Mughal design of a stylized
poppy plant in staggered rows. A complete floorspread of this design is VAM
I.M.77-1938. Other fragments are in
the Calico Museum, Ahmedabad (acc.
no. 652, Irwin and Hall 1971, no.23,
pl.9), and another in the Boston Museum
of Fine Art (acc.no.66.866, Heeramaneck cat.no.268), and the Indische
Museum, Berlin.   VM

227
Piece of chintz
Cotton, stencilled, painted and dyed.
Length : 85 cm, *Width* : 45 cm
Probably Golconda, 17th century.
VAM : Circ. 344A-1932 Given by Pro-
fessor K. de B. Codrington.
White ground with multi-colour design
of two different fanciful flowering
plants, repeating alternately in staggered rows. From a floorspread or
garment piece.
Another fragment (I.M. 57-1933) of the
same chintz was published by Irwin
(1970), no.4, pl.32   VM

228
Piece of chintz
Cotton, stencilled, painted and dyed.
Length : 56.5 cm, *Width* : 45.5 cm
Coromandel coast, Madras area, 17th
century.
VAM : Circ. 345A-1932. Given by Pro-
fessor K. de B. Codrington.
White ground, with multicoloured
design of a flowering plant repeating in
staggered rows. From a floorspread or
garment piece.
Another fragment (I.M. 58-1933) of the
same chintz was published by Irwin
(1970), no.5, pl.36.   VM

229
Floorspread
Silk and cotton mixed fabric, satin-
faced, embroidered with silk, silver and
silver-gilt thread.
Length : 245 cm, *Width* : 151 cm
Mughal, 18th century
Lent by Mr R. Goodall.
Red field, blue borders, embroidered
with multicoloured silks, silver and
silver-gilt thread in a variety of stitches,
with a pattern of scrolling leafy stems
and flowerheads, based on a central
medallion with quarter-medallions in
the corners of the field. Main (central)
border design of flowerheads and
foliage, flanked by narrower borders of
small stylized rosette and leaf pattern.
Guard borders of tiny leaf motif.   VM

230
Canopy
Mixed silk and cotton fabric, satin-
faced, embroidered with silks and silver
and silver-gilt thread.
Approx. 97.5 cm sq
Probably Gujarat or Deccan, 19th
century.
Lent by Mrs L. Holmes and Mr H.
Ginsburg.
Peach-coloured field embroidered in
coloured silks, mainly satin stitch, and
couched metal thread with a symmetrical design of stylized flowers and
foliage radiating from a central lotus
medallion. Green ground border with
scrolling stems and similar flowerheads.
Large areas of couching are worked in a
massive basket pattern.
Probably made for the roof of a shrine,
the embroidery design with its central
lotus medallion and large corner
palmettes, is indebted to prototypes of
c.1725-50. The presence of European-
style twisted embroidery thread, used in
conjunction with the traditional Indian
floss (untwisted) silk, suggests that the
work in fact dates from the later 19th
century, a view reinforced by the colour
combinations in the embroidery, and by
the type of tinselled braid which
squares off the sides.

230

231
Multi-niched prayer mat
Fine cotton, stencilled, printed, painted
and dyed.
Length : 410.2cm, *Width* : 134.4cm
Burhanpur, Khandesh; late 17th/early
18th century.
VAM : I.S.56-1950
White ground, with design of five
flowered niches and system of borders
(for reasons of space, some of the
niches may not be shown) in reds,
violets, greens and yellows, with red
outlines. Each niche is isolated from its
neighbours by an area of plain red
ground colour which also marks the
selvedges. This may indicate that the
length was in fact yardage from which
individual mats could be cut out, but
multi-niched flat-weave and pile prayer
mats are found.
The clarity and vibrance of the colours,
with their precise and delicate outlines,
make this an outstanding example of
Burhanpur chintz, a school which for
many represents the highest achievement of cotton painting and printing.
An almost identical piece in the VAM is
I.M.23-1936 (four niches). There are
also examples in the Calico Museum of
Textiles, Ahmedabad (acc.no.121,
Irwin & Hall 1971, no.17, pl.8), the
Metropolitan Museum of Art, New
York and the Textile Museum, Wash-
ington D.C.   VM

232
Prayer mat
Cotton, embroidered with silk.
Length : 117cm, *Width* : 81.25cm
Mughal, made by Gujarati professional
embroiderers under court patronage;
probably c.1650-1700.
VAM : I.S.168-1950
White ground, embroidered with continuous bands of closely-aligned chain-
stitch mainly in reds and soft blues and
greens; patterned with a cusped,
acanthus-edged niche containing a realistic but symmetrical lily plant, flanked
at the base by a pair of small symmetrical rose(?) plants and two different
pairs of minute plantlets. Floral scroll
borders and spandrels. Chinese cloud
motifs hover like winged insects in the
space around the lily.
A High Mughal design of a kind seen
also in manuscripts, pile carpets and
architectural details, the prayer mat is
an outstanding example of 'Cambay'
professional chain-stitch embroidery,
with its subtle use of light and shade to
lend variety to a limited colour palette.
The embroidered *qanats* in the back-

ground of no.71 are of the same school.
See also nos.252-3.
Bibliography : Irwin (1950), pl.6.   VM

233
Prayer mat
Silk and cotton fabric (satin-faced),
embroidered with silk.
Length : 112.3cm, *Width* : 74.5cm
Provincial Mughal, 1801-2
Lent by Mrs L. Holmes.
White ground (now yellowed), shell-
quilted in undyed silk, with trellised
spandrels, niche, and repeating sprig
design in red, pink and green silk; green
and red-embroidered roundel with
shi'ite inscription and the *sanah* date
1216 (1801-2 AD). Floral scroll border,
missing at the bottom.
An interesting object in which the
rather coarse needlework of a provincial
court is combined with mastery of the
colour palette and skilled placing of
motifs to produce a highly successful
embroidery.

234
Dari (mat)
Cotton flat-weave.
Length : 100cm, *Width* : 84.8cm
Rajasthan, (Ajmer), c.1880
VAM : 2133-1883 I.S.
Made as a Muslim prayer mat, with
triple-arched niche enclosing a plain
red field and surrounded by a striped
ikat design in blue, red and white.
Frinded sides. With the *dari* seen in
no.235 and most other objects regis-
tered by the Indian dept. in 1883 (a
number of which are included in this
catalogue) it was acquired by C. Purdon
Clarke on a special purchasing tour of
India, 1881-2, in search of material to
supply deficiencies in the collections.
Portions of at least two separate multi-
niched prayer mats in the *dari* technique are retained in the Jamma Masjid
(principal mosque) at Bijapur in the
Deccan. They are of austere design,
with a repeating simple niche in dull red
or indigo blue on an unbleached
ground. The niches are broad and low,
each with a trident symbol, possibly
representing a mosque lamp, at its
apex. Their custodians believe them to
be of considerable age, but their history
is apparently undocumented. One is
illustrated with other prayer carpets
then at the mosque by Cousens (1916)
pl.24. The mosque dates from 1576. VM

231

232

90

235
Dari (mat)
Cotton flat-weave.
Length : 220.2cm, *Width* : 135.5cm
North India, c.1880
VAM : 2457-1883 I.S.
Striped *ikat* design, blue, red, white and beige. Fringed ends. Unlike pile carpets, which were introduced by the Mughals and only attainable by the rich, the flat-woven mats known as *daris* or *satrangis* are probably of ancient origin in India. They were usually of cotton, though woollen examples are known, with simple striped or chequered patterns. Larger, grander versions made for the courts sometimes included stylized flower, bird and animal motifs, but these are rare. The basic colour scheme was (indigo) blue and white, to which red and beige might be added. Cheap, durable, light to roll up and carry, widely available, *daris* were used by people of all religions, castes and occupations to sit or sleep on, or spread out merchandise in the bazaar. They are a familiar feature of Mughal and Rajput paintings. The *dari* seen here, though made as late as 1880. shows a traditional Indian *ikat* design and colour scheme which is closely related to that of garment pieces in the Buddhist wall paintings of Ajanta Cave I (c.5th century AD). A *dari* for specifically Muslim use can be seen in no.234   VM

236
Saddle cloth
Cotton, embroidered with silver-gilt thread, and appliqued with velvet.
Length : 53.25cm, *Width* : 119.5cm
Hyderabad, Deccan, from the Hyderabad *toshkhana*; early 18th century.
VAM : I.M.68-1927
The entire ground is covered with twisted silver-gilt thread, couched with a diagonal effect. Against this background is appliqued a trellis and flower-head design with central and corner cartouches, in red, blue, green and yellow velvet. Kincob lining. In the Hyderabad toshkhana the saddle cloth formed part of a group of textiles associated with the reign of Asaf Jah I, first Nizam of Hyderabad (1724-48).
Bibliography : Irwin, (1950), pl.2.   VM

91

235

236

237
Tipu Sultan's saddle cloth
Velvet, embroidered with silver gilt thread, wire and spangles (*zardozi* work).
Length : 142.2cm, *Width* : 143.5cm
Deccan, mid-18th century, formerly in the collection of Tipu Sultan at Seringapatam
VAM : 784-1864
Rich red ground with pattern in massive gold raised embroidery. While elements of the design owe something to Turkish ornament, influenced in its turn by Chinese ceramics, the main inspiration seems to be the large palmettes of Safavid carpets, probably transmitted via an intermediate source such as the designs for European woven textiles of the earlier 18th century. Variants of the theme also occur in South Indian chintzes made for the Dutch market about this time. Deccani textiles, perhaps more than those of any other part of India, were strongly influenced by designs and fabrics imported from abroad, particularly from Europe and the Near East. Even the technique of *zardozi* embroidery, now looked on as a typically Indian court style, is said to have been learned from the Portuguese. The cloth retains its original striped *masru* lining and heavy fringe of silver-gilt thread. VM

238
Saddle cloth
Silk and cotton fabric, satin faced, with brocaded border of silk and silver-gilt thread (kincob).
Length : 76.5cm, *Width* : 106cm
West India (probably Ahmedabad or Surat), late 18th/early 19th century
Private collection.
Pale orange *masru* ground, with shaped border design of arabesque stems and rosettes in dark blue, red, green, white, gold, etc. The saddle cloth remains uncut as it left the loom. The border design appears to be an earlier version of one common to a group of Ahmedabad saddlecloths of about 1850. VM

239
Rumal (cover for a ceremonial gift)
Cotton, stencilled, painted and dyed.
Length : 82.3cm, *Width* : 67.3cm
Golconda, c.1630-40
Lent by the Boston Museum of Fine Arts, 66.230.
Purple ground field, with design in a wide range of brilliant colours apparently unfaded, showing a group of *peris* (Persian fairies) with patterned garments dancing or playing musical instruments.
The group is dominated by a dancing male *peri*, placed slightly off-centre, shown front-view with head in left profile. In the top right corner is another male dancer in a similar pose. Both wear the knee-length coat called *chakdar jama*, its hem cut into several long points, which passed out of fashion in the late 16th century, though later examples are known. The other eight *peris* are shown kneeling, facing one dancer or the other, their bodies in three-quarter view and faces in profile, scattered about the field, some with long trumpets and others with large cymbals. In the bottom left corner is a herd of gazelles lying in a rocky land-scape. The rest of the field is crowded with birds, animals, flowering plants and exotic trees growing from tall cone-shaped patterned rocks and bearing an assortment of mysterious flowers, fruits and foliage in the unique Golconda idiom.
Border with repeating design of car-touches, Maltese crosses and foiliated arabesques in several colours on an orange ground. Narrow guard border, white scroll on a red ground. Plain red edges all round.
Other examples of this Golconda group can be seen in nos.240-2.
Bibliography : Irwin (1959), p.32, pl.A (colour); Cavallo in Boston (Heeramaneck, 1966), no.50 and col. plate. VM

240
Rumal (cover for a ceremonial gift)
Cotton, stencilled, painted and dyed.
Length : 93cm, *Width* : 64.2cm
Golconda, c.1640-50
Lent by the Metropolitan Museum of Art, New York. 28.159.2.
White field, with design in red, brown, blue, violet, yellow and green, showing groups of figures, mainly in Persian and Indian dress, in scenes of courtly life, interspersed with the usual Golconda flora and fauna. The central figure is a prince reclining against a pile of cushions, with a hawk on his wrist, and an attendant massaging his feet. Red ground border of arabesque stems with leaves and palmettes.
Bibliography : Irwin (1959), p.45, pl.XIV, fig.18.

238

239

241
Rumal (cover for a ceremonial gift)
Cotton, stencilled, painted and dyed.
Length : 92.4cm, *Width* : 64.2cm
Golconda, c.1640-50
Lent by the Metropolitan Museum of
Art, New York. 28.159.1.
Red field, with design in red, blue,
yellow and green, showing scenes of
courtly life with groups of figures
mainly in Indian and Persian dress,
against a background of flora and fauna.
Many of the courtly figures recline on
floorspreads surrounded by attendants
and musicians. To the bottom right a
hunter in Portuguese dress returns
from shooting, carrying a gun and two
rabbits, followed by a servant carrying a
deer.
Border of arabesques with palmettes
and cartouches.
Bibliography : Irwin (1959), pp.44-5,
pl.XIII, fig.17   VM

242
Rumal (cover for a ceremonial gift)
Cotton, stencilled, painted and dyed.
Length : 89.5cm, *Width* : 62cm
Golconda, c.1625-50
VAM : I.S.34-1969. Given by Mrs C.E.
Bussell.
Red ground with design in brown,
violets, reds, etc. There is considerable
but uniform fading which does not
seriously detract from the appearance
of the cloth. Black areas have been
largely eaten away by the iron mordant
(fixing agent needed to make certain
colours fast), a condition noticeable in
many textiles and pile carpets prepared
in this way. The *rumal* has been
minutely darned in the past over most
of its surface to consolidate worn areas.
The design is based on a central
flowered and foliate medallion, with a
quarter-medallion repeated in each
corner of the field. The field is
patterned with groups of figures,
human and animal, showing scenes of
courtly life, mainly from Indian and
Indo-Persian sources : elephants with
riders, a prince carousing, dancers and
musicians, lovers, a dervish, etc., interspersed with typical Golconda flora and
fauna.   VM

243
Rumal (cover for a ceremonial gift)
Cotton, stencilled, painted and dyed.
Length : 82.5cm, *Width* : 45.5cm
Western India, 18th century.
VAM : I.M. 35-1935
Green ground with design in reds,
violets, green, yellow and brown, with

black outlines. The pattern is based on
a central medallion, closely patterned
with flowers, foliage, fruit and birds,
including a turkey, with a cartouche
similarly patterned in each corner of the
field. A symmetrical arrangement of a
stylized flowering plant flanked by a
pair of parrots is repeated six times
around the edge of the field, two on
each long side and one at each end.
Scroll border.
An almost identical but larger *rumal* in
the Calico Museum, Ahmedabad,
(acc.no.71) was published by Irwin and
Hall (1970) no.25, pl.12. Another in the
Metropolitan Museum of Art, New
York, (acc.no.28.162.1) was published
by J. Breck in MMA Bulletin XXIII,
p.311.   VM

244
Rumal
Muslin, embroidered with coloured
silks and metal thread.
Punjab Hills (Chamba State), mid-19th
century.
Lent by the Metropolitan Museum of
Art, 31.82.3.
White ground, embroidered in pastel-
coloured floss silks and silver thread
with hunting scenes. Chamba rumals,
their designs influenced by contemporary Pahari paintings, were traditionally embroidered by ladies of the
zenana, and used to spread over
ceremonial gifts.   VM

245
**Nazar (small cover for a ceremonial
gift)**
Muslin, embroidered with silk.
Approx. 30.4cm square
Rajasthan, from the Jaipur *toshkhana*,
late 18th/early 19th century.
VAM : I.M.53-1933
White ground, embroidered in satin
stitch with pastel-coloured floss silks.
Field pattern of a trellis with simple
repeating flowering plant motif. Floral
scroll border. A typical later Mughal-
influenced embroidery style and technique of which surviving examples are
fairly numerous. Another attractive
variant of the same theme is a pillow
cover dated 1745 AD, still in the Jaipur
collection (Singh, 1979, no.2524, plate
53B).   VM

240

93

244

246

Handkerchief or cover for a gift
Muslin, blockprinted with gum and gold leaf.
Approx. 30.4cm square
Rajasthan or Deccan, probably late 18th century
Lent anonymously.
Clear coarse muslin, with all-over pattern of swirling clouds or waves outlined in dotted gold leaf. Simple linear border at each end. 'Handkerchief' in this context would imply a costume accessory to be held in the hand and waved like a fly whisk in the presence of a dignitary; it might also be used to mop the brow. VM

247

Firman cases
Leather, stamped, painted and gilt.
Length : 23cm, *Width* : 10.4cm approx.
Mughal, probably 18th century.
VAM : I.M.234-236-1923
Containers for official letters and proclamations – *firmans* – issued by the Mughals and their vassals, and shaped like our soft slip-cases for spectacles, with fold-over flap tops, these *firman* cases have patterns like those on contemporary textiles : one horizontally striped, with scrolling flowered border, one with a repeating iris plant, and another with a small diaper sprig. They were originally lined with fine taffeta, mainly pigment-painted with trellis designs. Most of the linings have perished. See also no.248 VM

248

Firman cases
Silk and gold brocade.
Length : 30.4cm, *Width* : 5cm
Mughal, probably late 17th/early 18th century.
Lent anonymously.
Gold ground with flowers and foliage in pale orange, green and blue.
Long narrow cases probably improvised out of brocade left over from a furnishing fabric. See also no.247 VM

249

Two knuckle pad covers for shields
Cotton, embroidered with silks and silver and silver-gilt thread.
Approx. 15.5cm square
Rajasthan, from the Jaipur collection, 18th century.
VAM : I.M.106 and 107-1924
Rajput pictorial embroideries in the idiom of no.250. I.M.106 shows a court lady with a peacock and 107 a prince with a lady in a palace garden. Origin-

ally both cloths would have been completely covered with needlework; much of the background detail of the lady with the peacock has disintegrated, making it less interesting as a composition than the garden scene, which is more complete.
Similar knuckle pad embroideries in the Jaipur collection are mentioned by Irwin and Hall, 1973, no.16, with reference to a related purse (acc.no.304) in the Calico Museum.
Bibliography : Clarke (1927), pl.1; Irwin in Ashton (ed.), London (1950), nos.1076 and 1077; Irwin (1950), pls.7 and 8. VM

250

Strip of pictorial embroidery
Cotton, embroidered with silks and silver and silver-gilt thread.
Length : 149cm, *Width* : 28cm
Rajasthan, 18th century
Lent by Mr Steven P. Huyler.
The multicoloured embroidery, with its skilful use of shading and metallic effects to give emphasis to outlines, is mainly in chain stitch, closely worked to cover the entire ground fabric. It forms a horizontal strip picture of Rajput courtly life, on the left hunters in pursuit of lions in a rocky terrain, and on the right ladies walking in a palace garden.
Probably from a *gadi* set (furnishings for the royal dais), there is a smaller fragment in the same style in the Calico Museum, Ahmedabad (acc.no.697, Irwin and Hall, 1973, no.15, colour plate IV). The same authors also refer to a complete *gadi* set at Jaipur. C. Singh, 1979, p.xlii, suggests a link with Bundi paintings of the early 18th century, and dates the set around 1730, when a sister of Jai Singh II was married to Rao Budh Singh of Bundi. See also no.249.
Bibliography : Silverstein, (1981). VM

251

Huqqa snake cover and mat
Cloth, embroidered with coloured silk and silver and silver-gilt thread.
Length : 99.5cm (cover), *Diameter* : 52cm (mat)
Mughal style, mid-18th century.
Lent by the National Trust, Powis Castle.
The *huqqa* snake is the long flexible tube through which the smoke is drawn. In use, it was standard practice for the upper part of the snake to be covered with a decorative tubular textile, and for the *huqqa* itself to stand on a matching

mat, usually round or banjo-shaped. The *huqqa* furnishings seen here are from a collection brought from India by the first Lord Clive – 'Clive of India' – and listed in the inventories made for his widow in 1775. Professional embroiderers producing work of this kind, with flowering plant motifs in coloured silks on a ground covered with couched metal thread, would have been found at many provincial centres in India at the time, particularly where there was a Mughal-influenced court. Of Clive's twenty-odd years in the service of the East India Company, the first few were spent in the Madras area, but thereafter his associations were mainly with Bengal, where Dacca and Murshidabad were important embroidery centres. Another likely source of the work was the capital of Oudh (Lucknow or Faizabad) where arts and crafts were enjoying a renaissance at the court of Shuja ud-daula (1753-75). The East India Company, and Clive himself, were very much involved with the affairs of Oudh. A painting of another East India Company official, one of the many Europeans resident there in the 1780s, shows him using a *huqqa* with furnishings embroidered in the same style (Welch (1978), pl.37). A person of Clive's consequence would probably have employed embroiderers attached to his own household. VM

252

Riding coat
Satin, embroidered with silk.
Length : 97cm
Mughal, probably made for a prince of the house of Jahangir, early 17th century.
VAM : I.S.18-1947
White ground, embroidered with coloured silks in fine chain stitch, in shades of blue, yellow, green and brown, with a repeating pattern of animals, birds and winged insects in a rocky landscape of trees and flowers, with the great cats seen devouring their prey, or reposing peacefully in the shade. The design parallels that of Jahangir period manuscript borders, derived from Herati prototypes, but individual flowering plants such as poppies and daffodils are depicted with a realism and prominence unusual in painted landscape borders.
The knee-length coat is open in front, meeting edge to edge, with no sleeves or collar. The upper part is shaped to the waist, and the skirts flared on either side, with vertical placket slits and hem

slit on either side. A border of scrolling leafy stems and flowerheads surrounds the armholes, placket openings and edges of the garment except for the area round the neck and upper front, where it ends abruptly about half way between waist and neck. The embroidery was probably worked by Gujaratis already practised in assimilating and subtly Indianising Persian concepts. Fine chain stitch was a speciality of 'Cambay' embroiderers (cf.nos.232 and 253), their mastery of this cool palette, so appropriate to the subject and utterly alien to better-known tradition of heavily shaded brilliant pinks and blues, (cf embroidery in the background of no.71), gives some indication of the versatility of craftsmen long accustomed to pleasing foreign patrons. The standard suggests an origin in the imperial workshops. Like other articles of Mughal court dress, such coats were tailored in Persian style, and often worn with a fur tippet round the neck, which may explain the missing section of border. Variants appear as riding coats in many Mughal paintings, some patterned with the tiger stripe borrowed from Ottoman textiles. Coats with landscape designs are less plentiful, but several examples are known, including the painting of the emperor Babur sitting in a chair reading (no.38) and the falconer (no.34). The fabrics usually appear to be brocades; none of the designs is as detailed or realistic as this embroidery.
The Mughal emperors bestowed a dress of honour on persons they wished to distinguish. This, the *Khil'at*, included a coat called *nadiri* ('rarity'). Jahangir, like his father Akbar, was very interested in dress, and designed a special *nadiri* 'of length from the waist down to below the thighs, and it has no sleeves'. Nothing was known by the vendor of our coat as to its history. She was not aware of any family link with India.
Bibliography : Irwin, (1950), pl.1; Irwin in Ashton (ed.), London, (1950), no.1017, pl.66; Welch, (1963), pl.41 and colour detail. VM

94

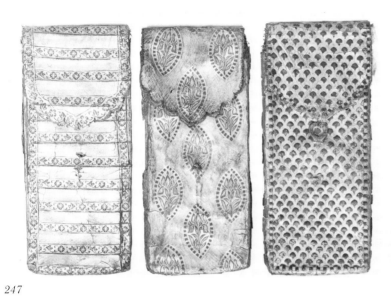

247

249

252

253
Falconer's glove
Leather; gauntlet embroidered with silk.
Length : 33cm
Sind or Gujarat, 17th century.
Lent by the National Museum, Copenhagen, EDc 30.
From the Royal Danish Kunstkammer collection, where it was catalogued in an inventory of 1690 as 'Een Indianske Handske'.
A panel of applied or inset leather following the shape of the gauntlet is worked with an arabesque design in the continuous bands of closely-aligned chain stitch which characterized a well known school of Western Indian professional embroidery in the 17th century (cf.nos.232 and 252).
Sind and Gujarat were famed for their embroidered leather work as early as 1300, when Marco Polo visited the region. Good specimens were still being produced in the mid-19th century.
A falconer in a glove something like this appears in no.34. A closer resemblance can be seen in a painting of c.1630, attributed to Govardhan. (Beach, (1978), pl.42).
Bibliography : Dam-Mikkelsen and Lundbaek (ed), (1980), p.130   VM

254
Woman's court dress (pairhan)
Gauze, appliquéd with tinsel braid, foil, spangles, beetles' wings, etc.
Mughal, 18th/early 19th century.
VAM : 5842 (I.S.)
Semi-transparent ground, with decoration in silver and silver-gilt braid, red and green tinfoil, irridescent beetles' wings, etc. Standard overdress of the Mughal period, with short, close-fitting bodice and sleeves and long full skirt, open-fronted to reveal tight trousers (*paijama*).   VM

255
Tipu Sultan's coat (jama)
Muslin, embroidered with flattened silver-gilt wire.
Length : 152.5cm
East or South India, late 18th century.
VAM : I.S.8-1968
White ground, self-striped clear and opaque, with diapered sprig design in applied flattened silver-gilt wire anchored with threads of yellow silk. Important centres of muslin manufacture included Bengal (Dacca and Santipur), Banaras, and Hyderabad, Deccan. Self-striped muslins very like this one were being made in the Hyderabad region in the mid-19th century.

Tipu is depicted wearing a similar muslin *jama* in a painting, now in the F.C.O., by the British artist G.F. Cherry, who visited Seringapatam in 1792.   VM

256
Tipu Sultan's shoes
Velvet, embroidered with silver wire, etc.
South India, late 18th century.
Lent by the National Trust, Powis Castle.
Red velvet uppers, broad at the toes and tapering to a point which is turned up and coiled within itself. Embroidery of silver wire, thread, glass beads, etc. Similar beadwork appears on the textile covering of a Tipu rosewater sprinkler in a private collection, and on a mango-shaped powder-flask which probably also comes from the Deccan. Shoes of this style were standard wear for Muslim dignitaries in India at the time; their decoration often included seed pearls.   VM

257
Man's coat (jama)
Cotton, printed, painted and dyed.
Length : 150cm
Khandesh, Burhanpur, 18th century; tailored for the Hyderabad *toshkhana*.
VAM : I.M.312-1921
Fine white cotton, with repeating design of a flowering plant in violet and two greens within a trellis permanently impressed by hot wires (see also nos.259, 263,280).
It is hard to envisage chintz piece-goods design more accomplished and successful than this garment with its sophisticated colour scheme and faultless layout, particularly striking where the motif has been accommodated to the tailored outline of the necktie lappets.
      VM

258
Boy's coat
Cotton, embroidered with silk and silver-gilt thread.
Length : 105cm
Rajput, under Mughal influence, probably late 18th century.
Lent by the National Museum, New Delhi; 56.23.18.
White ground, with repeating floral sprig design in coloured silks outlined in silver-gilt thread. Ink inscription in Hindi.   VM

258

259

Boy's coat

Shawlcloth (*pashmina* fabric).
Length : 91.5cm
Kashmir, probably worn at the courts of Oudh or Hyderabad, late 18th/early 19th century.
VAM : I.M.35-1934
Rich yellow ground, with woven diaper sprigs mainly in blue, enclosed by a trellis pattern permanently impressed by hot wires (see also nos.257, 263, 280).
Tailored shawlcloth garments of this kind were made up from *jamawar* lengths woven for the purpose. They were particularly favoured for winter wear at the Muslim courts of Oudh and Hyderabad. The same small diaper sprig is found on shawls and girdle ends of the late 18th century, including some dated *jamawar* fragments from the Hyderabad toshkhana in the VAM, (I.S.3-5-1969) and is conspicuous in portraits of the Oudh dynasty at this period. VM

260

Boy's coat (angarkha)

Brocaded silk and silver and silver-gilt thread ('kincob').
Length : 87.6cm
Probably Banaras, mid-19th century.
VAM : I.M.286-1920
Pale yellow ground, with floral diaper sprig mainly in blue and purple, in a silver trellis. A gold-ground kincob with stylized rosettes in silver on tightly scrolled slender black stems borders the edges of the garment, which has added cuffs of Persian velvet with leaf and flower pattern in colours on a black ground.

As a tailored garment, the *angarkha* is primarily an article of Muslim court dress, though like the *jama* and other tailored costumes it was adopted by non-Muslims.

A Banaras brocade of virtually identical pattern but different colour scheme in the B.K.B., is illustrated in Krishna, 1966, fig.19. A closely related example from Banaras, was collected by Forbes Watson (2nd series, no.413, London, 1873-80). This *angarkha* comes from a specialist collection of Western Indian textiles, most of which are folk embroideries from Kach and Saurashtra; the brocade was attributed to Ahmedabad. While it is possible that the design was used in both centres, the fact that the border trimming is also an apparently Banaras brocade shifts the weight of probability to Banaras. VM

261

Boy's coat, trousers and cloak

Block-printed in cotton.
Coat length : 89cm, *trousers* : 91cm, *cloak* : 101cm
North India (probably Sanganer, near Jaipur, Rajasthan), early 19th century.
Lent by the National Museum, New Delhi; 56.23.1 and 15.
Pale yellow ground, block-printed in blue, red, black, etc., with a repeating *buta* design. Coat and cloak wadded with cotton wool, a means of added warmth generally adopted in India for winter clothes and bedding in preference to using heavier material. VM

262

Boy's cap

Printed and painted cotton, wadded.
Length : 19cm, *Width* : 20cm
Rajasthan, probably late 18th century.
Lent by the National Museum, New Delhi; 56.4.227
Yellow-green ground, patterned with simple flower sprig in red, white and green, widely spaced and repeating in staggered rows.
Mughal princes wore caps of this style, possibly inspired by prints showing European royal infants in similar headgear.
See also no.263 VM

263

Boy's cap

Printed cotton
Length : 20cm, *Width* : 19.5cm
Rajasthan, late 18th/early 19th century.
Lent by the National Museum, New Delhi; 56.4/196.
Yellow ground, with closely-spaced diaper sprig in dark blue-green, enclosed by a trellis pattern permanently impressed by hot wires (see also nos.257, 259, 280).
A cap of similar shape is described in no.262 VM

264

Turban piece

Muslin, embroidered with coloured silks and silver-gilt thread.
Length : 129cm, *Width* : 18cm
Mughal/Rajput style, late 18th/early 19th century.
Keir Collection.
White ground, now stained and faded, with band of diapered floral sprigs mainly in pink, green and dark blue chain stitch, running down the centre, against a field pattern of fine silver-gilt spots in straight stitch. Border of scrolling flowered stems.
Similar turban pieces in the VAM are I.M.27 and 28-1936, Irwin (1950), pl.9a. Another, in the Calico Museum, Ahmedabad, acc.no.118, was published by Irwin and Hall (1973), (no.23, pl.14A) VM

97

260

261

265

Part of a sari

Woven silk and silver and silver-gilt thread (kincob)

Probably Ahmedabad or North West Deccan (Surat/Aurangabad), late 18th century.

Lent by the Bharat Kala Bhavan, Banaras, 9868.

Red field, diapered with gold *butis* laid sideways, stylized into a cone shape but still recognisable as flower sprigs. Gold ground end panel (*pallav*) patterned with a row of twelve identical stylized flowering plants, with realistic foliage and flowers of orange, pink and dark blue with contrasting outlines, the main stem rendered as a cypress tree with inclined top and a pair of broad serrated green leaves at the base. Above this section is a band with a row of twelve elephants, alternately purple with two pink riders and red with two orange riders; a flower sprig in similar colours alternates with the elephants. Three identical borders with scrolling leafy flowered stems outline and separate the bands, and have their own very narrow guard borders of repeating chevrons. Some details in silver.

The main design and layout are virtually identical to that of a *sari* end in the Metropolitan Museum of Art, New York, (acc.no.28.50). The flower motif in the broad guard borders is slightly different. Another closely related piece is a turban cloth in the B.K.B. (acc.no.146) which has the same main flowering plant motif in the lower band, while in the upper one a smaller, different flowering plant replaces the elephants. Another *sari* end in the B.K.B (Krishna, 1966, fig.20) retains the elephant band, but substitutes for the large plant seen in the lower section of all the other pieces a small plant almost identical to that of the upper band in the turban, though the colour scheme is different.

The silk weavers of Gujarat had established craft guilds more than a thousand years before the reign of the Mughal Emperor Akbar (1558-1605), when Ahmedabad looms began to supply the Mughal court with the costly brocades of silk and metal thread called *kamkhab* (a word of confused etymology received into English as kincob.) During the Mughal period the workshops produced a variety of goods, including tent hangings (cats.205, 206) and court girdles (cats.268-273), in which Safavid traditions were re-interpreted with uniquely Indian insight

to create the Mughal style. Mughal influence is also seen in the layout and ornament of garment pieces made, like this one, under Hindu patronage. VM

266

Ornhi end

Woven silk and silver and silver-gilt thread (kincob).

Width : 139cm, *Diameter* : 52cm

Central India, possibly Chanderi, probably late 18th/early 19th century.

Private Collection, Eire.

Only a gold-ground end border – *pallav* – of this large veil remains. It is divided into two sections, horizontally, each containing a row of eight stylized flowering plants, identical except that a plant with orange flowerheads alternates with a silverheaded one, while the plants in the upper row are smaller than those below, and have only five blooms each to eleven in the lower section. The flowerheads are shown in profile, inclining to the right; a pair of broad serrated blue-green leaves at the base of each main stem is depicted front view. The general effect of the shape approximates to that of the Kashmir shawl cone of the same period. Broad border with stylized rosettes and leaves, and a narrower one with scrolling stems and profile flowerheads as in the plants. The stems and silver flowerheads are outlined in black, the orange in yellow. The small plants include a detail in red. Garment pieces of this kind, which were kincobs for the Hindu market, women's *saris* and *ornhis* and men's scarves and turbans, were usually made with a gauze or muslin field of soft, subtle red, blue or green, plain or self-patterned with stripes, chequers or a trellis, sometimes with details in gold. There would be a gold-ground *pallav* like this one at either end. The work is associated with several places in Central India, of which Chanderi is the most renowned. Closely related examples from Burhanpur in the VAM, dating from the mid-19th century, show increasing stylization of the plant motif, harsher colours and more elaborate borders. Their fields are usually of silk gauze. Chanderi fields were more typically – though not invariably – of muslin. The field of this *ornhi* (no longer extant) was of muslin, and the *pallav* design appears to have strong links with that of a documented head-dress in the Jaipur collection (Singh, 1979, Colour plate I), dated 1791. VM

267

Patka (court girdle)

Woven silk and silver-gilt thread.

Length : 472cm, *Width* : 61cm

Deccani or Safavid, formerly in the Hyderabad *toshkhana*, 18th century (before 1746).

VAM : T.49-1923

Field patterned with horizontal stripes, gold rosettes on a tan ground alternating with scrolling leafy flowered stems in colours on a gold ground. End panels patterned with a row of five symmetrical flowering fruited plants in green, blue, yellow and white on a gold ground. Borders of delicate scrolling stems with flowers, fruit and foliage as in the panels. Fringed ends.

The *patka* bears the seal of Asaf Jah, Nizam-ul-Mulk, first Nizam of Hyderabad, dated AH 1159 (1746AD). Less obviously Indian than nos.268-273, this *patka* was possibly imported from Persia, which for centuries supplied luxury textiles to the courts of the Deccan. The flowered stripes of the field are, however, closely comparable with designs in a silk weaver's pattern book (no.171), of which other sections strongly suggest an Indian origin.

Bibliography : London (1976), no.97 and illus. VM

268

Patka (court girdle)

Woven silk and silver-gilt thread.

Length : 322.5cm, *Width* : 51cm

Mughal, probably early 18th century.

VAM : 317-1907

Red field, self-patterned with a tiny diaper lozenge. Ends patterned with a row of six flowering plants with orange blooms and green foliage on a gold ground. Borders of scrolling stems with similar flowerheads.

Bibliography : London (1976), no.96 and illus. VM

269

Patka (court girdle)

Woven silk and silver-gilt thread.

Length : 4.355m, *Width* : 72.2cm

Mughal, 18th century

Lent by the Boston Museum of Fine Arts; 66.858. Gift of John Goelet.

Dark green field, with twelve horizontal bands of continuous chevrons near the ends. End panels patterned with a row of four elongated poppy-like flowering plants on a gold ground, each plant carrying eight birds of two kinds – probably parrots and peacocks – and having its main stem 'tied' with a Chinese cloud motif near the base.

Borders of scrolling stems and flowerheads. Netted fringed ends.

A *patka* of apparently identical design was illustrated in *Marg* Vol.I, no.3, 1946-7. A detail of another of similar composition, but with a grapevine instead of a poppy motif, was illustrated by Kahlenberg, in Pal (ed.), 1972, pl.XCIX. VM

270

Patka (court girdle)

Woven silk and silver-gilt thread.

Mughal, 18th century

Lent by the Bharat Kala Bhawan Museum; 9928.

Blue-green field, self-patterned with a tiny chequer motif. Ends patterned with a row of naturalistic flowering plants, probably chrysanthemums, with full-blown white flowerhead and single bud, and light green foliage with darker outlines, on a gold ground. Borders with scrolling stems and flowerheads. VM

271

Patka (court girdle)

Woven silk and silver-gilt thread

Length 119.5cm, *Width* : 51cm

Mughal, 18th century

Lent by the National Museum, New Delhi; 60.1158.

Red ground, with design in silver-gilt thread. Ends and borders patterned with an ogival trellis and repeating sprig, field with horizontal bands of double tiger stripes, the bands separated by double horizontal lines. Fringed ends.

The tiger stripe, borrowed from earlier Ottoman textiles, occurs in a number of surviving Mughal period girdles. One, with a very similar field pattern, except that the dividing bands are filled with scrolling stems and flowerheads, is illustrated as the background to a sword in pl.76 *The Art of India and Pakistan*, ed. Ashton, London (1950). VM

272

Patka (court girdle)

Woven silk and silver-gilt thread

Length : 380cm, *Width* : 49.5cm

Mughal, 18th century

Lent by the National Museum, New Delhi; 60.1157.

Red field, with tiny gold diaper pattern creating a trellis effect. Ends and borders diapered with a 'Chinese cloud' motif in gold, outlined in dark blue, on a gold ground. Fringed ends.

A *patka* with a different field pattern, but an almost identical cloud motif, in the Jaipur collection, is no.1669, pl.35A, of Singh (1979). VM

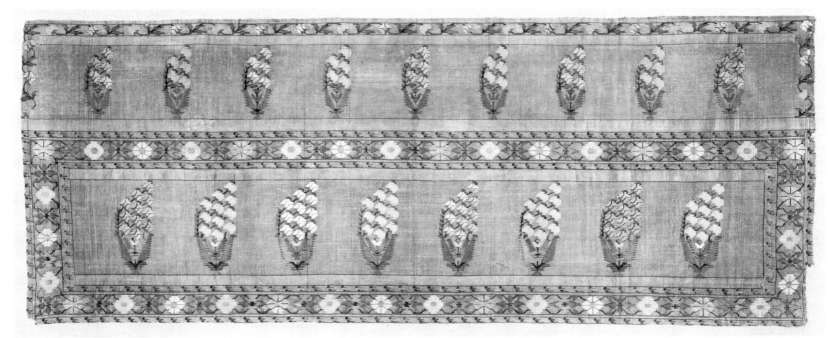

266

273
Patka (court girdle)
Woven silk and silver-gilt thread.
Length : 2.745m, *Width* : 52cm
Mughal, 18th century
Lent by the Boston Museum of Fine
Arts; 66.863.
Violet field, self-patterned with
repeating design of paired chevrons
or tiger stripes. Ends patterned with
a trellis enclosing bunches of white
grapes on a gold ground. Borders with
scrolling vine and bunches of grapes,
also on gold. Fringed ends.
Bibliography : Welch (1963), Cat.64
and illus.; Boston (Heeramaneck)
(1966), no.265 and illus.　　　VM

274
Patka (court girdle)
Cotton, embroidered with silk and
silver-gilt thread.
Length : 248m, *Width* : 50.5cm
Deccan, from the Hyderabad *toshkhana*, 18th century.
Lent by the National Museum, New
Delhi; 51.28/56.
White ground, ends and borders
embroidered mainly in yellow, orange
and dark blue silk, in satin stitch, with
details in silver-gilt thread. The pattern
is a row of six naturalistic delicate leafy
plants with no flowers. Border of scrolling stems with the same foliage. An
effective and unusual colour scheme
with skilful use of shading.
The *patka* bears stamps and inscriptions of the Hyderabad *toshkhana*.　VM

275
Patka (court girdle)
Muslin, embroidered with silk and
silver-gilt thread.
Length : 243cm, *Width* : 56cm
Mughal style, 18th century
VAM : I.M.29-1936
Semi-transparent ground, ends and
borders embroidered in pink, red and
green silk, in satin stitch, with details in
silver-gilt thread. The pattern is a row
of six flower sprays, stylized into a
shape probably influenced by contemporary jewelled turban ornaments.
Border of scrolling stems and flowerheads like those in the sprays.　　VM

276
Patka (court girdle)
Cotton, stencilled, painted and dyed.
Length : 533cm, *Width* : 71cm
Probably Burhanpur, Khandesh, late
17th/early 18th century.
VAM : I.S.94-1948
White ground, ends patterned with row
of five cypress trees, stylized into
elegant elongated green cones, with
filler pattern of fern or seaweed in red.
Main border of scrolling stems and
leaves, with miniature cypress cones
instead of flowerheads. This pattern, in
the same green and red colour scheme,
is repeated on a smaller scale in the
narrow borders.
There is an identical *patka* in the
Textile Museum, Washington,
TM6.111.　　　　　　　　　　　VM

269 (detail)

277
Patka (court girdle)
Cotton, stencilled, painted and dyed.
Length : 330cm, *Width* : 79cm
Burhanpur or Golconda, from the
Hyderabad *toshkhana*.
VAM : I.M.70-1927
Buff ground, ends patterned with row of
eight gracefully curved tulips, each with
two red flowers and a bud. Borders
patterned with tulip leaves and heads.
The outlines of the design are
embroidered with silver-gilt thread. VM

278
Piece goods
Masru (mixed silk and cotton) fabric.
Length : 651cm, *Width* : 66.8cm
East India (Bengal), late 18th century.
Lent by the M.S. Man Singh II Museum,
Jaipur; Tc.62.75.
Red and yellow striped pattern. A
sewn-on label inscribed in ink in Hindi
characters states that the cloth was
purchased from Seth Govardhandas,
V.S.1855 (1798 AD), price 13 rupis
13½ annas. A very ordinary, typical
Bengal fabric of simple striped design
produced in large quantities for the
home and export markets over a period
of centuries. Striped *masru* was often
used as a lining for more costly textiles.
In isolation it is virtually impossible to
date, so occasional documented pieces
such as this one from the Jaipur City

Palace stores are of considerable
interest.
The cloth merchant Seth Govardhandas
is the subject of the portrait no.152.
Bibliography : Singh (1979), no.583. VM

279
Length of piece goods (yardage)
Cotton, block printed, painted and
dyed.
Length : 9.86m, *Width* : 65cm
Burhanpur or Rajasthan, dated 1772.
VAM : I.S.64-1978
Yardage of this kind was intended for
jamas (cf.no.257). Cream ground,
patterned with a flowering plant in
staggered rows, probably a stylized
poppy, the petals yellow, outlined and
detailed in purple, purple seed pod,
green stem and foliage outlined in
purple. Green obtained by overpainting
yellow on dyed indigo, which shows on
the back. The often fugitive yellow
survives virtually intact.
A Hindi inscription in one corner states
that the cloth was made for a Hindu raja
in 1772. By this time the Mughal *jama*
was standard wear at most Rajput
courts. Theoretically Muslims tied their
jamas on the right and Hindus on the
left but this distinction was not always
observed.
A fragment from another *jama* length
can be seen in no.280. VM

280
Fragment of piece goods
Cotton, block printed, painted and dyed.
Length : 50.8cm, *Width* : 22.8cm
Probably Burhanpur, formerly in the
Hyderabad *toshkhana*, 18th century.
VAM : I.M.51-1924
Flowering plant, probably a rose, with
yellow flowers and buds, outlined and
detailed in orange, with green stem and
foliage, repeating in an impressed
trellis (see also nos.257, 259, 263).
A complete chintz *jama* from the
Hyderabad *toshkhana* can be seen in
no.257, and a chintz *jama* length of
somewhat similar style from an un-
recorded *toshkhana* in no.279. VM

281
Fragment of piece goods
Clear, coarse muslin, block printed,
painted and dyed.
Length 30.5cm, *Width* : 21.6cm
Deccan, from the Hyderabad *toshkhana*, 18th century.
VAM : I.M.50-1924
Clear ground, with vertical striped
design in which a slender, delicate leaf
and stem in muted violet with reddish
outlines alternates with gold obliques
applied by the gum and gold leaf
technique.
Probably from a woman's court dress
like the *pairhan* (no.254). Transparent
overdresses of gold-striped muslin or
gauze appear in many paintings of the
period, worn over long tight trousers.
The presence of a seam suggests that
this was part of a dress rather than a
turban.
Another Deccani muslin appears in
no.246 VM

282
Fragment of a shawl border
Pashmina fabric.
Height : 18cm, *Width* : 49cm
Kashmir, late 17th/early 18th century.
Lent by the Jagdish and Kamla Mittal
Museum of Indian Art, Hyderabad.
White ground, patterned with a row of
naturalistic flowering plants. A com-
paratively rare survival of about the
same date as no.283, and a complete
shawl in the Boston Museum of Fine
Arts (Irwin (1973), pls.5 and 6).

283
Fragment of a shawl border
Pashmina fabric.
Width : 36.8cm, *Height* : 14.6cm
Kashmir, late 17th/early 18th century.
VAM : I.S.70-1954. Given by Miss Gira
Sarabhai.

White ground, patterned with a row of
naturalistic flowering plants in two
blues, two greens and red. Guard
borders of two stylized rosettes,
repeating alternately.
There is another fragment of this shawl
border in the Calico Museum, Ahmedabad. The pieces are probably from a
shawl said to have been conferred as a
khil'at (dress of honour) on a chief of
Bikaner by one of the later Mughal
emperors.
Cf.no.282 and Irwin (1973), nos.5 and
6.
Bibliography : Delhi (1911), p.35,
pl.XV(d); Irwin (1973), no.1.

284
Shawl
Pashmina fabric.
Length : 218.4cm, *Width* : 132.1cm
Kashmir, early 18th century.
Lent by the Textile Museum, Washing-
ton D.C.; TM.6.11.
Peach or salmon ground, plain field and
patterned with a row of leafy flowering
tree-like plants in a field in blues and
green all slightly inclined to the left. A
remarkably complete early shawl of
unusual design and subtle colouring.
We know from the *Ain-i-Akbari* that
shawls were made in a wide range of
ground colours. The French traveller
Thevenot, a 17th century visitor to
India, remarked in 1666 that a dead leaf
colour 'feuille morte' was fashionable.
A number of colours could be so
described, including the rich, orange-
yellow much used as a ground colour for
many surviving shawl fabrics of the late
18th century (cf.no.259). This subtle
shade is another possible candidate.
The unusual design of the plants is
matched by that of a VAM shawl fragment (I.S.13-1972) from a collection of
discarded textiles used to line the 'Rich
War Dress of Tipu Sahib', now in the
Royal collections. VM

285
Shawl
Pashmina fabric.
Length : 252cm, *Width* : 126cm
Kashmir, late 17th/early 18th century.
Lent by the National Museum of India,
New Delhi; 59.304.
White ground, plain field, ends pat-
terned with a row of graceful semi-
naturalistic poppy plants with red
blooms and green foliage. There is a
virtually identical shawl in the Jagdish
& Kamla Mittal Museum of Indian Art,
Hyderabad. VM

100

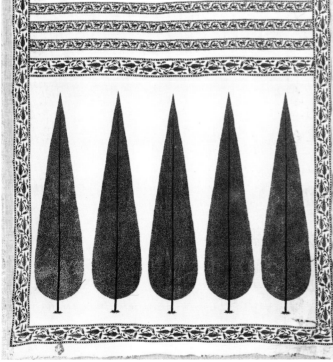

276 (detail)

286
Shawl
Pashmina fabric.
Kashmir, 1st half of 18th century.
Lent by the Bharat Kala Bhavan,
Banaras, 8006.
Pale olive ground, plain field, ends
patterned with a row of semi-naturalistic
poppy plants in red, yellow, green etc.
VM

287
**Fragment of a shawl border (one
flowering plant)**
Pashmina fabric.
Height : 27.9cm, *Width* : 11.4cm
Kashmir, early 18th century.
VAM : I.M.48-1924
White ground with multi-coloured
flowerheads and foliage.
A tall robust plant of several closely-
packed flowerheads, this *buta* shows
the increasing stylization of its period,
when the delicate realistic plant of the
late 17th/early 18th century had begun
its progress towards the ultimate stylization of the floral cone copied by
European shawl manufacturers and
known even in India as the Paisley.
Bibliography : Irwin (1973), pl.2.   VM

288
Shawl
Pashmina fabric.
Length : 284.5cm, *Width* : 132.1cm
Kashmir, late 18th century.
VAM : I.M.17-1915
White ground, plain field, ends patterned with a row of stylized flowering
plants predominantly in red and blue,
with touches of yellow, green etc. Good
colour preservation. Now well on its
way to complete stylization, they use
the type of Kashmir shawl design
popularized in Europe at the end of the
18th century by fashionable women
including the Empress Josephine and
Lady Hamilton. It appears in many
portraits of the period, including a
number of Ingres.
Bibliography : Irwin (1973), no.11.   VM

289
Shawl
Pashmina fabric.
Length : 315cm, *Width* : 130cm
Kashmir, late 18th/early 19th century.
Lent by the Jagdish and Kamla Mittal
Museum of Indian Art, Hyderabad.
White ground, plain field, ends pattern-
ed with three staggered rows of floral
butas, completely stylized into the
classic cone shape, in brilliant and
apparently unfaded colours, green, blue,
red, yellow etc., with a small bud motif

repeating between each cone.
A type of design which remained current
over a long period.
There is a virtually identical shawl in
the National Museum, New Delhi,
58.35/4.
VM

290
Shawl
Pashmina fabric.
Length : 320cm, *Width* : 132cm
Kashmir, probably second half of the
18th century.
Lent by the Jagdish and Kamla Mittal
Museum of Indian Art, Hyderabad.
White ground, plain field, ends patterned with *shikargarh* (hunting) scenes, in
brilliant unfaded colours.
An extremely unusual design, and
consequently hard to date. Needle-
embroidered *shikargarh* shawls are
fairly common in the 19th century but
the pattern is extremely rare in woven
pashmina fabrics. There is another fine
example, with a slightly different
shikargarh design in the same style, on
a red ground, in the Bharat Kala
Bhavan, Banaras.   VM

291
Patka (court girdle)
Pashmina fabric with gilded details
Length : 276.9cm, *Width* : 71.1cm
Kashmir, formerly in the Jaipur *toshkhana*, second half of the 18th century.
VAM : I.S.23-1967
Pea green ground, plain field, ends patterned with a small diaper flower sprig
in pink with detail in red. Green foliage
borders of scrolling stems with green
leaves and pink flower heads. The outlines of all the flower motifs have been
gilded with gold leaf and rubbed down
on gum applied by woodblocks, a technique also used to detail contemporary
chintzes, and as a decorative medium in
its own right in no.208.
Too narrow for a shawl, this fine *pashmina patka* appears unfaded and in
almost new condition. Like many other
textiles in the Jaipur *toshkhana*, it was
probably an unused gift. Shawls and
girdles were stock articles of presentation in the Mughal period, and princes
received far more than they could ever
expect to wear.
Shawl cloth *patkas* with sprigged ends
were fashionable court wear in North
India in the second half of the 18th
century. They are noticeable in Tilly
Kettle's portrait of Shuja ud-Daula,
Nawab Wazir of Oudh, and his sons,
around 1770.
Bibliography : Irwin (1973), no.7.   VM

283

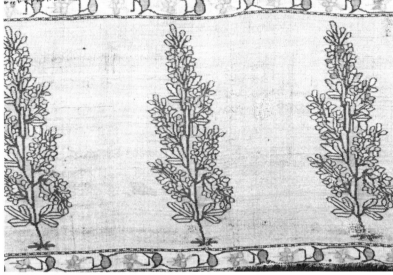

285 (detail)

290 (detail)

292

Stocking, sock and glove
Knitted from shawl wool.
Length : (stocking) 70cm, (sock) 27cm, (glove) 21.5cm
North India, probably mid-19th century.
VAM : I.M.51, 148A and 145-1926
Stocking : knee length, with triangular top made to cover the front of the knee. Red ground, leg and foot, patterned with flower sprigs in horizontal rows, a row of black and white flowers alternating with red and white, both with yellow and green foliage. Green ground toe cap with flowers in red, black and yellow. Vertical striped knee section in red and yellow, with designs in blue, yellow and black. The sections are defined by borders of stems and flower-heads in several colours. Lining of light brown worsted wool.
Ankle sock : yellow ground, with repeating sprig in beige and light blue with black stems and leaves creating a trellis effect. Small-scale diaper in the same colours on the sole. Three borders round the ankle, a central one with yellow ground and repeating rosette in light brown with black stems and centres, flanked by two with white ground and repeating red and green rosettes with black stems.
Glove : yellow ground with horizontal rows of scrolling black stems, squared into a key or battlement design, a row with red and white rosettes repeating alternately with grey and white. Red finger tips, defined by borders with a red zig-zag on yellow, a design which also edges the glove ends abruptly with no gauntlet section.
Knitted woollens, in colours and patterns related to those of shawl fabrics, were produced in several centres of North India under European influence in the 19th century. Knitting is not one of the traditional crafts of India, but like lace-making and chenille work, was introduced by Europeans. The date of introduction is uncertain but Warren Hastings (1732-1818) owned a pair of gloves of this kind. Knitted ankle socks were worn by *parda* (purdah) ladies in winter when Fanny Parks travelled about North India in 1835 (Parks (1850), vol.I, p.456).
For a pair of knitted stockings tasselled and incorporating gilt yarns in the wool, see Cavallo in Boston (Heeramaneck, 1966), no. and pl.275.   VM

293

Hawk's hood
Leather, covered with cloth embroidered in silver and silver-gilt thread.
Length : 7.5cm, *Width* : 6.3cm
Punjab (Hoshiarpur), 19th century.
VAM : 2442-1883
Bright blue cloth, now worn in places, with design of birds and animals in silver and gold. A traditional design which has changed little over the centuries.
Like their European contemporaries, the Mughal Emperors were fond of falconry. Trained birds of prey with their keepers and accessories are a favourite theme in Mughal painting (see no.34). Occasionally the ruler himself was depicted wearing a falconer's glove (no.85). See also no.253.   VM

294

Pachisi board
Cloth, embroidered with silk and silver-gilt thread.
78cm square approx.
Sind (probably Lahore or Hyderabad); made for the Paris Exhibition of 1855
VAM : 4537 I.S.
Red ground, embroidered with coloured floss silks (mainly in satin stitch) and couched silver-gilt thread, outlining the playing area, which is cruciform and divided into squares. Floral borders and corner devices.
Pachisi or *chaupar*, a game like ludo, has been popular in India for centuries and may be of indigenous origin. The 'boards' are often, like this one, made of cloth, and the pieces – four for each player – are little cones usually of wood or ivory (no.539). The game is often depicted in paintings (cf.no.101).   VM

295

Flag
Satin-faced fabric embroidered with silver gilt thread, wire and spangles.
Length : 155cm, *Width* : 127cm
Lucknow, early 19th century.
VAM : 41-1870
Silk and cotton mixed fabric, dark blue centre, bordered with red and yellow. Embroidered on both sides with central and corner devices of the Indo-European kind which Robert Home confected for the King of Oudh, including nereids whose lower halves are the fish symbols of state, and crowns of the type favoured by Ghazi-ud-din Haidar. (See the photographs of Home drawings in this section).   VM

296

Wood blocks for textile printing
(1) *Length* : 16.5cm, *Width* : 11.4cm
(2) *Length* : 12.1cm, *Width* : 5.7cm
(3) *Length* : 7.6cm, *Width* : 1.9cm
Indian, 19th century
VAM : IPN 668; 6803 I.S.; I.M.202-1914.
Block printing, on its own and in association with the related techniques of cotton painting and resist dyeing, is a traditional handicraft in many parts of India. Block printed export cottons from Gujarat ranging in date from the 15th to the 19th centuries are among textiles excavated at Fostat in Egypt. The French merchant Georges Roques left an account of block printing at Ahmedabad in 1678, and Pethapur, near Ahmedabad, remains an important centre of block-cutting in the late 20th century. Of several block printing centres in North India, probably the best known today is Sanganer, near Jaipur in Rajasthan, the source of nos.261 and 263, and the printed muslins seen in 'ethnic' dress shops in recent years (written 1982). At Burhanpur, Khandesh, meticulously-cut printing blocks were combined with painting and dyeing techniques to produce the finest chintzes of the late 17th/ early 18th century (no.231). A similar combination was employed in some of the Coromandel chintzes, especially prayer mats and other furnishings made under Persian influence in the Masulipatam area for the Islamic market in the 19th century. Number 169 shows block printers at work.   VM

Decorative arts

The enormous wealth of the Mughal emperors was a magnet which attracted craftsmen of many countries to the royal ateliers. The Mughal workshops (*karkhana*) were attached to the major centres of government such as Agra, Delhi and Lahore, and in them artisans such as goldsmiths, painters and weavers produced the artefacts for the court. The craftsmen often worked in family units (for example, the Lahore astrolabe makers (no.496)), fathers training their sons and passing on the skills developed over generations.

The provincial centres followed the Mughal model, each workshop answering to the needs of a particular noble or ruler. There were also commercial centres for particular products traded with the rest of India and exported to Iran, the Middle East and, with the increasing involvement of the European East India Companies, to the West. Thus Kashmir had an old-established shawl industry, Golconda was famed for its chintzes, Gujarat for its inlaid mother-of-pearl wares and carved wood, and Cambay for its hardstone carving.

As the empire became firmly established, the wealth of the conquered rulers was added to the royal coffers. The system whereby the property of nobles reverted to the Crown on their death increased the accumulation, and a steady flow of gifts introduced exotic elements such as Venetian glass, Italian metalwork and European arms. William Hawkins, a visitor to the court in the early 17th century, described the contents of the treasury in detail, his account probably based on the reports of the Jesuits there. His comments show the abundance and quality of the precious stones alone: 'There was a diamant cutter of my acquaintance that was sent for to cut a diamant of three mettegals and a halfe, who demanded a small foule diamant to make powder, wherewith to cut the other diamant. They brought him a chest, as he said, of three spannes long and a spanne and half broad, and a spanne and halfe deepe, full of diamants of all sizes and sorts; yet could he find never any one for his purpose, but one five rotties, which was not very foule neither.' (Foster (1921) p.112).

The keen interest that the Mughals took in precious stones is clear not only from the journals of outsiders to the court, but also from their own writings. That they had dynastic significance is shown by the carefully engraved imperial titles on some of the precious stones surviving in several collections today, for instance the spinel (no.297) in the V&A. Gemstones were used lavishly for setting into objects of precious metal or of jade, usually cut and polished *en cabochon* or carved. Diamonds were cleaved, or left in their natural form if octahedral, but facetting does not seem to have been as popular as it was in contemporary Europe. Jewels, hardstones like jade and crystal, and precious metal were used on vessels and arms throughout the Mughal period, reflecting the wealth of the patrons commissioning them but also the constant need for the exchange of gifts. Gifts were presented to the emperor at the twice-yearly weighing ceremonies or,

for example, when seeking particular favours, and to any noble or official who might stand in the way of making the path of diplomacy or trade run smoothly. Presentations to the emperor had to be particularly carefully chosen as each was examined and its value assessed, as witness Jahangir's punctilious accounting throughout his memoirs. These gifts were reciprocated; richly decorated weapons, costly articles of clothing and emblems of office or rank such as jewelled penboxes (no.370) or turban ornaments (no.308) were presented by the emperors, princes, or nobles on suitable occasions.

Sir Thomas Roe, the ambassador of James I to Jahangir, had been supplied with gifts for the emperor but these had been woefully inadequate. His account of his stay constantly refers to the struggle to find suitable offerings for the emperor and his court, the greed with which the new shipments from England were seized upon (a consignment was once purloined by Khurram before it even reached Roe) and the necessity for occasionally giving away his own personal possessions when Company supplies were temporarily exhausted. This could also happen when Jahangir had seen something which particularly appealed to him. Such royal gifts had a bearing on the Mughal style. It is a truism that Mughal painting is the result of a fusion of indigenous Indian and imported Iranian and European styles. Less attention has been given to exactly the same process in the decorative arts. The ceaseless flow of European artefacts to the court, the strong Iranian cultural and political ties, and the arrival of European and Iranian artisans who were taken into the emperor's workshops to join the Indian Hindu and Muslim craftsmen already there, had a profound influence on the style and decoration of objects, and also seem to have been responsible for the creation of entirely new industries.

Examination of the development of just one kind of motif, the floral arabesque, illustrates this mingling of disparate influences. Floral arabesques, in a multiplicity of forms, dominate the decoration of architecture and the crafts of the late 16th and early 17th century. In its earliest forms, dependence on Safavid prototypes is so strong that an Indian origin can barely be discerned. Gradually, however, the flowers become more naturalistic as indigenous Indian influence asserts itself. Also noticeable is a symmetrical angularity inter-rupting the fluidity of the scroll patterns, the result of contact with the art of the Italian Renaissance. This can be seen on the borders of the carved stone friezes of Shah Jahan's monuments (no.4a) and, in the 18th century, on the carved border of a shield (459). Cartouches of Italianate design are also on tiles (no.5) and carpets (no.201) of the mid-17th century.

Floral naturalism reaches a peak in the reign of Shah Jahan. The marble friezes on the Taj Mahal and Fort at Agra are carved with rows of flowering plants, their leaves and petals curled over, with Chinese clouds, butterflies and insects filling the spaces between. The source of the design is generally taken to be European herbals (see Skelton (1972)) which, in Jahangir's reign, provided the model for the many flower studies he commissioned. Iranian painting also had a strong influence, and in Shah Jahan's reign the motif permeated the decorative arts. It was carved on jade (no.357), inlaid in ivory on wooden boxes, chased on precious metal (no.323) and woven and embroidered on textiles. The naturalism of the earliest versions gradually stiffens into single, repeated motifs within lobed and cusped arches or cartouches, the representation of the flowers being more stylised. The delicately inlaid *pietra dura* of the buildings of Shah Jahan's reign was in itself an innovation in architectural decoration; the Florentine panel of Orpheus in the *Diwan-i 'Am* at Agra suggesting its Italian source.

Other new, or resurgent craft industries can be ascribed to the Mughal period. Enamel of extremely high quality was produced by the Mughal craftsmen and it is possible that this was a technique introduced from Europe. At a period when enamelled jewellery was fashionable in Europe, Jahangir notes in his memoirs the receipt of European jewels from the governor of Surat, Muqarrab Khan, and European jewellers such as Augustin of Bordeaux were known to have been in the service of the Mughal emperors and princes. People like him may well have been responsible for the enamel on the thumb ring (no.303) and jade wand (no.358) which are wholly European in style. Whatever the origins of enamelling in India, the techique was soon sufficiently well-developed to vie with the best European work and was used consistently throughout the Mughal period.

It is also probable that European craftsmen made the cameos (nos 376 & 377) shown in the exhibition, though the technical expertise for small scale hardstone carving of extreme finesse was certainly not lacking in India. Carved gemstones have already been mentioned, but jade and crystal also reached a peak of excellence under the Mughals, though the techniques of hardstone carving had been used in India from historical times. The use of jade, however, seems to be the result of Timurid influence. Jahangir owned several Timurid jades (see Skelton (1972) p.102) but by the reign of Shah Jahan, the industry was well-established and jades in an identifiable Mughal style were being produced. Perhaps the finest is Shah Jahan's wine-cup dated to 1657 (no.356). Agate and crystal artefacts were also made in quantity, Cambay being an important centre. Hardstones were used as embellishments to arms (no.416), jewellery (no.309) and metal wares (no.367) as well as for complete objects.

Glass-making, too, was known in India from antiquity, but there is no evidence so far for large scale production of a variety of glass wares until the Mughal period. The Italian writer Clemente Tosi notes Gujarat as a glass centre in his handbook for missionaries published in 1669 (see Lightbown (1969) p.253) and the *A'in-i Akbari* Bihar and Alwar. The range of glass products on the existing evidence seems to have been limited and the technical methods generally unadventurous.

327

328

Huqqa bases, spherical or bell-shaped (see no.475) are the most common surviving objects, dating usually from the 18th century or later. The quality of the metal is poor though the colour may be attractive, the decorative techniques deriving from the skills of the manuscript painter rather than of the glass blower (no.396). Lead glass items were acquired from Europe (no.385) and in the 19th century, according to one commentator, glass was exported to India from England in blocks and blown there.

The vast field of Indian arms and armour reveals the same blend of outside influences on an existing style or form to create entirely new fashions. India had its own indigenous punch dagger (no.425) and sword forms (for example no.431) and for centuries had been known for the export of high quality steel. In the western Islamic world this steel was made into beautifully watered, finely balanced, razor-sharp yet pliable blades which were clearly highly prized in India, and Iranian swordsmiths must have been employed by the Mughals.

The Indian element is perhaps most marked in arms decoration, for example in the profusion of animal scenes, carved on blades (no.421), and on ivory primers (no.440), inlaid on hilts (no.435) with animals also sometimes being carved in the round to form part of the structure of the weapon itself. Perhaps unique is the gun made for Tipu Sultan with its tiger stock, formerly in the collection of Lord Cornwallis (no.464). Firearms and ordnance are more clearly subject to European influence, the result of numbers of European gunsmiths and founders working in any court anxious to maintain a good arsenal to keep its enemies at bay or to increase its sphere of influence. In the exhibition, their effect is seen particularly on weapons from Tipu Sultan's court, which, though having strongly Indian decoration, have forms and firing mechanisms of the most modern European type of the time.

Metalwares for domestic and ritual use survive in quantity, though in the absence of inscribed and dated pieces establishing a historical sequence presents problems. The range of technical ingenuity and expertise is great, even though the methods of production were small scale, and used tools and equipment of the utmost simplicity (no.321). Early Mughal metalwares have marked Iranian influence, whether in the form, as in the Prince of Wales Museum bowl (no.488), or in the decoration, as in the late 16th century vase (no.489).

A standard 17th century Safavid shape is also borrowed for two other bowls in the exhibition (no.497 and no.479). The second is of *bidri* ware, *bidri* being the name of a technique peculiar to India and taking its name from Bidar in the Deccan, where it is thought to have originated. Objects are cast from an alloy of zinc with an admixture of copper and tin, often with a varying proportion of lead. They are then inlaid with silver or brass, occasionally with gold, and subsequently coated with a paste of mud containing sal ammoniac. When the

336 Box for betel; Lucknow, mid 19th century

coating is removed, the metal is left a rich matt black which provides a foil to the brightly shining inlay. If the industry began in the Deccan, by the 18th century *bidri* was also being produced in Lucknow, Purnea and Murshidabad, with small centres of production elsewhere.

The study of Mughal decorative arts, excepting textiles, is in its infancy with dates of objects often assigned on stylistic grounds only. The exhibition therefore has included objects noted in the inventories of public and private European collections thus giving proven dates of at least the 17th or 18th century. The most important of these are from the National Museum, Copenhagen and from Powis Castle. The Danish collection is based on the Royal Kunstkammer founded by Frederick III in about 1650, to which was added the collection of Ole Worm (1588-1654), called the Museum Wormianum. Worm started to publish short catalogues in the 1640's to facilitate exchanges of his objects for those of friends and colleagues, and the earliest Kunstkammer inventory dates from 1673-4. From this date the whole collection was subject to inventory checks when new Intendants were appointed. The many additions to the Museum led to the founding of the Royal Ethnographical Museum in 1849 and from 1921 it was an independent section of the National Museum. In 1981 the Department published a catalogue of the collection, fully illustrated and giving all the available inventory information.

The Powis collection was formed by Clive of India and his son and daughter-in-law, the Powis heiress, Lady Powis in particular having been a keen collector during her stay in India. Inventories, lists of goods shipped home, and other papers have been made available by Christopher Rowell of the National Trust and give valuable information about when the items came into the collection. Lady Powis was an avid collector of material related to Tipu Sultan, of which there is a wealth in public and private collections, though the association with him, with the important exception of inscribed weapons, rests usually on little more than oral tradition. Lady Powis's papers show her to have sought out 'Tipu relics' immediately after the seige of Seringapatam in 1799 and her notebook, now at Powis Castle, gives the information that the throne finial was given to her by Lord Wellesley who also gave the *huma* bird from the canopy to Queen Charlotte.

SS

Arts of the goldsmith

297
The Carew Spinel
Spinel; vertical bore-hole for attachment pin with a diamond at top and bottom, two ties of silk and gold thread.
Length : 4cm, *Width* : 2.3cm
Weight : 133.5 carats
Engraved with the titles of Jahangir, Shah Jahan, and Aurangzeb and the dates 1021 (1612-3), 1039 (1629-30) and 1077 (1666).
VAM : I.M. 243-1922
Bequeathed by the Rt. Hon. Julia Mary, Lady Carew.
The inscriptions read:
1 *Jahangir Shah Akbar Shahi*
2 *Jahangir Shah Akbar Shah* 1021
3 *Sahib-i qiran-i sani 1039 sanah 2* (the title of Shah Jahan and the regnal year 2)
4 *'Alamgir Shah 107(7) sanah 10* (the title of Aurangzeb and the regnal year 10)
The stone was bought in Tehran by a relative of Lady Carew some time before 1870.
Bibliography : Ball (1894); Hambly (1968) pl.107. SS

298
Pendant whistle
Rock crystal mounted with gems in a gold setting.
Length : 10.5cm
Mughal (?), late 16th century

Lent by the Rijksmuseum, Amsterdam. The pendant is modelled on European whistles in the form of a dolphin but in this case the head resembles the traditional Indian water-monster (*makara*). Such pendants appear in Europe to have evolved from nautical or hunting whistles and were worn in the sixteenth century as emblems of rank. The circumstances in which such an object might have been made in India are not clear. There is evidence that Captains of ships sometimes commissioned their badges while overseas (see Parke Bernet (1967), lot 21) but it is possible that it could have been made at the court in emulation of examples worn by the European nobility.
Bibliography : Du Ry (1972), p.255; La Roërie (1935); Parke-Bernet (1967) lot 21; Hackenbroch (1979) illus. 288, 305, 315, 633; Princely Magnificence, p.119. RC

299
The Canning jewel
Enamelled gold set with gems.
Height : 4 inches, *Width* : 2¾ inches
Flemish or Italian with Indian additions. Late 16th century.
VAM : M 2697-1931
The pendant is made up of enamelled gold set with a baroque pearl, table-, point- and rose-cut diamonds, a table-cut ruby and two cabochon rubies, a ruby carved as a lotus flower, and hung with an Indian pendant set with cabochon rubies. Three large pearls are suspended from it.

This is traditionally supposed to have been a gift from a Medici Grand Duke to one of the Mughal emperors, but this is unlikely as the Medici never sent an embassy to the Mughal courts. The carved ruby, which may date from the early 1600's, and the ruby-set pendant are, however, evidence that the piece must have found its way to India. Its later history is also unclear, it supposedly having formed part of the treasure of the King of Delhi captured after the Indian Mutiny; there is no documentary proof of this and it is not recognisable in the catalogue of the treasure which was auctioned by Messrs. Hamilton & Sons of Calcutta. Somehow, however, it came into the collection of Lord Canning, who saw the treasure while it was in Allahabad on the way to Calcutta. It then passed through the collection of Lord Clanricarde to the 6th Earl of Harewood, who sold it at Sotheby's on 16th July 1931. It was bought by Mrs. E. Harnkess, who presented it to the Museum.
Bibliography : Hackenbroch (1979), p.240, fig.646. AS-C

300
Pendant
White jade set with rubies and emeralds in gold, mounted in enamelled gold.
Length : 3.3cm, *Width* : (including attachment rings) 3.2cm
Northern India; 17th or 18th century.
VAM : 02534 (IS)
From the collection of Col. Charles

Seton Guthrie.
The gemstones are carved in the form of two birds perched in a tree, above which are three Chinese clouds. The scene painted on the enamel on the back, shows a male, turbanned figure mounted on a horse with a spear in his hand, riding past rocks and a city, towards a lion. In front of him are cranes and ducks in a river. There are several plant forms engraved in the gold under the translucent green enamel of the river; the landscape and rider are enamelled in opaque white, with outline details painted in black and yellow. SS

301 WITHDRAWN
Pendant
Gold, jewelled and enamelled.
Mughal, mid 18th century
Lent by the Bharat Kala Bhavan, Banaras.
The front is of emerald carved in relief (*munabbat*) with a flowering plant, surrounded by diamonds set in gold squares. The reverse of the pendant is richly enamelled with a design of flowers and a vase in blue, red, green and gold on a white ground. Two small birds in profile fill the spaces at each edge. A spinel and an emerald bead hang from the bottom.
The pendant has been attributed to Jaipur, but is of more refined quality than securely documented Jaipur pieces. The motif on a flowering plant in a vase was taken up in Rajasthan from the Mughal architectural decor-

298

299

300

ative repertoire and is found in both painting and marble relief in the palace of Amber. This pendant may possibly be an example of the Mughal style of enamelling soon after its introduction to Jaipur.

Bibliography : *Chhavi* (1971), p.124-5, pl.15 and fig.258; Black (1974), p.206. RS

302
Order of Merit
Gold pendant enamelled and jewelled and set with a water-colour painting of Ranjit Singh.
Length : 9.1cm, *Width* : 4.8cm
Punjab; 1837-39
VAM : I.S. 92-1981
Formerly in the collection of Ranjit Singh's son, Dalip Singh. According to Singh (1979) p.53, Maharaja Ranjit Singh (17-1839) instituted the 'Star of the Prosperity of the Punjab' (*Kaukab-i Iqbal-i Punjab*) in March 1837 on the occasion of the wedding of his grandson, Prince Naunihal Singh. The decoration had three grades differentiated by having diamonds (first class), diamonds and emeralds (second class) or, as here, emeralds only (third class). The pendant is star-shaped with ten 'rays'; in the centre behind glass is a circular portrait of Ranjit Singh enthroned and holding a bow and arrow as emblems of State. A durbar scene of the Maharaja in the Chester Beatty Library, Dublin (see W.G. Archer (1966) fig.15) is perhaps the sort of painting this miniature portrait was taken from. The pendant is enamelled on the back in translucent green with a floral scroll in opaque white, yellow, pale pink and pale green. The bell beneath the suspension ring is enamelled in translucent red and green with opaque white. The pendant would have been worn hanging from a gold and scarlet silk riband.
General Allard, the French military adventurer in the service of Ranjit Singh, can be seen wearing this kind of decoration in a painting of 1838 (Welch (1978) no.55).
Bibliography : Christie's (London) : *Objects of Vertu and Russian Works of Art* Tuesday 24 February 1981 no.25. SS

303
Thumb ring
Gold, chased and engraved and set with rubies and emeralds, the inside enamelled in opaque white, turquoise, pale green and black.
Length : 3.7cm, *Diam.* : 3cm
Northern India; first half of the 17th century.

VAM : I.M. 207-1920
The engraved and chased decoration on the thumb ring, though slightly coarser, compares with that on the spoon (322) in the exhibition. The colours and design of the enamel on the inside of the ring are influenced by European Renaissance jewellery. The shape is almost identical to that of Shah Jahan's thumb ring (355).
Bibliography : Hambly (1968) pl.109. SS

304
Thumb ring
White jade set with carved rubies and emeralds in gold.
Length : 4.1cm, *Width* : 3.2cm
Mughal; 17th century, probably first half.
VAM : 02522 (I.S.)
From the collection of Col. Charles Seton Guthrie.
This, like the jewelled gold thumb ring (303) is almost identical in shape to Shah Jahan's jade thumb ring dated 1632. SS

305
Thumb ring
Almandine garnet set with diamonds in gold.
Length : 4cm, *Diam.* : 3.1cm
Mughal, 17th century
VAM : 02530 (I.S.)
From the collection of Col. Charles Seton Guthrie.

306
Thumb ring
Gold, set with diamonds and enamelled in translucent blue and green with opaque black and white.
Length : 3.9cm, *Width* : 3cm
Mughal, 18th century, probably second half
VAM : 02528 (I.S.)
From the collection of Col. Charles Seton Guthrie.
A thumb ring of similar shape is illustrated on f.33 of the Gentil album (89) dated to c.1770. SS

307
The crown of the Emperor Bahadur Shah II
Gold set with jewels
Height : 27.5cm, *Diam.* : 17.7 x 16.4cm
Mughal, second quarter of the 19th century
Lent from Windsor Castle by Her Majesty The Queen.
The crown is loosely based on a European model with the circlet and standards of sheet gold decorated in repoussé and set with floral rosettes of

turquoises, rubies and diamonds around the circlet. The standards are capped with pearls and small emeralds with large perforated emeralds and small bullion tassels dependent from them. Two crossing arches of sheet gold set with diamonds enclose a gold filigree cap above which is an aigrette of white feathers surmounted by pearls, emeralds and rubies with three small bullion tassels. The inside of the crown is lined with crimson velvet and white cotton decorated with flowers.
The crown was sold to Queen Victoria for £500 by Robert Tytler, who had bought it in an auction following the Indian Mutiny. It resembles the crown depicted in the portrait of Bahadur Shah (no.109) which has several other aigrettes and decorations obscuring it.
Bibliography : Collier (1966), p.242. RS

308
Turban ornament
Gold, set with gemstones, the stem enamelled in translucent green.
Length : 16.8cm, *Width* : 5.8cm
Mughal, early 18th century
VAM : I.M. 240-1923
It seems likely that the jewelled aigrette, used as a turban ornament, became fashionable in India as a result of European influence. Turban decoration in the 16th century and first two decades of the 17th century had been in the form of feather plumes held in place by jewelled brooches, similar to Iranian ornaments. This type can be seen on one of the trays of jewels in the painting of the weighing ceremony (40). With the arrival of portraits of Europeans, notably James I, wearing jewelled aigrettes a new imitative fashion developed in India.
The portrait of Shah Jahan (41) shows him holding a turban ornament and is perhaps the earliest representation of this new jewel which, in different forms, remained popular until the end of the Mughal period (311).
This example is in the form of a floral spray and is set with rubies, diamonds, emeralds and pale beryls on one side and rubies, emeralds and pale beryls on the other. SS

309
Turban ornament
White jade in two sections, set with carved rubies, emeralds and rock crystal in gold, a pendent pearl at the top, the back carved.
Length : 19.7cm, *Width* : 4.6cm
Mughal, first half of the 18th century

VAM : 02569 (I.S.)
From the collection of Colonel Charles Seton Guthrie.
Each petal, and the central boss of the rosette, is set with a separate, carved ruby. The foliate upper section has emeralds, rubies and crystals cut to fit each leaf with as many as seven small, shaped rubies on one leaf, though most have only one or two. The veins of the leaves have then been carved on to the shaped gemstones before setting. The back is carved in low relief, with the plume holder carved from the same piece of jade as the main section of the jewel. A small ring is on the stem and would be used to attach the ornament to a turban.
Bibliography : Hendley (1906) part I pl.4 no.15; Hall (1971) pl.204b; Black (1974) illustrated on p.205. SS

304

308

310
Turban ornament
Gold, enamelled and set on the front with diamonds, rubies and foiled gemstones.
Length : 17.6cm, *Width* : 5.8cm
Northern India, late 18th-early 19th century.
Lent by The David Collection, Copenhagen : 2/1981.
The jewel has three attachment rings, and a plume-holder on the back.   SS

311
Turban ornament (sarpech)
Rubies and diamonds set in gold; the back enamelled.
Height : 15.7cm, *Length* : 22.5cm
Deccan, probably Hyderabad, 19th century
Private collection.
The turban ornament is made up of six pieces hinged in five places to take the shape of the wearer's head. The design is of a row of three flowers, made up of rubies and flat cut diamonds set in chased gold, with two end pieces suggestive of leaves. Eight spinels hang from the flowers, and another depends from the plume (*jigha*). The back is enamelled in an unusual colour scheme of pale opaque green, opaque white and translucent green enamel on gold in a pattern of leaves and petals. There is a holder for a heron-feather plume (*kalgi*) and two pierced rectangular lugs, probably so that the considerable weight of the piece may be supported by being

fixed to the turban. There is also a long tasselled cord to wrap around the head to secure the *sarpech*.
Bibliography : (for a similar example) Hyderabad Government (1954), pl. f.p.118.   RC

312
Turban ornament (turra)
Pearls and diamonds set in gold with enamel.
Length : 14.5cm, *Diam. of rosette* : 3.3cm
Deccan, probably Hyderabad, 19th century
Private collection.
This ornament would have been worn at the side of a turban, hanging down past the ear. It may have been worn as part of a set with a *sarpech*, and perhaps inserted into the cord by which the *sarpech* is secured (see Worswick and Embree (1976), p.20 for contemporary photographs). It is made up of three main parts : a rosette of diamonds set in gold and surrounded by pendent pearls, which screws into a curving enamelled stem by which the ornament would be secured into the turban or cord. From the diamond and enamelled bud at the bottom of the rosette hang five strings of seed pearls, from which depend more pearls and diamonds set in gold with enamelled backs.
The back of the diamond rosette is decorated with translucent green and red and opaque white enamel.
Bibliography : Hyderabad Government (1954), pl. f.p.118.   RC

313
Armlet
Gold, enamelled and set with rubies, diamonds and carved emeralds.
Diameter : 11.5cm
Mughal, 17th century
Lent by the State Hermitage, Leningrad.

314
Bracelet (dastband)
Rubies and diamonds set in gold, the back enamelled.
Length : 18.6cm, *Width* : 3.3cm
Deccan, probably Hyderabad, 19th century
Private collection.
This bracelet matches the *sarpech* (no.311) and was evidently part of the same *saropa*. It is made up of three strings of rosettes of rubies wired to gold with flat-cut diamonds. There is a large central rosette of rectangular shape with a diamond at its centre, and surrounded by diamond leaves set in gold. The small rosettes are separated

by pairs of gold and diamond leaves and the two rectangular pieces of the clasp are secured by a gold screw with a ruby in its head. The reverse of the rosettes have opaque white flowers enamelled in gold, while the leaves have opaque green enamel on the back and translucent green enamel on the sides.
The pieces of the bracelet are wired together in order to make it flexible.
Bibliography : Hyderabad Government (1954), pl.f.p.118.   RC

315
Armlets, a pair
Gold, set with rubies and diamonds, enamelled; the *makara*-head terminals have onyx eyes and ruby tongues.
Diameter : 12cm
Rajasthan (Jaipur); second half of the 19th century
Lent by The David Collection, Copenhagen : 3a-b/1981.
Bibliography : see Jacob and Hendley (1886) pl.24 for other examples of this type of armlet.   SS

316
Armlet
Gold, polychrome enamelled, set with rubies and diamonds, the *makara*-head terminals with ruby tongues and onyx eyes.
Width : 6.6cm
Rajasthan (Jaipur); c.1850
VAM : 119-1852
Purchased from the Great Exhibition of 1851 where it was described as 'modern'.   SS

310

311

312

314

315

318

317 WITHDRAWN
Bangle
Gold, enamelled and set with diamonds.
Banaras, 19th century
Lent by the Bharat Kala Bhavan,
Banaras.
The bracelet is painted in pink enamel
on opaque white with translucent green,
and its terminals are in the form of
elephants' heads with trunks entwined.
The use of painted pink enamel is
unique to Banaras; unlike the enamel of
Jaipur and other centres which has a
long tradition of craftsmanship, Banaras
pink enamel (*gulabi minakari*) had a
short span of manufacture lasting only
about 150 years, up to the death of its
last hereditary master, Babbu Singh, in
about 1923, although its now under-
going a revival. The pink colour is
applied with rose attar (*gulab*).
Bibliography : *Chhavi* (1971), pp.327-
34, pl.27.   RC

318
Pair of ear ornaments
Silver and gold filigree set with dia-
monds, hung with seed pearls, green
glass beads and a pendent emerald,
pearl strings with ruby and emerald
beads, gold thread tassels.
Length : 18cm
Northern India, mid 19th century
VAM : 03254 (I.S.)
Bibliography : Hendley (1906) part I
pl.5 no.24.   SS

319
Plaque from a necklace
Emerald
Weight : 182 carats
Mughal or Jaipur, mid-18th century
Private collection.
This large emerald, one of a series
which formed a necklace, is carved on
both sides, on the front with a many-
flowered plant, and on the back with a
lotus-flower rosette.
The flowering plant here is no longer
treated naturalistically but symmetrically fills the whole of its frame. It is
said that this stone formed part of a
necklace owned by the Emperor
'Alamgir and this may be corroborated
by a similarity of decorative treatment
in the case of another large square
emerald in an American private collection which bears the date 1107 AH
(1695 AD). The lotus medallion is often
found on the underside of hardstone
vessels and in architecture (see no.12).
Bibliography : Caplan (1968), p.1336. RS

320
Necklace
Seed pearl strings, pendants of gold,
enamelled and set with gemstones and
green glass beads.
Length : 34.5cm
Northern India, c.1850
VAM : 03306 (I.S.)
The crescent pendants and triangular
sections are set with natural white
sapphires and rock crystal, some foiled;
the lower pendants are set with garnets.
The enamel is translucent red and
opaque white in a chevron pattern.
Bibliography : Hendley (1908) part IX
pl.105, no.735; Black (1974) illustrated
on p.204.   SS

321
Set of tools for engraving
1   *silai   gharai   chamkai*
2   *parkal* (compass)
3   stones for sharpening tools.
**Set of tools and utensils for enamel-
ling acquired from Jaipur craftsmen**
1   Kiln
2   Pestle and mortar, iron.
3   Pestle and mortar, agate.
4   Tongs
5   Forceps
6   *chimta* and *chimti* : small and large
    tongs for putting the objects into
    the kiln.
7   *patra* : brass palette for the colours.
8   *qalam* : paint brush
9   *takwa* : needle
10 *abrak* : a sheet of mica on which the
    object rests for placing in the kiln.
11 *karchha* : a long iron spoon onto
    which the object and the sheet of
    mica are placed to be put inside the
    kiln.
12 *shan* or *korand* : a stick of corun-
    dum powder and shellac, used to
    rub down the enamel after each
    stage of firing.
13 *banqual* : wooden blow-pipe used to
    control the temperature on the
    enamel.
14 *bartha* : a mixture of powdered
    glass and shellac used for the final
    smoothing-off.
15 *rang* : raw material from Lahore for
    use in Jaipur. These colours, red
    and blue, were acquired about 150
    years ago by Jaipur enamellers.
16 raw material from Amritsar in six
    colours: turquoise, yellow, apple
    green, dark blue, pale blue and green.
17 Traditional designs from the 18th
    and 19th centuries.
Lent by Mr Mumin Latif
Bibliography : Latif (1982) pp.102-3,
109-10.   ML

322
Spoon
Gold, engraved and set with rubies, emeralds and diamonds.
Length : 18.6cm
Mughal, late 16th or early 17th century.
VAM : IM 173-1910
The spoon is a masterpiece of the goldsmith's art and gives a rare glimpse of the splendour of the artefacts being produced in the royal Mughal workshops towards the end of Akbar's reign or early into the reign of his son. European influence is seen in the form of the spoon, whilst the decoration is strongly Iranian, with as yet little reflection of the indigenous Indian traditions except in the engraving of the gold between the gemstones on the back of the bowl. The knop and the edge of the back of the bowl are set with small natural octahedral diamonds, and the finial is a large point-cut diamond.
Bibliography : Welch (1963) pl.20; Gascoigne (1971) p.226.   SS

323
Beaker and cover
Silver, the inside gilt, raised with cast finial, chased and engraved decoration.
Height : 14.2cm, *Diameter* : 8.3cm
Mughal, second half of the 17th century.
VAM : IS 31-1961
The Mughal silversmith has taken the shape from a European beaker, altering the profile slightly and giving it a cover of Indian form. The European prototype may have come to India by way of foreign merchants. Anxious to secure trading privileges, they were well aware of the need to smooth the path of diplomacy with gifts to the emperor and his nobles. The floral decoration of this piece is in a horizontal format derived from architectural stone carving and the borders of illuminated manuscripts; the hatched ground of the flowers may have been intended to hold enamel, perhaps with gold wire in the stems.
Bibliography : Welch (1963) pl.61; Skelton (1970) pl.3a; VAM (1978) fig.31. SS

324
Jar and cover
Gold with champlevé enamel
Height : 14.4cm, *Diameter* : 10.2cm
Mughal, c.1700
Lent by the Cleveland Museum of Art (purchased from the J.H. Wade Fund): 62.206
The vessel is decorated with *basse-taille* enamel in which the principal motifs are in white on a translucent green ground. The flower and trellis decoration on the

sides of the body is confined to these colours but the decoration on the shoulder and narcissus flowers on the tall flared neck incorporate translucent yellow which also appears on the lid together with surface painting of pink on white flower petals. There is an enamelled flower encircled by leaves and petals below the foot ring. The lid decoration is an unusually early example of pink painted enamel in India, but the painting technique was already known there and may have dropped out of use until its revival in Benares and Sind at the close of the 18th century.
Bibliography : Welch (1963) p.172 no.62.   SS

325
Rosewater sprinkler (gulabpash)
Gold, inlaid with rubies, emeralds and pearls.
Height : 28cm
India; 17th century
Lent by the State Hermitage, Leningrad.

326
Dish
Gold, enamelled in translucent red and green on an opaque white ground, set with rubies, emeralds and diamonds.
Diameter : 19cm
Northern India; 17th century
Lent by the State Hermitage, Leningrad.

327
Box
Gold, octagonal, enamelled in translucent green and red on an opaque white ground.
Height : 7.5cm
Northern India; 17th century
Lent by the State Hermitage, Leningrad.

328
Dish
Gold, octagonal, set with spinels and emeralds, enamelled in opaque white, translucent red and green.
Diameter : 29cm
Northern India; 17th century
Lent by the State Hermitage, Leningrad.

329
Box and cover
Gold with champlevé enamel.
Height : 3.8cm, *Width* : 5.6cm
Mughal, c.1700
Lent by Mr. and Mrs. James Alsdorf, Chicago.

The box and cover are decorated with floral scrolls in opaque white enamel on a translucent green ground. There is a rosette on the bottom of the box. On the dome of the lid and on the underside of the box part of the decoration is without enamel, the gold merely being chased to represent floral elements. A fitted yellow velvet case not exhibited, suggests that it was formally in the Imre Schwaiger collection.   RS

330
Box and cover with tray
Enamelled gold
Box height : (*with cover*) 10.0cm,
Width : 13.5cm
Tray width : 28.5cm
Mughal, 18th century
Lent anonymously.
The box and tray are octagonal in plan and the cover is semi-domed with a flat octagonal top.
The upper surface of the tray and outside of the box share a field decoration of flowering plants resembling dianthus with poppy foliage against an opaque white ground. On the tray this is contained within an arcade of leaves springing from radiating cypress trees. The rims of both the tray and the cover are decorated with rows of repeated leaves. In addition to the opaque white the colours are translucent red and green.   RS

331
Box, cover and stand
Silver, partly gilt and chased with stamped and ring-matted decoration.
Box: *Height* : 8.4cm, *Length* : 14.3cm, *Width* : 10.2cm
Stand: *Length* : 29.9cm, *Width* : 24cm
Mughal, 18th century (in the Clive collection by 1766)
Lent by the National Trust, Powis Castle.
This forms part of a set of objects at Powis Castle which includes one other box and stand, also for *pan*, and two pairs of rosewater sprinklers and stands, all of which appear in lists of goods sent to Lady Clive from India. A note on the lists gives the date of receipt, 1 January, 1766, and describes them as: '2 Silver Beettle Boxes and Bottoms gilt 2 Silver Rose Water Bottles and Bottoms gilt.' (papers in the India Office Library Box XVIII no.8).
Bibliography : Rivett-Carnac (1902) pl.103, 107.   SS

332
Box and cover (pandan)
Silver, partly gilt, with champlevé enamel in translucent green and cobalt blue, and opaque yellow.
Height : 6.7cm, *Width* : 10.5cm
Diameter : 8.9cm
Lucknow; first half of the 18th century
Reputed to have belonged to the last king of Oudh, Wajid 'Ali Shah (1847-1912)
VAM : IM 30-1912
Gift of Queen Mary, having been presented to her during the Delhi Coronation Durbar and Indian tour of 1911-12. The shape of this box is similar to that of the silver box from Powis Castle, in the collection of Lord Clive by 1766.   SS

333
Dish
Gold, enamelled and set with red and white gems.
Diameter : 31.0cm
Jaipur, late 18th or early 19th century.
Lent anonymously.
The dish is decorated with a central rosette of precious stones surrounded by three concentric bands of floral scrolls of which the inner is enamelled and the others set with gems. Enamelled acanthus leaves radiate around the *cavetto* and the rim is set with a row of rubies. The enamel colours are translucent red, green and dark blue with opaque white, mid- and pale blue.   RS

334
Betel nut cutters
Silver, gilt, with translucent and opaque enamel.
Lucknow; third quarter of the 18th century
Lent by the National Trust, Powis Castle.
Betel nut is the main ingredient of *pan* and is cut finely before being mixed with the lime and aromatic spices that fill the betel leaf to make a quid for chewing. Wherever *pan* is used, betel nut cutters are made, and range from the sturdy and utilitarian to the more refined and decorative, as exemplified by this pair.
They are probably the ones referred to in an account of the property of Lord Clive at Claremont made about 1774: 'A curious pair of bettlenut Cracker', listed again in an inventory of his Indian curiosities dated 17 March 1775 (Powis mss.).   SS

324 (base)

329

113

324

331

332

334

335

Pan set

Silver and silver filigree, partly gilt, enamelled and set with semi-precious stones.

Pan box height : 9.7cm,

Diameter : 11.3cm, *Spice containers heights* : 3.1cm, *Diameter* : 5.7cm

Lucknow; late 18th century

Lent by the National Trust, Powis Castle.

The four small circular boxes would hold the spices for the quid of sliced areca nut (see 334) which would then be put into the large box to be offered to guests.   SS

336

Betel-box (husndan)

Silver-gilt, with chased and engraved decoration.

Height : 19cm, *Diameter* : 14.3cm

N. India, Lucknow, mid-19th century.

Lent by the Jagdish and Kamla Mittal Museum of Indian Art, Hyderabad. (no.76.1324).

This betel container has a circular body and a domed cover surmounted by a removable peacock which incorporates a spoon. It is in three tiers, the top part serving as a perfume container. The middle tray is for betel leaves, and the lower section contains a tray with compartments for areca nuts and other ingredients.

The *husndan* became popular in Lucknow as a reaction against the increasingly large and cumbersome *pandan* which served as a portable treasure house for women as well as a betel container. Generally small in size, it was adopted at first by ladies not given to excessive outward display, but soon became generally popular.

Bibliography : Sharar (1975), p.223 & pl.29.   RC

337

Box and cover

Silver filigree, circular, lobed and cusped.

Height : 5cm, *Diameter* : 16cm

Possibly Deccan (Karimnagar); 18th century (in the Clive collection by 1775).

Lent by the National Trust, Powis Castle.

The box and cover is mentioned in the inventory of 17 March 1775 of Clive's collection as one of 'Two Philligree Dressing Boxes' and is a rare example of proven 18th century Indian filigree work. The filigree industry of Karimnagar, in present-day Andhra Pradesh, still survives. According to craftsmen

interviewed for the *1961 Census of India*, it has been established for about 200 years, though its origins are obscure (Sekhar 1961).   SS

338

Qur'an box

Silver with niello decoration.

Deccan, Hyderabad; early 18th century

Lent by the Jagdish and Kamla Mittal Museum, Hyderabad: 76-1537.

The box is rectangular, with two loops for a carrying strap at each end. The sides and hinged top have a qur'anic inscription in elegant *riqa* script surrounded by borders of floral arabesques. The ends are decorated with flowering plants and chevrons on the loops. Such boxes were made for small copies of the qur'an which the owner could carry with him at all times.   RS

339

Huqqa base with tobacco bowl and mouthpiece

Silver, partly gilt, enamelled and set with diamonds and rubies.

Height : 16.9cm, *Diameter* : 15.3cm

Mughal (Lucknow?); 18th century (in the collection of Clive of India, probably by 1766).

Lent by the National Trust, Powis Castle.

This sumptuous *huqqa* is enamelled in translucent blue and green on the body and neck, and set with jewels. The bottom has a central rosette enamelled in blue, green and purple. Encircling the rosette is a border of flowers, similar to those set with jewels on the body but here enamelled in yellow and purple on the same rich blue ground. This is perhaps the *huqqa* received by Lady Clive from India in 1766: 'Two hookahs One set with Topazes and Rubies' (Powis mss). It is in inventories of c.1774 and 17 March 1775 of Clive's property: 'A blue enamelled Hooka, consisting of five pieces set with Topazes & Rubies the Bottom round' (Powis mss). The five pieces are the *huqqa* base, tobacco bowl and cover with intermediate ring, and a mouthpiece, all enamelled and set with jewels.

Bibliography : Rivett-Carnac (1902) pl.101, 102.   SS

340

Huqqa base

Silver, partly gilt, enamelled.

Height : 18.5cm, *Diameter* : 18.5cm

Northern India, probably Lucknow; late 18th or early 19th century.

VAM : 122-1886 (IS)

Bought from the Colonial and Indian Exhibition, 1886.

The main decoration on the body is a broad frieze of six cartouches containing identical flowering plants, with a narrow floral scroll border above and below. The narrow borders which divide the registers of decoration are found repeatedly on 18th and 19th century pieces known to be from Lucknow and the translucent blue and green enamel is characteristic of wares from that centre.

SS

341

Flask

Silver, partly gilt, chased and engraved.

Height : 24.5cm, *Diameter* : 14.1cm

Rajasthan (?); mid-18th century.

Lent by the Jagdish and Kamla Mittal Museum of Indian Art, Hyderabad: 76.1289.

The flask has a tall narrow neck with a rounded body resting on a low, splayed, pierced ring foot. The body is decorated with spiralling bands which are alternately narrow and undecorated, or broad with a floral scroll. The scroll is 'inhabited' by birds, monkeys and other animals, all in a lively, if slightly naive style, on a ring-matted ground. On the neck is a continuous pattern of cusped and lobed cartouches containing flowers and animals. On the moulding at the top of the neck is a border of lotus petals. The shape of this flask is well-known from contemporary paintings but centres of silver manufacture before the 19th century have yet to be studied and clearly identified.   SS

342

Bottle and stopper

Zinc with chased and engraved silver neck and stopper.

Height : 39cm

Mughal, first half of the 18th century

Lent by the National Museum, Copenhagen, Department of Ethnography : EEc1.

This bottle would have been used for water which was chilled for drinking by immersing the bottle in a vat of water and saltpetre. The water outside the bottle, chilled by the saltpetre, would gradually cool the water inside.

Bibliography : Dam-Mikkelsen and Lundbaek (1980) p.101 and 102 which notes the bottle in inventories of 1741 and 1775.   SS

343

Basin

Silver, partly gilt, enamelled in translucent blue, green and purple.

Height : 13.3cm, *Diameter rim* : 31.6cm, *Diameter body* : 19.1cm

Lucknow; mid-19th century

Lent by the David Collection, Copenhagen.

The pierced cover for the opening has an openwork finial. The body is ribbed, with broad petal borders at top and bottom in high relief, and rests on four feet.   SS

344

Perfume tree

Silver, partly gilt

Height : 31.4cm,

Diameter of stand : 22.9cm

Northern India; probably mid-19th century

VAM : 836-1891

Each of the mangoes on the tree is a perfume container with an applicator spoon concealed inside. A peacock stands on the topmost branch, and the tree is supported by a circular stand on three feet.   SS

114

337

338

115

341

343

342

344

345

345
Ewer
Silver, partly gilt with chased and engraved decoration on a ring-matted ground.
Height : 33.3 cm, *Diameter* : 17.8 cm
Lucknow; bought from the Paris Exposition Universelle of 1867 as 'modern' work.
VAM : 778-1869

346
Tiger-head finial from the throne of Tipu Sultan (r.1784-99)
Gold on a wooden core, set with rubies, diamonds and emeralds.
Height : 8.3 cm, *Width base* : 4.7 cm
Mysore; late 18th century
Lent by the National Trust, Powis Castle.
This was one of the finials from Tipu's throne (94) taken after the fall of Seringapatam in 1799 and auctioned in India. It belonged to the 2nd Lady Clive, Countess of Powis, who was an inveterate hunter of Tipu 'relics'. Her notebook at Powis lists various miscellaneous items to be given away or bequeathed and contains the entry: 'An (?) Or Moulu Basket containing a head in pure Gold set with Precious Stones and one of the 8 heads which were on Tippoo Sultan's Throne at Seringapatam given me by Ld. Wellesley'. On the base of the stand is a gilt metal ring with an engraved inscription: 'Tiger's head which formed part of Tippoo's throne with H.A. Powis's love.'
A second throne finial was bought by Surgeon-Major Pulteney Mein at the sale after the fall of the fortress (illustrated in *Oriental Art* vol.XX no.4 (1974) p.357) and was the property of one of his descendants until 1974.
Bibliography : illustrated in Forrest (1970) fig.14b and in Courtney fig.47. SS

347
Tiger head from the throne of Tipu Sultan (r.1784-99)
Gold on a wooden core, eyes and teeth of crystal.
Mysore; late 18th century
Lent from Windsor Castle by Her Majesty the Queen.
This was bought in Seringapatam, after the fall of the fortress, by the Marquess Wellesley, Governor General, together with the *huma* bird from the canopy which is now also at Windsor Castle.
A copy of a letter giving an eye-witness account of the sale of the throne is in the Indian Department of the V & A.
It notes that Lord Harris originally acquired the head and sold it at auction where the writer of the letter, Pulteney Mein, bought it, selling it later to Marquess Wellesley who sent it to the Court of Directors. He also says the head 'supported the platform and the throne above'. The water colour of the throne (94) is not entirely accurate and Forrest (1970) notes that De La Tour's *History of Ayder Ali* (1774) has a version which is probably more reliable.
Bibliography : Forrest (1970) fig.15b. SS

348
Cage with clockwork singing bird
Silver; bird with traces of irridescent plumage.
Height : 30 cm, *Diameter* : 16.5 cm max.
Nabha; made by Nathooram the watchmaker; mid-19th century
VAM : 01226 IS
The cage bears an engraved silver label inscribed:
NATTOORAM
WATCHMAKER
NABHA
This object was exhibited with other mechanical curiosities by the Raja of Nabha in the London International Exhibition of 1872 (Miscellaneous Section, cat. no.3133 (771)). The entry explains: 'on touching a spring, after the machinery has been wound up, the bird sings, flaps its wings, moves its head, and turns upon its perch.'
The Raja of Nabha's fondness for automata was not unusual. Many Indian rulers, from the Mughal emperors down, shared this weakness. Some, like the Mirza Maharao Lakho of Kach (reigned 1741-61), devoted special rooms in their palaces to housing such material. VM

349 WITHDRAWN
Thumb ring
Nephrite jade, formerly with gold inlay set with precious stones.
Inscribed *shah salim* on the inside.
Mughal, c.1600
Lent by the Bharat Kala Bhavan, Banaras.
This thumb ring of whitish nephrite is the earliest Mughal jade object known to have been made in India. It was made for Prince Salim, as Jahangir was known before he came to the throne. It has a pattern of floral arabesques of Safavid inspiration, which was once inlaid with gold set with gems.
Bibliography : *Chhavi* (971), p.112, pl.8.

350

Wine cup of the Emperor Jahangir

Mottled grey-green nephrite jade.
Height: 7.4cm, *Diameter of rim* 7.4cm
Inscribed with two Persian quatrains
and the titles of Jahangir (see below)
together with the regnal and *hijri* dates
2 and 1016, which coincide between
24 April 1607 and 19 March 1608.
Mughal, c.1607-8
On loan to the Brooklyn Museum from
the Guennol Collection, GL 78.22.
The shape is evidently adapted from
that of a Chinese porcelain bowl with a
foot-ring and slightly flared walls. The
decoration consists solely of the three
bands of inscriptions within pairs of
horizontal lines enclosing rows of stars.
The central inscription in *tughra* style
suls characters reads: 'By command of
His Majesty, the Great Khaqan, Lord of
the Kings of the World, Manifestor of
Divine Favours in the Offices of Cali-
phate and Kingship, the Sun in the
Firmament of World Sovereignty, the
Moon in the Sky of Justice and Felicity,
Abu'l-Muzaffar, son of King Akbar,
Nur ad-Din Muhammad Jahangir the
Emperor, Warrior of the Faith, the form
of the cup attained completion (in the)
year 1016'.
The Persian quatrain above this is in
four cartouches alternating with quatre-
foils containing the inscription: 'The
wine cup / of the Emperor / of the Age /
second (regnal) year'. The verse itself
may perhaps be rendered:
See, this cup's body imbued with spirit –
A jasmine leaf suffused with purple (of
the Judas tree).
No no, I err! Through extreme gracious-
ness the cup
Is watery (i.e. yields water), pregnant
with flowing fire (wine).
The lower quatrain reads:
'Through wine, the tulip grows on thy
face.
It is like a rose petal: dew grows from it.
If the hand which took the cup from
thine
Should become dust, a cup will grow
from it'.
On one side the colour of the jade has
altered to mottled grey and creamy
white, presumably due to fire. This is
the earliest known cup made for Jahangir and during this formative period of
Indian jade carving his craftsmen were
still dependent upon metal and porcelain
prototypes.
Bibliography: Sotheby & Co. (16 Dec.
1971), lot 70; Skelton (1972), pp.103-4,
pl.26d. RS

351

The Emperor Jahangir's wine cup

Nephrite jade.
Height: 3.8cm, *Diameter*: 8.8cm
Transoxania or Iran, 15-16th century;
the inscription added in 1022 AH/
1613-14 AD
VAM: IM 152-1924
The cup is of dark green jade, with a
shallow curved bowl, low ring foot and
one handle in the form of the head of a
peacock or phoenix. At the bottom of
the interior of the bowl is a lotus flower
carved in relief. The cup is inscribed
around the rim with four cartouches
containing the verse, in Persian, 'From
King Jahangir, the world found order.
By the ray of his justice, the age was
illuminated. From the reflection of red
wine, may the cup of jade be always like
a ruby' (i.e. may it always be full). In the
centre of one side is a small quatrefoil
cartouche bearing the date 'year 1022'
(1613-14 AD), and on the other is a
similar cartouche dating the inscription
to the eighth regnal year of Jahangir
(15 March 1613 – 10 February 1614).
From marks on the surface of the jade,
it is evident that there were formerly
two handles. The cup itself is almost
certainly pre-Mughal, and is probably
late Timurid or early Safavid work.
Unlike the Timurids, the Safavid rulers
of Iran appear not to have been ardent
patrons of jade carving, but the sophistication of this cup slightly favours an
attribution to early 16th century Iran.
Bibliography: Skelton (1962), fig.11:
Irwin (1968), fig.11. RS

352

The Emperor Jahangir's inkpot

Signed by Mumin Jahangiri. Dark green
nephrite jade with a gold lid and chain.
Height: 6.4cm, *Diameter*: 7.9cm
Mughal, dated 1028 AH (1618-19 AD).
Lent by the Metropolitan Museum of
Art, New York. 29.145.2 (The Sylmaris
Collection, gift of George Coe Graves,
1929).
The inkpot of dark green jade is
engraved in intaglio with four ogival
cartouches containing flowering plants.
The cartouches are linked by four
smaller ones containing a Persian
inscription in *nasta'liq* characters: 'For
King Jahangir (son of) King Akbar in
the fourteenth year of Jahangir's reign
corresponding with the year 1028 of the
Flight the form (of the pot) attained
completion'. Above and below each
inscription is a wisp of Chinese cloud
pattern.
The underside of the foot is concave,

and engraved in Persian: *'amil-i mumin
jahangiri* 'The work of Mumin (in the
service of) Jahangir'.
Bibliography: Bulletin of the Metropolitan Museum of Art (1930), p.22;
Islamic jade (1966), p.164, fig.2; Welch
(1979), no.79. RC

350

351

353

Amulet (ta'wiz)
Grey nephrite jade with a ruby; inscribed in Arabic *mashallah la haula wa la quwwata illa bi'llah istaghfiru 'llah al-'azm al-'ali sana 1029;* 'May God preserve us. There is no power nor strength except in God, the Great, the Exalted. Year 1029 (1619 AD)'.
Mughal, dated 1029 AH/1619 AD
Lent by the Chester Beatty Library, Dublin.
This protective amulet with a pious formula and a ruby set in its centre dates from the time of Jahangir, and may have been made for the Emperor himself. At this period, jade was a rare and highly-valued commodity in India, and jade objects would have been owned only by a small number of people at the highest level of society.
Bibliography : James (1981), abb.1. RC

354

Perfume phial
Nephrite jade with silver mounts.
Length : 6.2cm, *Diameter* : 1.5cm
Inscribed around the top: *az jahangir shah akbar shah yashm-i* (undeciphered) *sanah-i julus 21 sanah-i hijri 1036.*
'By order of King Jahangir (son of) King Akbar, [undeciphered] jade. Regnal year 21, Hijri year 1036 (1626/7 AD)'.
Lent by the Prince of Wales Museum, Bombay.
This small bottle is carved in white jade in the form of a flower bud with elongated petals emerging from a ring of sepals. It is inscribed in five sections around the top, with the name of Jahangir, who owned it.
Although the organic style of jade carving reached its peak during the reign of Shah Jahan (see no.356), the trend had already started in Jahangir's reign, and this bottle is its earliest manifestation. It has been suggested (by Rai Krishna Dasa) that it is a receptacle for cotton wool with which scribes cleaned their pen-nibs, but its delicate shape and association with fragrant flowers seem more appropriate to a container for perfume.
Bibliography : Skelton (1972), p.105. RC

355

Thumb ring of Shah Jahan
White jade inscribed in gold within a cartouche.
Length : 4.1cm, *Width* : 3.2cm
Mughal, probably Delhi or Agra; dated 1632.
VAM : 1023-1871
From the Waterton collection.

The inscription reads *'saheb-i qiran-i sani'* and has the *hijra* year 1042 and the numeral 5. 'The Second Lord of the Auspicious Conjunction' was the title adopted by Shah Jahan in emulation of his ancestor Timur. The single numeral 5 indicates the regnal year and this, with the *hijra* year, gives a date between 19 July and 14 December 1632.
A similar ring of darkish green jade in the Salar Jung Musum, Hyderabad, bears the inscription in an identical cartouche but it is dated to the fourth regnal year, 1040 (see Nigam (1979) fig.29). The fourth year of Shah Jahan's reign began on 5 January 1631 and the *hijra* year ended on 29 July. RS

355a

Drinking cup
Nephrite jade.
Height : 6.3cm, *Length* : 17.8cm, *Width* : 11.8cm
Inscribed with the Persian couplet, in a lobed cartouche
shai-yi shahanshah giti sitan
shah jahan sani sahib qiran
'Article of the King of Kings, the World Conquerer
Shah Jahan, the Second Lord of the Conjunction'
and the dates 1057 (AH) and 21 (regnal) = 1647-48AD
Mughal, c.1647 or earlier
Lent by the British Museum, Department of Oriental Antiquities, Oscar Raphael Bequest, 1945.10-17-259.
The cup is carved from mottled green nephrite in the shape of a halved turban gourd (*cucurbita maxima*), split longitudinally with ribs between its five lobes. A rib moulding follows the rim and forms the stem of two pairs of leaves resembling scrolling half-palmettes, which meet opposite the 'turban' projection, where the stem would join the gourd in nature. The vessel is supported by a base of five overlapping spear-shaped leaves. Although the cup has hitherto been attributed to the date of its inscription it is possible that it could have been made as early as the end of Jahangir's reign when organic forms were first being copied in jade (cf. no.354).
A Turkish copy of the object exists, which may indicate that the cup later passed out of the Mughal Treasury and came into Ottoman possession. The copy, inscribed as being of Turkish workmanship, has hitherto been assumed to have been made in India (see Maynard (1963), p.88 fig.1, Welch (1963), pp.104, 170, pl.50).

Bibliography : Wilkinson (1934), p.187; Skelton (1962), p.44, fig.4, p.89; *idem.* (1966), pp.109-110 fig.8; Palmer (1967), p.63, pl.39; Grube (1967), p.160, fig.104. RS

356

Shah Jahan's wine cup
White nephrite jade, inscribed with the monogram of Shah Jahan *sahib-i qiran-i sani* 'Second Lord of the (auspicious) Conjunction'.
Length : 18.7cm, *Width* : 14cm
Mughal, dated 1067 AH (1657 AD)
VAM : IS 12-1962
The shape of the cup is based on that of a halved fruit or gourd, which tapers asymmetrically to the handle in the form of a realistically carved goat's head. The bowl is lobed and rests on a foot of lotus petals and acanthus leaves. This superbly designed and executed work is perhaps the finest known example of Mughal hardstone carving, and was probably made specifically for the Emperor himself, whose monogram would have been applied as soon as the cup was submitted for his approval. The overall design of the cup owes much of its inspiration to foreign models: the use of the gourd form for the bowl is basically Chinese, the pedestal support and acanthus leaves are European in origin, the fusion of animal and vegetal elements recalls European Mannerist hardstone carvings, while the use of lotus petals is characteristic of Hindu art. The fusion of all these disparate elements coupled with the realistic portrayal of natural forms typifies the essential features of Mughal art.
Bibliography : Skelton (1966); Irwin (1968), figs.12 & 13; Welch (1963), fig.5; Zebrowski (1981), fig.209. RC

357

Wine cup
Nephrite jade
Length : 13.3cm, *Width* : 8.2cm
Mughal, period of Shah Jahan (1628-58).
VAM : 02561 I.S.
The cup is of asymmetrical lobed form recalling a halved gourd and a leaf tapering towards a stem. Like the Shah Jahan cup (no.356), the bowl is carved in five tapering lobes which converge towards the spiral stem that forms the cup's handle. From the base of the stem emerge five acanthus leaves, one of which curls outwards to form a tiny volute projecting from the side of the cup in an echo of the shape of the

handle. Also like the Shah Jahan cup, the base is formed by a raised lotus blossom: its stem rises from behind the acanthus leaves, and it is flanked by two narcissus flowers. RC

358

Back-scratcher
Nephrite jade, in two shades of green, enamelled silver mounts, set with an imitation ruby.
Length : 58.4cm
Mughal; period of Shah Jahan (1628-58)
VAM : 02606 (IS)
From the collection of Col. Charles Seton Guthrie.
The shaft is cylindrical and of light green jade. The terminals, of flower and bud form, are of lighter colour and rejoined to the shaft by enamelled silver mounts. The flower head, with its curling petals, is related to the relief decoration of the buildings of Shah Jahan's reign. The imitation ruby at the centre of the flower has a claw setting and is probably a 19th century replacement. The silver mounts enamelled in translucent green, are in the style of European work of the late 16th or early 17th century and may be the work of a European craftsman at the court of Shah Jahan.
Bibliography : Skelton (1962) fig.12. RS

359

Crutch handle
Nephrite jade set with gems
Length : 13cm
Mughal, mid 17th century.
Private collection.
The handle is from a short prop (*zafar takieh* or 'cushion of victory') as used by mystics in meditation or rulers holding court. The staff very often conceals a blade for the owner's self protection. The handle is curved, to take the weight of the body under the shoulder, and terminates in two addorsed ibex heads joined at the necks with acanthus leaves carved in low relief at the junction of the shaft (missing). The carving of the heads is particularly sensitive and naturalistic with halters and tethering ropes skilfully depicted. The eyes are of banded agate in gold settings and there were five colourless gemstones set in silver on the heads and necks, of which one is missing and one replaced. RS

118

353   *355a*

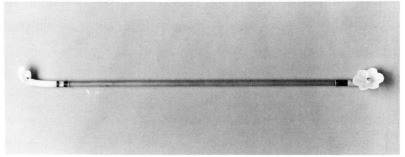

358

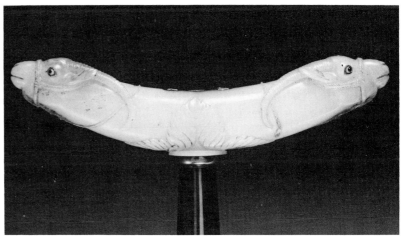

357   *359*

360
Covered potiche
Green nephrite jade flecked with brown.
Height : 11 cm, *Diameter (max)* : 11 cm
Mughal, c.1675
Lent by the British Museum
1945.10-17.258
The body is of flattened globular form
with a flared neck and ring base. There
are two handles in the shape of acanthus
leaves with pendant buds, and two rows
of acanthus leaves surround the base
and the shoulder of the pot. The neck is
decorated with overlapping lotus petals
carved in relief. The lid has a lotus bud
handle and is carved with lotus petals.
The whole piece is carved with precision
and delicacy on very thin jade.   RC

361
Plate
Nephrite jade.
Diameter : 25.2 cm
Mughal, late 17th century
Private collection.
The plate is of pale green jade with a
shallow cavetto. It is decorated with a
band around the interior edge, of serrated leaves which form pointed arches
over single flowering plants. Another
flower emerges from between the leaves.
There is a small many-petalled lotus
rosette in the centre. On the outside
edge of the cavetto is another, narrower
band of decoration, also of serrated
leaves with flowers springing from the
base of the stems.   RC

362
Wine pot
Green nephrite jade inlaid with enamelled gold.
Height : 10.4 cm, *Diameter* : 11.6 cm
Mughal, late 17th century, the enamel
added later, perhaps early 18th century.
VAM : 02594 & A I.S.
A wine vessel of squat, rounded shape
with a spout, a short flared neck and a
domed lid with a round handle. There is
a low foot formed of a lotus medallion
carved in shallow relief. The decoration
is of inlaid plant motifs (mostly poppies)
in red translucent enamel on gold with
touches of black and white opaque
enamel, with green opaque enamel in
the centre of the knob on the lid. Some
marking on the surface of the jade
opposite the spout may indicate that
there was once a handle, which was
removed probably before the addition
of the enamel.
Bibliography : Skelton (1962), fig.10;
Hambly (1968), fig.80.   RC

363
Hilt from a sword
Nephrite jade
Length : 13.2 cm
Mughal, late 17th century
Private collection.
The hilt is of green nephrite jade tinged
with ochre, the pommel carved in the
form of a camel's head. Finger grips are
provided by two ridges on the concave
edge. The base is carved in relief with
acanthus leaves and a lily flower. The
eye sockets of the camel are finely
engraved, but this has been obscured
by the clumsy re-insertion of rubies in a
gold setting.
Naturalistically carved animal heads,
more usually of horses or wild goats,
were favourite subjects for the decoration of weapon hilts at this time.   RS

364
Priming flask
Nephrite jade
Length : 13.7 cm x *greatest diameter*
3.3 cm
Mughal; 3rd quarter of the 17th century.
Private collection.
The jade flask is horn-shaped with a
convex cap closing its widest end. The
nozzle has been carved as the mouth of
a carp and the body of the flask is
carved with three poppy plants in low
relief with a fourth concentrically
arranged on the cap. The nephrite jade
is of a pale green colour with grey
speckled inclusions which have been
used by the craftsman to give a naturalistic colour to the throat of the fish. The
suspension chain is silver gilt.   RS

365
Spoon
Nephrite jade
Length : 16.2 cm
Mughal, c.1700
Private collection.
The bowl and handle are separately
made and joined with a dowel. Three
leaves are carved in relief on the under-
side of the bowl. The fragile curved
handle resembles a stem and terminates
with a spherical finial.   RS

366
Huqqa base
Nephrite jade, inlaid with coloured
nephrite, lapis lazuli and rubies set in
gold.
Height : 18.3 cm, *Diameter* : 17.0 cm
Mughal, c.1700
Lent by the British Museum,
1956.7-24.1.
The bowl is round with a flared neck,

which was made separately and joined
to the bowl, the join being concealed by
a gold thread. The surface of the bowl is
decorated with a trellis pattern of split
leaves joined by rosettes of dark green
nephrite, each rosette set with a small
ruby. Within each section of the trellis
is an iris flower of lapis lazuli. All the
leaves and flowers are carved to suggest
veins and petals. The neck is capped by
a rim of darker green jade and there is a
scrolling decoration of inlaid gold and
rubies around the top of the neck and
the flange which protrudes from it.
This *huqqa* bowl is one of a pair owned
by the British Museum. They rest on
elaborate French ormulu stands (not
exhibited) which were made in the late
18th century. They were owned by
William Beckford of Fonthill Abbey,
the noted collector, writer and recluse
(see no.90). Three other similar
huqqa bases are known: one in the
Victoria & Albert Museum (02593 I.S.),
one in the collection of the Maharana of
Mewar (Watt (1903), pl.75, no.7), and
another in a private collection in
England (Zebrowski (1981), fig.205). It
is probable that all these examples are
from the same workshop.
Bibliography : Skelton (1962), fig.7;
Palmer (1967), pl.44.   RC

367
Bottle with lid
Pale green nephrite jade mounted with
gold and set with rubies and emeralds.
Height : 25.3 cm, *Width* : 11.2 cm
Mughal, early 18th century
Private collection.
The bottle has a globular body, a tall
flared neck with a domed lid, and a
ribbed foot. The body is made up of
eight convex plaques held together by
vertical gold bands set with table-cut
emeralds. The top of the body is joined
to the neck by a band of chased gold
with a collar of alternate cabochon
rubies and table-cut emeralds in petal-
shaped settings.
The whole bottle is richly decorated
with gold inlay set with more rubies and
emeralds. On the body and upper part
of the neck, this is in a trellis pattern,
with rubies on the former and alternate
rubies and emeralds on the latter. On
the lid is an arabesque of gold set with
rubies and emeralds around the central
finial of gold with a ruby in a claw
setting. The interior of the lid, neck and
foot is lined with sheet gold. Inside the
neck is a grille of gold openwork forming
a six-petalled flower with a ruby at its
centre. A Persian inscription engraved

on the foot gives the weight as 93 *tolas*
and 10 *masas*. The present weight of
the vessel is 1123.1 grams, which gives
a value of 184.7 grains troy per *tola*.
This vessel is unusual not merely in the
opulence of its decoration but also in
two aspects of its craftsmanship. Firstly,
the construction of its globular body in
so many parts is surprising in view of
the fact that the technique of hollowing
out an interior of this type had been
thoroughly mastered by Indian carvers.
Secondly, the gems are mainly set by
the claw principle – discreetly in most
cases, but very conspicuously in the
case of the finial to the lid and inside
the neck. This is a European technique,
rare in India before the nineteenth
century, and still not generally employed
by traditional craftsmen. The rich
decorative effect and mode of chasing
the settings are paralleled on Muhammad Shah's enamelled throne in the
Topkapi Saray, and it is to the
emperor's reign that the bottle can
perhaps be ascribed.
Bibliography : Skelton (1962), no.9;
Irwin (1968), fig.18.   RS

368
Box and cover
Nephrite jade with silver mounts and
lock
Height : 5.7 cm, *Length* : 15.2 cm,
Width : 10.8 cm
Mughal, early 18th century
VAM : C.1947 & A – 1910
The box is leaf shaped in plan with
vertical sides and a domed lid held by a
hinge. The nephrite is carved in relief
with floral scrolls on the sides and a
vase containing a symmetrically stylised
flowering plant on the lid. It was presumably a container for *pan*.
The chased silver mounts and padlock
are later additions. For a comparable
example see Welch (1963), pl.55.   RS

369
Wine-cup
Pale greyish-green jade
Height : 5.2 cm, *Diameter* : 3.7 cm
Mughal, 18th century
VAM : 610-1874
From the collection of William Tayler,
an East India Company Civil Servant in
Bengal from 1829-1859.
The shape of this stem-cup derives
from Chinese porcelain, which was
keenly collected by the Mughal
emperors (cf. 401-3) and at the Muslim
courts of the Deccan.   SS

360

361

363

366

368

370

Pen box and cover

White nephrite jade, with diamonds, rubies and emeralds set in gold.
Length : 20.9cm, *Width* : 8.8cm
Mughal, late 18th century
VAM : 02549 I.S.

The interior of the box is in four compartments, the two smaller ones being ink-wells. The two open sections contain a matching set of writing accoutrements: a jade and jewelled knife, for trimming the nib, a small jade and jewelled spoon (for pouring ink?) and a pen holder, also of jade set with rubies and emeralds. RC

371

Thumb ring

Black hardstone
Inscribed in Persian: *as jahangir shah-i akbar shah* 'For King Jahangir (son of) King Akbar'.
Mughal, early 17th century
Lent by the Bharat Kala Bhavan, Banaras
Bibliography : *Chhavi* (1971), p.112, pl.8.

372

Wine cup of the Emperor Jahangir

Rock crystal (quartz) stained green
Height : 7.3cm, *Diameter* :12.1cm
Inscribed with Persian verses and dated (see below).
Mughal, 1021 AH/1612-13 AD
Private collection.

The cup is hemispherical with a flared foot and the walls are decorated with eight ogival cartouches, alternating in size, in which flowering plants are shown in relief by removal of the background. Thus, unlike later Mughal jade carvings, the floral decoration is flush with the surface rather than modelled in relief. The central zone containing these medallions is enclosed by two horizontal bands containing verse inscriptions in cartouches with cusped ends separated by quatrefoils. Beneath the footring are engraved a lotus rosette surrounded by smaller rosettes.

The six couplets of Persian verse may be read as follows:
(a) Upper band beneath rim:
This is the cup of water (of life), nourisher of the soul,
Of King Jahangir (son) of King Akbar,
Who can see from its shadow the dome of heaven.
(It is) the world-displaying cup (i.e. Jamshid's cup showing the events) on the face of the Earth.
Having poured the cup of his munificence over the world
He has caused the fountain of the spirit to flow.

Since this cup was completed at his command
May it be full of the Water of Life for ever.
(b) Lower band above foot:
May the seven climes be according to his desire;
May his cup be passed around eternally.
Its *hijri* year is obtained from the imprint 'The seventh year of the king's reign'. The date given in the chronogram formed by the last line *sanah haft-i julus-i padshahi* is AH 1021, which overlaps the seventh regnal year between 19 March 1612 and 20 February 1613. Previously it has been read as 1022 by inserting the second *alif* in the last word, where in poetry it is optional.

This early Mughal example of stained quartz carving is unique, although Goodchild (1908), pp.150-2, refers to the Indians' secret method of uniformly staining quartz. It was perhaps intended as a substitute for jade, which was a rare commodity in India in the early 17th century. Another unique feature is the mode of decoration which perhaps imitates the chasing of metal vessels, thus reflecting the experimental character of Mughal hardstone carving at this time. The cup formerly belonged to Sir Stephen Courtauld in Umtali who acquired it from Ganeshi Lall in Calcutta in 1926. The vendors stated that its previous owners included Sardar Mohamed Yakub Khan, Amir Sayed 'Ali Khan (Afghan) and the Amir of Bokhara (c.1875) for whom a fitted leather case was made (not exhibited).
Bibliography : Skelton (1972), p.104, fig.26e; Sotheby & Co. 23rd April 1979, lot 129. RS

372

373

Bowl

Rock crystal
Height : 8.2cm, *Diameter* : 12.8cm
Mughal, mid 17th century
VAM : 986-1875 I.S.

The bowl is carved in low relief with a design of lilies, whose stems divide the surface of the bowl into a series of vertical lobes. The alternate flowerheads and buds of the lilies form a

border around the rim of the bowl, and there is a border of acanthus leaves around the base.

This delicately carved bowl was probably made during the reign of Shah Jahan (1628-58), under whose patronage the art of hardstone carving reached its peak (cf. no.356).
Bibliography : Hambly (1968), fig.75. RC

373

374

Box and lid

Rock crystal, jewelled with gold settings and silver mounts.
Height : 8.9cm, *Length* : 13.0cm,
Width : 10.1cm
Mughal, early 18th century
VAM : 1671-1882 (Wells Bequest)

The box is of oval plan and convex section with a flared foot and the lid slightly domed to support a flat rectangular top. The sides and lid are set with rubies and emeralds in gold which is carved in a manner similar to that of the jade-inlaid bottle (no.367). Gold stems on the sides link eight jewelled rosettes and pairs of jewelled leaf sprays. The lid has jewelled sprigs surrounding and enclosed by a gold band containing a row of small rubies.*
There are related boxes in the British Museum and the Topkapi Saray Müzesi, Istanbul.
Bibliography : Skelton (1962), fig.8; Hambly (1968), pl.79; Latif (1982) p.157, no.12.

*The silver mounts and hinges attaching the lid are of later workmanship. RS

374

375

Relief portrait bust of Shah Jahan

by a Northern European craftsman at the Mughal court, c.1630-40.
Alabaster with polychrome
Height : 11.5cm, *Width* : 8.4cm
Lent by the Rijksprentenkabinet of the Rijksmuseum, Amsterdam, no.12249.

The Emperor is shown richly jewelled in profile at the *jharokha* window where he made his public appearances, his hand resting on the cloth covering the balcony rail. It has been suggested by Herman Goetz (1958 (p.45)) that the sculptor was Italian but the legacy of 15th-16th century Italian art is almost certainly transmitted here by a Franco-Flemish hand. The model for the portrait is clearly a Mughal miniature as in the case of the cameos (nos. 376-379), but the frame moulding is of European inspiration.
Bibliography : Amsterdam (1973), no.865. RS

375

376

Cameo

Sardonyx
Height : 2.3cm, *Width* : 2.0cm
Work of a European at the Mughal court, c.1630-40.
VAM : IS 14-1974

This oval portrait cameo of Shah Jahan shows him at about the age of forty-five and was presumably made by one of the emperor's European lapidaries after a Mughal painting. RS

122

376

377
Cameo
Sardonyx with enamelled gold setting
Height : 6.7cm, *Width* : 7.2cm
Inscribed in Persian: *shabih-i sahib-i qiran-i sani shah jahan padshah-i ghazi* and at the bottom: *amal-i kan atamm* 'Likeness of the Second Lord of the (Auspicous) Conjunction, Shah Jahan, the King, Warrior of the Faith' – 'Work of Kan Attam (Supreme Engraver)'.
Probably the work of a European at the Mughal court, c.1630-40.
Lent by the Bibliothèque Nationale, Paris.
The cameo depicts Shah Jahan as a prince attacking a lion, which mauls Jahangir's officer, Anup Ray. The event occurred in December 1610, when Anup Ray was savaged while bravely defending Jahangir from a lion during a hunt. The incident is also depicted in Mughal miniatures including f.134v. of the Windsor Library manuscript of the *Badshah Nama*. None of the published paintings showing this subject provide a precise model for the cameo but part of its composition is shared with a miniature in the Baroda Museum (P.G.5c-111).
The title *Kan Atamm* may well have been awarded to a European as in the case of Austin of Bordeaux, who was given the title *Hunarmand* (Skilful) by Jahangir.

European travellers mention a number of French and Italian jewellers and lapidaries at the court under Jahangir and Shah Jahan and although the sources do not clearly suggest a possible candidate for this title, he was clearly an accomplished exponent of cameo carving.
Bibliography : Babelon (1879), I, pp.197-8, no.366, II, pl.XLII; Goetz (1959), p.224; Hambly (1968), fig.12; Gascoigne (1971), p.195; Paris (1971), no.301; Paris (1977), no.702; *Tuzuk*, I, pp.186-7; Gangoly (1961), p.17, pl.IV; Ivanov, *et al.* (1962), pls.64-5.　　RS

378
Cameo
Sardonyx set in jade with gold wire
Length : 4.1cm, *Width* : 3.4cm
Perhaps Mediterranean work in the East (c. 1st – 2nd centuries AD), the setting Mughal; mid 17th century.
Lent by Mr. Richard Falkiner.
The three-layer sardonyx is carved in high relief to show a frolicking horse with its rear legs turned upwards in the manner of Scythian metal ornaments. The choice of material and quality of carving suggest early Imperial Roman workmanship although the treatment of the head is unusually sensitive. If it was made by a Mediterranean craftsman in the Kushan Empire, where animal-style ornaments were known, it could well have entered Mughal possession via Afghanistan, where Roman and Kushano-Roman objects have been found. The white jade setting, in the form of an oval button, is carved on the front with lotus petals framing the cameo and two pointed leaves joined by stems recalling the S-curve of the horse. The leaves are raised and drilled to provide loops for fixing the ornament to a coat or turban.
Bibliography : Paris (1975), pl.184.　　RS

379
Cameo
Sardonyx
Height : 2.9cm, *Width* : 4.0cm
Mughal (?), second quarter of the 17th century.
Lent by the Bibliothèque Nationale, Paris.
The subject of the cameo is a sleeping lion, which is far more stylised and rhythmic in outline than the lion represented on no.377. It has hitherto been regarded as a Sassanian example but recently the possibility of its having been made at the Mughal court has been suggested, and it is included here for comparison with the three known examples that have Mughal associations (nos.376-378).
Bibliography : Babelon (1897), I, p.196, no.364; II, pl.XLII.　　RS

379

380
Seal
Agate
Diameter : 3.5cm
Inscribed in Persian: *sharaf ud-din husain banda-yi 'adil badshah ghazi 1057*. 'Sharaf ud-Din Husain servant of the Just Emperor, Warrior of the Faith 1057 AH.'
Mughal, 1057/1647-8
Lent by the National Museum, New Delhi, 56.57/5.
This is evidently the personal seal of a minor office-holder under Shah Jahan. If this is the seal of Sharaf ud-Din, a son of Bahramand Khan, who was replaced as News Writer in the Khan-i Saman's Office in the 33rd year of Aurangzeb (1689), he would have been in the Imperial Service for over 40 years. (See *Ma'athir-ul-Umara* I, pp.366 and 665.)
　　RS

381
Bowl
Agate with metal rim
Height : 5.7cm, *Width* : 12.1cm
Mughal, mid 17th century.
Lent by the Los Angeles County Museum of Art (from the Nasli and Alice Heeramaneck collection).
This bowl is of honey-coloured agate in

six lobes, with a gilt metal rim and a plain round foot.
Although its design is simple, it has a sensuous quality of outline and material.
Bibliography : Welch (1964), fig.52 and p.104; Boston (1966), no.226.　　RC

382
Thumb ring
Agate with two circular inclusions
Length : 3.1cm, *Width* : 2.9cm
Mughal, 17th century
VAM : IS 42-1981
From the collection of Sir Andrew Fountaine (1676-1753) of Narford Hall. Sir Andrew Fountaine was a noted 18th century connoisseur who built up collections of porcelain, paintings, books and other objects. He was a friend of various luminaries of the period, including Jonathan Swift who mentions 'sauntering at china-shops and booksellers' with Fountaine in *Journal to Stella*; 'china-shops' in this case meant places where porcelain and curiosities from the East were sold.　　SS

382

383
Perfume bottle
Agate with gold and enamel
Length : 7cm,
Mughal, mid 18th century
Lent by the National Museum, New Delhi. 62.602.
This small agate bottle is carved in the shape of a mango. The gold stopper, which has milled sides to the knob, fits into a circular gold collar surrounding the opening. A gold rosette is fixed to one side of the bottle. The gold surfaces are enamelled with flowers in translucent green and red with opaque white.
RS

377

378

384
Leopard's head finial
Agate, inlaid with gemstones
Height : 8.5cm, *Width* : 10.5cm
Ascribed to Mughal India, 17th or 18th
century.
Lent by the British Museum, Dept. of
Oriental Antiquities OA-10617.
The finial is perhaps from the arm of a
throne. A cylindrical hollow underneath,
a groove at the back and holes for pins
at the top and back were provided for
fixing it in place. It is carved to show a
snarling mask, its eyes inlaid with
emeralds and citrines (?).
The head has formerly been identified
as that of a tiger and a suggestion made
that it formed part of Tipu Sultan's
throne (Forrest, 1970, p.357). This is
not possible (cf. nos 346, 347) and the
Indian origin of the object is also not
beyond doubt. Despite the coarseness
of execution, the object is nevertheless
impressive, and its exhibition with
other Mughal hardstones may help to
resolve the uncertainty of its origin and
date. It is believed to have formed part
of the Townley collection.   RS

124

384

Glass & ceramics

385
Huqqa
Glass bowl with ring to keep it stable.
Height : 40cm
Mughal, c.1700-1765
Lent by the National Museum, Copenhagen, Department of Ethnography:
EEc5
Analysis of the *huqqa* bowl shows it to
be lead glass and therefore a European
product of not earlier than about the
turn of the 18th century (cf.394).
The *huqqa* is a water pipe, the bowl
usually of spherical or bell shape, with a
detachable tobacco bowl and a long
tube through which the cooled smoke is
drawn. In its simplest form a *huqqa* may
be merely a coco-nut shell with a reed
stem and without a 'snake' or tube, but
the exhibition includes only the more
courtly examples. The tube may be
bound with silk, as here, or have a
separate cloth cover designed *en suite*
with the *huqqa* mat (251). The *huqqa*
bowl can be of various media, the most
splendid here being that from Powis
with its tobacco bowl, cover and intermediate ring all of silver, enamelled and
set with gems. Also in silver and enamelled is a *huqqa* base from Lucknow
(340) with other examples from elsewhere in *bidri* (472), brass (504), pottery
(405) and glass (386).
Tobacco appears to have been introduced to the Mughal court at the end of
Akbar's reign. In 1604 Asad Beg, one of
the emperor's officers, returned from a
mission to Bijapur and notes in his
memoirs:
'In Bijapur I had found some tobacco.
Never having seen the like in India, I
brought some with me, and prepared a
handsome pipe of jewel work' which he
then presented to Akbar. He concludes
his account: 'As I had brought a large
supply of tobacco and pipes, I sent
some to several of the nobles, while
others sent to ask for some; indeed all,
without exception, wanted some, and
the practice was introduced. After that
the merchants began to sell it, so the
custom of smoking spread rapidly. His
Majesty, however, did not adopt it.'
(Elliot 1953 pp.102-4).
Bibliography : Dam-Mikkelsen and
Lundbaek (1980) p.103 which notes the
huqqa having been in inventories of
1765-1771, and 1775.   SS

385

386

386

Huqqa base

Clear glass painted with lotuses in red, yellow and green, outlined in gold.
Height : 19.1cm, *Diameter* : 17.6cm
Mughal, 18th century
Lent by Los Angeles County Museum. From the Nasli M. Heeramaneck Collection, Museum Associates Purchase: M.76.2.12.
Bibliography : Welch (1963) pl.81; Beach (1966) no.234; Dikshit (1969) pl.XIb.SS

387

Huqqa base

Green glass with gilt floral decoration.
Height : 19.1cm
Mughal, first half of the 18th century
Lent by the Trustees of the British Museum: 1961.10-16.1. Bequeathed to the museum by Louis C.G. Clarke. The *huqqa* base is almost identical in shape and size to the V & A example (388) with its compressed spherical body, broad neck and pronounced kick in the base. The decoration on the body is a broad frieze containing poppy plants within narrow horizontal borders, with 4 single flowers on the neck.
Bibliography : Ashton (1948) no.1236(b) p.233; Pinder-Wilson (1962); Harden (1968) no.162; Zebrowski in Gray (1981) fig.204.   SS

388

Huqqa base

Green glass, painted in gold and yellow.
Height : 18.9-19.5cm, *Diameter* : 17.8cm
Mughal, first half of the 18th century
VAM : IM 15-1930
The *huqqa* base has a leaf design reserved against the green metal. Pale yellow, painted directly on to the glass, indicates the veins of the leaves.
A *huqqa* base with similar decoration, though of a completely different shape, is in the Salar Jung Museum, Hyderabad (see Dikshit (1969) pl.XXIIA).
Bibliography : VAM : Annual Review 1930 fig.25; Ashton (1950) p.233 no.1236(b); Dikshit (1969) pl.VI; VAM *Indian Art* 1978 p.23   SS

389

Huqqa base

Clear glass with applied decoration, gilt.
Height : 17.4cm, *Diameter* : 16.4cm
Mughal, 18th century
VAM : IM 109-1923
The decoration on this piece derives from metalwork, with pieces of glass, foil-backed to imitate precious stones, set into glass 'cloisons'. The beaded borders are of applied white glass.
Bibliography : Dikshit (1969) pl.VIIA.SS

390

Huqqa base

Purple glass with gilt and painted applied decoration.
Height : 18.5cm,
Diameter : base 16.8cm
Mughal, first half of the 17th century
Lent anonymously.
The main floral decoration on the body and neck, and the borders of palmettes, beads and floral scrolls are all of delicately applied white glass which has then been painted with yellow, green, orange and gold. Narrow chevron borders and the collar on the neck are painted in gold directly onto the purple metal.   SS

391

Huqqa base

Slightly cloudy colourless glass with cobalt blue trailed decoration, gilt.
Height : 16.2cm, *Diameter* : 15.4cm
Mughal, second half of 18th century
VAM : IM 91-1948
Bibliography : Dikshit (1969) pl.XIVD.
SS

392

Huqqa base

Clear glass encased in pale cobalt blue, part cut back, with gilt decoration.
Height : 17cm
Mughal, first half of the 18th century
Lent by Pilkington Glass Museum: 1974/7.
Bibliography : illustrated in *Journal of Glass Studies* New York 1974 vol.XVI p.127 and in Newman (1977) p.153.   SS

393

Ewer

Cobalt blue glass with painted gold decoration.
Height : 28.2cm
Mughal, 18th century
Lent by the Trustees of the British Museum, London: S343.
Bequeathed to the Museum by Felix Slade in 1868.
The decoration of flowers within foliate cartouches is in horizontal registers between narrow borders. These consist of two thin gold bands which contain triangles or lozenges, themselves containing stylised leaves or leaf sections. This border is identical to those on the bottle and cups (397 and 398), which with the similarity of some of the floral decoration suggests the same centre of manufacture.
Bibliography : Nesbitt (1871) pl.XI; Harden (1968) no.163.   SS

125

388   *389*

391   *392*

393

394

Rosewater sprinkler (gulabpash)

Lead glass, the bowl mould-blown, the neck attached separately.

Height : 28.2cm, *Diameter* : 10.5cm

Probably English; first half of the 18th century

VAM : 13-1893

Although this rosewater sprinkler was acquired in Bijapur as 16th century Indian work, analysis in the V & A has shown it to be lead glass and therefore not earlier than about the turn of the 18th century, by which time Ravenscroft's discoveries had been perfected. During this century a considerable trade developed in English glass made for the East with, for example, *Rheads Weekly Journal* of 17 September, 1737 reporting the exportation of 6306 pieces to India (see Buckley 1932).

Bibliography : Cole (1883) pl.XXXVIII; Dikshit (1969) p.99 and pl.XXIXB: see also Digby (1973) pp.88-89. SS

394

395

Bottle

Opaque pale cobalt blue glass, mould blown with floral design in relief painted in pink, yellow, white, green and gold.

Height : 13.7cm, *Width* : 6.6cm

Western India or Deccan; 18th century

VAM : 1891ᵃ-1855

Bibliography : Dikshit (1969) p.108 and plates XXXIII, XXXV B and C. cf. Pope (1938-9) Part VI pl.1451 D; see Digby (1973) pp.94-5. SS

395

396

Bottle with silver cap

Opaque cobalt blue glass with polychrome gilt decoration, the cap made from a Dutch coin mounted in silver.

Height : 13.8cm, *Width* : 6cm

Western India or Deccan; 18th century

VAM : 14-1867

The cap is made from a 6 stuivers coin of the Netherlands (Provinces of Holland and W. Friesland) c.1671-4, according to the Department of Coins and Medals at the British Museum. This bottle, and the one preceding it, represents a type which has been described as Dutch production for the Indian market. Despite a passing resemblance to 'case' bottles of the Netherlands, and the presence of Dutch coins forming part of the silver caps on this and three other V & A examples (all acquired from the same collection in 1867), these are all almost certainly wholly Indian. The stamp on the silver cap is Dutch but indicates

396

that the object is of foreign manufacture and was in the Netherlands between 1814, when this type of mark was introduced (Tardy p.322), and its acquisition by the museum. The imperfect metal of the body would not be characteristic of 18th century European wares and the painting is Indian in style. The figural scenes on two faces depict Leyla and Majnun, the other sides having floral decoration.

Bibliography : Dikshit (1969) Plates XXXIII, XXXIV A, C & D. SS

397

Bottle

Cobalt blue glass mould-blown with painted gold decoration.

Height : 18cm

Mughal, early 18th century

VAM : C.143-1936

From the Wilfred Buckley Collection of glass given by Mrs Buckley in memory of her husband.

The bottle has a rectangular body, each side painted with a vase holding a profusion of flowers standing on a fruit-laden tray. The vase on each of the wider panels has an animal head and crown incised into the gold. The cups (398) and saucer (399) were all acquired together and the decoration of the cups and bottle is closely comparable. Digby (p.94) notes a pair of bottles found in association with a cup in the Musée de Verre, Lièges (*Journal of Glass Studies*

397

XI 1969 p.119 no.59).

Bibliography : exhibited at the Persian exhibition of 1931 (no.299E); Pope vol.VI pl.1449B. SS

398

Two cups

Cobalt blue glass with painted gold decoration.

Diameter : 7cm

Mughal, early 18th century

VAM : C.140 and 141-1936

From the Wilfred Buckley Collection of glass given by Mrs Buckley in memory of her husband.

The cups were acquired, with the bottle and saucer (397 and 399) from the glass dealer, A. Churchill.

Bibliography : exhibited at the Persian exhibition of 1931 at the Royal Academy (no.299D); Pope vol.VI pl.1449. SS

399

Saucer

Blue glass with painted gold decoration.

Diameter : 14cm

Mughal, early 18th century

VAM : C.142-1936

From the Wilfred Buckley Collection of glass given by Mrs Buckley in memory of her husband.

Bibliography : exhibited at the Persian exhibition of 1931 at the Royal Academy (no.299F); Pope vol.VI pl.1449. SS

400

Bowl, cover and stand
Blue glass with painted gold decoration.
Height : (pot and cover) 12.6cm
Diameter : (stand) 11.5cm
Mughal, 18th century
Lent by the Trustees of the British
Museum: 78.12-30.324.
Bequeathed to the Museum by
J. Henderson, Esq. in 1878.   SS

401

Dish from Jahangir's household
Porcelain with yellow glaze.
Diameter : 21.5cm
Engraved on the footring in Persian
tughra script; *shah jahangir-i akbar
shah* 'King Jahangir (son) of King
Akbar', *1021* (1612-13 AD and below,
28 tola 2 masha.
Chinese; mark and period of Hung Chih
(1488-1505)
VAM : 551-1878
The inscriptions are illustrated by J.A.
Pope (1956), pl.6J. A comparable dish
is in the Avery Brundage Collection, see
S. Valenstein (1970), no.29, p.57. The
actual weight of this dish is 336.1 grams
giving a value of 184.14 grains Troy to
the *tola*.   RS

402

**Dish from the household of Shah
Jahan**
Porcelain with blue and white
decoration.
Diameter : 43.3cm
Inscribed on the underside with a circular *waqf* seal of Shah 'Abbas Safavi
and engraved outside the foot: *shah
jahan ibn jahangir shah 1053* 'Shah

Jahan son of Jahangir Shah, 1053/
1643-4.'
Chinese; early 15th century
On loan to the Metropolitan Museum of
Art, New York.
The dish has a foliate rim decorated
with waves, fungus and flower sprays
alternating on the *cavetto* and three
bunches of grapes with vine leaves and
tendrils in the centre. The underside of
the *cavetto* has twelve floral sprays.
Evidently it was donated by Shah
'Abbas I to the shrine of Shah Safi at
Ardebil and subsequently found its way
into the possession of Shah Jahan. A
companion plate still remains in the
Ardebil collection. A further inscription
on the foot-rim gives the weight as 251
tolas (8lbs Troy).
Bibliography : Rubin (1975), pp.287-
290; Pope (1956), pl.37; B. Gray
(1967), pp.21-37; A. Wardwell & R.D.
Mowry (1981), p.69; Christie's (15 July
1981), lot 73.   RS

403

Pilgrim flask
Porcelain
Height : 20.5cm
Engraved with the name of the Mughal
emperor 'Alamgir (Aurangzeb) and the
date 1070 AH/1659-60 AD.
Chinese, early 15th century
Lent by the British Museum, Depart-
ment of Oriental Antiquities (Sedgwick
Bequest), 1968-4.22-32.
The flask is decorated in mottled under-
glaze blue with a peony design and lotus
petals at the base and neck, which has
been cut down.
Bibliography : Burlington Fine Arts

Club (1910), pl.XXXVI, L23; Burlington
House (1935-6), no.1470; Oriental
Ceramics Society (1953), no.44;
Koyama (1974), vol.V, pl.160.   RS

404

Cup and saucer (gobelet-litron)
Porcelain, with shaped panels of polychrome painted flowers and other
ornament reserved on a yellow ground.
Cup: *Height* : 7cm *Diameter* : 6.5cm
Saucer: *Height* : 3.5cm,
Diameter : 13.5cm
Sèvres, 1786; from a set presented to
Tipu Sultan by Louis XVI.
Lent by the National Trust, Powis Castle.
The cup and saucer each have an inter-
laced 'L' on the base containing the
letters 'ii' for 1786 above a quaver in
blue enamel. This quaver is the mark of
the painter Antoine-Toussaint Cornaille
(worked at Sèvres 1755-92 and 1794-
1800). The cup and saucer both have
incised marks '41' on the bottom and
the cup also has '7'.
The set of twelve cups and saucers,
with grounds of different colours, formed
part of the presents sent to Tipu Sultan
by Louis XVI following the arrival in
1788 of three ambassadors from Mysore
bringing gifts from the Sultan to the
King of France. The records of the
Manufactures Royales refer to the
porcelain '*à fleurs, sans figures d'hommes
ni d'animaux.*'
Bibliography : Brunet (1961) pp.275-
283.   VM

405

Huqqa base
Jasper ware, blue with white applied
decoration in Wedgwood style.
Height : 18.8cm, *Diameter* : 18.6cm
Made by Turner & Co. of Lane End,
Staffordshire; impressed mark on the
base: TURNER
English; late 18th century or early 19th
century
Lent anonymously.
John Turner established a factory at
Lane End, Longton in Staffordshire
which maintained production until
1829. John Turner seems to have
discovered jasper independently of
Wedgwood and the composition of early
Turner wares was slightly different.
Generally, Turner products have a more
vitreous appearance, though Hillier
notes that most of the classical reliefs
used as decoration were copied from
Wedgwood designs. By 1781 Turner
had a shop, warehouse and workrooms
in Fleet Street and a draft for a news-
paper advertisement for these premises

comments: 'Captains and others going
to the East Indies will find here a more
general assortment of goods properly
adapted for that Country than at any
other house in the Kingdom – with this
singular advantage, that they may have
new Patterns done to their own fancy at
a very short notice for every voyage.'
(see Hillier, 1965).   SS

127

405

398 & 399

Arms & armour

406
Knife (kard)
Blade length : 17.7cm, *Hilt length* :
29.9cm
Watered steel blade inlaid with gold,
jade hilt; inscribed on the back of the
ferrule in gold: *sahib-i qiran-i sani, 2*
Mughal, c.1620-30
Private collection.
The grip is cylindrical, tapering slightly,
flat at the back, the pommel carved as
the head of a youth wearing a ruff and
single drop earrings, with his hair in
snail-shell curls. The blade is finely
watered and inlaid with a royal umbrella
mark in gold. The ferrule is inlaid in
gold with a band of floral scroll and the
chamfers with a pair of fish. The back of
the blade at the fort is inlaid with a row
of gold quatrefoils. In knives of this
type the scabbard extends to the
pommel. This is seen in the portrait of
Prince Salim (no.50) where a similar
kard is shown with a youthful head
forming the pommel.
It is plausible that the hilt of this knife
was made for Jahangir in about 1620
and that the blade was replaced early in
Shah Jahan's reign.
Howard Ricketts suggests that the head
may have been copied from a Goanese
ivory of Christ as the Good Shepherd.
Formerly in the collection of Samuel
Morse (inventor of the Morse code). RS

407
Dagger and scabbard
The hilt crystal set with rubies and
emeralds, the blade watered steel inlaid
with gold, the scabbard covered with
silk brocade, gilt locket and chape.
Length : 29.8cm
Mughal, 17th century
Lent by The David Collection, Copenhagen: 33/79.
The crystal hilt has a pommel in the
form of a camel's head, its trappings
and eyes set with rubies and emeralds
in gold. The grip is inlaid with delicate
floral sprays of chased gold set with
rubies and emeralds and there is chased
gold floral decoration on the blade at
the forte. SS

408
Knife (kard?)
Steel with jewelled jade hilt
Length : 25cm,
Blade length : 15.4cm
Mughal, mid-17th century
Private collection.

The watered steel blade has inlaid *koftgari* decoration of floriate scrolls at the
bolster. The elegant hilt terminates in a
wild goat's head with eyes and a ruby
collar set in gold.
Such small personal knives were housed
in the sheath of larger knives or weapons.
RS

409
Dagger and scabbard
The hilt white jade set with a ruby and
inlaid with enamelled gold, steel blade
overlaid with gold, wood scabbard
covered with red velvet, gilt locket and
tassels of gold and silver thread and
coloured silks.
Length : 41cm, *Blade length* : 26.7cm,
Scabbard length : 33.5cm
Mughal, 17th century
Lent by the National Trust, Powis
Castle.
The white jade hilt has a ram's head
pommel, carved and set with onyx eyes
and a large ruby in gold. The grip is
inlaid with two gold flowers, enamelled
in translucent red and green with opaque
white. The blade is watered steel with
gold overlaid scroll decoration on the
back. The blade's steel bolsters are
overlaid with gold birds.
The dagger is in an inventory of c.1774
listing Clive's possessions at Claremont
('A curious Dagger w^h Goatshead
curiously carv'd large Ruby on the head
and 2 Sardonyx Eyes') and again in an
inventory dated 17 March 1775 of his
Indian curiosities (manuscripts at
Powis Castle). SS

410
Dagger (khanjar)
Steel with ivory hilt
Length : 38.5cm, *Blade length* : 26cm
Mughal, late 17th century
Private collection.
The finely watered recurved steel blade
has a cusped re-inforcement at the fort
which is decorated with floral arabesques in two colours of gold on a
cross-hatched ground, the centre flowers
having silver stamens.
The ivory hilt has a cusped quillon
block with acanthus leaves and poppy
flowers carved in relief. The pommel
takes the form of a horse's head with
inlaid eyes. Polychrome stains have
been applied to the relief detail. The
blade has been re-ground. RS

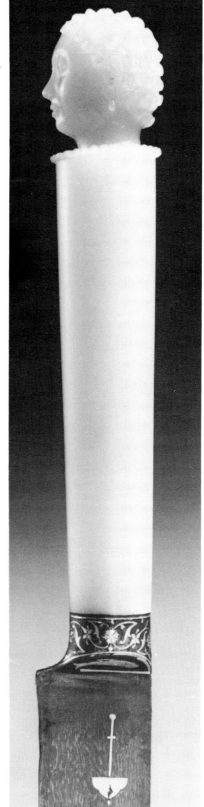

407

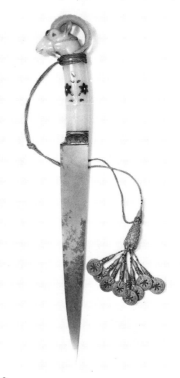

406   409

411
Dagger
Steel with jade hilt and enamelled sheath
Length : 31cm
Mughal or Deccani, first half of the 18th century
Lent by the British Museum, Henderson Bequest, 78.12-30.875.
The fine watered steel blade has three ribs on each side terminating in lily flowers and bracts at the fort. The jade hilt is carved as a horse's head at the pommel with inlaid eyes. The quillon block has relief carving of split acanthus leaves and lily flowers. The velvet covered sheath has an enamelled gold locket and chape.
According to the previous owner, the dagger was given by Haidar 'Ali of Mysore (d.1782) to Sir Hector Munro.
RS

412
Dagger and scabbard
The hilt white jade set with rubies, diamonds and emeralds in gold, the blade steel. The scabbard covered with red velvet with jewelled jade locket and chape.
Length : 39cm, *Blade length* : 26.2cm, *Scabbard length* : 31.5cm
Mughal, late 17th century
Lent by the National Trust, Powis Castle.
This is probably the dagger in the inventory of Lord Clive's possessions at Claremont of c.1774: 'A Curious Dagger w^h Jadd handle mounted w^h Diamonds Rubies & Emeralds set in Gold' and again in a list of Clive's Indian Curiosities dated 17 March 1775 (both manuscripts at Powis Castle).   SS

413
Dagger and scabbard
The hilt of pale greyish-green jade with ribbed baluster grip and carved floral decoration, the blade watered steel, the scabbard covered with red velvet with gilt metal locket and chape.
Length : 37.5cm, *Blade length* : 23.5cm, *Scabbard length* : 27cm
Mughal, late 17th – early 18th century
Lent by the National Trust, Powis Castle.
The decoration of carved irises and palmettes is reminiscent of architectural carved marble and uses an architectural form in its baluster grip. The hilt originally had a jade knuckle guard which has been broken off and lost.   SS

414
Dagger and scabbard
The hilt of pale greyish-green jade; the blade of steel; the scabbard covered with red velvet and with jade locket and chape.
Length : 37.5cm, *Blade length* : 23.5cm, *Scabbard length* : 27cm
Mughal, 18th century
Lent by the National Trust, Powis Castle, POW/G/8.
The pommel is in the form of five lotus buds; the hilt and chape are both carved with lotus-flower decoration.

415
Knife and scabbard
The hilt pale green jade set with emeralds, rubies and a diamond, the blade watered and overlaid with gold, the scabbard wood, covered with green velvet, enamelled gold locket and chape.
Length : 25cm, *Blade length* : 16.7cm
Mughal, 17th century
Lent by the Trustees of the British Museum, Department of Oriental Antiquities: 78.12-30.923.
Bequest of J. Henderson, Esq., 1878.
Knives of this type are seen in paintings from the reign of Jahangir onwards, hanging from the belt, usually with a group of thumbrings attached by separate cords.
The hilt of this example has silk tassels with four pale green jade pendants; the locket and chape are enamelled in translucent red and two shades of green on a white ground.   SS

129

413

411

412

414

416

Dagger

Watered steel blade, hilt of blade with rubies and emeralds set in gold.

Length : 23cm, *Width* : 4cm

Mughal, c.1625

Private collection.

The finely watered blade has a central rib and is decorated on the fort with a floral arabesque executed in *koftgari* on cross-hatching. The hilt has separate short straight quillons with a collar that may have been imitated from an early 17th century English model. One of the quillon ends is convex, the other concave. The hilt and the sheath are of pale green jade inlaid with rubies and emeralds set in gold. There is a design of birds flying or perched on a lattice of stems. The scabbard is edged with rows of rubies. Both locket and chape are formed of rubies and emeralds set in gold, which in the case of the locket is finely chased with foliate decoration (cf.nos.303 and 322 and also Norman (1971), fig.1).

The bifurcated pommel is typical of knives worn during Jahangir's reign (see also no.417) and perhaps has some distant relationship with Italian and Spanish 'ear' daggers and Near Eastern types such as the Turkish *yataghan*, which may have influenced the development of both the European and Indian examples. Possibly the Turkish form originated from the use of natural bones with the joints serving as pommels. Daggers such as this one may be seen in several paintings of the time of Jahangir, such as *Jahangir entertaining Shah Abbas* (Freer Gallery, Washington), *Prince Khurram being weighed* (British Museum) [no.40], and *The Princes of the house of Timur* (Chester Beatty Library) [no.53]. RS

417

Dagger

Steel with jewel-encrusted crystal hilt.

Length : 29cm

Mughal, early 17th century

Lent by the Maharaja Sawai Man Singh Museum, Jaipur, no.1275.

The dagger is a *kard* with a watered blade and floral *koftgari* decoration on the bolster. The rock crystal hilt has a bifurcated pommel of the type associated with the Emperor Jahangir (see no.416). This has been re-inlaid with cabuchon rubies and sapphires set in gold wire. A knife of this type is shown on a tray in a painting of Jahangir weighing Prince Khurram (no.40). RS

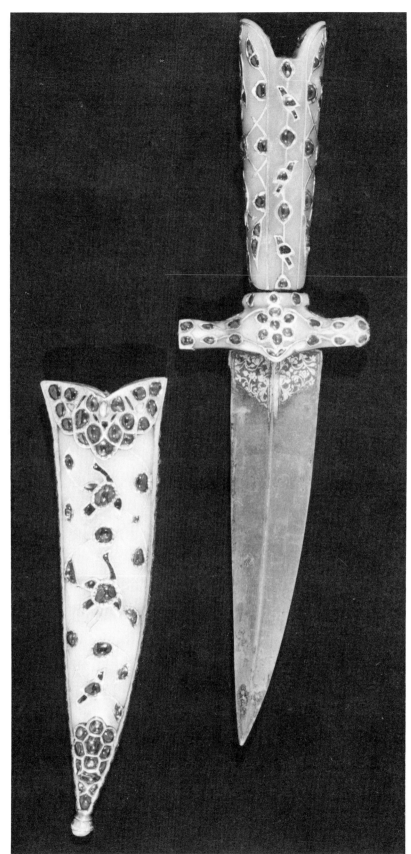

416

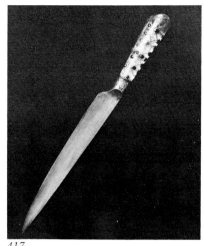

417

418

Dagger (khanjar)

Plain recurved steel blade with enamelled gold hilt, locket and chape.

North Indian (Mughal or Rajput), second half of the 18th century.

Private collection.

The principal motif of the hilt and scabbard mounts is a diaper of translucent green lotus leaves with opaque blue and white flowers at the foot of each. The pommel and quillon block are decorated with acanthus leaves in the same colours and set with rubies. The locket and chape have the same palette with the addition of translucent red on the button, finials and locket rim and suspension ring. The scabbard is covered with worn green velvet. The dagger is said to have once been in the treasury of the Nizams of Hyderabad. For a related piece see Spink & Sons (1980), no.16. RS

419

Dagger (khanjar)

Steel with ivory hilt

Length : 37cm, *Blade length* : 24.2cm

Deccani (Bijapur) or perhaps Mughal, early 17th century

Lent by the Jagdish and Kamla Mittal Museum of Indian Art, Hyderabad 76.1527.

The ribbed watered steel blade has a slight double curve. The hilt is carved in low relief to show floral arabesque against a black-stained ground. RS

420

Dagger hilt

Iron with traces of gilding

Height : 12.4cm, *Width* : 9cm

Mughal or Deccani; 16th-17th century

Private collection.

The hilt is detached from a *jamdhar*, the

418

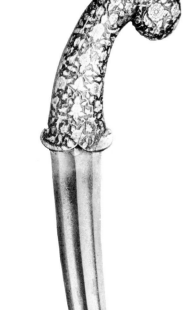

419

420

grip decorated with a series of mouldings from which sepals radiate where it meets the curved pommel and guard. The pommel is surmounted by a pair of leopards, carved in openwork.　RS

421
Dagger
Steel, the hilt with twisted grip, lotus bud finial and animal-head quillons, traces of gold overlaid decoration, the blade watered, with carved scenes on both faces at the forte.
Length : 31 cm, *Blade length* : 20.2 cm
Mughal, early 17th century
VAM : IS 86-1981
The blade has a well-defined central rib on each face and an armour-piercing point. At the forte on each face is a scene carved in low relief and lightly chased: on one side a figure mounted on an elephant spears an attacking tiger, on the other, an elephant and horse, both with riders, are shown fighting. Beneath the tiger are drilled numerals. The quillons and finial are overlaid with gold on a cross-hatched ground (see Bauer in Elgood (1979) for notes on this technique) and there are also traces of gold on the grip.　SS

131

421

422
Dagger
Steel, the hilt with relief decoration of flowers and cypress trees, traces of gilding, the blade watered.
Length : 34.9cm, *Blade length* : 20.9cm
Mughal, second half of the 17th century
Lent anonymously. SS

422a
Dagger (peshkabz)
Steel blade with silver hilt.
Mughal, 17th century
Lent by Maharana Sawai Man Singh II Museum, Jaipur. Mus. No.1748.
The pommel of the dagger is in the form of a ram's head with tightly curled fleece and curling horns. It was formerly in the armoury of the palace at Amber. It is very similar to the one worn by Maharana Jawan Singh of Mewar in no.156.
Bibliography : Welch (1963), no.68. RC

423
Dagger
Steel with moulded, pierced and chased decoration.
Length : 33.7cm, *Blade length* : 21cm
Mughal, 17th century or later
VAM : 371-1875
The hilt has a baluster grip surmounted by addorsed human heads; the quillons terminate in animal-heads. One of these is an elephant whose trunk forms the knuckle guard. The upper straight, down-turned quillons are similar to daggers of the Jahangir period but this may be a later example. The hilt has a pierced finial between confronted elephants modelled in the round. The blade has a narrow central rib and carved and chased palmettes at the forte.
SS

424
Dagger (katar)
Steel with gilt decoration
Length : 32cm
Mughal, 17th century (in the Kunstkammer collection by 1674)
Lent by the National Museum, Copenhagen, Department of Ethnography: EDb39b.
Bibliography : Dam-Mikkelsen and Lundbaek (1980) p.106 and 107 which notes the dagger in inventories for 1674 and 1690. SS

425
Dagger (katar)
Steel, watered, with relief decoration on the blade.
Length : 52cm
Mughal, 17th century (in the Kunstkammer collection by 1674).
Lent by the National Museum, Copenhagen, Department of Ethnography: EDb40.
Bibliography : Dam-Mikkelsen and Lundbaek (1980) p.106 and 107 which notes the dagger in inventories for 1674 and 1690. SS

426
Dagger (katar)
Steel
Length : 49.3cm, *Blade length* : 34.2cm
Mughal or Deccani; 1106 AH (1694/5 AD) or 1160 AH (1747 AD)
Private collection.
The blade has been cut down from a *firangi* sword and is inlaid in gold with the Arabic letter *he*. The hilt is decorated with bold iris flowers and scrolling leaves in *koftgari* and inscribed *ya fattah ya razzaq saneh 116*, 'Oh Conqueror! Oh Provider! Year 116'. RS

427
Knife
Steel with lac-inlaid brass hilt
Length : 38.5cm, *Blade length* : 26.6cm
N. India, probably Moradabad; c.1770
Lent anonymously.
The steel blade has traces of silver on the bolster. Its hilt is of chased brass decorated with various birds, animals and plants in landscapes divided by streams, horizontally on one side and diagonally on the other. Such landscapes are more usually found in *koftgari* and Lucknow enamelled hilts. RS

428
Sword of Dara Shikuh
Steel, the hilt overlaid with gold, the watered blade with stamped and gold-inlaid inscriptions, wood scabbard covered with green velvet and red brocaded cloth covering a dagger sheath, sword belt of gold and silver brocade, the locket, chape and sword-belt mounts gold enamelled in green.
Sword length : 85.1cm, *Blade length* : 71.7cm, *Scabbard length* : 73.8cm
Mughal, inscribed as belonging to Dara Shikuh (1615-1659) stamped with a date 105(?)0/1640-1
VAM : IS 214-1964
Given by Lord Kitchener.
The blade has very fine black watering with fluting on both faces and is prob-

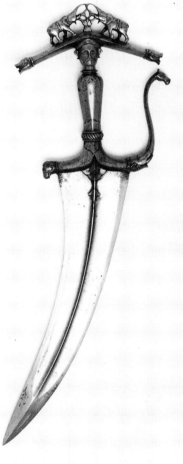

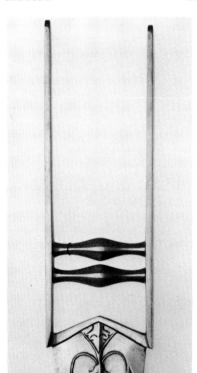

ably of Persian origin. The stamped inscription reads 'Dara Shikuhi' and has a partially defaced date which seems to be 1050, though the five is not entirely clear.

The gold-inlaid inscription on the back of the blade reads:

In tegh-i shahzada-i Dara Shikuhnam Kar-i hazar khasm ba yakdam konad tamam

'This sword of the Prince called Dara Shikuh

Takes care of a thousand enemies at one go'

(Inscription read by AS M-C).

Bibliography : Rawson (1952) pp.111-2; Varney (1958) figs.I and Ia and p.35; Rawson (1967) pl.66.   SS

429
Sword and scabbard

Steel, the hilt overlaid with gold, the watered blade with carved inscriptions overlaid with gold, the scabbard wood covered with green velvet, chape of steel overlaid with gold.

Length : 96.6cm, *Blade length* : 84cm, *Scabbard length* : 85.19cm

Mughal, period of Aurangzeb (1658-1707)

VAM : IS 227&a-1964

Given by Lord Kitchener.

The four inscriptions on the blade are carved within cartouches and, reading from the bottom up as the sword is held upward, are:

1 *Banda-i 'Alamgir/Padishah Ghazi*
'The servant of 'Alamgir/king and fighter for the faith'
2 *Sipahsalar/Firuzjang*
'Marshall/Firuzjang'
3 *'Amal-i Asadullah*
'The work of Asadullah'
4 *Ya qadi al-hajat* (Arabic; call to God)
'O Thou Judge of Necessities!'
(Inscriptions read by AS M-C).

Firuz Jang is possibly Mir Shihab al-din who came from Turkestan and entered into military service under Aurangzeb in his 12th regnal year. He was given the title Ghazi ud-din Khan in the 27th regnal year and Firuz Jang in the 28th. It was not until the 48th year of Aurangzeb's reign that he was made a *sipahsalar*.

Bibliography : Rawson (1952) p.106; Beveridge and Prashad (1979) vol.I p.587-92.   SS

430
Sword

The hilt steel with silver-inlaid floral scroll decoration, cloth covered grip, the blade steel of European manufacture bearing the mark of Christian V of Denmark (1670-1699).

Length : 91cm

Indian hilt, European blade; in the Kunstkammer collection by 1739.

Lent by the National Museum, Copenhagen, Department of Ethnography: EDb106.

Bibliography : Dam-Mikkelsen and Lundbaek (1980) p.108 and 109 which notes the sword in inventories for 1739 and 1775.   SS

431
Gauntlet sword (pata)

Steel

Length : 135cm, *Blade length* : 101.2cm

Mughal or Deccani; late 17th century

Private collection.

The flamboyant blade with orb mark is of 17th century German manufacture. The gauntlet, cuff and blade reinforcement are richly decorated with gold and silver *koftgari* of which the principal motifs are a border and cartouche pattern imitating chain mail links containing florets and a field design of squares divided diagonally to separate triangles containing split palmettes and parallel hatching. The padded blue silk lining appears to be original.   RS

432
Sword (khanda)

Steel with a brocade-covered scabbard

Length : 103cm, *Blade length* : 81.5cm

Central India; 18th century

Private collection.

The watered blade is re-inforced with ornamental plates and, together with the basket hilt and pommel spike, these are decorated with floral and foliate motifs in *koftgari*.

The scabbard is covered with its original gold brocade with a diaper of stylised tulips. The chape is of chased copper. RS

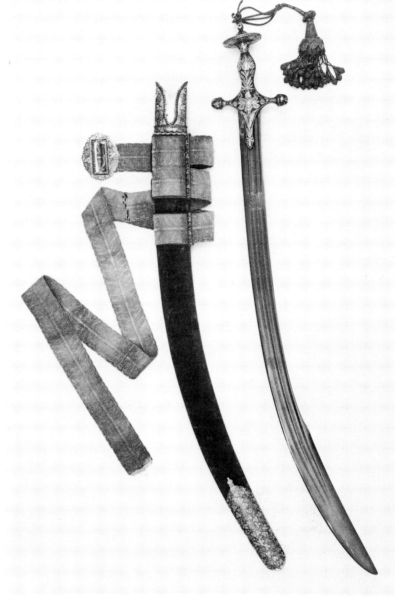

133

428

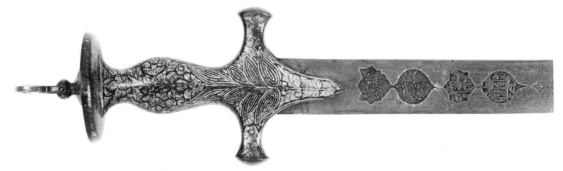

429

434

435

433
Sword and scabbard
The hilt silver, polychrome enamelled, the blade steel, the scabbard covered with tooled leather, gilt and with mounts of enamelled silver.
Length : 83.4cm, *Blade length* : 69.4cm, *Scabbard length* : 83.2cm
Lucknow; late 18th or early 19th century
VAM : 300-1876
The hilt has a ram's head pommel and quillons; similar examples in the V & A and Wallace Collection have terminals of bird, ewe and makara heads. Two swords with similar hilts have associations with Lucknow: one, in the Wallace Collection, bears the name of one of the Nawabs of Oudh, Shuja ad-Daula who ruled from 1753-1775 (Norman (1968) fig.5), and a second was taken at the siege of Lucknow in 1858 and is illustrated by Rawson (1967) pl.71.
Bibliography : Rawson (1952) p.132. SS

434
Sword hilt
Silver, partly gilt with translucent poly-chrome enamel.
Lucknow; second half of the 19th century
Length : 17.5cm, *Width* : 11cm
Lent anonymously.
For enamel of this type made about 1880 and exhibited at Simla see Cole (1881) pl.XVd. SS

435
Sword and scabbard
Steel, the hilt overlaid with gold and silver, the blade watered in ladder pattern, scabbard of velvet-covered wood with pierced and chased gilt chape.
Length : 91.4cm, *Blade length* : 78.6cm
Rajasthan; 19th century
VAM : IS 87-1981
The hilt has a pommel in the form of an elephant's head. A tiger, its back legs resting on one of the quillons, is attack-ing the elephant and is entwined in its trunk, thus forming the knuckle-guard. The hilt is overlaid with gold and silver to indicate the stripes of the tiger and the features of the elephant on the pommel. The elephant's trappings include a disc which has a sun symbol with human features within a crescent moon. The rest of the hilt is overlaid in gold with scenes of the hunt of a foliate scrolling ground. The scenes show a horseman spearing a wild boar, a man holding dagger and shield fending off a tiger, an elephant fighting with a tiger, and a tiger and a wild boar locked in combat. SS

436
Matchlock musket
Steel with painted wooden stock
Length : 167.5cm
Inscribed in *koftgari* on the barrel: *'The work of Haji Shafi . . . stan'*
North India, early 18th century
Private collection.
The russet iron barrel is decorated at the muzzle and breech with cross hatched *koftgari* decoration of inter-laced split palmette meandering stems. The stock is painted and lacquered with flowering scrolls on a green ground. The butt is carved in relief with repeated merlons, painted brown, outlined in white and red, and stylised parakeets, facing a central fleur-de-lys. RS

437
Matchlock gun
Wooden stock, covered with black lac and inlaid with ivory which has traces of red pigment.
Length : 175cm
Rajasthan; first half of the 18th century
VAM : 2642 (IS)
An almost identical gun is in the V & A and was presented by the Maharaja of Jaipur (Egerton (1880) no.442). A related example in the Maharaja of Jaipur Museum is said to have been made at Manpur, Gwalior. (Welch (1963) pl.71).
Bibliography : Egerton (1880) no.421. SS

438
Flintlock gun
The stock mounted with gilt metal, the barrel steel with gold overlaid decoration and inscription, polychrome painted enamel on gold at the breech end, tiger-head muzzle set with red and green stones, ivory ramrod.
Length : 160cm
Sind (Hyderabad); inscribed with the name of Mir Murad 'Ali Khan Talpur (ruled 1828-1833).
VAM : 143-1890
The inscriptions on the barrel read:
sarkar-i Mir Murad 'Ali Khan Talpur
'commissioned by Mir Murad 'Ali Khan Talpur'
Amal-i Hajji Mir Khan
'Made by Hajji Mir Khan'
There is also a stamped and gold-over-laid inscription which is illegible. The lock is English, engraved 'John Manton & Son, Patent'. According to Graham Rimer of the Tower of London, the patent is for the design of the rainproof pan and was taken out on July 21, 1815. The serial number on the lock is 7787 which dates it to 1820 (see Neal and

Back (1967) p.58). The enamel on the breech end of the stock is painted in bright pinks and oranges and is Persian in style.

Other examples of work by this craftsman are in the reserve collections of the V & A.

Bibliography : cf.Egerton (1880) no.733.
SS

439
Primer

Ivory, carved with birds, animals and human figures, traces of red pigment, brass stopper attachment.
Length : 27.2cm
Mughal, first of the 17th century.
Lent by the Historisches Museum, Dresden.

This, with one other example in Dresden, was in the collection of Prince Elector Johann Georg II of Saxony in 1658.

Its decoration is, like that on the other carved ivory primers in the exhibition, to do with hunting, but unlike the others deals specifically with birds rather than beasts. On one side are two duck hunters clutching their spoils with European figures on the other, one of whom holds a bird of prey.

Bibliography : Frenzel (1850) Y 381a; Ehrenthal (1896) M 252; Born (1942) figs 2 and 3; Schöbel (1975) no.169.   SS

440
Primer

Ivory, carved with animals of the hunt and mythical beasts, metal suspension chain and stopper attachment, gilt and enamelled details.
Length : 30cm
Mughal, 17th century
Lent by the National Museum, Copenhagen, Department of Ethnography : EDb 63.

Two other ivory primers are in the National Museum, one in an inventory of 1690 and both in one for 1737.

Bibliography : Dam-Mikkelsen and Lundbaek (1980) p.111 and 112, noting the primer in inventories for 1737-65 and 1775.   SS

437

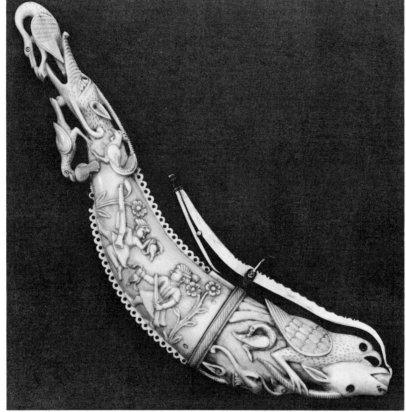

439

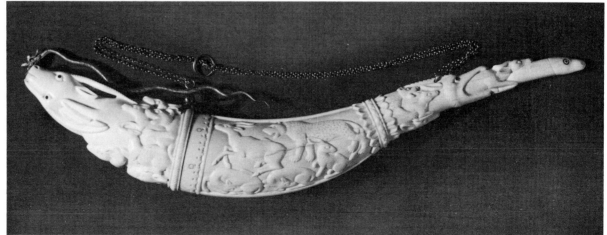

440

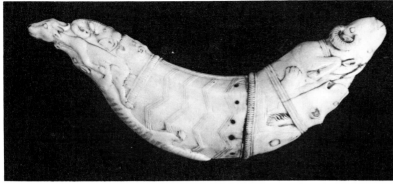

441

442

443

441
Primer
Ivory, carved, with traces of red pigment
and gilding, two metal rings.
Length : 16cm
Mughal, 17th century
VAM : Circ. 597-1923
The sensitively carved intertwined and
overlapping animals of the hunt include
an elephant, lions, ibex and ram. The
central section is plain except for chevron decoration in four bands. Micro-
scopic examination of the piece in the
conservation department of the V & A
showed that it was once extensively
painted and gilt. A similar primer is in
the Walters Art Gallery, Baltimore (see
Born (1942) fig.5). SS

442
Primer
Ibex horn with *makara* head of ivory
painted in green, white, red and black.
Length : 24.1cm
Lahore, late 18th or early 19th century.
VAM : 2599 (IS)
An ibex head issues from the mouth of
the *makara* to hold the stopper which is
in the shape of a lotus bud. A similar
primer is in the Egerton collection, now
housed at the Queens Park Art Gallery,
Manchester, but a winged female figure
takes the place of the ibex (Egerton
(1880) p.47 fig.5). Both examples were
collected before 1880, the V & A primer
having been acquired by the Indian
Museum in 1855 as from Lahore, and
Egerton having formed his collection
between 1855 and 1880.
Bibliography : Egerton (1880) no.683. SS

443
Powder horn
Nautilus shell inlaid with mother-of-
pearl and lac with an ivory finial.
Rajasthan (Kota), 19th century
Lent by Mr and Mrs James Alsdorf.
For a similar example sent to the Delhi
exhibition of 1902-3 see Watt (1904)
plate 43A no.6. SS

444

444
Powder horn
Horn, inlaid with lozenges of horn,
mother of pearl and ivory, silver and
brass mounts.
Length : 14.1cm
Rajasthan (Etawah, Kota), end of the
19th century.
VAM : IM 97-1927
For a similar example sent to the Delhi
exhibition of 1902-3 from Etawah, see
Watt (1904) pl.43A no.1. Kota at the
time of the exhibition was known as the
only centre for the manufacture of small,
decorative objects of wood or horn inlaid
with ivory, horn and mother of pearl. SS

445
Saddle-axe (tabarzin)
Axe-head of steel, champlevé carved
with decoration and inscription inlaid
with gold, the shaft cased in embossed
silver, partly gilt.
Length : 56.5cm, *Length head* : 14.3cm
Lahore, signed as the work of Lotf 'ali,
an Iranian artist, and dated 1150/
1737-8, but made as a forgery in India,
probably in the mid-19th century.
VAM : 111-1880
Four axes, signed and dated, are so far
known by Lotf 'ali Gholam, who worked
in Iran during the reign of Nader Shah
(1736-47). His work is distinctive in
style and of extremely high quality. The
decorative scheme of the axe-head here
copies that of the Iranian craftsman,
but the execution by comparison is poor
and elements of the decoration are
misunderstood. The inscribed date
would be plausible for a genuine piece
and implies that the work of Lotf 'ali
was well-known by Indian craftsmen
and his name, at least, was known by
their clients.
Bibliography : Melikian-Chirvani in
Elgood (1979) figs.42, 43 and 45 and
discussion *passim*. SS

446
Mace (gurz)
Steel with gold overlay, inscribed on the
shaft and head.
Length : 159cm
Northern India (Punjab), made for
Nawab Muhammad Bahawal Khan-i
'Abbasi, dated 1182/1768-9.
Lent by the Trustees of the British
Museum : OA-10637.
The inscription on the head reads
*sarkar-i muhammad bahawal khan-i
'abbasi* (commissioned by Muhammad
Bahawal Khan-i 'Abbasi); that on the
shaft gives only the name. He came
from the Afghan tribe of 'Abbasi Daud-

putras and founded the state of
Bahawalpur in the Punjab during the
disintegration of the Durrani empire.
RS

447
Mace
Steel, narrow raised fillets and palmettes
on the shaft, finely inlaid with gold.
Length : 58.5cm
Mughal, 18th century
VAM : 3526 (IS) SS

448
Elephant goad (ankus)
Steel
Length : 84cm
Deccan, early 18th century.
Inscribed with the name of Shah Amin
ud-Din 'Ali.
Lent by the Jagdish and Kamla Mittal
Museum of Indian Art, Hyderabad,
76.1530.
The shaft is octagonal and tapers
towards the two pointed blades, with a
knob at the end and a series of ring
moulding dividing its length into compartments. Within these the sides of the
shaft are chiselled with Quranic inscriptions in relief *naskhi* characters and an
inscription repeated on both sides of
the reinforcing plate of the curved
blade reads : Allah, Muhammad, 'Ali,
Shah Amin ud-Din 'Ali. This probably
refers to the *sufi shaikh* Sayid Shah
Amin ud-Din 'Ali Husaini who died in
1150 AH/1737-8 AD.
Bibliography : Bilgrami (1927), p.62. RS

449
Elephant goad (ankus)
Gold set with diamonds on blue, green
or red enamel with scenes of the hunt in
polychrome painted enamel on the grip.
Length : 54.5cm
Rajasthan (Jaipur), c.1870
VAM : 02693 (IS)
Acquired by the India Museum in 1871
from the International Exhibition,
London.
Hendley, in *Jeypore Enamels* (p.11),
notes that the *ankus* 'when made of
gold or enamel, is presented by rajas to
men of rank. It forms part of the *Khillat*
or dress of honour given by the Maharaja
of Jeypore to some of the higher nobles.'
Bibliography : London International
Exhibition 1871 cat. no.232; Egerton
(1880) no.391[a]; Watt (1904) p.462 and
pl.68A fig.3. SS

445

447

448

449

450
Composite bow
Leather covered, painted red, black and gold.
Length : 64cm
Mughal, 17th century
Lent by the National Museum of Denmark, Department of Ethnography : EDb6
The composite bow has a wooden core, faced with horn and backed with sinew, glued together. When the bow is drawn, the horn withstands extreme compression whereas the sinew stretches and pulls back sharply when the bowstring is released. In India, Paterson notes that the bow is completely covered with leather or lacquer, except for the extremities, to resist the humidity of the climate. The bow may have reached the Indus valley civilization about 2500 BC and was still in military use at the end of the Mughal period.
Bibliography : Dam-Mikkelsen and Lundbaek (1980) p.104 which notes the bow in inventories for 1689, 1690 and 1737; Paterson (1972) for general comments on the Indian composite bow. SS

451
Spear
Wood, painted green with gilt floral decoration, the heads steel, overlaid with gold at one end.
Length : 219cm
Lahore, c.1850
VAM : 114-1852
Bought from the Great Exhibition of 1851 as 'modern'. SS

452
Spear
Wood, painted red with gilt floral decoration, the heads steel, overlaid with gold.
Length : 229cm
Lahore, c.1850
VAM : 3159 (IS)
This was acquired by the Indian Museum and transferred to the South Kensington Museum in 1880. SS

453
Vambrace (dastana)
Steel plate with copper-gilt overlay.
Length : 35.2cm
Deccan (Golconda), c.1675
Lent by the Jagdish and Kamla Mittal Museum of Indian Art, Hyderabad, 76.1526.
The armguard is of the usual Deccani form curved out at the elbow with an eliptical transverse rib at the wrist. Its curved wrist-plate is hinged along nearly

half the length of the main plate and was originally closed by a long pin. It also has a transverse rib. Both plates are covered with gilt copper overlay with openwork decoration. On the main plate this comprises four rows of Arabic religious inscriptions on either side of the central rib and a transverse row containing the *Bismillah* at the wrist. The space between these inscriptions is occupied by an arched panel of openwork floral decoration incorporating the transverse rib. The wrist plate has similar floral decoration in a rectangular frame surrounded by a single band of inscriptions. RS

453

454
Vambrace (dastana)
Steel
Length : 45cm
Deccan, second half of the 17th century.
Private collection.
The steel is finely carved with curvilinear ribs terminating in *fleurs de lis* and split palmettes. The chain mail is missing but copper rivets remain. RS

455
Body armour
Four plates of steel with straps and buckles, overlaid with gold and with moulded and engraved decoration, velvet-backed, epaulettes of fabric.
Front and back plates : *Height* : 29.5cm
Width : 23.6cm
Side plates : *Height* : 25cm, *Width* : 20cm
Delhi, c.1865
VAM : 796-c-1869
Bought from the Exposition Universelle, Paris, 1867.
Hendley (1892 pl.29) illustrates armour of this type with similar, though coarser, iris decoration made at Delhi in about 1890. SS

137

458

138

456
Helmet
Steel damascened with gold.
Height: 17cm, *Width*: 15.2cm
Mughal, second half of the 17th century.
Lent by the Maharaja Sawai Man Singh II Museum, Jaipur, no.2.
The helmet is in the form of a turban with a reinforcing plate attached at the front. Its gold *koftgari* decoration copies the flowered brocade of the turban over which it is designed to be worn. Although Mughal and Rajput helmets (*top*) were normally modelled on the Iranian *kulah khud* there are a few known examples which imitate turban shapes. It is possible that some features of this may be influenced by 16th century Italian parade casques based on classical models.

Bibliography: Welch (1963), pl.69; Robinson (1967), pp.110-111.   RS

457
Helmet
Steel with moulded decoration, traces of gold overlay.
Height: 12.7cm, *Diameter*: 20.8cm
Mughal, 17th century (?)
Lent anonymously.
The helmet has low relief decoration of half palmettes within a series of octagonal frames. The top of the nasal bears the inscription *Ya Allah* ('O Allah') with *Ya Muhammad* ('O Muhammad') beneath; the bottom has the inscription *Ya 'Ali* ('O 'Ali'). Surviving traces of gold overlay indicate all the raised decoration and a narrow border round the rim was originally gilt. To the left and right of the nasal are two holders, now broken, for plumes (cf 458). The rim is pierced for a neck-guard of mail, now lost, and the finial is broken.   SS

458
Helmet
Steel overlaid with gold with three plumes of heron feathers in holders, the neck guard of brass and steel links.
Height: 19.5cm, *Diameter*: 21cm
Lahore, c.1850
VAM: 118ª-1852
Bought from the Great Exhibition of 1851 as 'modern'.   SS

459
Shield
Steel with four central bosses, carved and engraved decoration, overlaid with gold, inscribed; the back lined with red velvet, blue velvet knuckle pad, both embroidered with silver thread.
Diameter: 53cm
Mughal, dated 1120/1708-9
Lent by Robert Elgood.
The decoration on the shield divides into three sections: the centre with a rosette and four pierced steel bosses, bordered by a narrow band of low relief palmette decoration and gold-overlaid florets; a broad inner band, undecorated except for four cartouches containing inscriptions and with a palmette border; and an outer border with eight cartouches containing inscriptions and eight containing florets, the space between occupied by a scrolling pattern of bi-lobed half-palmettes. All this outer border is carved in low relief on a ring-matted ground. Three of the group of four cartouches enclose the 'Nadi 'Ali' or invocation to Ali, a Shiite prayer. The fourth reads *Sarkar-i Asif Khan*

459

'commissioned by Asif Khan' and the date 1120. The outer cartouches on the border enclose Sura II, v.255 of the Koran.
(Inscriptions read by AS M-C)   SS

460
Shield
Leather, painted with hunting scenes, gilt, four metal bosses.
Diameter: 62cm
Rajasthan (Mewar); inscribed with the name of Maharana Sangram Singh II (1690-1734)
Lent by the National Museum, Delhi: 62.2879
Another shield of similar design also belonging to Maharana Sangram Singh II is in the National Museum (62.2880).
Bibliography: Sharma and Tandon (1969).   SS

461
Shield
Leather, painted with flowering plants in red and green with gilt details on a white ground, four gilt pierced metal bosses.
Diameter: 53cm
Mughal, 18th century
Lent by the Executors of the Late Earl of Powis.
This appears in the Claremont inventory of Clive's possessions made in about 1774 ('A japand Shield mounted wʰ Gold') and in an inventory for 1775 (mss both at Powis Castle).   SS

Weapons of Tipu Sultan

Fire-arms
The fire-arms of Tipu Sultan are virtually unique in two respects. Firstly, although of local manufacture, they resemble the most up-to-date European patterns and feature many of the 'improvements' which abounded in the last quarter of the 18th century. In form they are a mixture of English and French, the decoration being of a restrained Indian flavour. Secondly, they are fully inscribed stating by whom they were made, the year, the town and often the Workshop, either Royal or Public. A series of control marks was used rather similar to hall marks, but these covered base metals also. Furthermore, in some instances the recommended charge was inscribed on the piece. His Cabinet of Arms may be compared with those of other princely houses but his is more unusual in that the form he adopted for all his fire-arms was entirely foreign while his tiger motif decoration was peculiar to the 'Tiger of Mysore.'   RW

462
Flint-lock Musketoon
Steel barrel inlaid with silver, wooden stock mounted with brass.
Length: 106cm, *Muzzle diameter*: 5cm
Mysore, Seringapatam; made by Shaykh Muhyi al-din and dated M1224/1795-6.
Lent by the Arms and Armour Museum,

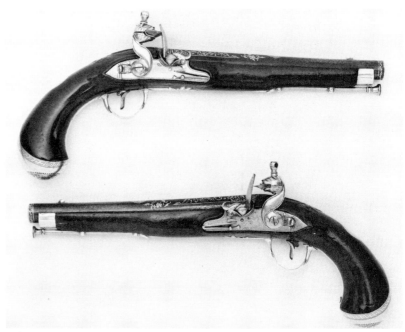

461

463

464

Stratford-upon-Avon.
The lock has a chiselled tiger-head cock and lock-plate in the form of a tiger-stripe. The stock has a carved apron at the tang.   RW

463
Pair of Flint-lock Pistols with left and right-hand locks
Steel barrels with wooden stocks, the barrels inlaid with gold and silver.
Length : 39cm, *Calibre* : 16 bore
Mysore, Seringapatam; made by Assad Amin and dated M1223/1794-5.
Lent by the Arms and Armour Museum, Stratford-upon-Avon.
The locks have chiselled tiger-head cocks; the stocks have carved aprons at the tang. The barrels are inlaid in gold and silver, bearing the same Persian quatrain as that on nos. 464 and 466 and have a 'tiger-head' motif composed of mirrored Arabic calligraphy : 'The Victorious Lion of God.'   RW

464
Flint-lock Sporting Gun for Super-imposed Load
Steel barrel inlaid with gold and silver, wooden stock mounted with silver and carved in the form of a tiger, inlaid with silver stripes.
Length : 138cm, *Calibre* : 14 bore
Mysore, Seringapatam; made by Asad Khan Muhammad and dated M1222/1793-4.
Lent by the Arms and Armour Museum, Stratford-upon-Avon.

Tigers predominate in the design of this gun, notably in the unique form of the stock which is a crouching tiger, carved in the round and inlaid with silver stripes. The lock, with partly internal cock, is in the form of a tiger, chiselled and inlaid with silver stripes and the safety catch is a crouching tiger. The double pan is fitted with a tap action for superimposed ignition. The cast and chased silver mounts depict tigers mauling human figures, probably intended to be Englishmen, and on the heel-plate are two tigers killing the double-headed eagle of the Hindu dynasty of Mysore. The barrel has gold and silver inlaid inscriptions and the same quatrain as no.466.
The gun was presented to Lord Cornwallis and came to the Arms and Armour Museum from the Earls of Pembroke, Wilton House.   RW

465
Flint-lock Sporting Gun
Steel barrel with wooden stock, the barrel inlaid with gold and silver decoration and inscriptions.
Length : 138cm, *Calibre* : 14 bore
Mysore, Seringapatam; made by Sayid Ma'sum and dated M1221/1792-3.
Lent by the Arms and Armour Museum, Stratford-upon-Avon.
The barrel is inlaid with a cheetah in pursuit of antelope and has a Persian quatrain which translates as:
'Like Timur Shah, Warrior of the Religion, Refuge of the Faith

He befriends the gun with his palm
And, as Moses with his staff, gives it the target
Of Pharaoh-like unbelievers in time of war.'
The lock has an internal mechanism and tiger-head safety catch. The stock is carved at the tang and comb and has a butt-trap for a socket bayonet.   RW

466
Flint-lock Duck-Gun
Steel barrel with wooden stock, mounted with silver and inscribed in silver and gold.
Length : 192cm, *Calibre* : 9 bore
Mysore, Seringapatam; made by Sayid Ma'sum and dated M1218/1789-90.
Lent by the Arms and Armour Museum, Stratford-upon-Avon.
The barrel is inlaid in gold and silver with the maker's name and a Persian quatrain which is translated as:
'The peerless gun of the Khusrau of India
Which with its shaft of forked lightning

Can seal the fate of the adversary
If it is aimed at his forehead.'
The lock has a chiselled tiger-head cock and the half-stock is carved at the tang and comb.   RW

140

467

467
Pair of cannon
Bronze with brass bearings.
Mysore (Seringapatam), late 18th
century.
Private collection.
The barrels are of green-patinated
bronze with muzzles, trunnions and
cascables cast as tigers' heads, finely
chased and matted. Cast in relief on the
chases are, in one case, the sword of 'Ali
and in the other, a broad bladed dagger
within tiger stripes. The muzzle astra-
gals are in form of chains edged with
alternate flower and leaf pattern, the
reinforce rings *en suite*. The dolphins
have tigers' heads. Almost identical
cannon are depicted in J. Vendramini's
engraving after Robert Ker Porter's
'The Storming of Seringapatam' (1803).
RS

468

468
Sabre (shamsher) of Tipu Sultan
Steel with gilt bronze hilt.
Length : 82.7cm, *Blade length* : 68.8cm
Mysore (Seringapatam); late 18th
century.
Lent anonymously.
The deeply curved single blade has
decoration of zig-zag lines in cross-
hatched *koftgari* on the back. The fort
bears a cartouche of gold cross-hatched
koftgari, inscribed with the *bismillah*
and the Arabic phrase 'Help is with
(Allah) and Victory is near'. Inscriptions
in two smaller panels are no longer
legible.
The gilt cast and chased bronze hilt is
typical of the personal weapons of Tipu
Sultan. Both the grip and knuckle guard
and quillons are decorated with tiger
stripes on a matted ground. The
pommel and quillon block are in the
form of large tiger heads. Smaller tiger
heads terminate the quillons and
knuckle guard.
For the hilt of a similar weapon at
Windsor see Egerton (1896), p.35.   RS

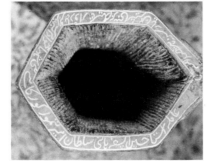

469

Base metal

469
Ewer
Alloy, inlaid with silver and brass (*bidri*),
overlaid inscription in silver.
Height : 28.5cm, *max.*, *Width* : 18.4cm
Deccan, 17th century
VAM : 1479-1904
The decoration, of floral and foliate
arabesques in silver and brass, derives
from Safavid Iran. The design is cut out
of sheet silver which is inlaid in small
sections into shaped depressions on the
ewer, the brass wire being used to
indicate details such as veins of leaves
and the centres of flowers.   SS
The inscription is on the top of the
hexagonal neck opening.
It begins *Amiluhu usta/husayn isfahani.
Sultan/amir Teymur Kurka/ni.* A
Persian distich follows, with the date on
the sixth side : *sanata hasht sad o noh*
'in the year 809'.
The inscription is meant to indicate
that the ewer was made for Timur by
Husayn Isfahani. That this is aprocry-
phal is evident from several details.
Firstly, the opening formula is supposedly a signature but reads *'amiluhu*
'the maker' rather than *'aml* 'made by'
which would be the standard formula.
Secondly, *usta* is a colloquial form of
ustad ('the master') which is never used
in the formulae of formal signatures
until the 18th century. 'Isfahani' is
oddly spelt for that period, with *sin*
instead of *sad*. Thirdly, the name of
Timur would necessarily be introduced
by his protocol if only in shortened
form; the way he is referred to suggests
that the man who wrote it was culling it
from a historical chronicle of the period
such as the *Habib os-Siyar*, unaware of
the proper form of address in a dedi-
catory inscription. Finally, the dating is
oddly given in a clumsy compromise
between Arabic *(sanata)* and Persian
(hasht sad o noh). If the set rules of
'Persian-Arabic' had been followed, a
complete Arabic phrase would be
inserted into a Persian sentence, or the
Arabic words would be used according
to Persian grammar.
The silver and brass on the ewer is
inlaid; the inscription is overlaid and
almost certainly an addition of the 19th
century when attempts were made to
create objects of historical interest
(cf445).   AS M-C
Bibliography : Zebrowski in Gray (1981)
fig.208.

470

470
Ewer
Alloy, inlaid with silver (*bidri*).
Height : 13.1cm, *Diameter body* : 10.6cm
Deccan (?), 17th century.
VAM : IS 11-1973
Given by Simon Digby, Esq.
The ewer has a ribbed body, circular
pedestal foot and chamfered spout,
with a low flaring neck. The decoration
consists of borders of split palmettes
and stylised flower heads, with petals
inlaid onto the neck rim and diagonal
strips on the base and moulding of the
foot.   RS

471

471
Ewer
Alloy, inlaid with silver and gold (*bidri*).
Height : 23cm
Deccan, late 17th century.
Lent by the Jagdish and Kamla Mittal
Museum of Indian Art, Hyderabad.
82.1
This ewer has a striking and unusual
design of a large silver iris on each side,
with three smaller flowers in the space
between them. The two irises are inlaid
with gold stamens. The lid is decorated
with flowers, and the straight spout has
alternate bands of trefoils and leaf
scrolls. The handle has a lotus bud at

472

one end and a stylised animal head at the top. The ewer rests on four feet patterned with chevrons.   RC

472
Huqqa base
Alloy, inlaid with silver and brass (*bidri*), compressed spherical body with squat neck.
Height : 18.6cm, *Diameter* : 16.8cm
Deccan or Northern India; second half of the 17th century.
VAM : IS 27-1980
The broad frieze of decoration on the body of this *huqqa* bowl has four cartouches containing identical flowering plants, the large flowers inlaid with silver and the stems and leaves with brass.   SS

473

473
Huqqa base
Alloy, inlaid with silver and brass (*bidri*).
Height : 18.7cm, *Diameter* : 17.9cm
Deccan, late 17th-early 18th century.
Lent anonymously.
The *huqqa* base has a compressed

spherical body with a squat neck and is similar in shape to the V & A example (472). The main decoration on the body is a double row of identical flowering plants on a ground of brass-inlaid water pattern.   SS

474
Huqqa base
Alloy, inlaid with silver (*bidri*).
Deccan, late 17th century.
Lent by the National Museum, New Delhi. 56.160/6.
This *huqqa* base is decorated with scenes depicting passages from the *Padmavati* : a mystical romance about the eponymous daughter of the king of Ceylon. The hero, Ratan Sen, is told of her beauty by a parrot, and embarks on a series of adventures in search of her. Eventually, through the intervention of Shiva, her father agrees to their marriage. The poem was written in Awadhi Hindi by the Sufi Malik Muhammad Jaisi in about 1540. Around the shoulder is a band decorated with animals and fishes.   RC

474

475
Huqqa base
Alloy, inlaid with silver (*bidri*).
Height : 16.8cm, *Diameter* : 15.8cm
Deccan (?), mid 18th century.
VAM : IS 39-1976
The *huqqa* base is inlaid with a design of peacock feathers.
The two most common forms of *huqqa* base in India have bodies either of compressed spherical shape, or, as in this example, of 'bell' shape. Both types can be seen in different media in the exhibition. The spherical *huqqa* base usually had a supporting ring to give it stability (385) either in rope, padded

fabric, or of the same material as the bowl itself. The bell shape appeared at about the turn of the century, its earliest representation so far being (as noted by Digby (1973) p.92) in the Marriage Procession painting (160) previously dated at c.1700 by Digby but dated in this exhibition at c.1680. Various modifications of the shape can be found throughout the 18th and 19th centuries, the splay of the bottom generally becoming more pronounced. Stands were sometimes made *en suite* which, in the 19th century, tended to become flattened rings into which the *huqqa* base fitted. Both forms of *huqqa* base were copied by European glass and ceramic manufacturers for export to India (e.g. no.405).   SS

475

476
Huqqa base
Alloy, inlaid with silver (*bidri*), the body of compressed spherical shape, ribbed.
Height : 16.4cm, *Diameter* : 14.7cm
India, 18th century.
VAM : 856-1874
Bought from the Tayler collection. William Tayler was an East India Company Civil Servant working in Bengal from 1829 to 1859.
The body of the *huqqa* base has alternate broad and narrow ribs, bearing respectively a floral scroll pattern and a small chevron. For a piece with identical shape and the same decorative scheme see KK Osterreichischen Handels-Museum (1895) pl.XXXVII.   SS

476

477
Huqqa base
Alloy, inlaid with silver (*bidri*).
Height : 17.7cm, *Diameter at base* : 16.9cm
Deccan, Bidar, mid-18th century.
Lent by the Jagdish and Kamla Mittal Museum of Indian Art, Hyderabad. 76.1241.
This bell-shaped *huqqa* base has a fluted body with a scalloped bottom edge and the unusual addition of three feet. Within the sections are vertical scrolling patterns of two alternate flower motifs, bounded by rows of chevrons. There is a serrated collar around the base of the neck, decorated with a fish design.   RC

477

480

481

482

478

Huqqa base

Alloy, inlaid with silver (*bidri*).
Height : 18.2cm, *Base diameter* : 17.3cm
Probably Bengal (Murshidabad or
Purnea); 18th century
Lent anonymously.

The Turner *huqqa* base (405) is an
example of Europeans adapting their
wares for the Indian market; this *bidri
huqqa* base shows the Indian craftsman
doing exactly the same thing for the
European market in India.

The *bidri* industry in Bengal, based in
Murshidabad and Purnea, had a
flourishing trade to large urban centres
like Calcutta and Dacca and must have
often executed commissions like this
for a customer who wished to have
initials incorporated into the design. SS

479

Basin

Alloy, inlaid with silver (*bidri*) in a floral
scroll on the body and a water pattern
on the neck.
Height : 12cm, *Body diameter* : 20.6cm
Deccan, 18th century.
Lent by the Trustees of the British
Museum, London : 1880-765.

The form of the basin is derived from
17th century Iranian wares; the decoration on the body of a scroll bearing
large flowers, fantastic rather than
naturalistic, owes a debt to Deccani textiles of the first half of the 18th century.
SS

480

Bowl

Alloy, inlaid with silver and brass (*bidri*).
Height : 6.2cm, *Diameter* : 14cm
Deccan, mid-17th century.
VAM : IS 10-1973
Given by Simon Digby, Esq.

The shape of the bowl derives ultimately from China, coming to India
either directly from imported Ming
porcelain, or from Chinese-influenced
Iranian metal wares.

The decoration is of foliate arabesque
scrolls containing dianthus flowers
alternately enclosed within large serrated leaves. RS

481

Plate

Alloy, inlaid with silver and brass (*bidri*).
Diameter : 30.4cm
Deccan, Bidar, late 17th century.
Lent by the Jagdish and Kamla Mittal
Museum of Indian Art, Hyderabad.
76.1228.

The design is of eight cartouches each
enclosing a flowering dianthus plant,

with a background of Chinese clouds.
The cartouches surround a blank central medallion. There is a shallow
cavetto decorated with a scrolling floral
design within a chevronned rim.

The decoration on the plate is in a
technique known as *teh-nishan* work
(P., lit : 'sitting on the bottom'), which is
a sort of deep *koftgari* technique, in
which the alloy is deeply engraved and
thick gold or silver, and brass in this
case, is hammered into the grooves,
then filed down to make a smooth
surface as opposed to ordinary *koftgari*,
in which the design is of very fine wire
hammered into shallow grooves. RC

482

Plate

Alloy, inlaid with brass (*bidri*).
Diameter : 32.5cm
Mughal, North India or Deccan, c.1700
AD
Lent by Simon Digby, Esq.

The decoration is of eight flowering
plants around a central medallion, with
smaller plants in the spaces between
them. They are enclosed by a narrow
rim of linked quatrefoils, and a cavetto
of floral scrolls. The flowering plants on
this piece recall the *pietra dura* decoration of the great mid-17th century
marble buildings of Agra and Delhi, but
have here acquired a baroque bravura. SD

483

Box and cover

Alloy, inlaid with silver and brass (*bidri*).
Height : 10.4cm, *Base diameter* 16.1cm
Deccan, late 17th – early 18th century.
Lent anonymously.

The box is circular with incurving sides
and a low domed cover which rises
slightly towards the centre. The box
and cover have identical brass foliate
scrolls, each bearing eight silver flowers.
At the centre of the top of the cover is a
rosette of feather-like leaves round
what was probably originally a flower
head, though the inlay is now missing.
Bibliography : Spink (1980) fig.9 (but
caption for fig.10); Zebrowski in Gray
(1982). SS

484

Box and cover

Alloy, inlaid with silver and brass (*bidri*).
Height : 13.2cm, *Base width* : 11.5cm
Mughal or Deccan, 18th century.
Lent by John Suidmak.

The box is octagonal with a pierced
cover and rests on four legs. The architectural form of the piece is adapted
from octagonal tomb buildings, with its

cover like a low dome resting on an octagonal drum with lotus-bud finials. On the base of the box is a drilled inscription in *devanagari* script (read by RS as giving the name of an owner, Dada ji Bhau Ka s..)　　　SS

484

485
Bottle (surahi) with silver gilt stopper
Alloy, inlaid with silver (*bidri*).
Height (without stopper) : 24.1cm
Body diameter : 14.4cm
Deccan (?), 18th century.
Lent by the National Trust, Powis Castle.
The compressed spherical body supports a tall, slightly flaring neck. The silver gilt stopper is attached by a chain to a silver ring round the base of the neck. The continuous pattern on the body and neck is of flower heads within interlocking foliate cartouches, framed within narrow scrolling or chevron borders.　　　SS

486
Darvish's staff
Alloy, inlaid with brass and silver (*bidri*), set with rubies, the terminals in the form of a hand and a *makara*-head.
Length : 38.7cm
Deccan, 18th century
Lent by the Trustees of the British Museum : 1895.6-3.96.
Presented by Sir A.W. Franks.
Stilettoes attached to the hand and the *makara*-head are concealed within the shaft. A similar example can be seen in the Gentil album (89; f.34, not shown) in association with axes, maces and a crutch (cf 359) and an example from Bidar is shown being carried by a Qalandar darvish in Gentil's atlas (87). SS

487
Weights for floor coverings, a pair
Alloy inlaid with silver and brass (*bidri*).
Height : 11cm, *Base width* : 11.7cm
Deccan, 18th century
VAM : I.S. 46 & A-1977
These weights would have been used to hold down the corners of floor coverings and, like the box and cover (484) derive their form from architecture. For examples of similar objects in the Salar Jung Museum, Hyderabad, see Gowd (1961) pl.13.　　　SS

485

486　　　*487*

488

Wine-bowl (jâm)

Copper, cast and turned, tinned; engraved with champlevé designs inlaid with black composition. Foot reinforced by inner shell.

Height : 15.7-16.45cm, *Diameter of opening* : 34.15-34.5cm

North-West India; 1590-1600 (?). Lent by the Trustees of the Prince of Wales Museum of Western India: 56.61. The wine bowl with hunting scenes is a key piece to the history of Mughal metalwork. In shape, general decorative programme and textual content, it follows the Western Iranian tradition. The footed bowl, rising at a low angle before curving upwards more steeply, with a strong moulding marking off the upper section, finds its closest parallels in a series of tinned copper bowls from Western Iran dated between 1608-9 and 1643-44 (Melikian-Chirvani (1982) p.328 pl.149 and p.334 pl.153). As on most Iranian pieces that include figurative decoration, a calligraphic frieze runs at the top, figurative scenes cover the main area in the centre, and the border of lobed escutcheons with pendant-like finials finishes off the composition in the lower section.

Considered in detail, however, the decoration departs from Western-Iranian standards. It is unusual for inscriptions on such bowls not to run in one continuous frieze. Instead, the upper section is broken up into twelve elongated four-lobed panels alternating with shorter panels. The former enclose a prayer in Arabic calling God's blessings on Muhammad, Fatima and the Twelve Imams – *Chaharda ma'sum* 'The Fourteen Protected Ones' – revered by the Shiites. In the shorter panels, the Shiite prayer (also in Arabic) known as the *Nadi 'Ali* ('Call unto 'Ali – he that makes wonders appear' etc.) leaves no doubt as to the Shiite faith of the intended recipient. Most unusual is the association of these two prayers – with Persian verses from a *Saqi-Name* or mystical poem in the form of an allegorical praise of wine (metre: *moteqareb*). The verses are engraved in two horizontal bands of *nasta'aliq* script framing the figurative scenes. The upper band begins: *Biya saqi an ab-e atesh khavas – Be man deh magar yabam az khod khalas* 'Come, Cupbearer, that fiery water of the Chosen Give it to me, perchance I might gain release from Self' and ends: *Biya saqi an mey^e hal avarad   Karamat fazayad kamal avarad   Be man deh ke bas Bidel*

oftade am   Va'zin har do bi hasel oftade am 'Come, Cupbearer, that wine brings the spiritual condition   It increases the divine gift and brings perfection   Give it to me for I have lost heart   And of these two I have been much deprived.' Bidel is almost certainly to be read as a nom-de-plume hitherto unnoticed, which, at that period, points to Bidel Gilani known to have lived in Jahangir's time. His *Divan* ('Collected poems') remains unpublished and comparison with his work, which I have failed to trace in manuscript form so far, is required before elaborating the point. Whatever the case, the verses are of great importance for determining the purpose of the bowl – a wine-bowl, in Persian *jâm* – and characterizing the religious leanings of the intended owner: their Sufi nature is made explicit by reference to a series of concepts that include *karamat*, 'the divine gift', the release from self, etc. The selection of the verses further suggests that the original owner was a member of the Royal House. They include such phrases as *Faridun-sefat*, 'endowed with the character of Faridun', a reference to one of the mythical kings of Ancient Iran frequently used as a way of identifying royal ownership together with other similar qualifications. They fit with the nature of the scenes – the royal hunt. In one, the rider in full gallop, spear in hand, wears the costume of the Shah Abbas period, including the characteristic fur cap. In the other, an elephant carrying a howdah is preceded by a runner in Hindustani garb. The combination of Western Iranian and Mughal characters is obviously intentional and reminds one of the famous miniature in the Freer Gallery celebrating the allegorical encounter of Shah Abbas and Jahangir. There is a further inscription, added after the bowl was completed. It is engraved at the bottom in a non-professional hand and is written in what I have called 'Arabic Persian' ie. Persian words arranged in Arabic grammatical order as is usual in the Iranian tradition for religious donation (*vaqf*) formulas. It records the dedication of the bowl to the shrine of Abu 'Abdullah al-Husayn and calls the curse of the Prophet Muhammad on whoever might 'covet' it. The date, apparently reading 991/25 January 1583 – 13 January 1584, seems too early. Further research into historical chronicles should eventually clarify this point.

Bibliography : Chandra (1955-57); Chandra (1974) pl.LXX.   ASM-C

488

488 (detail)

489

490

492

489
Vase
Brass, cast, with engraved champlevé decoration, the hatched ground filled with black composition.
Height : 12.3cm, *Diameter body* : 15.4cm
North-western India, probably Lahore, c.1580-1600
VAM : 21-1889 (IS)
All the inscriptions on the vase are in a bold, finely engraved *nashki*, the outside bearing invocations to the *Panj Ahl-e Beyt* or 'Five Members of the House' of Muhammad, and the inside Koranic verses. The decoration is based on Safavid designs of the period of Shah Tahmasp, but the shape is Indian. The vase would originally have had a spout. This is one of the earliest examples of metal wares so far known which is in the Safavid manner but which has strong Indian characteristics.
Bibliography : Melikian-Chirvani (to be published 1982) no.164, on which this entry is based. SS

490
Fragment of a mirror
White brass (H. *jasti*) inlaid with silver; inscribed in Persian with a couplet and the maker's name : *ustad muhamm [ad]* : 'the master Muhammad.'
Width : 14.6cm, *Approx. height* : 8.6cm
Deccan, 16th century
Lent by Simon Digby, Esq.
In the centre is a six-lobed interlacing medallion with arabesque decoration, enclosed by a band of floral decoration

inhabited by birds. The outer band has Persian inscriptions in cartouches, the first two being a couplet of verse, the third (fragmentary) cartouche containing the name of the craftsman.
The arabesque decoration closely follows Safavid Iranian models in style and quality of execution but comparison with a salver in the Mittal Museum (cat.no.491) suggests a Deccan provenance. RC

491
Salver
Copper, with traces of gilding.
Diameter : 60.5cm
Deccan, c.1600
Lent by the Jagdish and Kamla Mittal Museum of Indian Art, Hyderabad. (no.76.1442).
The decoration is in three concentric zones around a central medallion containing a *hamsa* amidst floral ornament. This is surrounded by a band containing a Shi'i version of the *kalima*, and the phrase *nasr min allah wa fath qar [ib]* : 'Deliverance is from God, victory is nigh', written in *suls* script. The next band is one of floral arabesque, and the outer band shows a lively portrayal of birds and animals against a floral arabesque background. Apart from the *hamsa*, the ornamental repertoire is characteristic of Timurid and Safavid decoration, although the elephants here are in a more Indian than Persian manner, and there is a rich flamboyance of execution which suggests Deccani workmanship. RC

492
Beggar's cup (kashkul)
Tinned copper.
Height : 8.9cm, *Length* : 22.2cm, *Width* : 10.1cm
Inscribed on the dragon heads i) *shaikh 'abd al-qadir*, ii) [not deciphered].
Deccan, Bijapur or Golconda, c.1600.
Lent by the Jagdish and Kamla Mittal Museum of Indian Art, Hyderabad : no.76.1430.
A characteristically boat-shaped *kashkul* with a dragon's head at either end, pierced for hanging from a chain. Decorated on the outside with half-medallions containing floral arabesques with lobed pendants between them. The interior is decorated with Arabic inscriptions in *naskhi* script : around the upper half is a band with roundels containing the names of the twelve *imams,* and in the centre an elliptical medallion inscribed with the Muslim confession of faith, surrounded by a band containing a Shi'i battle-cry. Both dragon-heads are inscribed in *nasta'liq* as above. It is not clear whether the inscription is an owner's name or refers to the celebrated twelfth century saint 'Abd ul-Qadir Gilani, founder of the important Sufi order which had many adherents in the Deccan.
The aristocracy often sought the company of sufis and showed them favour (see no.55). It is possible that this begging bowl was the gift of a wealthy patron to an esteemed *darvish*.
Bibliography : Welch (1973), no.42. RC

493
Box (pandan)
Enamelled copper.
Height : 7.2cm, *Diameter* : 13.8cm
Mughal, late 16th or early 17th century.
Lent by Simon Digby, Esq.
The lid and sides are decorated in powder-blue champlevé enamel, with naturalistic flowering plants in reserve. The eight lobes of the box form decorative panels divided by cypresses, formerly gilt, ascending to scalloped arches, the spandrels enamelled black with gilt leaves on them. At the centre of the lid is a white enamel roundel, with traces of flowers and leaves painted *impasto* on it. On the bottom of the box is a radiating interlaced design of blue and white flowers and leaves in champlevé enamel against the copper field. At the centre is an eight-pointed floral medallion originally filled with white enamel. The interior of the lid is enamelled in a type of cloisonné technique with a pattern of eight cypress trees converging on a central floral medallion.
This piece is recorded as having been acquired by a Mr. Stebbing in Delhi in 1928, and was exhibited at the Persian Exhibition of 1931 as 'Persian, 18th century'. The recorded provenance and the fact that these small lobed boxes are an Indian utensil without Persian parallels compel us to reject that attribution. No other comparable example in these techniques of enamelling has been recorded. The variegated flowering plants recall parallels in miniatures and suggest an early 17th century date. The naturalistically drawn flowers date from before the introduction in about 1620 of formalised floral designs as a major element in the Mughal repertoire of design. The lack of comparable pieces suggest that the technique of opaque enamelling fell out of favour when translucent enamelling on silver was introduced, possibly from Southern Germany, to the Mughal court.
Bibliography : London, Burlington House (1931), 309; Zebrowski (1981), fig.214 and p.185. SD

9a

9b

9 *(entry 208)*
a) **Velvet**
   Mughal, 17th century
   VAM : IM 30-1936

9 *(entry 259)*
b) **Boy's coat**
   Kashmir, late 18th-early 19th century
   VAM : IM 35-1934

10 *(entry 231)*
a) **Prayer mat**
   Burhanpur, Khandesh; late 17th-
   early 18th century
   VAM : IS 56-1950

10 *(entry 232)*
b) **Prayer mat**
   Mughal, c.1700
   VAM : IS 168-1950

494

495

494

Steel object with lion head, possibly a doorknocker or gun-carriage attachment

Steel, with some silver inlay.
Length : 14.2cm, *Width* : 5.2cm
Deccan, first half of 17th century.
Lent by Simon Digby, Esq.
This object of uncertain function has a lion's head at one end and a pair of rudimentary horses' heads joined by a solid iron bar at the other. There is a ram's head in the mouth of the lion, and on the back of the lion's head a lightly engraved palmette and leaves. On the back is an intaglio-carved flowering plant, which was probably formerly inlaid. On both sides, blessings on the Twelve Shi'i Imams are inscribed in *nasta'liq* script, the background chiselled to show the words in relief. The underside is inlaid in silver with a pattern of split leaves and dots.
The inscriptions in praise of the twelve imams suggest that this object was made in the Shi'a Muslim states of the Deccan. The flower on the back is also paralleled in some Deccani painting. Many different techniques of decoration have been used on this small object, which may indicate that it was a piece submitted by a craftsman to demonstrate his skills.
If it was intended as a door-knocker, it would probably have been for a religious building such as a shrine or *madrasa*.RC

495

Talismanic bowl

Brass
Height : 6.0cm, *Diameter*: 19.4cm
Mughal, first half of the 17th century.
Lent anonymously.
The bowl is inscribed with verses from the Qur'an including the *suran YaSin*, which fills the interior together with an arrangement of cabalistic numbers and letters. The twelve signs of the zodiac are engraved between the verses on the outside. Bowls of this type were used in the treatment of sickness.
Bibliography : A. Welch (1979) pp.186-7. RS

496

Celestial sphere

Brass, engraved and inlaid with silver and black composition.
Diameter : 13.1cm
Lahore, dated 1067/1656-7 and inscribed as the work of Ziya ol-Din Mohammad.
VAM : 2324-1883 (IS)
Bought for the South Kensington Museum in Bombay for £8 by Caspar Purdon Clarke in 1881-2.
The inscription is in Persian :
'Amal-e Aqall ol-'ebad Ziya ol-Din Mohammad ebn-e Qayem-Mohammad ebn-e Molla 'Isa ebn-e Sheykh Elahdad-e Ostorlabe-e Homayuni-e Lahuri Sana 1067 'The work of the most insignificant of slaves Ziya ol-Din Mohammad ebn-e Qayem-Mohammad ebn-e Molla 'Isa ebn-e Sheykh-e Elahdad, His Majesty's astrolabist, the Lahuri 1067.' (A.S. M-C)
Humayun is known, from the comments of Badauni and other authors, to have had a passionate interest in astronomy and employed Ziya ol-Din's ancestor, Sheykh Elahdad, as his astrolabist. Surviving dated instruments show that the family maintained production through the reigns of Akbar, Jahangir, Shah Jahan and Aurangzeb (see Linton no.166).
Bibliography : see Nadvi (1935) and Wiet (1936) for other astronomical instruments by this crafsman. Wiet lists an astrolabe in the Jaipur museum also dated 1067. SS

496

497

Wine bowl

Copper, formerly tinned, engraved design, inlaid with black composition on hatched ground.
Height : 9cm, *Body diameter* : 20.6-20.8cm
Kashmir or North-western India, 17th century.
VAM : 1317-1883 (I.S.)
The bowl is inscribed in *nasta'aliq* with verses from Hafez in a band on the neck within four cartouches separated by quatrefoils. The fifth cartouche on the neck was originally left empty, to be filled with the name of an eventual owner. The first name has been crossed out and another's added : *Sahibuhu Ala'ul* 'owned by Ala'ul.' Another owner's name appears : Merza 'Ali, the 'merza' spelt according to Indian rather than Iranian practice (see for instance, the tombstone of Babur's son Merza Hindal *EIM* 1923-4 p.7). The bowl is one of many examples of metal wares of Safavid type made in India, the Indian origin of this piece evident only in small details of ornament or orthography which would be unusual in an Iranian context.
Bibliography : Melikian-Chirvani (to be published 1982) no.167 on which this entry is based. SS

498

Box and cover

Brass, chased and engraved on a ring-matted ground.
Height : 33cm, *Diameter* : 34cm
Western India, first half of the 17th century.
Lent by the Trustees, Prince of Wales Museum of Western India, Bombay : 37.6.
The circular box has a high, stepped cover with a flat top, and fastens at the front with a hasp. The decoration on the walls of the box is a broad frieze of hunting scenes separated by narrow, curved, diagonal or undulating borders containing a water motif. The style of the figures is derived from Western

Indian painting of the early 17th century, which was influenced by Akbari Mughal miniature painting. The cover has four horizontal bands, the upper two and bottom one containing floral scrolls influenced by Chinese blue and white porcelain designs. The remaining band depicts a variety of animals, some with riders, contained within scrolls and framed between narrow vertical borders. These figures are in an archaic style derived from Western Indian Jain painting of the 16th century.
The piece has variously been described as a turban box or jewel casket, but its exact function is uncertain.
Bibliography : Chandra (1940); Gorakshkar (1979) p.27, no.226; Gascoigne (1971), p.56. RS

499

Vase

Bronze, cast, with ribbed body.
Height : 22.6cm, *Diameter* 14.8cm
Deccan (?), 17th c. (?)
Lent anonymously.
The vase has a spherical ribbed body, compressed at the bottom where it joins the pedestal ring foot. The neck flares out from a ring moulding and has softly chamfered sides. The ribs on the body are alternately broad and very narrow with a petal moulding at top and bottom of each broad rib. The neck has been broken off and repaired. SS

500

Spittoon

Bronze, cast.
Height : 7.8cm, *Body diameter* : 10.9cm
Mughal or Deccan, 17th century (?).
Lent anonymously.
Spittoons of various forms appear on many of the paintings in the exhibition showing rulers or nobles indulging in *pan*; the spittoon was a necessary utensil for this occupation. SS

501

Water bottle

Bronze, cast, with moulded and chased decoration.
Height : 21cm, *Width* : 23.6cm
Western India or Deccan, 17th century (?)
Lent anonymously.
The shape of this bottle, with its scrolling lotus-bud terminals, is based on a leather prototype, the moulded area in low relief round the neck probably deriving from appliqué work. The lightly chased decoration on this raised section is identical on both sides, consisting of palmettes within lobed and cusped

497

499

501

cartouches, and two linked roundels containing birds. To left and right on the body of the bottle are peacocks and there are chased palmettes below each scroll terminal. SS

502
Betel-box (pandan)
Brass, with traces of tinning.
Height : 9.8cm, *Width* : 15.5cm
Marwar, Rajasthan, 17th century.
Lent by Simon Digby, Esq.
The panels on the lid are set between arches; those on the sides are divided by cypress trees. The scenes in the panels depict a Raja or Sultan drinking with one or more ladies, the ladies drinking on their own, the ruler holding a parrot while a lady holds a flagon, and a couple riding a camel with a servant between them, possibly a reference to the Rajput folk tale of Dola and Maru. The vernacular style of the scenes on the box recalls the Ragamala paintings of Pali, Marwar, dated 1623 AD.
Bibliography : Singh (1960), p.76 ff.; Ebeling (1973), p.165-6. RC

503
Box and cover
Brass, raised; engraved and inlaid with lac.
Height : 9.1cm, *Diameter* : 14cm
Mughal, 18th century
VAM : 747-1889
The circular box and domed cover have twelve ribs, each with a flowering plant under a cusped or lobed arch. The flowers are filled with orange lac; other details are in black but both orange and black are partly missing. The top of the cover is a low projecting cone decorated with an orange and black rosette. The cover is attached to the box by a hinge, two chains and has a hasp fastening. SS

504
Huqqa base
Brass
Height : 18.1cm, *Width* : 15.4cm
Punjab, c.1700
Lent by Simon Digby, Esq.
This *huqqa*-base of depressed spherical shape is decorated with eight many-petalled lotus flowers within vegetal scrolls.
Shapes like this which were elsewhere produced in the *bidri* technique, or in glass or more precious materials, were usually made in the Punjab in solid brass. Brass *huqqas* continued to be made in the Punjab until the late 19th century, and were popular at the courts of the rulers of the Punjab hills.

The decoration on this example is probably incomplete. One lotus rosette is covered with fine hatched lines to indicate shading, whereas on the adjacent one this embellishment is incomplete. RC

505
Huqqa base
Brassy alloy, cast; engraved and originally inlaid with black lac, mostly missing.
Height : 16.5cm, *Body diameter* : 14.4cm
Punjab, late 18th or early 19th century.
VAM : 100-1898 (IS)
This has the same decorative scheme as a group of *huqqa* bases in the V & A collected by Caspar Purdon Clarke in 1881-2. These were all acquired for the museum and attributed to Kangra or Nurpur in the Punjab. The group also includes bell-shaped *huqqa* bases which probably do not date before the middle of the 19th century at the latest. Some of the border motifs on this *huqqa* base and those in the Purdon Clarke group are closely comparable but the engraving here is marked by its greater care and crispness and the date of the piece is perhaps earlier. SS

505

150

11 *(entry 213)*

a) **Wall from Tipu Sultan's tent**
Burhanpur, Khandesh, mid-18th
century
Lent by the Trustees of the Powis
Estate.

11 *(entry 309)*

b) **Turban ornament**
White jade set with rubies, emeralds
and crystals in gold.
Mughal, first half of the 18th century
VAM : 02569 (IS)

11 *(entry 330)*

c) **Box and cover**
Gold, enamelled
Mughal, 18th century
Lent anonymously

11 *(entry 330)*

d) **Stand for box and cover**
Gold, enamelled
Mughal, 18th century
Lent anonymously

11a

11b

11c

11d

12a

12b

12 *(entry 322)*
a) **Spoon**
   Gold, jewelled
   Mughal, late 16th-early 17th century
   VAM : IM 173-1910

12 *(entry 356)*
b) **Wine cup of Shah Jahan**
   White jade
   Mughal, dated 1657
   VAM : IS 12-1962

508

506
Ewer
Brass, cast; engraved, with traces of black lac.
Height : 33.5cm, *Width* : 20.6cm
Deccan (?), 18th century
Lent anonymously.
The ewer rests on a hexagonal pedestal foot and has a bulbous body with chamfered sides. The neck is hexagonal with a ring-moulding and everted rim. The cover is missing. The tall spout terminates in a flower and the crozier-shaped handle has an animal head at the top. The deeply engraved decoration, originally filled with black lac, consists of flowering plants between borders of floral scrolls with a broad band of half-palmettes on the foot. The shape is related to that of the *bidri* ewer (no.469) but this is clearly a later form.
SS

507
Ritual ewer
Golden brassy alloy, cast, with *lingam-yoni* spout, inscribed with the name of Tiwari Radha Krishnaji.
Height : 20.1cm, *Body diameter* : 14.5cm
Northern India, 18th century
Lent anonymously.
The inscription is engraved in *devanagari* and the name 'Tiwari' refers to a particular class of Brahmins entitled to read three Vedas. The spout is in the form of the *lingam-yoni*, the aniconic representation of the Shaivite divine couple. Almost identical spouts can be seen on a pair of ewers in the painting of Balwant Singh (166). The central section of the body has diagonal ribs moulded in low relief between horizontal and engraved lines, largely worn away at the top.
SS

506

508
Ewer and basin
Brass, cast, with engraved decoration.
Ewer height : 19.6cm, *Diameter 16.1cm*
Basin height : 13cm, *Diameter* : 28.8cm
Western India (?), 19th century.
Lent anonymously.
The ewer, its lid missing, is a late example of a shape copied from Iranian metal wares but which originally derived from China. The foot of the ewer fits exactly into the cavity of the basin but the deeply engraved scrolling decoration differs on each piece.
SS

509
Hawking drum
Damascened steel (*koftgari* work) with a red velvet belt embroidered with gold.
Diameter : 26cm
Sialkot, 19th century
VAM : 04044 I.S.
This type of drum was worn on the saddle and permitted the owner to transmit signals to his hunting falcon (cf.no.42).
RS

510

510
Two hooks in the form of peacocks' heads
Brass
Gujarat, 19th century
Lent by the National Museum, New Delhi, 69.330 a & b.
RC

Coins

511
Presentation coin (muhr)
Gold
Weight : 10.91 grams
Inscribed in Persian *sana-yi shesh-i julus shabih-i jihangir shah-i akbar shah*
'The sixth regnal year. The likeness of King Jahangir, (son of) King Akbar'.
Lent by the British Museum.
The coin has a portrait of Jahangir on the obverse and a lion on the reverse. The emperor is shown with a nimbus around his head, and he holds a goblet in one hand and a book in the other. Far from alluding to Jahangir's fondness for wine, the cup is probably intended as a symbol of kingship, a tradition also found in Sassanian art. The cup may also be an allusion to the Persian 'cup of Jamshid', in which all the world was mirrored (see also no.372). The book held in Jahangir's left hand may be another symbol of the emperor's omni-science. These portrait coins were made for presentation by the emperor to his most faithful and intimate fol-lowers, and were suspended by a chain around the neck, or fastened to the turban. Jahangir instituted the practice in his sixth regnal year (1611), from which this example dates, and it con-tinued until his ninth regnal year. They were known as *shast* or *shast o shabih* : 'token and likeness', and the bestowal of similar emblems of the ruler was also current in Akbar's reign.
Bibliography : Lane Poole (1885), no.315; Hodivala (1923), pp.147-170; Gupta (1969), p.126, no.285; Gascoigne (1971), p.139.
RC

512
Twelve zodiac coins
Gold
Weight : 10.9 grams each
Mughal, c.1618
Lent by the British Museum.
These coins show the astrological signs of the months in which they were minted. On the reverse is the Emperor's name and the place of minting. Jahangir records in his diary in his thirteenth regnal year that 'it entered my mind that in place of the month they should substitute the figure of the constellation which belonged to that month . . . This usage is my own, and has never been practised until now'.
(*Tuzuk*, II, pp.6-7).
Bibliography : Lane Poole (1885),

nos.322-383; Hodivala (1923), p.171; Gupta (1967), p.126, no.287. RC

513a
Gold coin (muhr)
Mint Agra. 971 AH/1563-64 AD. Inscribed on the obverse with the *kalima*, and on the reverse with the name and titles of the Emperor Akbar. Lent by Mr Richard Falkiner.

513b
Silver (rupees)
Akbar
(a) Mint Akbarpur Tanda. 974 AH/1566-67 AD. *Kalima*, royal titles, names of four Caliphs.
(b) Jaunpur. 977 AH/1569-70 AD. *Kalima*, royal titles, names of four Caliphs.
(c) Mintless type. 34th *Ilahi* year /1590-91 AD. Inscribed 'Allahu Akbar' (God is the greatest).
(d) Lahore. 39th *Ilahi* year/1595-96 AD. Inscribed *'Allahu Akbar'* (God is the greatest) May his glory shine.
Jahangir
(e) Lahore. 1015 AH. Inscribed with Persian couplet:
Shah Nur al-Din Jahangir son of Akbar Padishah
Made the face of gold to shine like the sun and moon
(f) Agra. Month *Adhar*, twelfth regnal year, also dated 1026 AH/1617-18 AD. Royal name and dates, floral ornaments.
(g) Lahore. 15th regnal year, 1051 AH/1641-42 AD. *Kalima* and royal titles, praise of the four Caliphs.
Aurangzeb
(h) Ajmer, *Dar al-Khayr* ('The Abode of Blessing'). 44th regnal year, 1111 AH/1699-1700 AD. Inscribed with Persian couplet :
Shah Aurangzeb-Alamgir
Struck money in the world like the shining sun
This coin was collected in Tehran from a hoard of early eighteenth century Mughal silver rupees, probably loot from Nadir Shah Afshar's invasion of India and sack of Delhi in 1739 AD. Coins (a) to (d), (f) to (h) lent by Mr Simon Digby. Coin (e) lent by Mr Richard Falkiner. SD

513(c)
Copper (dams and smaller fractions) of the Emperor Akbar
(a) *dam*. Ahmedabad, Dar al-saltanat ('Abode of the government'). 980 AH/1572-73 AD.
(b) Saharanpur. Month *Adhar*, 37th *Ilahi* year/1593-94 AD.

(c) *nim dam* ('half *dam*'). Srinagar (Kashmir). Date partly legible 4 x *Ilahi* year, i.e. in the decade after 1596 AD.
(d) *damra*. Mintless type. 33rd *Ilahi* year/1589-90 AD.
(e) Quarter *dam*. Mint, Urdu-i Zafar Qarin ('The royal camp joined to victory'). Undated. Coins which bear this mint-name were probably struck during the emperor's progresses. Square silver *jalalas* and copper *dams* of the *Hijri* year 1000 are common, and the silver coins were often imitated as talismans.
(f) *shanzdahum* (one-sixteenth of a notional *tanka* = ⅛ *dam*). Mint Delhi. Month *Shahrivar*, *Ilahi* year not visible. Lent by Mr Simon Digby. SD

514
Seal of Shah Jahan
Chased brass with modern ebony handle.
Diameter : 4.4cm
Inscribed in reverse : *shiab al-din muhammad shah jahan badshah-i ghazi. 1062.*
Mughal, 1062 AH/1651 AD.
Lent by the P. McMahon Collection, Dublin.
Various types of seal were required for the authentication of state documents. This example is larger than the 'Uzuk' seal (chagatai *uzuk* = 'ring') mentioned by writers such as Abu'l Fazl. An even larger type of Mughal seal, introduced under Akbar, contained the names of the Emperor's Timurid ancestors enclosed within small circles around his own name. Such 'pedigree' seals were originally intended for use on documents sent to foreign rulers.
Bibliography : *A'in-i Akbari* I,p.54. RC

Insignia

515
Lion
Bronze
Height : 43cm
Mughal, early 17th century.
Lent anonymously.
The lion sits in the 'sejant erect' pose of European heraldry with its fore paws raised as though intended to be a supporter flanking a shield. It resembles bronze lions of the German renaissance but has not been accepted as such and in the opinion of S.C. Welch it is of Mughal origin. If we accept this attribution the lion is likely to be from the top of a standard as seen in certain Mughal *durbar* paintings of Shah Jahan's reign (cf.no.68). According

to the presumably spurious Memoirs of Timur *'Malfuzat-i Timuri'* presented to Shah Jahan by Mir Abu Talib Husaini in 1637/8 Timur ordained that a standard called the *Sher-tugh* should be awarded to certain of his principle officers. This may be identical with the *sher-maratib*, a flag with lion on its flagstaff which Colonel Gentil saw displayed by the Nizam of Hyderabad in the late 18th century.
Bibliography : White (1783), pp.105-6; Irvine (1903), p.34. RS

516
Standard ('alam)
Gilt brass with a wooden pole.
Height : 47cm, *Width* : 30.4cm
Length of pole : 153cm
Inscribed in Arabic in the openwork panel : *nasr min allah wa fath qarib* 'Help is with God, and victory is nigh'.
Mughal, c.1800
VAM : 2538 I.S.
The standard is inscribed:
This Trophy was Presented to General Lake on the 14th day of September 1803 by the Hands of His Majesty Shah Aulum, Emperor of Agra and Delhi, with the titles of Prince of Delhi, in Consideration of the Gallant Victory attained over the French and Native Troops under the Command of Dowlat Rao Sindia.
Ashgar ul Mulk – The Hero of the Land.
General Gerard Lake Bhadur Futteh Jung. The Lord of the Age and the Victorious in War.
Sumsam a Dowla – The Sword of the State
Kahn Dawran Kahn – The Lord of the Land
Lord Lake was presented with this standard (and probably the others exhibited) by the Emperor for his part in the Second Maratha war of 1803. The 'Gallant Victory' over Sindia's forces would have been the Battle of Delhi, on September 13th, 1803, the inscription recording the presentation evidently being added at a later date. The Maratha army was commanded by the French general Perron. The Emperor, Shah 'Alam, had been in Perron's custody, but the army's defeat in this battle placed him under British protection. RC

517
Standard ('alam)
Gilt brass and wood
Height : 80.2cm, *Length of pole* : 150cm
Mughal, c.1800
VAM : 2541 I.S.

The standard is cut from a sheet of gilt brass and mounted on a wooden pole. Standards such as this one and nos.518-521 would have been carried in processions and at court in the retinue of the ruler and also of honoured dignitaries upon whom they would have been bestowed as marks of favour. The practice of bearing insignia as marks of sovereignty is a very ancient one; the form of the Mughal examples is probably derived from Central Asian prototypes. In the *Baburnama*, standards (*tug*) of various shapes are illustrated, and the present examples are derivatives of these and similar forms.
Bibliography : *A'in-i Akbari*, p.50; Hyderabad Government (1954), pl. facing p.76; Irvine (1962), p.32; Verma (1978) p.78, pls.LVI & LVII. RC

518
Standard ('alam)
Gilt brass, copper and wood.
Height : 15cm, *Diameter* : 16.5cm
Length of pole : 150.0cm
Mughal, c.1800
VAM : 2543 I.S.
This standard of flattened spherical shape is derived from the type known as *kawkaba* from Arabic 'star' which in earlier standards was displayed as a sphere hanging from the curved neck of a dragon standard. Examples of this type are illustrated in the *Baburnama*, fol.268 (VAM : I.M. 268-1913) where they are shown with the pole wrapped up in a fabric bag, which may also have been the case with the examples exhibited here.
Bibliography : *A'in-i Akbari*, p.50; Irvine (1962), p.32, pp.77-8, pl.LVI. RC

519
Fish standard (mahi)
Gilt brass, with horse-hair tassels, and modern body of gold-stencilled cotton.
Length of head : 66.2cm
Mughal, c.1800
VAM : 2542 I.S.
The fish standard was one of the very highest indicators of rank, only being granted to the most powerful officers of state. The head was supported horizontally on a pole, and the whole emblem would be carried on an elephant or camel in the retinue of the man honoured. It was sometimes accompanied by two copper gilt balls, in which case the ensemble is known as *mahi-o-maratib* 'fish and dignitaries'.
Bibliography : Delhi (1911), pl.XII, pp.27-29; Hyderabad Govt. (1954), pl. f.p.14; Irvine (1962), p.32. RC

153

13

13 *(entry 367)*
Bottle inlaid with jade and jewelled
Mughal, 18th century
Lent anonymously

14 *(entry 346)* Opposite page
a) **Tiger-head finial from the throne of Tipu Sultan**
Mysore, late 18th century
Lent by the National Trust, Powis Castle.

14 *(entry 339)*
b) **Pieces from a huqqa**
Silver, enamelled and jewelled.
Mughal, (Lucknow?), mid-18th century
Lent by the National Trust, Powis Castle.

14 *(entry 323)*
c) **Silver beaker and cover**
Mughal, second half of the 17th century
VAM : IS 31-1961

14 *(entry 340)*
d) **Huqqa base**
Silver, partly gilt and enamelled.
Lucknow (?), late 18th-early 19th century
VAM : 122-1886 (IS)

14a

14b

14c

14d

520

Standard ('alam)
Gilt brass, with wooden pole.
Height : 80.2cm, *Length of pole* :
150.0cm
Mughal, c.1800
VAM : 2539 I.S.   RC

521

Standard ('alam)
Gilt brass with wooden pole.
Height : 80cm, *Length of pole* : 150cm
Mughal, c.1800
VAM : 2540 I.S.
An identical standard to no.520.   RC

522

Ceremonial staff
The shaft of gold set with diamonds and
enamelled.
Length : 48.5cm
Rajasthan (Jaipur), second half of the
19th century
Lent by the David Collection, Copenhagen.
On the base of the staff is an embossed
enamelled tiger, its stripes set with
diamonds and its eyes with rubies.   SS

523

Peacock feather fan (morchal)
Peacock feathers with gold and silver
thread, set in a gilt copper holder.
Length : 116cm
Murshidabad, mid-19th century
VAM : 2488 (IS)
This type of highly decorative fly whisk
can be seen in many of the paintings in
the exhibition, for example, in the
Durbar of Aurangzeb (no.78) where
the *morchal* has a jewelled handle.
The fan was acquired by the Indian
Museum and transferred to the South
Kensington Museum in 1880.
Bibliography : Stronge in *Arts of Bengal*
(1979), no.223.   SS

524

Fly flapper (chaunri)
Yak's tail set in a chased and engraved
silver holder.
Length : 111cm
Calcutta, c.1855
VAM : 2491 (IS)
The *chaunri* was an ancient symbol of
royalty in India. Its continuing significance in Mughal times as a royal
emblem can be seen in a painting from
the V & A *Akbarnama* (no.26) and in
the 1761 painting of Maharana Ari
Singh (149). This example was acquired
in 1855 by the Indian Museum.
Bibliography : Stronge in *Arts of Bengal*
(1979), no.224.   SS

Wood & ivory

525

Cup
Rhinoceros horn.
Length : 15.1cm
Mughal, c.1525
Lent by the British Museum (Sloane
Collection 1713).
This cup is of boat shape with simple
decoration of a serrated band around
the rim, and another above the ribbed
foot. Its form may be based on a metal
prototype.
The Emperor Babur notes in his diary
in the year 1525-6 that he had a
drinking-cup (*ab-khwura kishti*) made
out of the horn of a rhinoceros; the word
kishti (P. 'boat') indicated that the cup
was of similar shape to this example,
and it is conjectured that this may be
the one that Babur had made.
The cup was formerly in the possession
of Sir Hans Sloane (1660-1753), whose
collection formed the basis of the
British Museum.   RC

526

Archer's thumbring (shast)
Ivory
Length : 4.2cm
Deccan, Golconda, late 17th century.
Lent by the Jagdish and Kamla Mittal
Museum of Indian Art, Hyderabad,
76.1499.
The ring is of unusual form in having an
obtuse-angled rather than curved tip.
It is carved in relief with a border con-
taining repeated acanthus leaves and a
series of trefoils from which depends a
foliate medallion enclosing a flower.
The back is carved with a flower and
leafy stems.   RS

527

Thumb ring in the form of a bird
Stained ivory, with inlaid eye.
Length : 5.3cm
Rajasthan or Western India, 17th-18th
century.
Lent by the Sainsbury Centre for Visual
Arts, University of East Anglia,
Norwich.
Bibliography : Sainsbury (ed.), (1978),
no.369.

528

Lord Clive's chess set
Ivory, partly stained.
Height (max.): 8.7cm, *(min.)* : 4.4cm
Bengal (Murshidabad), c.1760.
Lent by the National Trust, Powis
Castle.

525

526

527

528

The pieces are depicted as troops and standard-bearers dressed in Mughal costume of the period with long pleated *jamas* and cummerbunds. Another ivory chess set said to have been owned by Lord Clive was formerly in the collection of the late Col. Thomas Sutton.
Bibliography: Ashton (1950), pp.80-81, pl.74.   RS

529
Ceremonial staff (chub)
Ivory and silver.
Length: 83.5cm
North India, probably Bengal, c.1760.
Lent by the National Trust, Powis Castle.
The staff is of sections of turned ivory which broadens and becomes decagonal at the top, where it curves to form the neck of a tiger. The head is executed in silver and chased. Such batons of office were carried by an attendant called a *chub dar* 'stick bearer' who preceded persons of rank when they travelled.
The East India Vade-Mecum describes him as 'generally a man of some prudence, versed in all the ceremonies of court etiquette. He stands at the inner door of the audience, or receiving, apartment; announcing the approach of visitors, and conducting them to the presence.'
The staff is from the Clive collection and probably belonged to the first Lord Clive.   RS

530
Box
Ivory
Length: 24.2cm
Bengal, Murshidabad, late 18th century.
VAM: IM 212-1921
The sides of the box are carved in relief with ogival arches enclosing alternate animals and flowering plants, with half-rosettes in the spandrels of the arches. On the top of the box is a rectangular panel with a floral outer border and dotted guard band which depicts Krishna and his flute. The use of cusped arches and the modelling of the figure recalls the decoration on the terra-cotta temples of Bengal and on the silk saris of Baluchar.   RC

531
Box
Ivory
Length: 23cm
Bengal, Murshidabad, late 18th century.
Lent by H.M. The Queen.
The box is carved in relief on the sides with alternate human figures and

157

531

flowering plants within ogival cartouches. In the spaces between them are flying birds at the top, and crouched animals at the bottom. The lid is plain, and probably a replacement for an originally carved one. For a related box in the Cleveland Museum of Art, see Dwivedi (1976), p.122 and fig.106. It has been suggested that a similar box was made in Bijapur in the late 16th century, see Goetz (1945), pp.29-32, 85.   RC

532
Panel from a howdah
Ivory
Height: 10.2cm, *Width*: 31.0cm
Rajasthan, c.1820
Lent by the Rt. Hon. The Lord Reigate, PC.
The panel is carved in high relief to show two elephants in combat with mahouts clinging to their backs. A horseman goads one beast with his spear and a third mahout runs behind with a fire cracker. The carving can be connected with Rajput miniatures from Mewar and in particular the head-gear resembles that worn by the retinue of Colonel James Tod in a painting of c.1820 belonging to the Royal Asiatic Society.
Bibliography: Skelton (1959), p.5, fig.1.
RS

533
Pen box
Ivory
Length: 23cm
Mughal, Delhi, early 19th century.
VAM: 11-1893 (I.S.)
The box is decorated with a floral design carved in low relief. There are silver mounts and lock.   RC

534
Box
Ivory with silver mounts.
Length: 10.2cm, *Width*: 5.4cm
Delhi, 19th century
VAM: IM 35-1937
This box, decorated in relief with floral ornament, is said to have contained the miniature Qur'an (no.110) supposedly taken from Bahadur Shah's apartments after the siege of Delhi in 1857.   RC

535
Bottle in the shape of an aubergine
Stained ivory
Rajasthan, early 19th century.
Lent by the National Museum, New Delhi. 57.117.
This bottle is for *surma* or collyrium used as a cosmetic for the eyes. It is in the shape of an aubergine with its green stem and sepals, which unscrew to form the opening of the bottle.   RC

536
Cup
Turned ivory with painted floral decoration.
Rajasthan, early 19th century.
Lent by the National Museum, New Delhi. 57.116.

536

15 *(entry 362)*

b) **Pouring vessel with cover**
Green jade, inlaid with enamelled
gold.
Mughal, 18th century
VAM : 02594 (IS)

158

15 *(entry 387)*

a) **Huqqa bowl**
Glass painted with gold.
Mughal, first half of the 18th century
Lent by the Trustees of the British
Museum.

16a

16b

16c

16d

16 *(entry 559)*

a) **Wooden box, painted**
Western India, early 19th century
VAM : IM 6-1920

16 *(entry 548)*

b) **Jewel casket**
Papier mâché, painted and lacquered.
Deccan, c. 1660
VAM : 851-1889

16 *(entry 503)*

c) **Brass box and cover**
Engraved and inlaid with lac.
Mughal, 18th century
VAM : 747-1889

16 *(entry 469)*

d) **Ewer**
Bidri, inlaid with silver and brass.
Deccan, 17th century
VAM : 1479-1904

537
Box
Ivory, coloured with lac.
Height : 3.8cm, *Diameter* 5.6cm
Rajasthan, 19th century.
Lent by Mr and Mrs James Alsdorf, Chicago.
The box is circular in plan and convex in outline with a shallow foot. It was initially turned and then carved to produce shallow gadrooning around the perimeter. The handle of the lid is surrounded by a series of turned studs.
Around the edges of box and lid the surface of the ivory has been lightly drilled and lac applied in a pattern of rings and dots.   RS

538
Opium box
Wood, turned and lacquered, inlaid with ivory.
Western Rajasthan, 19th century.
Lent by the National Museum, New Delhi, 62-2707.
The box is decorated with three rows of stylised motifs, including birds, trees and camels.   RC

539
Chaupar set
Ivory.
Each piece : *Height* : 3.8cm, *Width* : 2.9cm
Rajasthan or Sind, 19th century
VAM : IS 02503-5 and 02507
The 16 domed ivory pieces are stained red, blue, yellow and green, with decoration of flowers in niches reserved against a coloured ground. (see nos.101 and 294).   RC

540
Two dice
Ivory, stained with red and blue markings.
Length : 8.1cm
Sind, 19th century
VAM : IS 08237.

541
Spinning disc
Ivory, stained red.
Diameter : 6cm
Sind, 19th century
VAM : IS 02432.

542
Rattle
Ivory, stained red.
Length : 13.1cm, *Diameter* : 2.8cm
Sind, 19th century
VAM : IS 02430
(see no.102).

160

537

538

543

543
Panel
Wood
Height : 6.1cm, *Length* : 49.7cm
Mughal or Rajput, late 16th century.
Lent by Mr. Howard Hodgkin.
The panel possibly formed part of a
wooden throne of the type represented
in the relief carving on its outer face.
This shows a Muslim king seated on a
throne watching pairs of warriors
engaged in duelling with *khandas* and
parrying shields. The king is attended
by three courtiers, one of whom ushers
two of the combatants into his presence. To the right, two mounted
elephants approach, preceded by a
retainer bearing a standard.   RS

544
Cabinet
Painted and lacquered wood.
Height : 20.3cm, *Width* : 28.5cm,
Depth : 22.1cm
Sind (?), early 17th century
Lent by the Ashmolean Museum,
Oxford, 1978.129.
The top and four sides are painted with
hunting scenes in a landscape of trees
and flowering plants. The mounted
huntsmen on the sides are wearing
Mughal costume and their faces are
shown in profile.
The painting of the top is perhaps by a
different artist, who paints faces in the
three-quarters view characteristic of
Persian painting.
Although there has been a tendency to
attribute such painted and lacquered
boxes to the Deccan it is more likely
that they were made in Sind which was
a major centre for the manufacture of
cabinets and also for painted and
lacquered bows during the early seventeenth century. Provincial versions of
the Mughal style of painting were
current in Sind and the lower Punjab
through the century, e.g. Titley (1977),
pl.23, and boxes decorated with hunting
scenes were still being made in Sind in
the 19th century; see Birdwood (1880),
pl.65.
Bibliography : Zebrowski (1982),
pls.1-4.   RS

545
Cabinet
Painted wood, *Height* : 16cm, *Width* :
26cm, *Diameter* : 17.8cm
Sind (?), early 17th century.
Lent by the Hon. Robert Erskine.
The cabinet has seven drawers and is
painted all over : on the back and one
end with scenes of a European hunting
party in a landscape with animals and
birds; on the other end with an angel
and a lady, with flowers and birds – a
scene probably based on European
paintings of the Annunciation; and the
top, which has been badly damaged, is
painted gold with the vestiges of a
central floral medallion. All the sides
are bordered with a band of scrolling
floral decoration. The fronts of the
drawers are all painted in olive green
with the same floral pattern as in the
borders, except for the deep central
drawer which shows two cranes against
a floral background. The sides of the
drawers are painted bright red with a
delicately drawn scrolling pattern of
green serrated leaves and flowers in
shades of red and green.   RC

546
Jewel casket
Papier mâché, painted and lacquered.
Height : 12cm, *Length* : 25.5cm,
Width : 25.5cm
Sind (?), early 17th century.
Lent by the Metropolitan Museum of
Art, New York.
(Rogers Fund, 1958), no.58.159.
The box is octagonal with domed lid
which is painted to show a court
festivity at which dancers perform. The
side panels are painted with figures
continuing the main theme including a
man and a female *vina* player sitting on
chairs.   RS

544 (back)

546

549

547
Cabinet
Wood, painted and lacquered.
Height : 23cm, *Length* : 30.2cm,
Diameter : 22cm
Sind (?), second half of the 17th century.
Private collection.
The box has two doors and six drawers arranged in three rows. Its original painted decoration survives only on the interior – the exterior having been lacquered black with red and white borders in England at a later date. Each door is painted with a flowering plant on a gold-leaf ground with wisps of green Chinese cloud. The lock plate, hinges and corner fittings are of gilt copper with chased foliate decoration on a ground of punched circles. There are four flattened ball feet of gilt copper. According to the owner's family tradition, the box descended through the Fotherley-Whitfield family from John Fotherley (1652-1702) of The Bury, Rickmansworth. RS

548
Jewel casket
Painted by Rahim Deccani.
Papier-mâché, painted and lacquered, with ivory edging at base.
Height : 9.6cm, *Length* : 13.6cm,
Width : 9.2cm
Deccani (Golconda), c.1660-70.
VAM : 851-1889.
The box has parallel sides and serpentine ends with a sliding lid. On one side a seated prince embraces a standing girl as he receives a cup from a female attendant. The other side shows a girl dancing while two others play a vina and drum (*dholak*). At one end a girl stands in the Salabhanjika pose watching an egret and at the other is a youth wearing European costume. On the top of the box is shown a lady reclining on a couch under a tree, attended by a maid and observed by a young man. The casket is attributed to Rahim Deccani on the basis of a signed painting by the same hand in the Chester Beatty Library, Dublin.
Bibliography : Kramrisch (1937), p.172, pl.XXI; Zebrowski (1981), p.181; Barrett (1958), pl.10. RS

549
Pen box (qalamdan)
Mother-of-pearl inlay on wood.
Length : 34.5cm, *Height* : 6.3cm
Inscribed with Persian verses referring to the art of calligraphy.
Mughal (Gujarat), early 17th century.
Lent by the Los Angeles County Museum of Art, Nasli M. Heeramaneck Collection, Gift of Joan Palevsky, M.73.5.340.
The wooden carcase is lacquered black against which the *nasta'liq* calligraphy of the verses appears in elongated hexagons along the top and sides. These are surrounded by bands of dense foliate arabesque within geometric borders. The drawer of the box is painted red and decorated with sprigs of flowers.
Bibliography : Pal (1973), p.180, no.363. RS

550
Chest
Shisham wood inlaid with mother-of-pearl.
Length : 69.9cm, *Width* : 38.2cm,
Height : 39.9cm
Mughal, 17th century
Lent by Mr. Howard Hodgkin.
This chest seems to be based on a Turkish design, and was possibly made for the Turkish market. It has a Turkish verse running in cartouches around the top, and the painting inside the drawers is of lilies and roses in Turkish style. The drawers also have cusped lacquered corner brackets, and a gold and black chevron design on the rims. There are some similar chests in the Topkapi Sarayi Müzesi in Istanbul, though the mother-of-pearl designs on them are Turkish in style, whereas this Indian example is decorated in the style of Gujarat, as is another in the Benaki

Museum, Athens.
Bibliography : Istanbul: Topkapi Sarayi (1956), no.21; Washington: Smithsonian Institute (1966), no.258. RC

551
Casket
Wood overlaid with mother-of-pearl in lac.
Height : 21.6cm, *Width* : 31.4cm,
Depth : 19.0cm
Western India, 17th century
Lent by the Ashmolean Museum, Oxford.
The casket is rectangular on a wooden plinth with four feet of cusped profile. The sides are decorated with medallions containing stylised interlaced foliate decoration, interspersed with palm trees and leafy fronds. The flat surface of the lid is executed in a similar style, but its sloping sides have geometric ornament of repeated hexagons and diamonds characteristic of Ottoman work. The piece was probably made for the Turkish market (cf.no.550). RS

552
Courtier's stick
Wood with mother-of-pearl overlaid in lac, silver mounts and an agate handle.
Length : 150.7cm
The agate handle is inscribed 'Carolus Rex AD 1632, Dieu et Mon Droit' and the silver mouldings 'Carolus Rex' and 'Natus Nov. 1600',
Mughal (Gujarat), 17th century with later additions.

Lent by The Marquess of Tavistock & The Trustees of Bedford Estates.
The stick is overlaid with a repeating pattern of stylised flowers within a trellis of diamond-shaped lozenges. The head is mounted with silver and is capped with a Western Indian agate crutch handle. Despite its inscriptions associating it with Charles I, the composite head is of uncertain date. The inscriptions themselves, accompanied on the handle by an engraved crown of late Georgian design, were probably added in about 1820. According to family tradition, the stick was given by King Charles I to William, 5th Earl of Bedford in 1647. RS

552a
Fencing stick
Painted wood, with pommel spike and ferrule of enamel on silver.
Length : 135cm
Lucknow, c.1780
VAM : I.S. 10-1980
The stick is painted all over in blue with scenes of Europeans in a landscape with animals and buildings. The painting style is strongly influenced by Chinese decorated porcelain, and is paralleled in album borders painted for Col. Polier in about 1780 (see no.90).
The shape of the handle is derived from the hilt of the Hindu *khanda* with the spiked ball pommel found in Central Indian and Rajput weapons. The silver mounts are decorated in the blue and green enamel characteristic of Lucknow.

550

The stick was probably used in *lakri*: combat with wooden sticks, and more specifically the Persian martial art known in India as *ali mad*, for which there was a school in Lucknow. The art was practised only by the aristocracy, as opposed to the Indian form known in Lucknow as *rustam khani*, which was popular with the ordinary people. This stick would certainly have been used by a member of the nobility.
Bibliography : Sharar (1975), pp.109-110; Hickman (1979).   RC

553
Darvish's staff (danda)
Wood
Length : 63.7cm, *Diameter* : 4.2cm
Deccan, 17th century
Lent by the Jagdish and Kamla Mittal Museum of Indian Art, 76.1431.
The staff is slightly curved at the top and is decorated in low relief in three zones separated by bands of foliate scroll. Each zone contains a spiral band of animals and birds chasing each other through flowering vegetation. A similar staff is shown being carried by a darvish on the map of Bidar in Colonel Gentil's atlas (no.87). Although both Muslim and Hindu mendicant ascetics professed worldly poverty, as implied by descriptions such as *faqir* and *darvish*, both meaning poor person, they sometimes carried expensive artifacts appropriate to their calling (see also no. 192). These were made to the order of wealthy patrons and either donated to favoured mendicants or perhaps carried by devotees whose poverty was purely symbolic.   RS

554
Games board (reversible)
Teak, veneered with ebony, citronwood, ivory and *sadeli* mosaic.
Length : 32.5cm, *Width* : 29.2cm
Sind, 17th century
VAM : 1961-1899
One side chequered with alternate squares of ebony and ivory, for chess, draughts, etc., each square with a *sadeli* disc. Borders of geometric ornament and scrolling flowered stems. Reverse patterned with nine rectangles, the central one with a large *sadeli* disc, and six others with *sadeli* lozenges. Each of the two remaining panels contains a small square compartment with raised sides. The rest of the surface on this side is patterned with scrolling leafy stems of ivory inlay. The board has raised edges. *Sadeli*, a mosaic of ivory, wood, horn, tin, etc., is sliced off bundles of facetted

rods which have been glued together so that the shaped pattern, often based on tiny hexagons, goes all the way through, on the principle of Tunbridge ware and English seaside rock. The resulting geometrical designs, in very thin slices, are glued into corresponding pre-cut shallow depressions on the surface of the object concerned, usually of wood or ivory. The technique, which probably originated in the ancient Middle East, was known to the Romans and is still familiar in Mediterranean countries. It was brought to Sind from Persia (where it is mainly associated with Shiraz) in the 16th/17th century, and used as decoration on boxes and related articles made under Portuguese patronage. It was also used in architectural woodwork. Sindi/ Indian examples of *sadeli* differ from the Persian prototype mainly in the use of silvery tin as the metal component, as opposed to brass, which gives Persian *sadeli* its much warmer tone. During the first half of the 18th century the craft seems virtually to have died out in Sind, probably due to the epidemics which wiped out thousands of craftsmen in Tatta, the city in which the cabinet makers were concentrated. According to information supplied to Sir George Birdwood by *sadeli* workers in Bombay, and published originally by him in the catalogue of the 1862 International Exhibition, the craft was re-introduced to Sind 'about a hundred years ago' [i.e., c.1760], by three Multanis who had it from Shiraz. They taught other craftsmen who settled in Bombay around 1800 and started the manufacture of European style bric-a-brac such as sandalwood and ivory work-boxes, with *sadeli* ornament. This revived *sadeli* became popular as Bombay Inlaid Work, or simply Bombay Boxes.
See no.555 for another 17th century example of Sindi *sadeli*.   VM

555
Cabinet
Inlaid wood.
Height : 16.2cm *Length* : 27.4cm, *Diameter* : 19.6cm
Sind, 17th century
VAM : 1598-1903
Top, front, back and sides inlaid in lighter wood, ivory (plain and stained green) and brass with symmetrical designs in which human and *peri* (Persian fairies/angels) figures confront each other in a setting of stylized flowering trees and birds. Inside the fall-front is a design of two confronted

tigers similarly placed. Borders of scrolling stems and flowerheads. Behind the fall-front is a series of drawers, a long one at the top, disguised as two, and beneath it a deep central drawer, with two shallow ones on either side. The drawer fronts are veneered with ivory incised with flower motifs. Chequer borders. Some drawers retain their ivory knobs. The fall-front is fitted with a brass-escutcheoned lock and iron key, and drop-handles are attached to the sides.
The towns of Sind, particularly Tatta, were famed in the 16th and 17th centuries for the manufacture of inlaid boxes and cabinets of basically European style, but decorated according to local traditions. Linschoten (about 1585) and Pelsaert (1626) were two of the European travellers who remarked on this trade, and the large quantities of such wares brought to Goa for the Portuguese market. The *sadeli* games board (no.554) also comes into this category.   VM

556
Cabinet
Rosewood, inlaid with ivory.
Width : 62.3cm, *Diameter* : 41.9cm, *Height* : 41.9cm
Deccan (probably Golconda); late 17th/ early 18th century.
Lent by Mr and Mrs W.Z. Lloyd.
The top, sides and double doors are patterned with a symmetrical design in which a palmette is repeated on an arabesque of stems and leaves, centred on a single rosette, within floral scroll borders. There are iron carrying handles, and hinges and escutcheons of silvery metal. The doors open to reveal a symmetrical arrangement of drawers, long and short, deep and shallow, with ivory pulls and inlay in which the figures of female attendants, separated by single flowering plants and bearing an assortment of objects such as trays, *rumals* and wands of office direct attention to the main scene on the deep central drawer, where a prince and a lady face each other seated on a floor-spread, each backed by a female attendant with fly-whisk. The scene is surmounted by a pointed niche with a single flowering plant repeated in each spandrel and under the apex. A shallow drawer immediately above it is balustraded to maintain the illusion of architecture. Inside each door the figure of a court official faces towards the central scene, a wand of office in his hand. He is flanked by three pairs of flowering

plants, a large pair in the centre with a smaller pair above and below. Below him a tiger crouches over its kill, a gazelle, flanked by a pair of stylized cypress trees. The scene is framed by the floral scroll border design which appears on the outside panels.
The cabinet has descended in the family of a Bristol merchant who traded with the Indies in the early 18th century. Several other examples of this interesting group have come to our notice in recent years. Figures in Deccani court dress of the later 17th century feature in most of them; whole areas such as the outer panels and insides of the doors are often patterned with rows of gracefully curved flowering plants; occasionally this motif replaces the human figures on the drawers. The ivory-inlayers' repertoire included other Indo-Persian elements such as stylized cypress entwined with willow boughs or sprays of blossoming plum, *Simurghs* carrying off elephants, tableaux in which courtly hunting scenes are interspersed with flora and fauna in the manner of Golconda chintzes (nos.239-242), and carpet-style borders perhaps reflecting the proximity of the Ellore weavers. A few of the cabinets show hunters in European dress, and subjects derived from classical sources via European engravings : the Labours of Hercules provided a favourite theme. Fairly early in the 18th century demand for this type of cabinet appears to have waned, as the prototype went out of fashion in Europe. It seems likely that in fact the main patronage was European, and that its heyday coincided with the craze for chintz hangings such as the diarist Evelyn saw at Lady Mordaunt's house in 1665 : '. . . a room hung with Pintado full of figures . . . representing Sundry Trades and occupations of the Indians, with their habits &c. . .'
By a strange coincidence the compartment effect created by the drawer fronts in 17th century European cabinets closely paralleled the traditional Hindu strip-picture arrangement of temple friezes and murals, echoed in cotton paintings such as nos.209 and 210. (Lady Mordaunt's hanging was probably a composition of this kind.) The Golconda ivory-inlaying tradition survived the eclipse of these cabinets and their figure subjects, in the furniture and boxes made under British patronage at Vizagapatam. Major John Corneille, who visited the town in 1756, remarked : 'Vizagaptam . . . hitherto the

principal settlement the English had in the Kingdom of Golconda . . . their chintz is esteemed the best in India for the brightness of its colours. The place is likewise remarkable for its inlay work, and justly, for they do it to the greatest perfection.'   VM

557
Sanduk (box and cover)
Wood, incised and lacquered.
Height : 23cm, *Diameter* : 21cm
Khanote, Sind, 19th century
VAM : 1645-1883
Circular design, with domed cover. Lacquered in various colours and incised with bold rosettes in horizontal bands. Similar designs and colour schemes appear on Sindi folk embroidery of the period.
True Sindi lac-work of this kind is sometimes confused with painted and varnished gesso ware in the manner of Kashmir, which was also made in Sind.
VM

557

558
Painted box for jewellery (?)
Painted and lacquered wood.
Length : 39cm, *Width* : 32.2cm, *Diameter* : 5.2cm
Central India, c.1825-50
Private collection.
The oval-shaped box, with a projecting section, has a swivelling lid and a well on its central axis inside, round which it is thought that jewellery (necklaces, etc.) may have been secured. The lid is painted with a scene of Shiva and Parvati seated beneath a *pipal* tree, attended by Ganesha, Hanuman and musicians on the right and by Rajput noblemen on the left. A lady at her toilet appears on the projecting section

below. The style has affinities with Mewar painting and with the Central Indian schools of Ratlam and Sitamau.
AT

559
Painted box
painted and lacquered wood.
Height : 31.1cm, *Length* : 39.7cm, *Width* : 27.9cm
Kutch or Gujarat, mid-19th century.
VAM : I.M. 6-1920
The box has a hinged lid, metal handles and catch and wooden feet. It is painted on the lid and front with durbar scenes, in which a raja sits on a European chair, attended by noblemen. On the rear side a tiger hunt is shown, and on the two shorter sides, a lady on a palace terrace.
AT

560
Yoyo (chakri)
Painted wood
Rajasthan, 19th century
Lent by the National Museum, New Delhi. 62/1753/2.
The yoyo is painted with scenes from a Rajput folk-tale. (See no.168).   RC

561
Opium box
Wood, turned and lacquered, inlaid with ivory.
Western Rajasthan, 19th century.
Lent by the National Museum, New Delhi, 62-2707.
The box is decorated with three rows of stylised motifs, including birds, trees and camels.   RC

562
Musical instrument (sarinda), formerly stringed
Carved ivory. The flowers and eyes of animals and people were formerly inlaid with gem-stones on gold : some traces of gold and some stones remain, and traces of black and red pigment.
Height : 67.3cm, *Width* : 19.7cm, *Diameter* : 14.6cm
North India, c.1800
Lent by Mr Bashir Mohamed.
The *sarinda* is a bowed instrument related to the *sarangi* and is said to have been popular in Bengal. This one was in the collection of Lt. Col. John Murray MacGregor (1745-1822), who was Auditor General of Bengal.   RC

563
Stringed instrument (taus)
The body in the form of a peacock (*taus*), lacquered wood with feathers in the tail; the neck fretted and partly

lacquered.
Height : 38.1cm, *Length* 103.5cm, *Width* : 12.7cm
North India, 19th century
VAM : IS 182-1882
The *taus* or *mayuri* is a bowed instrument related to the *dilruba*, said to be a cross between the *sarangi* and the *sitar*. There is also a *taus* or peacock variety of the North Indian version of India's classical plucked instrument, the *vina*.
RS

564
Stringed instrument (rabab)
The wooden body is covered with skin; the long neck terminates in a carved and inlaid head, with silver-mounted pegs for six strings.
Height : 104.6cm, *Width* : 34.2cm, *Diameter* : 21.5cm
North India, 19th century
VAM : IS 36-1890
The *rabab* was a bowed instrument of Near Eastern origin which developed also as a plucked instrument in India and is the forerunner of the modern *sarod*. It was a favourite instrument of Muslim musicians who specialised in devotional music in the classical tradition of Northern India. One of its most distinguished exponents was the sixteenth century master Tansen.
Bibliography : Gosvami, (1957), pl.f.176 and pp.298-300   RS

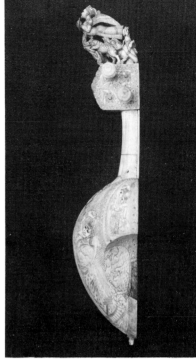

562

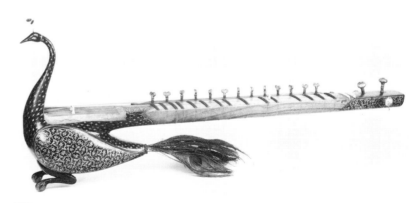

563

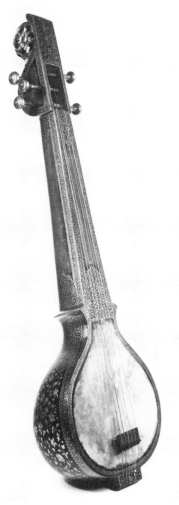

564

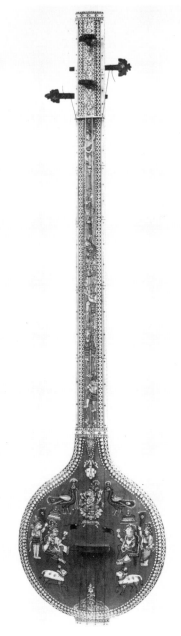

565

565

Musical instrument (tanpura), with keys for four strings

Painted wood, inlaid with darker wood and ivory, ornamented with paintings of various deities.

Height : 93.3 cm, *Width* : 34.2 cm, *Diameter* : 15.8 cm

Probably made at Sipri, Gwalior State, Central India, 19th century

VAM : I.M. 238-1922

On the front are depicted Ganesha, Sita being fanned by Lakshman, and Rama fanned by Hanuman; on the back are Shiva, Brahma and Krishna with the *gopis* (cow-girls). The neck is decorated with nautch girls and two male figures, one of whom plays a pipe. The *tanpura* is a plucked instrument designed to provide the drone accompaniment to an improvised melodic line.

Bibliography : Jenkins and Olsen (1976), p.27 (illustration)   RS

566

Pair of drums (tabla and banya)

Wood (*tabla*) and tinned copper (*banya*), with skin drum heads, stretched by thongs, with lacquered wood reels for tuning (*tabla*).

Height : 32 cm and 25.5 cm

North India, late 19th century.

VAM : I.S. 69 and 70-1890

Introduced during the Muslim period, the *tabla* is the most popular North Indian percussion instrument. It is played as the right hand drum of a pair, with the *banya* or bass drum on the left.

AT

Furniture

Before the period of European colonization there was no tradition of ordinary seat furniture in India. The concept of special elevated chairs for gods and kings was familiar, from the lotus thrones of the Hindu pantheon to the towering canopied daises of the Mughal emperors. Palaces were amply supplied with carpets, cushions and bolsters where princes could relax when they were not holding court. The first European chairs used by Indians were almost certainly individual items, seen as thrones. Fr. Monserrate, a Spanish Jesuit at the court of Akbar (1556-1605), noted in 1580 that the emperor liked to use a Portuguese-style velvet-covered throne. There is, however, little evidence to suggest that European-inspired chairs and sofas, in quantity, became standard furnishings in any Indian palace until far on in the 18th century. The catalyst was probably the establishment by high-ranking officials of the East India Companies of reception rooms furnished in the current European fashion with large suites of settees, side chairs and armchairs arranged against the walls, with the floorspace left clear for dancing or sauntering. If this is so, it comes as no surprise that among the first princely patrons of such a furniture convention were the Nawab of Arcot, who in 1772 presented Lady Harland, wife of the British Plenipotentiary to his court, with a handsome Chippendale-type armchair inlaid with ivory; and Mani Begam, widow of the Nawab of Murshidabad, who 'prepared an elegant display' of ivory couches, chairs and footstools for Warren Hastings in 1784. Each of their territories was close to a chief administrative centre of the East India Company, one in Madras, the other in Bengal. Each had a tradition of ivory carving, veneering, and – in the Madras area – inlaying in wood. Local craftsmen, accustomed for generations to working for foreign markets, had long been renowned for their ability to work from patterns – 'musters' – and copy unfamiliar objects. The chances are that the European-style furniture copied for patrons like the Nawab of Arcot had in fact been made locally, from imported pattern-books, and decorated with designs from the craftsmen's own repertoire, a combination which gave rise to some strange hybrids but was often very successful. At this stage Indian palace chairs and sofas were probably regarded by their owners as uncomfortable status symbols, reserved for entertaining Europeans, like the English front parlour of the 19th century kept for special occasions.

By the 1780s, it was not only the associates of the British who were cultivating seat furniture. In Mysore, it was reported that Haidar Ali and later his son Tipu Sultan (nos.94 and 96), whose European affiliations were mainly with France (no.404), owned chairs and sofas (no.568).

During the first half of the 19th century relatively restrained designs, based on English late Georgian and Regency prototypes, were in vogue (nos.112, 158, 570). Some armchairs included a distinctive Indian feature in which each arm, instead of meeting the back in the conventional way, continues round in a loop to join it from behind, so that seen from the side, arm and back merge into a continuous curve.

To judge from their frequent appearance in Sikh portraiture, armchairs of this type were much in evidence on formal occasions at the court of Lahore in the latter years of Maharaja Ranjit Singh (1780-1839), who, like the rulers of Oudh, encouraged European soldiers of fortune to enlist in his service (no.108). 'Sikh' armchairs were, however, also made and used far beyond the frontiers of the Punjab; in Calcutta for instance there was an expanding market for such furniture with the growing class of westernized Hindu merchants such as D'Oyley's 'Nob Kishen', who bought up large numbers of chairs at auctions in order to entertain Englishmen like Tom Raw (no.106).

At the same time a very different and highly decorated style enjoyed growing popularity with the extrovert and exuberant rulers of Oudh. A Lucknow painting of about 1760 (Binney (1973), no.96 colour plate) shows that already the princes of Oudh were cultivating elaborately carved semi-European-style chairs. This interest came to a head with the appointment of the Scottish artist Robert Home (1752-1834) as Court Painter to Ghazi-ud-din Haidar (1814-27), Nawab Wazir and – from 1819 – first King of Oudh. Home's duties were broadly interpreted and included designing quasi-European objects of many kinds, among them thrones, chairs and sofas loosely based on the more bizarre European styles such as that of the Egyptian Revival – the more sphinxes and griffins the better – but also taking Indian prototypes into account. What might be called School of Home designs were quickly assimilated into North Indian court tradition, spreading first to Benares, where the Maharaja's hereditary ivory carvers constructed improbable chairs and sofas (nos.188 and 572) of the kind happily described in Welch (1978) as looking as though they would have to be chased across the room...

By 1838 the last Mughal emperor, Bahadur Shah II (1837-58) had abandoned his mark II or III Peacock Throne for an ornate and decadent throne-chair made broad and low, a riot of sea-serpents, lions and acanthus leaves (no.109). Such designs certainly had their roots in Hindu tradition (e.g. the *Sinhasana* or lion-throne) and versions appear in North Indian paintings of the 18th century (Binney, opp. cit.) However, their 19th century re-vamping and widespread adoption at the courts of North India, even by the 'Refuge of Islam', were probably stimulated by Indo-European whimsies such as Robert Home created for the King of Oudh. Variants of the design were often encased in high relief embossed sheet silver (no.574) and gold, another tradition of ancient origin in India, seen with wonder by early European travellers, including the anonymous narrator of Cabral's *Voyages* who in 1500 noted the Zamorin of Calicut's 'large silver chair'. From about the middle of the 19th century 'silver' armchairs and sofas upholstered with deep-buttoned silk or velvet upholstery in the High Victorian taste gradually became standard furnishings in the palaces of Rajasthan. They were accompanied by exotic imports such as Belgian chairs, tables and four-poster beds made entirely of glass.

VM

567

Palanquin

Carved wood, lacquered green and gilt. Cane bottom.

Length: 165cm, *Width*: 94cm

Height: 80cm (headboard)

Probably Murshidabad, Bengal, mid-18th century.

Lent by the National Trust, Powis Castle.

Traditional low-sided construction, with raised headboard, scalloped edges, scrolled bracket feet, and X-shaped stretchers at either end, through the upper part of which would pass the long, curved bamboo carrying-pole from which the palanquin is suspended by ropes. The pole was usually covered with embroidered and tasselled cloth, and a canopy could be attached to shield the occupant from the sun. A mattress and cushions often completed the ensemble, which was carried by a minimum of four bearers. This palanquin, described in an inventory of 1775 as including 'a Bamboo and rich embroidered Furniture', was brought from Bengal by Clive of India (1725-74), and is believed to have been abandoned by Siraj-ud-daula on the field of Plassey in 1757. VM

568

Armchair

Ivory, carved, painted and gilt.

Height: 92.4cm

South India, possibly made for Tipu Sahib at Seringapatam, late 18th century.

VAM: 1075-1882

From a set originally comprising two settees and a large number of chairs, long dispersed. The Musuem has a pair of the armchairs; another pair and one settee were in a private collection in London in 1970. The set is traditionally associated with Tipu, Warren Hastings and Queen Charlotte. Our two armchairs appear to have come from the sale of Queen Charlotte's effects in 1819, and the other items from the Daylesford sale in 1853. Since they do not feature in the Daylesford inventory of 1799, it is possible that Warren Hastings, a known collector of ivory furniture, could have acquired them from the spoils of Seringapatam via his East India Company contacts. Although the Tipu association cannot be proved, there is contemporary evidence that he and his father Haidar Ali owned chairs and sofas, and it seems significant that most of the furniture traditionally associated with Tipu, both here and in Indian collections, is of this type. VM

569

Throne chair

Gilt wood, with gilt metal mounts.

Height: 93cm

Lucknow, about 1820

Lent by the Rt. Hon. the Earl Amherst

Based on a European prototype of the Egyptian Revival, the armchair incorporates in its back panel the fish symbols of Oudh. Brought to England by the first Earl Amherst, who was Governor General 1823-8, the chair is associate dwith Ghazi-ud-din Haidar, Nawab Wazir and first King of Oudh (1814-27). Furniture of this kind was designed for him by the Scottish artist Robert Home (1752-1834), whose career as Court Painter at Lucknow approximately spanned the reign. Photographs of designs from Home's Lucknow period are shown in this section. VM

570

Armchair and matching footstool

Embossed sheet silver on a wooden core.

Height: 93.6cm

North India (probably Punjab or Oudh), about 1820.

VAM: 2519 & 2520 I.S.

A more than usually restrained Indian interpretation of an English late Georgian design, this handsome chair is decorated with plaques of Lucknow enamel. While Lucknow was among the most important centres of European-inspired furniture making, documented Lucknow furniture tends to the exuberant and even bizarre. This plainer style is much more characteristic of the European-style chairs seen in Sikh paintings of the period. Its restraint may, however, suggest that it was made for an official of the East India Company, though the practice of covering seat furniture in embossed silver or gold is normally associated with Indian potentates, who would also have been more likely to favour the tiger and peacock design on the top rail. An interesting feature of this chair is that it is collapsible for travelling; all the sections are hinged or hooked so that the chair, completely solid and stable in use, can be folded flat if necessary. VM

571

The Golden Throne of Ranjit Singh

Sheets of embossed gold over a core of wood and resin.

Height: 94cm

Lahore, about 1830

571

VAM: 2518 I.S.

The Golden Throne is associated with Maharaja Ranjit Singh (1780-1839), 'Lion of the Punjab', who welded the factions of the Punjab into a Sikh nation. The disintegration which followed his death culminated in the Sikh Wars and finally, in 1849, British annexation of the Punjab. The throne was shipped to England in 1853 for the East India Company's Museum and eventually transferred to South Kensington.

The distinctive 'waisted' shape derives from Hindu tradition, seen also in the sculptured lotus thrones of the gods. Sikh paintings show at least 3 other thrones of this type in use at the Court of Lahore. This throne can be identified in a sketch of Ranjit Singh by W.G.Osborne, reproduced in his book *The Court and Camp of Runjeet Sing* (sic), London, 1840, and in Schoefft's oil-painting of Maharaja Sher Singh (1807-43), colour plate II of F.S. Aijazuddin's *Sikh Portraits by European Artists*, 1979. It also appears in an engraving of Indian Museum objects on display at Fife House, Whitehall, published in *The Illustrated London News*, Aug. 3rd 1861.

Another 'Golden Throne' of apparently almost identical appearance is published in *Calcutta 200 Years*, ed. N.K. Nayak, 1981, p.96. This throne is in Government House, Calcutta, and said to be associated with Tipu Sultan. VM

572

Sofa

Veneered and carved ivory, painted and gilt, over a wooden core.

Length: 253cm, *Diameter*: 77cm

Height: 124cm (back)

Banaras, probably about 1830.

Lent by the National Heritage Memorial Fund.

A lavish overstatement of an English Regency prototype, made for a Maharaja, the vast boat-shaped sofa has a triple-arched back pierced with latticework roundels topped by urn finials, above five ebony panels inlaid in ivory with Islamic designs. The ivory veneer of its framework is carved with a scrolling leaf-and-flower motif in colours and gilt. There are two lion/tiger mask finials at each end, and splayed legs with metal claw feet and castors. The velvet upholstery and brocade trimming were already dilapidated when the sofa was photographed in the Calcutta Exhibition of 1883-4, where it was displayed with other similar furniture by its owner, the Maharaja of Banaras. That upholstery

168

was later relaced, probably for Lord Curzon of Kedleston, who acquired the furniture while Viceroy of India, 1899-1904. During recent investigation, a fragment of the original blue velvet cover was found under a nailhead, and the latest uphostery colour is based on this. The trimming is Banaras brocade of the mid-19th century. VM

573
Charpai (bed) leg
Lacquered wood.
Height : 44cm, *Diameter* : 14cm (max.)
Jaipur, Rajasthan, mid-19th century.
VAM : 01342 I.S.
Trellis and flower pattern, mainly in orange, red and yellow with touches of green on a black ground. Ivory finial. Two undecorated roundels on the upper portion indicate where the side and end rails of the bed frame would have joined the leg.
The *charpai* is the archetypal all-purpose Indian bed, used by people of all ranks except the completely desti-tute whose only bed is the ground. However costly or humble the materials – ranging from sheet silver or gilt on a wooden core, through turned and carved ivory or wood variously decor-ated or inlaid, down to plain wood with-out any attempt at finish or ornament – the basic design is always the same : legs of approximately this shape, and a frame over which is stretched an inter-woven webbing of cords. Mattresses are not part of the traditional bed furniture, the occupant usually lying on a mat or quilt with another quilt as covering. The design of the *charpai* has not changed since the traveller Ibn Batuta described it about 1350: 'The beds in India are very light. A single man can carry one, and every traveller should have his own. The bed consists of four conical legs, on which four staves are laid; between they plait a sort of ribbon of silk or cotton. When you lie on it you need nothing else to render the bed sufficiently elastic.' VM

574
Throne (one of a pair)
Silver
Indian, mid-19th century.
Lent by Robin Wigington, Stratford-upon-Avon.
The teak frame is covered overall with silver sheet embossed with stylised grapes, vines, running foliage and at the cartouche shaped back peacocks and pennons flanking a vase of flowers framed by foliage. The serpentine seat-rail has at the centre a tiger's head. The four cabriole legs terminate in claw feet at the front and scrolls at the back. RW

575
Foot-stool (one of a pair)
Silver
Indian, late 19th century.
Lent by Robin Wigington, Stratford-upon-Avon.
The teak frame is covered overall with silver sheet embossed *en suite* with the throne. There is a tiger's head at the centre of each rail. The four cabriole legs terminate in claw feet. RW

573

574 & 575

576
Painted panel with Ragamala scenes
Gouache on wood
Height : 15.7cm, *Length* :137cm
Southern Rajasthan, late 17th century.
Lent by the National Museum of India, New Delhi. 76.485.
This panel with ten *Ragamala* subjects, or depictions of musical modes, may once have formed part of the decoration of a princely music room. The *ragas* and *raginis* shown are (left to right): *Kedara, Khambavati, Varari, Patamanjari, Vilaval, Bangali, Maru, Asavari, Desakh, Nata*. AT

577
Painted ceiling with procession, Rasamandala and Baramasa scenes
Gouache on wood
Length : 336cm, *Width* : 147cm
Patan region, Gujarat, late 18th or early 19th century.
Lent by the Hon. Robert Erskine.
This ceiling, consisting of 13 painted panels, belonged to a village house in the region of Patan, Gujarat. Its imagery, however, derives from court painting. The left side of the compo-sition shows figures on horses, camels, elephants, bullock-carts and a palan-quin, proceeding, amid floral decor-ation, towards the centre, where a *Rasamandala* circle of alternating male and female dancers appears. The right side contains a number of interior and exterior scenes, including an inscribed series of *Baramasa* scenes, conventional representations of the activities of lovers during the twelve months of the year. The upper half of this section contains depictions of the summer months of Vaisakh, Jeth, Asarh, Sravan, Bhadra-pada and Asoj, while the lower half shows the autumn and winter months of Karttik, Margasirsa, Paus, Magh, Phalgun, and Chaitra. AT

169

Glossary

A : Arabic
H : Hindi
P : Persian
S : Sanskrit

amir (A)
A chief or nobleman

angarkha (H)
A long tunic or coat worn by men

arati (H)
The act of swinging a lamp before an image

astragal
Moulding around the barrel of a cannon

barahmasa (H)
"Twelve months" : a series of poems, often illustrated, showing the behaviour of lovers during the different months of the year

bidri (H)
From the town of Bidar in the Deccan. A metal-working technique, in which silver, gold or brass is inlaid into an alloy base which is then blackened

bigha (H)
A measure of land equal to about ⅝ of an acre

bismillah (A)
"In the name of God" : the start of the invocation which concludes 'the Merciful, the Compassionate'

bolster
The raised piece of metal between the blade and hilt of a knife

buta (P)
Lit. 'flower' or 'bush'. A decorative motif, often called a cone, found mostly on textiles, especially Kashmir shawls

cascabel
Knob behind the breech of a cannon

chadar (P)
A tent, mantle or veil. In India, the term normally means a coverlet or shawl

charpai (P)
Lit. 'four-footed'. A bedstead

chaturmukhalingam (S)
A phallic emblem of Shiva bearing the four faces of the god

chauri, chaunri (H)
A fly-whisk made of hair set into a handle

chhatri (H)
A pavilion

chhipi (H)
A block-printer

dak (H)
Post or mail, or any system of travelling or conveyance in relays

damascening
A term used for at least three different processes for the decoration of iron and steel : 1) watering, whereby bars of varied hardness are forged together and etched to bring out the pattern 2) inlaying the metal with gold, silver or other metals 3) beating the applied metal on to a surface that has been prepared by cross-hatching or chasing with a burin or draw knife. See *koftgari*

dastana (P)
A glove or forearm guard (vambrace, *q.v.*)

dolphins
The handles cast on a cannon

darbar (P) (durbar)
Audience hall, or a royal audience

dhoti (H)
A cloth worn round the waist and passing between the legs

firangi (P)
Lit. 'Frankish', 'European'. A type of straight-bladed sword, either imported from Europe by the Portuguese, or made in imitation of them

gadi (H)
A cushion, especially the cushion or bolster on which the ruler sits

ganjifa (H)
A pack or game of cards

gorakhpanthi yogi (H)
A follower of Gorakh (fl. AD 1120), the most renowned of the Nathas. The Nath cult of Hindu asceticism flourished in Northern India, Nepal and Bengal from the 10th century AD

gulabpash (P)
Rosewater sprinkler

hamsa (H)
The sacred goose of Indian mythology

howdah (H)
A litter or seat for the back of an elephant

huma (P)
A mythical bird of good omen, said to forecast kingship for anyone whose head it overshadows

huqqa (P)
A type of pipe in which tobacco is smoked through water

husndan (A,P)
A decorative betel-box

jama (P)
A type of gown or coat

jamdhar (H)
Lit. 'death-bearer'. A type of dagger

jinn (A)
A spirit or demon

kalgi (P)
A heron-feather plume

kalima (A)
Lit. 'the Word'. The Muslim confession of faith : 'There is no god but God, and Muhammad is the prophet of God'

kard (P)
A type of Persian knife with straight tapering blade and a straight hilt with no guard

kashkul (P)
A beggar's cup or bowl

katar (H)
The characteristic Indian thrusting dagger with a double-edged blade and a transverse grip between two parallel bars

kathak (H)
From *katha* 'story'. A north Indian form of dance

khanda (H)
A type of sword

khanjar (A)
A dagger, of which the Indian type has a double-edged, single or double curved blade. The hilt is often shaped like a pistol-grip or carved as an animal's head, usually from hardstone or ivory

khil'at (A)
A robe of honour, or set of garments etc. bestowed by a ruler as a mark of favour

khimkhab (P) (kincob)
A brocaded fabric with gold or silver thread

koftgari (P)
The decoration of iron and steel by inlaying or applying gold or silver to a surface which has been deeply engraved to receive wire, or lightly hatched to retain wire or leaf. An inferior process substitutes the use of adhesives for engraving. These processes are often referred to as damascening (q.v.) or false damascening, the epithet 'false' sometimes being reserved for the process of surface application rather than inlaying. See also **damascening**

lingam (S)
The phallus, the symbolic form in which the god Shiva is normally worshipped

lingam-yoni
The aniconic representation of Shiva Mahadeva and the Goddess

lota (H)
A small, round, metal pot

madrasa (A)
Lit. 'place of learning'. An Islamic religious college

makara (S)
A mythical aquatic animal

mashru (A)
Lit. 'permitted by religious law (*shari'a*)'. A fabric of silk and cotton worn by Muslims, who are not permitted to pray in garments of pure silk

mihrab (A)
The prayer-niche of a mosque, which contains the *qibla* or indicator of the direction of Mecca

morchhal (H)
A fan or fly-whisk made of peacock feathers

naichaband (P)
A maker of tubes for *huqqas*

naqqara (P)
A kettle-drum

naqqarkhana (P)
The place at the porch of a palace

where drums are beaten at stated intervals

naqqash (A)
Designer or pattern-maker

naskhi (A)
A variety of cursive Arabic script

nasta'liq (A)
A style of cursive Arabic script

nautch (H)
A dance, or stage entertainment with dancing

padmasana (S)
The 'lotus position' adopted by ascetics during meditation

pallu (H)
Border, especially of a textile

pan (H)
The leaf of the betel plant, which is chewed with pieces of areca nut and lime

pandan (H,P)
A box in which betel is kept

pankha (H) (punkah)
A fan

parda (P) (purdah)
Lit. 'a curtain'. Concealment or privacy of women

parsi (P)
Lit. 'Persian'. A descendant of the Persian Zoroastrians who fled to India in the 7th and 8th centuries to escape Muslim persecution, and who retain the Zoroastrian religion

pashmina (P)
From Persian *pashm* 'wool'. Fine woollen cloth used especially for making Kashmir shawls

patka (H)
A sash worn round the waist

peri (P)
A fairy

pikdan (H,P)
A spittoon for the juice of the chewed betel leaf

puja (S)
The act of worship

qamargah (A,P)

The hunting-ring formed to enclose the game in the royal hunt

qanat (P)
A panel of a tent, also portable screens supported by a wood or bamboo framework

qur'an (A)
The holy book of the Muslims, the word of God conveyed through the Archangel Gabriel to the prophet Muhammad. It is written in classical Arabic

rabab (A)
A stringed instrument, bowed in the Near East, usually plucked in India. It has six strings, with or without sympathetic strings

rafugar (P)
Embroiderer and darner

raga, fem. **ragina** (S)
A musical mode providing a melodic framework upon which music is improvised according to set rules. A *ragini* is a subordinate mode

ragamala (S)
A 'garland of *ragas*', a collection of *ragas* in which they are personified as heroes and heroines and described in verses which were often illustrated

rasalila (S)
The amorous pastimes of Krishna with the cowherds (*gopis*); the play or work which describes them

rasamandala (S)
The circular dance, or dancing-ground, of Krishna and the cowherds (*gopis*)

rumal (P)
Lit. 'face-wiping'. A piece of cloth serving as a handkerchief, towel, covering for trays, etc.

sadeli (H)
Marquetry work, made in Ahmedabad, Baroda, Bombay and Surat. The materials used are ivory, horn, wood, and silver or tin. The technique was introduced from Iran in the 16th century

sadhu (S)
A Hindu ascetic

saf (A)
Lit. 'a row'. A multiple prayer mat with several juxtaposed niches

sanduq (A)
A chest or coffer

sardar (P)
Officer of rank, chief, nobleman

sarod (P)
A plucked stringed instrument with four to six strings and additional sympathetic strings

saropa (P)
Lit. 'head and foot'. A dress of honour, or set of personal ornaments bestowed by a ruler

shalagrama (S)
A pebble or fossilized mollusc-shell which is worshipped as an aniconic form of the god Vishnu

shamiana (P)
A canopy or awning

shamsher (P)
The characteristic Persian sword with a narrow curved blade sharpened only at the fore edge, a cross guard and the pommel projecting in the direction of the edge. Its curved edge renders it suitable for the 'draw cut'

shroff
From Arabic *sarraf* : moneychanger

simurgh (P)
A fabulous bird of Iranian origin, cognate with the Arabian *'anqa* and Chinese *feng*, which has influenced its representation in the arts of Persia and India

subah (A)
A province

suls (A. thuluth)
A cursive ornamental variety of the Arabic script

surah (A)
A chapter of the Qur'an [q.v.]

tabla (A)
The most widely-used type of Indian drum. It is made of wood and has a range of about an octave

ta'lim (A)
A coded pattern-guide used by weavers

talwar (H)
A type of sword developed in India during the Mughal period. The blade is slightly curved with the reverse sharp-

ened along a broader section near the tip, the fore edge blunt at the ricasso. The hilt usually has a disc pommel and domed quillons

tamasha (P)
Entertainment, spectacle

tanpura (P,H)
A musical instrument, usually having four strings, which provides a drone accompaniment to the voice or other instruments

tarahguru (A,S)
One who calls out the colours from the *ta'lim* [q.v.] for weavers

taslim (A)
A form of respectful salutation in which one touches the ground with the fingers and then places the palm of the hand on one's head

taus (A)
Peacock. Refers to stringed musical instruments whose resonating chamber is formed like the body of a peacock

tola (H)
A unit of weight used by jewellers

toshkhana (P)
A store for furnishings, wardrobe, etc

trunnions
The side projections on which a cannon is pivoted

vahana (S)
'Carrier' or 'bearer'. The animal or bird associated with the major Hindu deities

vambrace
Forearm guard, usually of two hinged steel plates with chain mail to protect the hand and wrist

vina (S)
The primary stringed instrument of classical Indian music which occurs in both North and South Indian varieties. It is fretted with four strings over the frets and three to provide a drone

zamindar (P)
Land-owner, landlord

zardozi (P)
Embroidery

zenana (P)
The women's living quarters, *harem*

Bibliography

Note
Bibliographical references in the text of this catalogue normally cite the author's surname and the date of publication (e.g. Ebeling (1973) for Ebeling, K., *Ragamala painting*, Basel, 1973). Exceptions are made in the case of certain translated historical texts, which are cited under their titles. In the following bibliography, catalogues of exhibitions and collections normally appear under the location and name of the institution concerned (e.g. Paris : Grand Palais). Titles of more than one book by the same author are listed chronologically by the dates of publication.

Abdul Aziz, *Thrones, tents and their furniture used by the Indian Mughals*, Lahore, n.d.

Abu'l-Fazl *see A'in-i Akbari, The*, and *Akbarnama, The*.

Aga-Oglu, M., 'A fragment of a rare Indian carpet', *Bulletin of the Detroit Institute of Arts*, vol.XIII, no.1, October 1931.

Ahmed, N., *Kitab-i-Nauras*, New Delhi, 1956.
—, 'Jahangir's album of art – Muraqqa-i-Gulshan – and its two Adilshahi paintings', *Indo-Islamica*, vol.30, 1977.

A'in-i Akbari, The, by Abu'l-Fazl, translated by H. Blochmann, 3rd ed., New Delhi, 1977.

Akbarnama, The, by Abu'l-Fazl, translated by H. Beveridge, Calcutta, 1902.

Allgrove, J., 'Carpets of the Central and Eastern Islamic Lands', *Encyclopaedia of Islam*, Leiden, 1980.

Alvi, M.A., and Rahman, A., *Jahangir the naturalist*, New Delhi, 1968.

American Art Association, *Sale of the Collection of Henry G. Marquand*, New York, 1902.

Amsterdam : Rijksmuseum, *Beeldhouwkunst in het Rijksmuseum*, Amsterdam, 1973.

Anon., 'Islamic Jade', *Apollo*, vol.LXXXIV, no.54 (n.s.), August 1966, p.164, fig.2.

Archer, M., *Patua painting*, London, 1947.
—, 'The social history of the nautch girl', *The Saturday Book*, vol.22, London, 1962, p.242 *et seq*.
—, 'The Talented Baronet : Sir Charles D'Oyly and his drawings of India', *The Connoisseur*, November 1970, pp.173-81.
—, 'Tilly Kettle and the Court of Oudh', *Apollo*, February 1972.
—, *Company drawings in the India Office Library*, London, 1972.
—, 'Colonel Gentil's Atlas : an early series of Company drawings', *India Office Library and Records Report*, London, 1978, pp.41-5.
—, *India and British portraiture 1770-1825*, London, 1979.
— and Archer, W.G., *Indian painting for the British, 1770-1880*, Oxford, 1955.

Archer, W.G., *Indian painting in the Punjab Hills*, London, 1952.
—, *Indian painting*, London, 1956.
—, *Central Indian painting*, London, 1958.
—, *Indian paintings from Rajasthan*, London, 1957; rev. ed. Calcutta, 1962.
—, *Indian paintings from the Punjab Hills*, 2 vols., London, 1973.

Ardeshir, A.C., 'Mughal Miniature Painting : The School of Jahangir', *Roopa Lekha*, vol.II, no.3, 1940.

Arnold, *Sir* T.W., and Wilkinson, J.V.S., *The Library of A. Chester Beatty : A Catalogue of the Indian Miniatures*, London, 1936.

Arts of Bengal, The (1979), *see* London : Whitechapel Art Gallery.

Ashton, *Sir* L. (ed.), *The Art of India and Pakistan*, London, 1950.

Atabay, B., *Fihrisht-i Muraqqa'at-i Kitabkaneh-i Sultanati*, Tehran, s.1353.

Babelon, E., *Catalogue des camées antiques et modernes de la Bibliothèque Nationale*, 2 vols., Paris, 1897.

Baburnama in English, The, translated by A. Beveridge, London, 1922.

Badshah Namah, The, by 'Abd Al-Hamid Lahawri, edited by Mawlawis Kabir Al-Din Ahmad and 'Abd Al-Rahim (Bibliotheca Indica), Calcutta, 1866-72.

Ball, V., 'A Description of two Large Spinal Rubies, with Persian Characters engraved upon them', *Proceedings of the Royal Irish Academy*, vol.III, no.2, (third series), 1894, pp.381-400.

Barrett, D., *Painting in the Deccan XVI-XVII Century*, London 1958.
— and Gray, B., *Paintings of India*, Lausanne, 1963.

Bauer, W.P., 'A scientific examination of the applied decoration of two Indian swords' *in* Elgood (1979), *q.v.*

Beach, M.C., 'Mughal and Rajput Minor Arts', *The Arts of India and Nepal : The Nasli and Alice Heeramaneck Collection*, Museum of Fine Arts, Boston, 1966.
—, *Rajput painting at Bundi and Kota*, Ascona, 1974.
—, *The Grand Mogul*, Williamstown, Mass., 1978.
—, *Reflections of India : Paintings from the 16th to the 19th century*, Royal Ontario Museum, Toronto, 1979.

Beattie, M.H., 'The Burrell Collection of Oriental rugs', *Oriental Art*, vol.VII, no.4, winter 1961.
—, *The Thyssen-Bornemisza Collection of Oriental rugs*, Castagnola, 1972.
—, 'A Legacy of Carpets', *The Connoisseur*, vol.191, no.770, April 1976, pp.254-65.

Beer, A.B., *Trade Goods . . . Indian Chintz in the Cooper-Hewitt Museum . . .*, Washington, 1970.

Bennett, I. (ed.), *Country Life Book of Rugs and Carpets of the World*, London, 1977.

Berlin : Museum für Indische Kunst, *Katalog, Ausgestellte Werke*, Berlin, 1971.

Bernier, F., *Travels in the Mogul Empire*, translated by A. Constable, London, 1891.

Bilgrami, S.A.A., *Landmarks of the Deccan*, Hyderabad, 1927.

Binney, E., *Indian Miniature Painting from the Collection of Edwin Binney, 3rd, I : The Mughal and Deccani Schools*, Portland, 1973.

Binyon, L., Wilkinson, J.V.S., and Gray, B., *Persian Miniature Painting*, London, 1933.

Birdwood, *Sir* G., 'History of Bombay Inlaid Work' [*sadeli* work], *Journal of the Bombay Asiatic Society*, vol.II, 1861-3.
—, *The Industrial Arts of India*, London 1880; reprinted London, 1971 (Reprint Press).

Black, J.A., *A History of Jewels*, London, 1974.

Blochet, E., *Musulman Painting*, London, 1929.
—, *Les peintures orientales de la collection Pozzi*, Paris, 1930.

Blunt, W., *The Art of Botanical Illustration*, London, 1950.

Bode, W. von, and Kühnel, E., *Antique rugs from the Near East*, 4th ed., London, 1970.

Bogdanov, L., 'The tomb of the Emperor Babur near Kabul', *Epigraphica Indo-Moslemica*, Calcutta, 1923-4.

Born, W., 'Ivory powder flasks from the Mughal period', *Ars Islamica*, vol.IX, 1942, pp.93-111.

Boston : Museum of Fine Arts, *The Arts of India and Nepal : The Nasli and Alice Heeramaneck Collection*, 1966.

Brown, P., *Indian Painting under the Mughals*, Oxford, 1924.

Brunet, M., 'Incidences de l'ambassade de Tippoo-Saib sur la porcelaine de Sèvres', *Cahiers de la ceramique*, no.24, 1961.

Brussels : Musées Royaux d'Art et d'Histoire, *L'art indien dans les collections belges*, 1969.

Buckley, F., 'Curious Old English Glasses : Glasses for the Eastern market', *Glass*, April 1932.

Bulletin of the Metropolitan Museum of Art (1930) *see* U., J.M.

Burlington Fine Arts Club, *Exhibition of Early Chinese Pottery and Porcelain*

172

1910, illustrated ed., London, 1911.

Caplan, A., 'An important carved emerald from the Mogul period of India', *Lapidary Journal,* February 1968.

Cavallo, A.S., 'Textiles', *The Arts of India and Nepal : The Nasli and Alice Heeramaneck Collection,* Museum of Fine Arts, Boston, 1966.

Chandra, M., 'A Brass Jewel Casket of Akbar-Jehangir Period', *Roopa Lekha,* vol.II, no.3, 1940, pp.9-13.
—, *Indian Art,* Bombay, 1974.
— and Khandalavala, K., 'Editorial Notes', *Lalit Kala,* nos.1-2, 1955-6, p.11 *et seq.*

Chandra, P., 'Two early Mughal metal cups', *Bulletin of the Prince of Wales Museum,* no.5, Bombay, 1955-7, pp.57-60 and plates.

Chhavi, Golden Jubilee Volume, Banaras, 1971.

Choudhury, A.R., *Bidri Ware,* Salar Jung Museum, Hyderabad, 1961.

Christie Manson and Woods, *Islamic and Indian manuscripts and miniatures,* London, 24 April 1980.
—, *Important Chinese Ceramics and Works of Art,* London, 15 July 1981, lot 73.

Clarke, C.S., *Indian Art and Letters,* vol.I, no.2, 1927.

Cleveland : Museum of Art, *The Handbook of the Cleveland Museum of Art,* 1969.

Cole, *Sir* H.H., *Fifty-one photographic illustrations taken by order of the Government of India of some selected objects shown at the third exhibition of native fine and industrial art opened at Simla . . . 24th September 1881,* London, 1883.

Collier, R., *The Indian Mutiny,* London, 1966.

Coomaraswamy, A.K., *The Arts and Crafts of India and Ceylon,* London, 1913.
—, *Catalogue of the Indian Collections in the Museum of Fine Arts, Boston, Part VI : Mughal Paintings,* Boston, 1930.

Corneille, J., *Journal of my service in India,* edited by Michael Edwardes, London, 1966.

Courtney, N., *The Tiger : Symbol of Freedom,* London, 1980.

Cousens, H., *Bijapur and its architectural remains,* Bombay, 1916.

Crowe, S., *et al., The Gardens of Mughul India,* London, 1972.

Culin, S., 'The Story of the Painted Curtain', *Good Furniture Magazine,* vol.XI, New York, 1981, pp.131-47.

Dahmen-Dallapiccola, A.L., *Ragamala-Miniaturen von 1475 bis 1700,* Wiesbaden, 1975.

Dam-Mikkelsen, B., and Lundbaek, T. (eds.), *Ethnographic Objects in the Royal Danish Kunstkammer 1650-1800,* National Museum, Copenhagen, 1980.

Das, A., 'Ustad Mansur', *Lalit Kala,* no.17, 1974, p.32 *et seq.*

Delhi : Coronation Durbar, *Catalogue of Loan Exhibition of Antiquities,* Delhi, 1911.

Digby, S., 'A corpus of "Mughal" glass', *Bulletin of the School of Oriental and African Studies,* vol. XXXVI, part I, 1973.

Dikshit, M.G., *History of Indian Glass,* Bombay, 1969.

Dimand, M.S., *Oriental Rugs in the Metropolitan Museum of Art,* New York, 1973.

D'Oyly, C., *Tom Raw, the griffin,* London, 1828.

Du Ry, C., *Art of Islam,* New York, 1972.

Eaton, R.M., *The Sufis of Bijapur 1300-1700,* Princeton, 1978.

Ebeling, K., *Ragamala painting,* Basel, 1973.

Egerton, W., *An illustrated handbook of Indian arms, being a classified and descriptive catalogue of the arms exhibited at the India Museum,* London, 1880.

Ehrenthal, M. von, *Führer durch das Königliche Historische Museum zu Dresden,* 1896.

Eiland, M.L., *Chinese and Exotic Rugs,* London,1979.

Elgood, R. (ed.), *Islamic Arms and Armour,* London, 1979.

Elliott, *Sir* H.M., and Dowson, J., The *History of India as told by its own historians : The Muhammadan Period,* 2nd ed., Calcutta, 1953.

Ellis, C.G., 'Ottoman Prayer Rugs', *Textile Museum Journal,* vol.II, no.4, December 1969.

Erdmann, K., 'Der Indische Knüpfteppich', *Indologen-Tagung,* 1959.
—, *700 years of Oriental Carpets,* translated by M.H. Beattie and H. Herzog, London, 1970.

Evans, J., *A History of Jewellery,* London, 1953.

Falk, T., 'Rothschild Collection of Mughal Miniatures', *Persian and Mughal Art,* edited by M. Goedhuis, London, 1976.
— and Archer, M., *Indian Miniatures in the India Office Library,* London, 1981.

Forrest, D., *Tiger of Mysore : the life and death of Tipu Sultan,* London, 1970.

Foster, *Sir* W., *Early Travels in India 1583-1619,* Oxford, 1921.
—, (ed.), *The Embassy of Sir Thomas Roe to the Court of the Great Mogul, 1615-19,* London, 1899; reprinted Nendeln 1967.

Freeman-Grenville, G.S.P., *The Muslim and Christian Calendars,* London, 1963.

French, J.C., *Himalayan Art,* London, 1931.

Frenzal, F.A., *Führer durch das Historische Museum zu Dresden,* 1850.

Ganz, P., *L'œuvre d'un amateur d'art : la collection de Monsieur F. Engel-Gros,* Geneva and Paris, 1925.

Gascoigne, B., *The Great Moghuls,* London, 1971.

Goetz, H., *The Indian and Persian Miniature Paintings in the Rijksprentenkabinet (Rijksmuseum),* Amsterdam, Amsterdam, 1958.
—, *India : Five thousand years of Indian Art,* London, 1959.

Goodchild, W., *Precious stones,* London, 1908.

Gorakshkar, S. (ed.), *Animal[s] in Indian Art,* Bombay, 1979.

Gosvami, O., *The Story of Indian Museums,* Bombay, 1957.

Gowd, K.V.N., 'Selected crafts of Andhra Pradesh : Bidri Ware', *Census of India 1961,* vol.II, part VII-A (3), pp.3-21 plus plate and two appendices of plates.

Gray, B., 'The Export of Chinese Porcelain to India', *Transactions of the Oriental Ceramic Society, 1964-66,* London, 1967, pp.21-37.
— (ed.), *The Arts of India,* Oxford, 1981.

Grube, E., *The World of Islam,* London, 1967, p.160, fig.104.

Gupta, P.L., *Coins,* New Delhi, 1969.

Hájek, L., *Indian Miniatures of the Moghul School,* London, 1960.

Hall, M., 'Indisches Kunsthandwerk', Indien und Südostasien, Berlin, 1971.

Hambly, G., *Cities of Mughal India,* London, 1968.

Harden, D.B., Painter, K.S., Pinder-Wilson, R.H., and Tait, H., *Masterpieces of Glass,* London, 1968.

Hasrat, B.J., *Dara Shikuh : Life and Works,* Calcutta, 1953.

Heeramaneck Collection *see* Boston : Museum of Fine Arts.

Hendley, T.H., *Damascening on steel or iron, as practised in India,* London, 1892.
—, 'Indian Jewellery', *Journal of Indian Art,* vol.XII, n.d.

Hickmann, R., *et al., Indische Albumblätter: Miniaturen und Kalligraphien aus der Zeit der Moghul-Kaiser,* Leipzig and Weimar, 1979.

Hillier, B., *Master Potters of the Industrial Revolution : The Turners of Lane End,* London, 1965.

Hodivala, S.H., *Historical studies in Mughal numismatics,* Calcutta, 1923.

Hoey, W., *A Monograph on Trade and Manufactures in Northern India,* Lucknow, 1880.

Hutchison, J., and Vogel, J.P., *History of the Panjab Hill States,* 2 vols., Lahore, 1933.

Hyderabad Government : Central Records Office, *The Chronology of Modern Hyderabad 1720-1890,* Hyderabad, 1954.

Irvine, W., *The Army of the Indian Moguls,* London, 1903.

Irwin, J.C., 'Textiles and the minor arts', *The Art of India and Pakistan,* edited by L. Ashton (catalogue of an exhibition held at the Royal Academy, 1947-8), London, 1950.
—, *Indian Embroidery,* London, 1951.
—, 'Golconda cotton paintings of the early 17th century', *Lalit Kala,* no.5, April 1959.
—, 'Mughal jades', *The Times of India Annual,* 1968.
—, *Origins of Chintz,* London, 1970.
—, *The Kashmir shawl,* London, 1973.
— and Hall, M., *Indian painted and printed fabrics,* Ahmedabad, 1970.
— and —, *Indian Embroideries,* Ahmedabad, 1973.

Istanbul: Topkapi Sarayi, *Eski çekmeceler* (Topkapi Sarayi Müzesi Yayinlari no.4), Istanbul, 1956.

Ivanov, A.A., Grek, T.V., and Akimushkin, O.F., *Al'bom indiyskikh i pyersidskikh miniatyur XVI-XVIII vv.* [Album of Indian and Persian Miniatures of the 16th-18th centuries], Moscow, 1962.

Jacob, S.S., and Hendley, T.H., *Jeypore Enamels,* London, 1886.

Jaisi, M.M., *Padmavati,* translated by A.G. Shirreff, Calcutta, 1944.

James, D., 'Koranverse in Miniature', *Kunst und Antiquitäten,* vol.II, 1981.
—, *Islamic Masterpieces of the Chester Beatty Library,* London, 1981.

Jayakar, P., 'A seventeenth century

satin tissue wall-hanging from Ahmedabad', *Lalit Kala,* 1-2, 1955-6, pp.108-12.

Jenkins, J., and Olsen, P.R., *Music and Musical Instruments in the World of Islam,* London, 1976.

Kahlenberg, M., 'A study of the development and use of the Mughal *patka* (sash)', *Aspects of Indian Art,* edited by P. Pal, Leiden, 1972.
—, 'The relationship between a Persian and Indian floral velvet in the Los Angeles County Museum of Art collection', *Los Angeles County Museum Bulletin,* 1973.

Karpinski, C., 'Kashmir to Paisley', *Bulletin of the Metropolitan Museum,* New York, November 1963

Keene, M., 'The Lapidary Arts in Islam: An Underappreciated Tradition', *Expedition,* University of Pennsylvania, The University Museum, 1982.

Khan, M.W.U., *Lahore and its important monuments,* Lahore, 1958.

Khandalavala, K., *Pahari miniature painting,* Bombay, 1958.
—, Chandra, M., and Chandra, P., *Miniature Painting : A Catalogue of the exhibition of the Sri Motichand Khajanchi Collection held by the Lalit Kala Akademi,* New Delhi, 1960.

Koch, E., 'The lost colonnade of Shah Jahan's bath in the Red Fort at Agra 1637', *Burlington Magazine,* vol.CXXIV, June or August 1982 (forthcoming).

Koyama, F. (ed.), *Toyo toji taikan. Oriental Ceramics : the world's great collections.* Vol.V Barrett, D., Dai-Ei Hakubutsukan. The British Museum, Tokyo, 1974.

Kramrisch, S., *A Survey of Painting in the Deccan,* Hyderabad, 1937.

Krishna, A., and Krishna, V., *Banaras Brocades,* New Delhi, 1966.

Krishnadasa, R., 'Mughal Miniatures', *The Lalit Kala series of Indian Art,* vol.I, Delhi, 1955.
—, 'The pink enamelling of Banaras', *Chhavi, Golden Jubilee Volume,* Banaras, 1971, pp.327-34.

Kurz, O., 'Folding chairs and Koran stands', *Islamic Art in the Metropolitan Museum of Art,* edited by R. Ettinghausen, New York, 1972, p.299 *et seq.*

La Roërie, G., 'The Admiral's Whistle', *The Mariner's Mirror : The Journal of the Society for Nautical Research,* vol.21, 1935, pp.198-204.

Latif, M., *Bijoux moghols,* Brussels, 1982.

Lee, S.E., *Rajput Painting,* New York, 1960.

Leeds : Temple Newsam House, *The Rug in Islamic Art* : catalogue by M.H. Beattie, 1964.

Leyden, R. von, *Ganjifa : The playing cards of India,* London, 1982.

Lightbown, R.W., 'Oriental Art and the Orient in late Renaissance and Baroque Italy', *Journal of the Warburg and Courtauld Institutes,* vol. XXXII, 1969.

Linton Collection *see* Nouveau Drouot.

London : British Museum, *Paintings from the Muslim Courts of India,* London, 1976.

London : Hayward Gallery, *The Arts of Islam,* catalogue edited by G. Michell and D. Jones, London, 1976.

London : Royal Academy of Arts, *Catalogue of the International Exhibition of Persian Art,* London, 1931.

London : Victoria and Albert Museum, *A guide to an exhibition of tapestries, carpets and furniture lent by the Earl of Dalkeith,* London, 1914.
—, *Indian Art* (departmental guide), London, 1978.
—, *Princely Magnificence* : catalogue of an exhibition of *Court Jewels of the Renaissance 1500-1630,* London, 1980.

London : Whitechapel Art Gallery, *The Arts of Bengal* (exhibition catalogue), London, 1979.

McEwen, E., 'The *chahar kham* or "four-curved" bow of India', *in* Elgood (1979).

McMullan, J.V., *Islamic carpets,* New

York Near Eastern Art Research Center, Inc., 1965.

Maathir-ul-umara, The, by Nawwab Samsam-ud-daula Shah Nawaz Khan and his son 'Abdul Hayy, translated by H. Beveridge and Baini Prashad, Calcutta, 1911-1952; reprinted Patna, 1979.

Mailey, J., 'Indian Textiles in the Museum's Collection', *Chronicle of the Museum for the Arts of Decoration of the Cooper Union,* vol.II, no.4, 1952.

Manrique, S., *Travels . . . 1629-1643,* translated by C.E. Luard and H. Hosten, Oxford, 1927.

Marteau, G., and Vever, H., *Miniatures persanes exposées au Musée des Arts Décoratifs,* 2 vols., Paris, 1912.

Martin, F.R., *A History of Oriental Carpets before 1800,* Vienna, 1908.
—, *The Miniature Painting and Painters of Persia, India and Turkey,* London, 1912.

Massey, R. and J., *The Music of India,* London, 1976.

Maynard, A., 'Chinese and Indian jade carvings in the collection of Sir Isaac and Lady Wolfson', *The Connoisseur,* vol.153, no.616, June 1963, p.88, fig.1.

Meer Hassan Ali, Mrs., *Observations on the Mussulmans of India,* edited by W. Crooke, Karachi, 1978.

Melikian-Chirvani, A.S., 'The tabarzins of Lotf 'ali', *in* Elgood (1979), pp.116-35 and appendix.
—, *Metalwork from Iranian Lands,* London, 1982.

Morley, G., 'On Applied Arts of India in Bharat Kala Bhavan', *Chhavi, Golden Jubilee Volume,* Banaras, 1971, pp.107-29.

Murphy, V., 'Furniture in India', *Discovering Antiques,* issue 65, 1971, p.1541 *et seq.*

Murray, H.J.R., *A History of board games other than chess,* Oxford, 1952.

Nadvi, S.S., 'Some Indian Astrolabemakers', *Islamic Culture,* vol.9,

Hyderabad, October 1935, pp.621-31.

Nakhshabi, Z., *Tales of a parrot,* translated and edited by M.A. Simsar, Graz, 1978.

Neal, W.K. and Back, D.H.L., *The Mantons : Gunmakers,* London, 1967.

Nesbitt, A., *Catalogue of Glass formed by Felix Slade, Esq.,* London, 1871.

Newman, H., *An Illustrated Dictionary of Glass,* London, 1977.

Nigam, M.L., *Jade Collection in the Salar Jung Museum,* Hyderabad, 1979.

Norman, A.V.B., 'Ornate Weapons of the Orient', *Country Life,* vol.CLXIV, 14 November 1968, pp.1245-8.
—, 'Swords and Daggers', *Discovering Antiques,* issue 65, 1971, pp.1554-5.

Nouveau Drouot, *Scientific Instruments/Rare Books : Leonard Linton Collection,* etc., Paris, 9 and 10 October 1980.

Oriental Ceramics Society, The, *Exhibition of Chinese blue and white porcelain from the 14th to the 19th century* (catalogue), 1953.
—, *Transactions,* vol.36, London, 1964-66.

Oxford : Ashmolean Museum, *Eastern Ceramics and other works of art from the collection of Gerald Reitlinger,* London, 1981.

Pal, P. (ed.), *Islamic Art,* Los Angeles County Museum of Art, 1973.

Palmer, J.P., *Jade,* London, 1967.

Pargiter, F.E., 'An Indian game : Heaven or Hell', *Journal of the Royal Asiatic Society,* 1916.

Paris : Grand Palais, *Or des Scythes,* 1975.
—, *L'Islam dans les collections nationales,* 1977.

Paris : Musée de l'Orangerie, *Les Arts de l'Islam des origines à 1700,* 1971.

Parks, F., *Wanderings of a Pilgrim in search of the Picturesque,* 2 vols., London, 1850.

Paterson, W.F., 'Archery in Moghul India : an illustrated manual of instruction in the collection of the Marquess of Bute', *Islamic Quarterly,* vol.XVI, 1/2, January-June 1972, pp.81-95.

Pinder-Wilson, R., *Islamic Art,* London, 1957.
—, 'A glass huqqa bowl', *British Museum Quarterly,* vol.XXV, London, 1962, pp.91-4 and pl.XXXVI.
—, *Paintings from the Muslim Courts of India,* British Museum, London, 1976.

Pope, A.U., and Ackerman, P., *A Survey of Persian Art from prehistoric times to the present,* 6 vols., London, 1938-9.

Pope, J.A., *Chinese Porcelains from the Ardebil Shrine,* Washington, 1956.

Princely Magnificence (1980) *see* London : Victoria and Albert Museum.

Rawson, P.S., *The Indian Sword : A catalogue raissone* [sic] *of the Indian collections in the Victoria and Albert Museum :* Unpublished M.A. thesis for the School of Oriental and African Studies, London, 1952.
—, *The Indian Sword,* Copenhagen, 1967.
—, *Indian Art,* London and New York, 1972, pp.152-3.

Rieu, C., *Catalogue of the Persian manuscripts in the British Museum,* 2 vols., London, 1881; reprinted 1966.

Rivett-Carbac, J.H., 'Specimens of Indian Metal Work', *Journal of Indian Art and Industry,* no.77, January 1902.

Rubin, I.E. (ed.), *The Guennol Collection,* vol.I, Metropolitan Museum of Art, New York, 1975.

Sainsbury, *Sir* R. (ed.), *The Sainsbury Centre for Visual Arts, University of East Anglia, Norwich,* Norwich, 1978.

Sainsbury, W.N., 'The Fine Arts in India in the Reign of James I', *The Fine Arts Quarterly Review,* vol.II, January-May 1864, pp.313-9.

Saksena, B.P., *History of Shahjahan of Dihli,* Allahabad, 1958.

Sarkar, J., *Mughal Administration,* revised edition, Calcutta, 1952.

Schöbel, J., *Princely Arms and Armour,* London, 1975.

Schulberg, L., *Historic India,* New York, 1968.

Schulz, P.W., *Die persisch-islamische Miniaturmalerei : ein Beitrag zur Kunstgeschichte Irans,* 2 vols., Leipzig, 1914.

Seïr Mutaqherin, The; or Review of Modern Times; being an History of India, as far down as the year 1783 . . . by Seid-Gholam-Hossein-Khan, translated by Nota-Manus, 4 vols., Calcutta, 1789; reprinted Lahore, 1975.

Sekhar, A.C., 'Filigree Industry of Karimnagar', *Census of India 1961,* vol.II, part VII-A (1).

Sharar, A.H., *Lucknow : The last phase of an Oriental culture,* London, 1975.

Sharma, O.P., *Indian Miniature Painting,* Brussels, 1974.
— and Tandon, B.N., 'A leather shield painted in the Mewar style in the collection of the National Museum, New Delhi', *Studies in Museology,* vol.V, Baroda, 1969, pp.60-71.

Sharma, Y.D., *Delhi and its Neighbourhood,* Archaeological Survey of India, New Delhi, 1964.

Silverstein, J., *Woven Winds : The Art of Textiles in India :* illustrated catalogue of an exhibition at The Gallery, Stratford, Ontario, 1981.

Singh, C., *Textiles and costumes from the Maharaja Sawai Man Singh II Museum,* Jaipur, 1979.

Singh, J., *Sher-e-Punjab : Maharaja Ranjit Singh,* Chandigarh, 1979.

Singh, K.S., 'An early Ragamala MS from Pali', *Lalit Kala,* no.7, 1960, p.76 *et seq.*

Skelton, R.W., 'The Tod Collection of Rajasthani paintings', *Roopa Lekha,* vol.XXX, 1959, pp.5-11.
—, 'Jades moghols', *L'Œil,* no.96, December 1962, p.44, fig.4, and p.89.
—, 'The Shah Jahan Cup', *V & A Museum Bulletin,* vol.II, no.3, July 1966, pp.109-10, fig.8.
—, 'The European impact on Mughal art', *Europe and the Indies, the Era of the Companies 1600-1824,* London, 1970.
—, 'Skills of the Indian Craftsmen', *Discovering Antiques,* issue 65, 1971, p.1545 *et seq.*
—, 'A Decorative Motif in Mughal Art', *Aspects of Indian Art,* edited by P. Pal, Leiden, 1972, p.147 *et seq.*
—, 'The relations between the Chinese and Indian jade carving traditions', *The Westward Influence of the Chinese arts from the 14th to the 18th century,* edited by W. Watson; Colloquies on Art and Archaeology in Asia, no.3, London, 1972.
—, 'Indian Painting of the Mughal Period', *Islamic Painting and the Arts of the Book,* edited by B.W. Robinson, London, 1976.
—, 'Persian carpet design in relation to miniature paintings and manuscript decoration', *Carpets of Central Persia* (colloquium), Sheffield City Art Galleries, 1978.
—, 'Shaykh Phul and the origins of Bundi painting', *Chhavi-2,* edited by A. Krishna, Banaras, 1981.

Sonday, M. and Kajitani, N., 'A type of Mughal sash', *Textile Museum Journal,* vol.III, no.1, Washington, December 1970.
— and —, 'A second type of Mughal sash', *Textile Museum Journal,* vol.III, no.2, Washington, December 1971.

Sotheby & Co., *Bibliotheca Phillippica. Medieval MSS,* new series, fourth part, London, 25-26 November 1968.
—, *Catalogue of an interesting collection of oriental miniatures,* London, 11 April 1972.
—, *Sale of Oriental Manuscripts and Miniatures,* London, 7 April 1975.

Soustiel, J. and David, M.C., *Miniatures de l'Inde,* 2, Paris, 1974.

Spink and Son, *Islamic Art from India,* London, 1980.

Spuhler, F., *Islamic Carpets and Textiles in the Keir Collection,* London, 1978.

Stchoukine, I., *La peinture indienne à l'époque des grands Moghols,* Paris, 1929.

—, 'Portraits Moghols, IV. La Collection du Baron Maurice de Rothschild', *Revue des arts asiatiques,* tome IX, no.IV, Paris, 1935, pp.190-208.

Stratford, Ontario : The Gallery *see* Silverstein, J.

Stronge, S., 'Decorative Arts', *The Arts of Bengal,* Whitechapel Gallery, London, 1979.

176 Tarapor, M., 'John Lockwood Kipling and British art education in India', *Victorian Studies,* vol.24, no.1, 1980.

Tardy, *Poinçons d'argent,* 11th ed., Paris, 1975.
—, *Les ivoires,* Paris, 1977.

Tavernier, J.B., *Travels in India . . .,* translated by V. Ball, edited by E. Crooke, Oxford, 1925.

Titley, N.M., Miniatures from Persian Manuscripts, London, 1977.

Tod, J., *Annals and antiquities of Rajasthan,* edited by W. Crooke, 3 vols., Oxford, 1920.

Topsfield, A., *Paintings from Rajasthan in the National Gallery of Victoria,* Melbourne, 1980.
—, 'Painting for the Rajput courts', *The Arts of India,* edited by Basil Gray, Oxford, 1981, pp.159-76.

Tuzuk-i-Jahangiri, The, translated by A. Rogers, edited by H. Beveridge, London, 1909, 1914.

U., J.M., 'A gift of jade', *Bulletin of the Metropolitan Museum of Art,* vol.XXV, no.1, January 1930, p.22.

Vallenstein, S., *Ming Porcelain,* New York, 1970.

Varney, R.J., 'Enamelling in Rajasthan', *Roopa Lekha,* vol.XXIX, nos.1 and 2, December 1958.

Vienna : K.K. Österreichisches Handelsmuseum, *Sammlung von Abbildungen türkischer, arabischer, persischer, centralasiatischer und indischer Metallobjecte,* Vienna, 1895.

Vogel, J.P., *Tile mosaics of the Lahore Fort,* 1920; reprinted Karachi, n.d.

Ward, W.E., 'Two Rajput paintings and a Rajput textile', *Bulletin of the Cleveland Museum of Art,* vol.XLIII, 1956.

Wardwell, A., and Mowry, R.D., *Handbook of the Mr. and Mrs. John D. Rockefeller 3rd Collection,* Asia Society, New York, 1981.

Washington: Smithsonian Institution, *Art Treasures of Turkey,* Washington, 1966.

Watson, O., 'An Islamic "lacquered" dish' [including notes on technique of Indian wares], *Percival David Foundation Colloquy no.11,* London, 1982.

Watt, *Sir G., Indian Art at Delhi, 1903,* Calcutta, 1903.

Welch, A., *Shah 'Abbas and the Arts of Isfahan,* Asia Society, New York, 1973.
—, *Calligraphy in the Arts of the Muslim World,* Asia Society, New York, 1979.

Welch, S.C., *The Art of Mughal India,* Asia Society, New York, 1963.
—, *Indian drawings and painted sketches,* New York, 1976.
—, *Imperial Mughal Painting,* New York, 1978a.
—, *Room for Wonder: Indian painting during the British period, 1760-1880,* New York, 1978b.
— and Beach, M.C., *Gods, thrones and peacocks,* New York, 1965.

White, J. (ed.), *Political and military institutes of Tamerlane,* Oxford, 1783.

Wiet, G., 'Une famille de fabricants d'astrolabes', *Bulletin de l'Institut Français d'Archéologie Orientale,* vol.XXXVI, Cairo, 1936, pp.98-9.

Wilkinson, J.V.S., 'Shah Jahan's drinking vessel', *The Burlington Magazine,* vol.LXIV, 1934, p.187.

Williamson, T., *East-India vade-mecum,* 2 vols., London, 1810.

Worswick, C. and Embree, A., *The last empire : photography in British India, 1855-1911, New York, 1977.*

Zara, L., *Jade,* London, 1969.

Zebrowski, M., 'Decorative Arts of the Mughal Period', *in* Gray (1981).
—, 'Bidri ware', *Hali,* January 1982.
—, 'Indian lacquerwork and the antecedents of the Qajar style', *Percival David Foundation Colloquy no.11,* London, 1982.